DISSONANT LIVES

T0346725

Dissonant Lives

*Generations and violence through
the German dictatorships*

Volume I
Imperialism through Nazism

MARY FULBROOK

OXFORD

UNIVERSITY PRESS

OXFORD
UNIVERSITY PRESS

Great Clarendon Street, Oxford, OX2 6DP,
United Kingdom

Oxford University Press is a department of the University of Oxford.
It furthers the University's objective of excellence in research, scholarship,
and education by publishing worldwide. Oxford is a registered trade mark of
Oxford University Press in the UK and in certain other countries

First published as a single volume hardback 2011
First published in paperback 2017

Impression: 1

Published in the United States of America by Oxford University Press
198 Madison Avenue, New York, NY 10016, United States of America

British Library Cataloguing in Publication Data
Data available

Library of Congress Control Number: 2017940549

ISBN 978–0–19–879952–8

Printed in Great Britain by
Bell & Bain Ltd., Glasgow

Preface

This book is not a standard 'history of Germany' in the twentieth century, or even of the German dictatorships, but rather is concerned with the ways in which Germans of different ages and life stages variously lived through and across the major historical ruptures that peculiarly marked that century: it is about collective patterns of experience and individual passages through the violent eruptions of wars and post-war periods, and through the succeeding dictatorships of Nazism and communism. It explores the experiences and perceptions of selected individuals, and analyses the ways in which major historical events, and changing structures of constraint and opportunity, affected the course of their lives and their outlooks.

For this project, the concept of social generations has been used as a tool of analysis, in order to explore how the 'same' historical period can be experienced quite differently according to social age or life stage at the time, to understand how certain cohorts disproportionately rose to prominence in the historical record of particular regimes at certain times, and to see the ways in which earlier periods of history had lingering implications in later presents. I have thus sought to trace not only individual lives but also the collective patterns that may under certain histori-cal circumstances, although not always, be seen among those born in roughly the same era. 'Generation' is sometimes more and sometimes less significant for the ways in which key moments or periods of history are experienced; it is not always important, and sometimes not at all, yet people are themselves on occasion keenly aware of how just how different their own lives might have been had they been born just a few years earlier or later. This is particularly the case in a country beset, as Germany was, by violence, warfare, and radical historical ruptures, with major changes of highly ideological regimes, where people repeatedly faced massive challenges and repeatedly were brought to account for their own biographies and their own recent pasts. So generation is, in a sense, a hidden factor in historical experience which warrants more explicit and systematic attention than it has frequently been given.

My attempt to write 'history from within' has meant a primary focus on what people themselves wrote and said about their lives—sources that are often termed 'ego-documents'. These should, on the one hand, never be seen as adequate guides to 'how it really was', to adopt a favourite Rankean phrase, since the worm's-eye view is rarely a good vantage point for mapping out the shape of the wood as whole, and particularly not when those in charge of the wood are past masters at deception and manipulation of the inhabitants; but on the other hand, such subjective perceptions and self-representations themselves form a crucial part of that history, and indeed help to shape it. In exploring the degrees of dissonance between what people confess to themselves and others in private letters and diaries, and their acts in public under particular regimes, a new approach may be developed to under-standing the German dictatorships in terms of varying degrees of 'availability for mobilization' by intrusive and demanding regimes, and more or less willing 'enactment' of roles by their citizens, adopting manners of speaking and behaving as appropriate to their surroundings. This too forms a crucial, if often hidden, part of understanding stability and change, affecting what it was or was not possible for those in positions of power to achieve.

The book attempts, then, to combine an exploration of the subjective perceptions and lived experiences of succeeding generations with an analysis of changing historical structures and developments. The standard historical narrative of the period, in terms at least of the basic chronology of major events and high politics, is taken for granted as a relatively familiar if highly contested backdrop to the exploration that follows. The work covers such a vast span, beset by innumerable historical controversies, that I have thought it best to keep footnote references to relevant secondary literature to a minimum and only to suggest, on occasion, where to go for further reading on any particular period or problem.

In writing the book, I often had the sense of trying to paint shifting shadows, or capture the wind by observing distant ripples in the trees. Yet this aspect of perceived and experienced history is central to the ways in which people live and behave, and hence has massive implications for understanding the character particularly of dictatorial regimes, where outer behaviour and private reflections are intrinsically related, yet often run quite at odds with each other. Moreover, even a dictatorship which is ultimately predicated on force and physical containment requires its functionary classes to put policies into effect; and policies of waging an aggressive war of expansion or committing acts of organized genocide on an unprecedented scale require the mobilization or cooperation of millions of people.

This last point is perhaps the hardest to confront. For, in writing about people who lived through what, from a comfortable vantage point in the early twenty-first century, seem like almost impossible times, facing at best only a 'choice' between the 'lesser of two evils', I feel I have frequently hit up against the limits of history as a discipline. There is only so much we can know, understand, explain, or describe. Nevertheless, what follows is an attempt to bring aspects of Germany's dictatorial past to the present in ways which make intelligible some of the worst features of German history in the twentieth century, and clarify some of their longer-term implications for those lucky enough to survive or to be born later; or rather, to make another kind of sense out of this past, and hence to contribute to a fuller understanding of aspects of what, ultimately, remains beyond comprehension. The attempt has frequently made me feel deeply humbled; I hope the results will nevertheless prove illuminating.

Acknowledgements

I have many debts of gratitude which it is a pleasure to acknowledge. The Leverhulme Trust awarded me a three-year Major Research Fellowship, giving me leave from UCL to become, for once, almost completely free from other university duties and able to immerse myself in research and writing. The Leverhulme Trust also provided travel funding for archival research and undertaking some additional oral history interviews. The research for this book would simply not have been possible without such generous support. Archivists have been unfailingly helpful, and I would like to thank staff in the following archives for their assistance: the German Federal Archive (Bundesarchiv) in Berlin, the Central Institute (Zentrale Stelle) in Ludwigsburg, the State Archive Berlin (Landesarchiv Berlin), the Kempowski Archive in the Academy of Arts (Akademie der Künste), the Secret State Archive of Prussian Cultural Heritage (Geheimes Staatsarchiv Preussischer Kulturbesitz), the Field Post Collection of the Museum of Communication (Feldpostsammlung Museum für Kommunikation) in Berlin, the Rhineland State Archive (Landschaftsverband Rheinland) near Cologne, the Archive of the Library of Contemporary History (Bibliothek für Zeitgeschichte) in Stuttgart, the manuscript collection at the Houghton Library of Harvard University, and the Katowice State Archive (Archivum Państwowe w Katowicach) in Poland; particular thanks are due to the German Diary Archive (Deutsches Tagebuch Archiv) in Emmendingen (where staff opened up for me when the archive was technically closed, in deepest August) and to the Local Archive (Heimatarchiv) Schöneberg in Berlin, both of which allowed me not only to have unfettered physical access to their collections but also to the office photocopier.

This book in part grew out of an earlier research project on the GDR 1961–1979, funded by the Arts and Humanities Research Council (AHRC), which I would like to thank again for its support. I also continue to benefit from Silvia Dallinger's work as an Honorary Research Assistant. Esther von Richthofen, Angela Brock, and Erica Fulbrook provided assistance with oral history interviews in German; and Marta Szymska assisted me with interviews in Polish. Christa von Richthofen and Anne-Franziska von Schweinitz were of considerable help in opening up the world of the German aristocracy, and providing materials, contacts, and leads for oral history interviews with aristocrats who remained in the GDR after 1945. Bodo Förster and the Sophie Scholl Schule in Berlin generously shared the history of their school with me, and put me in contact with the former secretary of the Old Girls Association, Inge Cohn-Lampert. For reasons relating both to themes and constraints of space, oral-history interviews have been only selectively alluded to here, and will be deployed more extensively in forthcoming related publications which expand on some of the issues raised in this book. I am particularly grateful to all those individuals who were willing to share their personal experiences in oral-history interviews, bearing witness to their lives through challenging times; and to those families who let me read letters and diaries of close relatives and friends. For reasons of the anonymity which has been preserved in quotations in the text, where pseudonyms or initial letters in place of surnames have been used, I shall not thank them explicitly by name here.

There is always a danger among historians, when acknowledging debts, of seeking to weigh up the many multiple influences on the shaping of a project; I shall resist the temptation here to list individually those with whom I have talked through the issues addressed in this book, and whom I would like collectively to thank in this context. My colleagues at UCL have been extremely supportive during my period of absence from most of the routine travails of academic life. It has been a particular pleasure to have continued to supervise a group of highly talented UCL graduate students, many of whom have been working on related topics, and to have benefited from stimulating discussions in our many informal workshops and conferences. The German Historical Institute London has been a constant companion, providing assistance and support for both jointly and separately organised conferences; I would like to thank its staff and particularly its director, Andreas Gestrich, for all they have done during this time. Christiane Wienand and Julia Wagner also helped in organizing joint conferences with the GHIL on themes relating to this book, and I would like here to express my thanks to them and also my gratitude to the Gerda Henkel Stiftung, the German History Society, and the Marie Curie Foundation through the UCL Centre for European Studies, for additional conference support. I have, in the course of this project, also benefited greatly from discussions with colleagues nationally and internationally, in the context of lectures and conferences in a wide variety of places across the world. Finally, I would like to thank Christopher Wheeler and the anonymous reader for OUP for their very perceptive comments, Matthew Cotton for hanging on as it took ever longer to complete, and John Nichols for straying well beyond his comfort zones of music and literature and taking the time to pick up typographical errors in the manuscript while I struggled to complete the translation of quotations. This task proved extraordinarily challenging, not so much because it was not clear what the German meant or implied, but rather because of the often heavily context-laden tone of utterances deriving from the German dictatorships, where the relevant English words or phrases often seemed to provide little by way of equivalence in wider connotations and tone. On occasion, I have therefore commented on the difficulties of translation and suggested alternatives.

I dedicate this book to my family, in the widest sense. All our lives and identities have been shaped, in one way or another, by the kinds of forces that I have only been able to begin to explore in this book. I dedicate it to the memories of my father, a Canadian, whose own father went missing under mysterious circumstances in the Great War, in 1917, hugely affecting his own outlook and passage through life; my mother, who fled Nazi Germany in the 1930s, equally massively affecting the future course of her life; and my brother Howard, who, born in Wales and utterly British, as an adult settled in Germany; I would so much have liked to have been able to share it with them. I dedicate it also to my other brother Hanno, whose disrupted pan-European childhood and sense of lost relatives were so much part of the developments described here; and to Howard's wife and children, Germans who have grown up in the shadow of a culture of imposed shame without any personal guilt. Our own tangled family histories reveal just how complex the issues are, and how ridiculous it can be to make simplistic generalizations about 'the Germans'. Most of all, I dedicate this book to my husband Julian, and to our three children, Conrad, Erica, and Carl. Julian, as always, not only put up with my obsessive interest in the past, but also (more or less) willingly exposed himself to some of the accompanying sagas of research trips in Germany, Poland, and the USA, and even devoted a 'summer holiday' to ploughing through and constructively commenting on a full draft of the manuscript; Erica gave me invaluable assistance with oral-history interviews in Germany; Conrad and Lara filmed interviews in Poland; and Carl shared much of my indulgence in the past in Berlin; and all of them lovingly bore with me and supported me while I was at times immersed in the research to the exclusion of life in the present.

Contents

1

Introduction

Violence and generations through the German dictatorships

Truly, I live in times of darkness!
. . .
What sort of times are these, when
A conversation about trees is virtually a crime
Because it entails silence about so much wrongdoing!
. . .
You, who will arise after the flood
In which we drowned
Think
When you speak of our failings
Also about the dark times
That you escaped.
. . .
Yet of course we also know:
Hatred even of baseness
Distorts our own features.
Anger even about injustice
Makes our own voice rough. Oh, we
Who wanted to prepare the ground for friendliness
Could not ourselves be friendly.
You however, when the stage has been reached
When human beings help one another,
Think of us
With consideration.

(Bertolt Brecht)[1]

The central challenge of understanding twentieth-century German history can arguably be summarized in one word: Auschwitz. And around this one word—which stands, of course, for far more than Nazi Germany's largest industrial extermination centre and concentration camp—there are many other, more wide-ranging

---

[1] Bertolt Brecht, 'An die Nachgeborenen', my translation. The German original can be found in Karl Carstens (ed.), *Deutsche Gedichte* (C. Bertelsmann Verlag, 1983).

questions. Not only the immediate and obvious questions: who were those directly responsible for unleashing the policy of mass murder; who were the perpetrators and facilitators; and how could it come to be in a highly cultured, 'civilized' nation? Were there indeed, as some would claim, continuities between the military culture of Imperial Germany, with genocidal practices in its African colonies, and the violent 'colonization' of Poland some forty years later? What precisely was the impact of the Great War on the cultures of violence of the 1920s and 1930s, and what role did these play in the development of Nazi rule? But also, in the longer term: how did people who lived through and beyond the 'age of extremes' interpret, confront and respond to the multiple challenges of their times? How were those Germans who lived through periods of major economic, social and political crisis affected by their experiences—and how did they reconfigure their roles and identities across rapid changes of regime and in highly uncertain times? What were the more distant reverberations, even among those born much later, into quite different circumstances? How did living through Germany's 'second dictatorship', the German Democratic Republic (GDR), dominated by the Communist power against whom the Germans had fought and by whom they had been defeated, affect behaviour patterns and social identities, and what implications did these experiences have for interpretations of the Nazi past? In what ways do the experiences, memories, and collective representations of two German dictatorships continue to affect Germans even in the united, democratic Federal Republic of Germany formed with the collapse of the GDR in 1990? In short: 'Auschwitz' must inevitably stand, in Germany, for a past that was memorably and controversially termed the 'past which will not pass away'.[2]

Millions of Germans of course had nothing to do with Hitler's project of exterminating Europe's Jews as well as many others on 'racial' grounds; and many lives remained apparently untouched by foreknowledge of the as yet unthinkable, or by the later and highly diverse legacies of Auschwitz. Even so, both the crises preceding and the immediate and longer-term consequences of the Nazi regime deeply affected all those who lived through even a small portion of this turbulent century. The reverberations of the wars of aggression and mass genocide unleashed by Germany have affected, however distantly, millions of people throughout the century.

This book seeks to view the dictatorial regimes of twentieth-century Germany 'from within'. Taking a deeper look at the life stories of individual Germans from a range of periods and backgrounds may help to provide a new understanding of the ways in which not only the character of the German state, economy, and social structure changed over the century, but also the very character of people themselves. Exploring the interactions between individual perceptions as captured through an ever changing 'inner eye' (which is itself of course socially and culturally

    [2] Ernst Nolte, 'Die Vergangenheit, die nicht vergehen will. Eine Rede, die geschrieben, aber nicht gehalten werden konnte', *Frankfurter Allgemeine Zeitung*, 6 June 1986, reprinted in *'Historikerstreit': Die Dokumentation der Kontroverse um die Einzigartigkeit der nationalsozialistischen Judenvernichtung* (Munich: Piper, 1987).

shaped), and the flux of social relations and political demands, may help us to understand the formation and transformation of 'social selves'. This book focuses on ordinary lives, in the sense of people who were not themselves policymakers and shapers, not at the pinnacle of any political hierarchy; but at the same time, it argues that there is no such thing as 'ordinary Germans' in any general sense. People are very much shaped by the times and places into which they were born and through which they grew up. Yet it was also possible for individuals—within the very variable constraints of both their circumstances and their subjective perceptions—to make active choices about their routes through life.

Political instability and radical changes of regime meant that Germans frequently had to change their outward allegiances, or at least adapt their behaviour patterns, in order to pursue what they construed as their personal life projects. Aspirations, opportunities, constraints, were dramatically affected by changing circumstances across the major political divides of 1918, 1933, 1945, and 1989–90. The World Wars initiated by Germany brought about the physical mutilation, psychological scarring, and premature deaths of tens of millions of people, and radically affected the shape of international as well as German politics and society for half a century or more. People were affected, too, by the no less fundamental but often less immediately discernible shifts in social and economic structures and cultural traditions. What it was that individuals thought they wanted to achieve in life, and the ways in which they pursued their goals, were not only radically affected by the period, place, and social location into which they were born, but also by the moment of their birth, and their 'social age' at the time of major historical events—age-related chances could make the difference between violent early death, or long and relatively peaceful life; between becoming a Nazi or becoming a communist; between believing in God and giving birth to numerous children or believing only in life on earth, taking the pill, and assuming a woman should be able to pursue a career of her own choosing.

For those living through these demanding times—characterized by violence, war, revolution, and mobilization in service of radically different ideological causes—any attempt to steer a personal course was doomed at one time or another to hit up against constraints and penalties. The varying demands of politically intrusive, ideologically driven regimes, and the character of the lives—and deaths—of individuals were intrinsically interrelated. We can only begin to comprehend the century that produced Auschwitz if we try to understand the ways in which individuals lived through these turbulent times.

I. TRADITIONS AND LEGACIES OF VIOLENCE

Genocide was not a uniquely German invention. There is no claim here that other countries, other peoples, have not committed or been victims of appalling acts of inhumanity, carried out in a variety of ways in different places. But the extraordinary escalation of a state-sanctioned resort to violence as a political tool, and the widespread willingness to participate in brutal killings and in a bureaucratic machinery ultimately geared to extermination during Hitler's war, nevertheless remain to be explained, as do the consequences for Germans after the war.

Auschwitz was a product of a very specific history, characterized by extreme political instability and the widespread use of violence as a political tool even well before the Nazi dictatorship. The latter cannot be adequately understood without looking in some depth at its prehistory; far from being some extraordinarily powerful and evil force effectively 'outside of history' (captured in such phrases as a 'spanner in the works', or inflated through an excessive concentration on the individual personality at the expense of historical context), Hitler emerged from the turmoil of the Great War and was only able to amass political support under the very specific historical conditions of Germany in the 1920s and early 1930s. Those who were willing to enact the Nazi project, to carry the functions of the Nazi state once Hitler was in power, were themselves, too, shaped by the legacies of Imperial and Weimar Germany. To understand Auschwitz, it is important to understand the perceptions and actions of those who made it possible—beyond the clearly central level of key decision-makers and power holders. But it is important also to understand the impact living through this period had on the people who, in different ways and at different stages of their own lives, variously contested, sustained, and participated in the workings of the Nazi state.

Beyond Auschwitz lay the two post-war German states—both designed, in very different ways, to ensure that war and genocide could never again proceed from German soil. While the Federal Republic of Germany, founded in the Western zones of occupation under the influence particularly of Britain and America (as well as their junior partner, France), became eventually a stable and economically productive democracy, in the Soviet zone of occupation in what is now eastern Germany, a new communist dictatorship, the German Democratic Republic (GDR), was erected in place of the former Nazi regime. In East Germany during the Cold War new processes of mass mobilization took place under very different ideological colours from those of the preceding decades: Hitler's rabid racism and anti-Bolshevism was replaced in the GDR by communist anti-fascism. And the GDR, in turn, collapsed forty years after its foundation, with the 'gentle revolution' of autumn 1989 followed by accession to an enlarged Federal Republic of Germany in 1990; those living through the 'second German dictatorship' were faced by further challenges of accounting for and recounting their past.

Generations in Germany thus lived through radical and rapid changes of regime—often socialized under one, making their lives under another, reflecting on their past under a third. At each stage, they had to behave, and to present their actions both to themselves and to others, under massively different ideological and political conditions. Anyone living through these extraordinary historical periods was inevitably challenged and marked by their experiences, and particularly so when they lived under dictatorial conditions that radically constrained what kinds of 'selves' they could develop.

I have chosen in this book to focus specifically on the significance of generations in the transitions into, through, and out of Nazism and communism: two regimes which tried energetically to mould and remake their citizens in forms shaped by powerful, interventionist ideologies, backed up by significant reserves of power and repression for those who refused to conform or did not fit ideologically driven ideals. The transitions of 1918, 1933, and 1945 were common for Germans living in both East and West; but the final transition of the 'short' twentieth century, 1989–90, had a peculiarly powerful impact on the social self only for former GDR citizens, whose state was absorbed into an enlarged Federal Republic: with this transition, for them, the whole social world and web of relationships which had in large part constructed, constrained and sustained their identities also disappeared. The puzzles of generation formation and the transformation of social selves are thus presented most acutely in the successive ideological transitions from Nazism through communism to a capitalist democracy. West Germans only needed to perform one flip in this process—with also some significant continuities across the 1945 political divide, it should be noted, in both personnel and social and economic structures, for all the upheavals of the post-war period—while East Germans faced a far greater set of transformations, both in the scale and character of the transformations required after 1945 and in the upheavals after 1989. What concerns me most in this context, therefore, are patterns of accommodation to dictatorial regimes of opposing political colours, and the shifts across major mo-ments of historical ruptures. The comparisons developed here diachronically, across a long stretch of time, could well be supplemented, of course, by glances across the inner-German border at simultaneous developments in what was rarely called the 'other Germany' (an appellation generally retained by West Germans for the East, rather than vice versa); but the full realization of such a project, with systematic comparisons of generation formation in the two German states of the Cold War period, would require a major extension that would more than burst the bounds of this particular project.[3] The general line of inquiry, and the theoretical approach developed here, can of course be applied far more generally: not merely to West and as well as East Germany, but indeed to any other society at any time. The contours of the rapidly succeeding German states, and the character of the massive historical ruptures in twentieth-century Germany, perhaps allow us to see most clearly, both in detail and in high relief, more general processes which are at work far more broadly in other places and other times. The uniqueness of this singular history should not obscure the fact that major historical upheavals and challenges, and varying less-visible pressures and constraints, always help to shape the social behaviour, 'character', and self-representations of different communities at any given time.[4]

There have been innumerable attempts at answering the central questions of routes into and (for those lucky enough to survive) out of 'Auschwitz', understood as the epitome of modern industrial violence and the nadir of German history. It is only too evident that there can be no fully adequate mode of representation or explanation;

---

[3] It is interesting that very few Western textbooks or histories of 'Germany' before 1989 seemed to feel any need to make more than the merest gesture towards incorporating GDR history into a larger narrative, generally satisfying themselves with a few comments about the loss of the 'Soviet zone' and the significance of the Wall and repression, but barely giving more than the minimum of space to any deeper discussion.

[4] I shall be exploring some of these issues further in my work on *Reckoning with the Nazi Past*, part of an AHRC-funded project on *Reverberations of the Second World War in Europe*.

that, in face of the ultimate moral inexplicability of the gas chambers, all attempts at historical explanation will be at best partial. But this does not mean that some kinds of approach are not more adequate than others. While touching on these broader issues, it should be emphasized at the outset that this book is not concerned with the by now familiar (if still highly controversial) questions of policy formation and high politics, but rather with the ways in which ordinary people were involved in and affected by the wider systems that made Auschwitz possible, and those that followed. It is also important to stress that among the least adequate approaches to 'explaining Auschwitz' are those that seek to make generalizations about 'the Germans' or 'German traditions'. One of the major arguments of this work is that the question of which traditions, norms, and patterns of behaviour became predominant, which patterns of behaviour were fostered and which values suppressed, was very much a contested and always contingent matter; in this sense, the political context was always crucial.

II. A SENSE OF GENERATION: AGE-RELATED CHALLENGES AND UNRESOLVED ISSUES

The notion of social generations allows us to explore the extent to which, and the ways in which, people are shaped by their times, and in turn affect the times through which they live. But there are a wide variety of ways in which this slippery term is used, so some preliminary clarification is essential.

The most obvious, long-term general usage of the term is in the 'biological' sense, referring simply to family generations—grandparents, parents, children and so on—and linguistically rooted in the word for procreation. In the social sense, the term is used more broadly, in a variety of ways. It may refer to what are seen as age-related conflicts (rather than conflicts rooted in class, race, religion, gender, or other relevant attributes): for example, over life styles, leisure pursuits, sexuality, mutual duties and responsibilities relating to care of the young or the old, and so on. Similarly, a 'generational claim' may be made when articulate members of a particular age group feel a need to define themselves as distinct from others who are older or younger. These sorts of 'generational discourse' tend to arise when people are highly aware of, or sensitive to, rapid changes of social relations and cultural value systems, or when there are age-related conflicts over social activities or the distribution of resources. In recent media inflation, there has been something of a game of 'coining the generation', with slaphappy labelling for any phenomenon which might help to enhance sales figures or audience viewing rates in a Western culture obsessed by lifestyles.

In more theoretically self-aware senses, the term is also used in a variety of ways, partly driven by methodological concerns and partly by substantive questions.[5] The

---

[5] There is a growing literature on the concept of generations, with which I do not intend to engage explicitly here. See for a range of approaches and further references: Mark Roseman (ed.), *Generations in Conflict* (Cambridge: Cambridge University Press, 1995); Jürgen Reulecke (ed.), in collaboration with Elisabeth Müller-Lückner, *Generationalität und Lebensgeschichte im 20. Jahrhundert* (Munich: R. Oldenbourg Verlag, 2003); Ulrike Jureit and Michael Wildt (eds.), *Generationen* (Hamburg: Hamburger Edition, 2005); Ulrike Jureit, *Generationenforschung* (Vandenhoeck and Ruprecht,

notion of 'cohorts', those born within particular time periods, may be useful as an analytic tool simply for investigating the ways in which succeeding age groups had different experiences or characteristics, with an open mind about possible findings. Coming from quite another perspective, the notion of generation is often used to refer to 'second' and 'third generations' with respect to collectives such as 'immigrants', 'perpetrators' or 'victims/survivors', where the key experiences or characteristics of the 'original' group are held to have continuing implications for their children and grandchildren, irrespective of differences of age across members of any of these groups. 'Social generations' in a more general sense are often assumed to have characteristics in common by virtue of common experiences at a particular life stage, particularly in periods of radical political and social change. The classical formulation of this approach was to be found in Karl Mannheim's influential concept, which emphasized 'key formative experiences' (*Schlüsselerlebnisse*) which allegedly stamped their mark on members of a cohort, cutting across social or religious differences, at a crucial stage in youth; to be a 'social generation' in the full sense of the term, such formative experiences should also give rise to a later subjective sense of common collective identity.[6] Subjectively, the concept may be used by groups of contemporaries seeking to claim a role for themselves, as speaking for a wider cohort, or as a spearhead of cultural change. Sometimes both of these approaches overlap, with cross-fertilization between collective self-appellations and outsiders' analyses, as in the notion of the (left-wing) radicals known as '68ers', or the (largely right-wing) radicals of the Weimar Republic claiming to speak for a 'Front Generation' after the Great War.

Not all of these uses of the term are relevant in the current context, where the primary focus is on exploring the ways in which people lived through the German dictatorships. Here, for pragmatic purposes, the concept of generation is used in two quite specific senses.

The first has to do with what might be called 'sore-thumb generations' or 'cohort clusters'. These are members of particular cohorts which 'stick out' in the historical record, groups of people born within a few years of each other who tend to play a highly visible historical role in some way, with striking differences in their outlooks and actions from those born a few years earlier or a few years later. The prevalence of such 'cohort clusters' in particular positions at particular times is something which needs to be explained in some detail: to appeal simply to 'common generational experiences' fails to explain anything at all, since the distinctive cluster may or may not be typical of the wider cohort from which it is drawn, many members of

---

2006); and on historical approaches to generation formations in Germany, see e.g. Walter Jaide, *Generationen eines Jahrhunderts. Wechsel der Jugendgenerationen im Jahrhunderttrend. Zur Geschichte der Jugend in Deutschland 1871 bis 1985* (Opladen: Leske und Budrich, 1988); and on generations in different areas of Europe, see e.g. Dieter Dowe (ed), *Jugendprotest und Generationenkonflikt in Europa im 20. Jahrhundert. Deutschland, England, Frankreich und Italien im Vergleich* (Bonn: Verlag Neue Gesellschaft, 1986); and Stephen Lovell (ed.), *Generations in Twentieth-Century Europe* (Basingstoke: Palgrave Macmillan, November 2007).

[6] Karl Mannheim, 'Das Problem der Generationen' in Mannheim, *Wissenssoziologie* (Berlin: Luchterhand, 1964; orig. 1928), pp. 509–65.

which may not have developed in similar ways or drawn similar conclusions from their experiences. It is also worth noting that members of 'sore-thumb cohort clusters' may not be at all aware, subjectively, of participating in any kind of common generational experience. This is, then, a category imposed by external analysis, which may or may not find echoes in the subjective consciousness and discourse of those involved. In this particular usage, the notion of cohort clusters is a category designed solely to highlight the existence of statistical prevalence and curious patterns, which themselves require further exploration and explanation. Common experiences while young may, as we shall see, turn out to have less to do with later patterns of behaviour than do other factors, including differential birth and death rates, or post-war social and political opportunities.

In analysing the German dictatorships, it is highly striking that there are two particular cohorts that 'stick out' in this way. Even more strikingly, they are both, in some respects, what might be called 'war-youth generations': those either too young to fight in, or to take much responsibility during, the Great War; and those either too young to fight in, or to take much responsibility during, the Second World War. Members of both of these cohorts were nevertheless old enough consciously to witness and to draw what they presumed to be the lessons for the future of the two World Wars inaugurated and lost by Germany while they were still young. Both those born in the first decade or so of the twentieth century, and those born in the later 1920s and early 1930s, were radicalized by their generally indirect experiences of war as teenagers: both came to play highly active, historically significant political roles in later periods.

The first 'war-youth generation', born roughly from 1900–14, took the lessons of the Great War to mean radical commitment to new ideological causes—on both the right and the left. This was a highly politicized, but also highly divided generation. It remained divided: while one part played a major role in supporting the Third Reich, a smaller section of this cohort, bitterly opposed to and persecuted by the Nazis, took up key political roles in the communist cause once the opportunity presented itself in the GDR.

The second 'war-youth generation', whom I shall call the '1929ers', were those born from the mid-1920s through to the early 1930s, who were socialized entirely within the framework of Hitler's Third Reich. While a group of 1929ers stand out as significant in the public life of the Federal Republic of Germany, particularly in roles as 'public intellectuals', their most startling prominence was achieved, across the board, in the GDR, where members of the 1929er cohort became the most committed communists, not only populating significant positions across the range of institutions of state and society but also at lower levels and at the grass roots providing much of what support there was for the GDR. As curious as it seems, these younger members of what is often seen in an unduly undifferentiated fashion as one long 'Hitler Youth generation' were to become both the backbone of the East German communist functionary system and also, even among the wider population, generally the most supportive of the new communist system, the least religious, and the most nostalgic for the GDR after its collapse in 1989. In the GDR context at least, the 1929ers were far more homogeneous in outlook and attitude than the older members of East German society, among whom deep pre-war divisions persisted in radically altered circumstances. So these two 'sore-thumb generations' seem to demand much closer inspection: their striking prevalence in support of later ideological causes which were very different from the worlds in which they had been socialized requires exploration.

The second sense in which the concept of generation is used here is rather broader: it has to do with the differential impact of the times people live through and the significance of their 'social age' at time of particular historical contexts and developments. I am not in any way suggesting that common patterns of socialization, let alone any 'key formative experiences', necessarily produce similar *outcomes*, but rather seeking to draw attention to the importance of common *challenges* at a particular life stage—to which individuals may respond very differently—and, equally significantly, of *unresolved issues*, which become salient under later circumstances.

People of course face challenges throughout their lives—dealing with births or bereavements, sitting exams, forming relationships, making moves, applying for new positions—but these may remain quite haphazard in their distribution and patterning in any given area at any given time. Common challenges, however—arising, for example, from economic depression, civil war, mobilization for war abroad, repression by a dictatorial power, radically new social policies—are faced when major historical events massively intrude on what people consider to be their 'private lives'. Such challenges may be experienced by different cohorts in distinctive ways related to biological and social life-stages. Older people will face the demands made on them by a newly imposed dictatorship in different ways than will younger individuals, who have less by way of prior experience on which to base independent evaluations of a new ideology; similarly, children will have a different experience of war than adults in positions of responsibility at home or at the front, or elderly people with rather different resources and strategies for survival. Such age-related distinctions will of course be cross-cut by other distinctions which may be of far greater relevance: political commitments and 'race' radically divided German society in the Third Reich; politics continued, under totally different ideological colours, to cross-cut all else in the GDR; class and status, and in different ways gender, regional and religious differences, always cross-cut distinctions of generation. Yet the issue of generation remains an intriguing one, getting to the heart, as it does, of the possibilities of malleability and (self-)transformation of human beings in ways which are heavily patterned, if never entirely determined, by changing historical environments.

There are a variety of possible responses to common challenges, depending both on social location and on cultural and personal characteristics. Thus, some people will have greater 'structural' degrees of freedom than others, a wider range of opportunities to negotiate and navigate their own path through the circumstances which face them; others, by virtue, for example, of a lower social status, more restricted resources, or access to positions of power and influence, will have far less choice over where they are sent and what they are required to do. Thus, there are widely differing degrees of what might be called 'structural availability for mobilization'. Similarly, some milieus will be far more in tune with, or compatible with, whatever a given regime is trying to do at any particular time; others will be designated as oppositional, unacceptable, or simply impervious to penetration by whatever the dominant idea system demands at the time. This means that there are also varying degrees of what might be called 'cultural availability for mobilization'. Beyond these two aspects, however, it is also vital to note that individuals differ in terms of their own moral outlooks, personalities, willingness to compromise or conform, their capacity for independent thought, and their courage to take a stand, even under conditions of utmost risk. Even those who appear, in terms of their structural location, to have very limited degrees of freedom, in fact are often prepared to take a strong stand on the basis of personal moral convictions. In contrast, for example, the aristocratic officer class in the Third Reich—a group who, in terms of position, potentially had the highest degree of leeway—for the most part compromised and cooperated with Hitler's policies almost up to the end; and it was only a small fraction who dared to join in the oppositional activities around the July Plot of 1944 that could have toppled Hitler and terminated the war.

The level of individual perceptions and individual responsibility therefore cannot be written out of any concept of generations. But here there are major methodo- logical and theoretical issues to be addressed. It is important to distinguish between the 'inner self', the 'monitoring eye', and outer behaviour patterns; yet it is extraordinarily difficult for historians to gain access to the former. Moreover, even when there are apparently good historical sources, it is clear that the ways in which an individual thinks about and self-reflexively monitors his or her own 'performances' at any given time is in itself a historical product: there is no abstract 'authentic self', untainted by historical and social setting; even the most apparently 'private' ruminations, such as diary entries written only for the author's own benefit, are in quite large measure constituted by the discourses, aspirations, and characteristics which that setting has inculcated within the individual, whether in terms of internalization and unconscious acceptance, or in terms of resistance, discomfort, and partial reaction against, while yet simultaneously thinking in the very terms of the cultural codes and moral frameworks of the moment. This is, in a sense, the mystery of socialization: that individuals sense themselves to be unique, timeless souls, and yet reflect and enact, 'authentically', a role constituted within or against the terms of their times. Furthermore, any analysis of individual life stories over time, and particularly across major historical transitions, rapidly shows the ways in which individuals themselves are aware of a changing historical 'self'. What they share in common with others by way of assumptions, ways of thinking, concepts that serve to define the character of their world, values, aspirations, help to constitute what might be called a 'social self', irrespective of individual differ- ences in personality and aptitudes.

So with generations, we do have to be in some ways concerned with changing 'social selves'; but at the same time we have to remember that these too entail degrees of individual moral responsibility. 'Inner selves'—however socially and culturally constituted and informed—are also acting selves with varying experiences of distance from or harmony with the historical conditions in which they live; and individuals have degrees of choice about the ways in which they make their lives through often uncomfortable times. The ways in which they represent their choices and experiences are however highly coloured by the varying discourses of the day, and the ends they seek to achieve within any given context.

The second part of this sort of generation formation concerns 'unresolved issues': that is, the widespread salience of specific, selected aspects of experience at a later date. Such unresolved issues may consist in uncomfortable legacies of a persistent physical or psychological nature—the long-term effects of war wounds, traumatic experiences, loss of family and friends, a lasting sense of 'before' and 'after', difficulties with trust, and so on. Or they may consist in occasional challenges to which a response must be given: moments when particular actions are brought to account under a subsequent regime, or moments when a particular cultural development calls up repressed memories, and public debate reawakens old scars. They may be worked out through explicit, public, articulate debates; or they may remain inchoate, bubbling along at an informal level in the circles of families and friends, or even largely unspoken, revealed only in emotional reactions, patterns of behaviour, failures to connect, or 'active silences'. After the extraordinary violence of the first half of the twentieth century, culminating in the most brutal atrocities in war and the mass murder of millions of civilians on grounds of 'race', such evasions and silences always accompanied explicit controversies.

There is always fluidity in any moment of construction of a collective identity on the basis of generationally defined common experiences. Writing a history of 'social generations' is a bit like trying to paint a sky full of clouds which are constantly shifting in density, shape, relationship, sometimes barely existent at all and at other times looming over the landscape in ways which are inescapable. Generations are not 'essentialist' entities, always there to be negotiated: they are not continually existing collective actors. Both subjectively perceived and 'remembered' experience, and a collective discourse in a situation where certain 'memories' are selected as relevant, come together to form moments when a 'generational identity' may be experienced. But even then it is always experienced within a life full of other roles and identities, some of which may be far more important for those concerned— political, moral, religious, cultural, gender, class and ethnic identities may well take precedence for most people most of the time, not to mention everyday roles within family, locality, places of work and leisure, and so on. Yet interpretation of and confrontation with certain experiences may be patterned on generational lines, particularly in twentieth-century Germany where individual lives were so deeply affected by rapid, multiple, dramatic historical transitions; and the manner of later construction of these experiences, however personal the memories, is always 'con-taminated' or informed by later contexts of remembrance.

When exploring the question of social generations, then, one has to explore not only how individuals reacted to the challenges of the worlds in which they made their lives, but also the broader contexts of their perceptions, 'experiences', and later patterns of recounting or 'making sense of' their lives. For twentieth-century Germans, the central defining events for generation formation relate to the wars unleashed by Germany in 1914 and 1939, and to the extraordinarily intrusive, proactively mobilising, ideologically driven dictatorships of Nazism and Communism. The two World Wars and the radical regime changes across this century of violence made massive demands on and cut dramatic caesurae in the lives of those born during these turbulent times—experiences which were generationally patterned. The difficulty is in connecting the broader historical contexts and structures—the stuff of 'real history'—with the changing perceptions and culturally informed subjectivities of those whose lives were shaped by these historical contexts and who in turn helped to affect how things developed.

III. 'MOBILIZATION' AND INDIVIDUAL MOTIVES

One of the keys to understanding the impact and legacies of the two German dictatorships is that of mobilization; and this mobilization was highly distinctive with respect to the generations that acted as the prime 'carriers' of each. Effectively, both were sustained and supported disproportionately by the two 'war-youth generations'. These generations, and the puzzles they present—their historical prominence requires explanation, rather than providing any easy answers—are central to the analysis of the twentieth-century German dictatorships. In short, what we have to explain is the question of why certain groups were more readily mobilized in service of particular ideological causes than others.

The Third Reich was led by self-proclaimed members of the 'front generation' (among them, of course, Hitler, though there are problems with the designation of this alleged 'generation'), and largely 'carried' by the war-youth generation, those too young to have been directly involved but old enough to have had some direct personal knowledge of what the Great War meant for German society. It was most enthusiastically supported by what one might call the 'first Hitler Youth Generation', those born during and in the early years after the Great War. It is particularly among these last two groups—roughly, those born between 1900 and 1924—that the greatest enthusiasm for and active participation in the Nazi project is disproportionately to be found. In this sense, these are 'sore-thumb generations': despite deep internal divisions and the prevalence of strongly opposing views, their profile in the historical record sticks out as disproportionate in comparison with that of older or younger age groups in ways which require deeper historical exploration. We can say *that* they supported Nazism particularly strongly or actively; we still need to explain in some detail *why* this was so.[7] It requires a very careful generational analysis to determine why the most active carriers and supporters of Nazism were disproportionately drawn from among the 'younger' adults among the newly defined 'racial community' (*Volksgemeinschaft*) of Nazi Germany, and not from the self-proclaimed and in fact highly diverse 'front generation', from which of course a small proportion of right-wing leaders were drawn. Moreover, given the prevalence

[7] See also Michael Wildt, *Generation des Unbedingten* (Hamburg: Hamburger Edition, 2002).

of younger cohorts, who had not personally been involved in the Great War, in the later translation of Nazi ideology into violence in reality, questions must be raised about the alleged military 'cultures of violence' transmitted across time in Germany; some have suggested lines of continuity from the suppression of uprisings in the German colonies in the early 1900s, through atrocities committed following the invasion of Belgium and France in 1914, to the acts of terror in Poland following the outbreak of the Second World War in 1939.[8] When possible lines of transmission of 'cultures of violence' are explored in more detail, these younger cohorts appear to be generations 'carrying the torch' for those who were slightly older, rather than there being any significant continuities of personnel or some reified 'cultural tradition' of violence. A focus on the people who acted as carriers, and the political configurations which allowed some projects to rise to dominance over others, thus may help to clarify some of the issues involved. This book, then, argues against any disembodied notion of 'continuities' in mentalities or cultures, and focuses attention rather on changing historical agents under particular social and political circumstances.

Despite the differentially strong support for Nazism among those too young to have fought in the Great War, it has to be remembered that these were also radically divided generations, and increasingly so on both political and 'racial' lines. It is necessary to combine an analysis of generational experience and its subjective processing with a political analysis of the changing balance of forces through the 1920s and 1930s. This is particularly significant in light of the very rapid 'nazification' of German society after 1933, with implications for the mentalities, behaviour patterns, and new constructions of the self among enthusiasts and conformists on the one hand, and the dissidents and outcasts of Nazi society on the other. The Third Reich was a deeply intrusive regime which had fundamental implications for all who lived through it; the category of 'bystander' is arguably one of the least helpful of all in seeking to understand this period.

Living through the Third Reich also seems to have had key implications for one of the subsequent regimes, the German Democratic Republic (GDR), when viewed in generational terms. And again, curiously, it appears to have been a new, second 'war-youth generation', this time with reference not to the Great War but rather Hitler's war, who provided the most active and committed supporters of the new communist regime—although here we see some extraordinary twists of ideology and leaps of conversion.

Politically, the GDR was initially led by a tiny minority of committed communists drawn from the deeply divided front generation, with a tail of younger

---

[8] On these questions, see particularly Isabel Hull, *Absolute Destruction: Military culture and the practices of war in Imperial Germany* (Ithaca and London: Cornell University Press, 2005); John Horne and Alan Kramer, *German Atrocities: A history of denial* (New Haven and London: Yale University Press, 2001); see also Alan Kramer, *Dynamic of Destruction: Culture and mass killing in the First World War* (Oxford: Oxford University Press, 2007). The book by David Olusoga and Casper Erichsen, *The Kaiser's Holocaust: Germany's forgotten genocide and the colonial roots of Nazism* (London: Faber and Faber, 2010) unfortunately appeared too late for me to take into account in this work.

supporters and later leaders (including Erich Honecker) drawn from the first war-youth generation. Their distinction was in the depths of their communist commitment, their survival through the Third Reich (and indeed through Stalin's purges, if in exile in the Soviet Union), and thus, in some sense, in the generational experiences of the deep divisions of the earlier twentieth century, the classic 'age of extremes'.[9] The founding fathers of the GDR were, however, but a tiny minority of their cohort: the little splinter that still sought to fight the battles of earlier decades. The vast majority of their cohorts had, by contrast, been either active supporters of Nazism or had gone along with or somehow passively survived through the Nazi regime, insofar as they were not 'racially' excluded from the 'national community' or *Volksgemeinschaft*. While one might seek to adduce the generational experiences of those growing up during the Great War and the turmoil of its aftermath to explain generationally differential support for the Third Reich, one could hardly suggest that the succeeding communist dictatorship was massively supported by these cohorts, the majority of whom had not merely been steeped in the anti-communist, or 'anti-Bolshevik', ideology of Nazism, but had also been actively implicated in or beneficiaries of the associated racist and murderous practices. Their dislike and fear of the newly imposed communist regime with Soviet backing had major historical roots. And positions with respect to Nazism came to override earlier distinctions between generations: whether or not one had fought in the Great War paled into insignificance compared with the question of whether or not one had been an active Nazi. All those who had been sufficiently old during the Third Reich to have faced its challenges as adults became, effectively, now a 'KZ generation': whether having survived, actively sustained or benefited from Nazi rule, or whether having opposed or been victimized by the regime, all those who had been adults in the Third Reich were subsequently in some respects defined by having lived through this period in ways that those just a few years younger, children and teenagers during the Third Reich, were not.

The real puzzle emerges with respect to those a little bit younger: the cohorts born, roughly, from the later 1920s through to 1932, the 'second Hitler Youth generation' or those whom I prefer to call the '1929ers'. They are also sometimes known, at least as far as males among them are concerned, as the 'air force auxiliary generation' (*Flakhelfergeneration*) or, in another variant sometimes used to refer to intellectuals from these cohorts in the Federal Republic of Germany, the '1945ers'.[10] If the leaders of the GDR were but a tiny minority of older political

---

[9] Eric Hobsbawm, *Age of Extremes: The short twentieth century 1914–1991* (London: Penguin, 1994).

[10] For 'public intellectuals' in the Federal Republic, see e.g. Dirk Moses, *German Intellectuals and the Nazi Past* (Cambridge: Cambridge University Press, 2007); and Christina von Hodenberg, *Konsens und Krise. Eine Geschichte der westdeutschen Medienöffentlichkeit 1945–1973* (Göttingen: Wallstein Verlag, 2006). For a pioneering analysis revealing the significance of this age group for the GDR, see Lutz Niethammer, Alexander von Plato, and Dorothee Wierling, *Die volkseigene Erfahrung* (Berlin: Rowohlt, 1991).

activists, with massive backing from the occupying Soviet power, the long-term carriers of communism were drawn from the far broader group of those who had just reached the brink of adulthood at the time of foundation of the GDR. An analysis of 'Who was who in the GDR' (*Wer war wer in der DDR*) reveals that the communist state was functionally carried by a very narrow age range—the '1929ers'.[11] And an analysis of professed attitudes towards and memories of the GDR among different cohorts early in the twenty-first century reveals that the most striking support of, and evidence of active participation in, the organizational structures and political institutions of the GDR was to be found among precisely these 1929ers.[12] The differences in participation among the functional elites with respect to those just a few years older can be to a large extent explained by demography: there were very low birth rates in the Great War and differentially high death rates in the Second World War for these cohorts. But it is less easy to explain attitudinal differences among those who did survive.

Most striking, however, are the differences between the 1929ers and those born shortly afterwards, in the baby-boom years of the Third Reich, with its combination of a return to full employment and pro-natalist policies. Those large cohorts born during the Third Reich—the now much discussed generation of 'war children' (*Kriegskinder*), too young to have been fully socialized by the Hitler Youth or the formal education system, some of them direct 'witnesses of war' but far too young to have participated actively in war—not only played a disproportionately small role in the GDR regime, but also had the least positive attitudes towards the communist dictatorship, both at the time and later. Yet they tended on the whole to retreat into silence, or excelled in 'expressive' activities such as art and music, rather than being practically involved in the functioning of the system. Their relative 'absence' from political or functionary positions cannot be explained in terms of either post-war demography or politically channelled opportunity structures. They were, in numerical terms, abundant, alive, and well; nor did they face any 'blocked opportunities' through the early filling of posts by the slightly older 1929ers, since the mass flights to the West and the high turnover of personnel up to the building of the Wall in 1961 continued to provide ample opportunities for advancement among those politically untainted by Nazism by virtue of age, and relatively willing and committed, or at least prepared to conform in the ways required of them. 'Blocked opportunities' only became a serious issue with the

---

[11] Helmut Müller-Enbergs, Jan Wielgohs, and Dieter Hoffman (eds.), *Wer war wer in der DDR? Ein biographisches Lexikon* (Berlin: Christoph Links Verlag and Bundeszentrale für politische Bildung, 2001 edn). For further details, see Ch. 6, below, and M. Fulbrook, 'Generationen und Kohorten in der DDR. Protagonisten und Widersacher des DDR-Systems aus der Perspektive biographischer Daten' in Annegret Schüle, Thomas Ahbe, and Rainer Gries (eds.), *Die DDR aus generationengeschichtlicher Perspektive. Eine Inventur* (Universitätsverlag Leipzig, 2005), pp. 113–30.

[12] See further M. Fulbrook, '"Normalisation" in retrospect: East German perspectives on their own lives' in Fulbrook (ed.), *Power and Society in the GDR, 1961–1979: The 'normalisation of rule'?* (New York: Berghahn, 2009).

social stagnation of the 1970s and 1980s, affecting the prospects of cohorts born after the war but not those born during the Third Reich.[13]

How then should one try to explain these striking generational patterns of disproportionate participation and absence with respect to the Nazi and communist regimes? It is necessary to combine some kind of overview, including analysis of structures and generalizations about trends, processes, and exceptions, with selective in-depth probing into individual patterns of perception and response to the varying challenges of the day.

IV. 'INDIVIDUAL' LIVES

These developments, and the ways in which they were not merely perceived but enacted, indeed bitterly fought and contested, by contemporaries from a range of social and political positions, can be explored and arguably better understood by pursuing the differing paths of individuals living through the various transitions from imperialism through Nazism and communism. There is a vast range of sources for exploring the subjective experiences, perceptions, and inner ruminations of individuals, not all of which have as yet been adequately exploited by historians, let alone set together in a broad sweep across the century. This book draws on a wide variety of materials often known as 'ego-documents' or 'testaments to the self', including published and unpublished diaries, autobiographical essays and memoirs, letters to and from the front during the Second World War or across the 'Iron Curtain' dividing post-war Germany, and life stories derived from oral history interviews, as well as a myriad of archival sources. There is no suggestion that such sources can tell us 'how it really was'; contemporaries are often not the best guides to their own societies and often have little insight into the wider structures within which they live. But they do tell us a lot about changing perceptions and constructions of the social world, about ways in which people wanted to present themselves in different contexts, about inner conflicts and also about ambivalences and difficulties. And hence they provide insights into how particular societies functioned and changed; how people interacted with the wider political circumstances of their lives; and how they were affected by the momentous events of the century, carrying the traces and impact of earlier periods forwards, with implications for subsequent actions and attitudes, as well as transmission to those born later.

It may immediately be objected that individuals are not 'typical'. No claim is made here about any spurious 'typicality' for those whose lives have received attention in this book, although I have tried to trawl widely and ensure that a relatively broad range of voices and perspectives can be heard at any given period.

---

[13] See e.g. Ralph Jessen, 'Mobility and blockage during the 1970s' in Konrad Jarausch (ed.), *Dictatorship as Experience: Towards a socio-cultural history of the GDR* (New York: Berghahn, 1999), Ch. 18; and more generally on the transformation of East German social structure and social classes, M. Fulbrook, *The People's State: East German society from Hitler to Honecker* (New Haven and London: Yale University Press, 2005).

The significance of intertwining an exploration of individual lives with more general trends and patterns is rather different, and can be highly illuminating for several reasons.

First, in cases where the sources are adequate, this approach allows us to gain a deeper understanding of changing frameworks of perception over time: not merely changing vocabularies of expression, as dominant discourses and ways of seeing the world shifted, but also changing patterns of (self-)justification across major historical and political divides. Thus we do not have to wonder whether the vicissitudes of survival and suppression of documentation have left distinctive paper trails, prioritizing certain kinds of account over others, from which we construct a disembodied narrative of 'change', not knowing whether the 'culture' is changing, or whether some individuals are later simply keeping their mouths shut while others gain greater publicity. Where there is sufficient material we can, in short, probe aspects of changing views and discourses within the space of one person's life, as expressed in different contexts over a period of time.

Secondly, and perhaps particularly where an individual might be held to be far from 'typical', we can use such material to probe precisely what are the often hidden expectations and normative frameworks of a given historical context. This is very obviously the case where a person hits up against the normative and juridical borders of a regime, coming into conflict with whichever authorities disapprove of the conduct or attitudes of the individual in question. Thus the tracing of individual lives can be helpful in probing the boundaries and limits, the unspoken assumptions and hidden norms of behaviour, that might—precisely in their very 'normality' or taken for granted status in the period—go un-remarked or unnoticed in the diaries and letters of those who conformed and saw 'nothing special' to talk about.

Thirdly, exploring the development of individual lives allows us to explore the ways in which people are only in part a 'product of their times': it allows us to reach a better understanding of the kinds of moral choices facing people, of the ways in which they constructed or explained these choices to themselves, and the possible routes of action that were within their mental horizons. We can then better understand how people chose certain patterns of action and not others; without entering into the hoary questions around any concept of 'free will', it is important to understand the ways in which people historically perceived constraints and evaluated priorities, in choosing (or not even thinking about) how to act, particularly when they acted in ways with which we can barely empathize, let alone sympathize or admire. For all the emphasis on birth cohorts and generational groupings, and on the social and historical construction and shaping of social roles, this analysis is predicated on the view that there is an irreducible core of individuality, however hard that may be theoretically to define and however historically bounded and constructed the expressions of 'individuality' may be. Yet each individual could only operate within a historically situated, socially and culturally defined, and politically constrained field of forces, and it is within the domain of the historian to explore just how the 'inner self', as socially expressed in letters, diaries, memoirs, developed in constant interaction with an 'outer' environment from which the seeing eye might experience greater or lesser degrees of distance. People might develop very different senses of identity, or adopt different roles and personae simultaneously, under different circumstances; an exploration of the expressions of 'inner self' and observed behaviour patterns can help us to understand the changing historical constraints and opportunities all the better.

Finally, and not least in importance, a focus on selected lives over longer periods of time can be of help in exploring the longer-term consequences that certain patterns of behaviour, perhaps disproportionately fostered under one regime but condemned by a subsequent state, may have had for conceptions of self, attitudes, and values, and ways of representing a particular past to others, including to later generations. In this way, it is possible to gain a clearer understanding of the less-obvious legacies of particular historical moments for later ways of thinking, making choices, and acting. 'Coming to terms with' an ever receding past, a transient present, and a constantly overhauled future, is an integral part of the transmission of values and social relations. 'Memory', or at least the ways in which people recount their actions under different contexts, is an intrinsic part of later social and cultural relations, and is thus integral to the project of understanding generational shifts not only across twentieth-century Germany, but has far wider relevance for other times and places.

V. DISSONANT LIVES THROUGH THE GERMAN DICTATORSHIPS

The two German dictatorships are rarely set together in terms of continuities across 1945, a divide which has been more easily, or at least in the Western historiography more frequently, crossed with respect to the transition from the Third Reich to the Western Federal Republic of Germany; and insofar as they are set within the same framework, the approach is generally that of key events and changes in political and social history across a radical historical caesura, and not that of the lingering consequences for and effects on the people living through this period. A generational approach can, by contrast, help to explore the ways in which such states affected those who lived through them and moreover, in the particular twisted history of twentieth-century Germany, made the transition from one to the other. Through what follows, episodes and developments in individual lives are explored, some in greater depth and some only briefly, with an eye to the ways in which perceptions, choices, and behaviours were not only shaped by the changing circumstances of their times, but also in turn actually made certain developments, certain types of politics and society, more possible than others.

Throughout, a key theme is that of the changing character and consequences of different kinds of violence, as well as the ways in which violence was experienced differently by people of different ages. For this, it is important to start where many of the people who carried the Nazi project in the Third Reich themselves started: in the early twentieth century. The major focus of this book is on patterns of living through the two German dictatorships, but these cannot be understood without exploring the experiential context of what came before: the legacies of Imperial

Germany and defeat in the Great War, and the political instability and economic upheavals of the Weimar years, are the essential backdrop to exploring the massive disruption to German lives wrought by Hitler's attempts to create a 'racially pure' society that would dominate the world. When alleged 'continuities' in German traditions of militarism or cultures of violence are explored, it becomes very clear that particular political conditions and unique historical circumstances rendered some people far more susceptible to the lures of radical politics than others, and allowed certain forces to become dominant while others were suppressed. Chapters 2 and 3 trace some of the diverse ways in which individuals were variously involved in or affected by the trajectory of violence before 1933, from genocidal practices in Germany's African colonies, through the Great War and the radicalization of politics in the paramilitary movements of the 1920s, to the appointment of Hitler as Chancellor in 1933. It rapidly becomes clear that what ultimately emerged was by no means foreordained. Furthermore, and more importantly in this context, nor were people's responses to these challenges prefigured: the debates and disagreements in a deeply divided society were intense. The fact that the radical right eventually gained the upper hand in 1933 did not preclude the equally radicalized left-wing splinters of the first war-youth generation from returning to the historical stage at a later juncture, when the balance of power internationally tipped in their favour in what became East Germany after the Second World War.

Once Hitler had appropriated a monopoly of state-sanctioned force in the 1930s, however, the possibilities for contestation were radically constrained. The stain of racism that spread through German society in the 'peace-time' years of the Third Reich contaminated all who came into contact with this phenomenon, one way or another, as explored in Chapter 4. A key argument here is that what I have called the 'formation of two worlds' was in itself a form of hidden violence— at least, in the sense that many of those 'perpetrating' it, without necessarily being involved in or approving of acts of physical violence, were frequently unaware of the full impact and hurtfulness of their actions against those who were progressively excluded from the circle of fellow citizens (and ultimately, unless they were very lucky, from the land of the living entirely). Those who were young adults in the early 1930s were uniquely poised to make their careers with and within a Nazi state that was radically purging and excluding all its real and imagined opponents, on 'racial' or political grounds; many others, less committed but unwilling to face the risks of open disaffection, were prepared in public to 'go along' with the game they now felt they had to play—but with the consequence of further exclusion of those designated as outcast from the circle of fellow citizens. The apparent antinomy between repression and enthusiasm—giving rise to repeated debates about the balance of consensus, conformity, and coercion in Nazi Germany—is dissolved once we realize the extent to which people were able to disassociate their inner reservations from outward accommodation to both the perceived and the undeniably real and unavoidable demands of the regime. And again, it becomes apparent that responses were interestingly patterned not only by all the obvious factors ('race', class, religion, region, morality), but also by age: generation crucially affected the character and degrees of exposure to Nazi influences and pressures, the levels of enthusiasm and willingness or otherwise to conform, and the longer-term implications of experiences before, during, and after the Third Reich. This period and what came afterwards also cannot be adequately understood without a sense of what war meant for millions of Germans of different backgrounds and generations. Once Hitler's policies—which were imbued with violence all along—exploded into an aggressive war of expansion and annihilation, the mobilization of those included in the Nazi 'racial community' was far wider, embracing even those who were less than willing participants in the process, inexorably affecting their own sense of self and community. Chapter 5 makes an attempt, again, not merely to rehearse the horrendous developments of war and extermination during these years but to explore the ways in which people were differentially involved and how they conceived their experiences, with different implications for self-understandings and the possibilities for shaping later post-war lives.

The book could have ended just there, in 1945. But it did not, for a number of reasons. The legacies of Nazism for post-1945 Germany—and indeed for Germany still today—can only be fully comprehended if we explore the ways in which history did not simply come to an end, or simply start afresh, at the 'zero hour' of 1945. People's lives are messier and more continuous than the narratives of history books that confine and contain historical periods within the dates of particular political systems; and the age at which individuals crossed this greatest of historical divides made a massive difference to the ways in which they engaged with what came afterwards, thus shaping what was or was not historically possible in the post-war world. This point is true for both of the German states founded on the soil of the defeated Third Reich, and its implications have been increasingly explored for the West German state, the Federal Republic of Germany. Our understanding of the succeeding German dictatorship in East Germany is, however, equally if not even more likely to be enhanced by setting it within the context of the broader understandings of history that this approach allows. The GDR is so easily and frequently seen simply as an imposition out of the sky, as it were, by the occupying Soviet forces, instantly rendering all those Germans under Soviet control innocent victims of communist oppression; but it may be nuanced rather differently in the light of the approach suggested here. Volume II opens with a brief summary of the curious, generationally patterned character of differential support for the GDR, which is then, in the following chapters, explored further in terms of subjective experiences and perceptions in changing circumstances. Subsequent chapters variously explore the ways in which people of different generations sought to establish a degree of what they saw as 'normality' after a period of unprecedented suffering and violence; how they sought to build new lives and construct a better future while still dealing with the legacies of the past; and how, increasingly, the drab present of 'actually existing socialism' began to crumble, inaugurating the final major transition of the century, the 'gentle revolution' of 1989 and the demise of the GDR through unification with the West in 1990.

The Third Reich unleashed unrivalled destruction, radically transforming or truncating the lives of millions of people across the world, and lasted a mere dozen years. It has become a mountain in history. The GDR, by contrast (consigned by some historians to the status not even of a foothill but merely a 'footnote in history'), struggled along for forty years, attempting to create a more equal and just society of 'workers and peasants', under the constant paranoid surveillance of the State Security Service or Stasi, and behind the massive fortifications of concrete, barbed wire, and machine guns that formed the 'Iron Curtain' between Cold War East and West. This was long enough for generations to be born, come to maturity, and make their adult lives under conditions which they increasingly—despite the obvious barriers in a divided Germany—began to take for granted as a new form of what they saw as everyday 'normality'. For the first time for the best part of a century, generations lived through decades of peace; and while fears of a Third World War were very present through the 1950s, in the years of détente (before the renewed superpower tensions in Europe from the late 1970s), people even began to feel there was a secure future, in a context which might not be ideal but in which they sought to make the best of their lives. For East Germans, in a relatively guilt-free context as far as official representations of the past were concerned, 'coming to terms' with the communist present very often took precedence over any concern for the Nazi past. Even so, the past remained always to some extent present, particularly when precipitated by commemorations, life events, or the quest for advantages or avoidance of disadvantage. For many older East Germans, memories of times prior to division, and the character of defeat and occupation introduced notes of dissonance into the life stories of those expected to buy into the new myth of 'liberation', and continued animosities were exacerbated a by a sense of loss of years of one's own life and damage suffered which could never be redeemed. Living through this regime, too, where violence was in a sense concentrated at the literal and metaphorical borders of the regime—the Wall and the Stasi stand as shorthand for visible physical repression as well as hidden control through surveillance and manipulation—had a further impact on the patterning of inter-personal relations and social selves. Moreover, the sheer extent of social and economic transformation during the relatively lengthy lifespan of the GDR—surviving for more than three times as long as either of its immediate predecessors—requires exploration. Here again, the generational dynamics are complex yet crucial.

Particularly interesting about the history of twentieth-century Germany is the way in which the Nazi regime was replaced by a dictatorship of quite opposite ideological colours in the communist GDR. While the vast majority of members of older generations were officially exonerated by the new communist regime in what was now a self-proclaimed 'anti-fascist state', their own experiences and actions were not adequately represented in the new state. They had to come to terms with it—or, particularly if among those groups adversely affected by communist policies, or with relatives in the West, or seeing better economic and professional chances, seek to flee before the last hole in the border was sealed with the erection of the Berlin Wall in August 1961. But others were remarkably, surprisingly supportive—a feature that has to date been far less well explored, let alone explained, than the familiar history of dissent and flight. Moreover, the support came from what might at first seem highly unlikely quarters. One of the oddest features of GDR history is that those who had been most exposed to Nazi propaganda, those who had been socialized entirely within the period of Hitler Youth organizations, became the most stalwart supporters and institutional carriers of the new communist state. The tales they heard in the family were perhaps not the tales that were officially proclaimed; and, with the need for sudden radical conversion from Nazism to communism, there was arguably from the outset a sense of inbuilt dissonance. Yet they made a clean break with a past in which many felt they had been 'betrayed' and sought to build anew. They were, in the end, not entirely successful even in the terms of their own visions and ideals of the 'better Germany'; but they remained, even after the end of the GDR—which coincided with their own entry into retirement—the most nostalgic for aspects of its unique society and what they saw as its distinctive achievements.

The East German dictatorship was characterized not only by its difficult birth and early years, marked by upheaval and violence; it also witnessed a period of relative 'normalization of rule', in which a degree of increasing predictability and routinization fed into a sense of stagnation, before the decline during the 1980s and the sudden demise of the GDR in the 'gentle revolution' of 1989. And it was those who had been socialized entirely within the GDR, born in the early 1950s, who were at the forefront of the often highly idealistic attempts to transform it from within, and which ultimately brought it down with the collapse of communism. Yet Germans lived through this last great rupture, eventuating in unification with the Western Federal Republic of Germany in 1990, and later looked back on their lives, in ways that were somewhat at odds with their enthusiasm for the revolutionary challenges of autumn 1989.

* * * * *

These cases raise central questions about twentieth-century German history. Put very simply, they point to questions about the long-term preconditions and the eventual ways in which genocide could take place in a highly advanced society which prided itself on its level of 'civilization'; they point to questions about how individuals conceived of their behaviour at the time, how they dealt with state-sanctioned incidents of violence, and how they sought to confront, or evade, accounts of their own roles in it afterwards; and they point to questions about how the violent pasts of twentieth-century Germany were not only represented and dealt with in later decades, but also shaped patterns of behaviour and attitudes across generations, with continuing reverberations right up to the present. These levels are inchoate, far more difficult to grasp and define than are the obvious points of political history, with moments of policy formation, events, and decisions; but the attempt to write 'history from within', discussed more explicitly as a theoretical approach in the concluding chapter of Volume II, promises to yield a deeper understanding of the most significant questions of recent German, and indeed world, history.

Selected aspects of an ever changing, ever reinterpreted past were always present, at whichever time of the century we look. Across each of these phases and historical ruptures, Germans repeatedly had to invent themselves anew, with ambivalent and complex attitudes towards a personal past that they had to recast in later representations of their own former roles. This could be achieved with varying measures of success depending both on earlier behaviours and later requirements, but always at some personal cost to a sense of a continuous self; and in a context where individuals frequently bore the physical and emotional scars of what had come before, carrying the legacies of their personal past in ways that could not always easily be realigned with the demands of the new. Most notable, perhaps, is the fact that at each major historical turning point—1933, 1945, 1989—it was the then young adults who were best placed to engage with the new projects of building a better future, whether or not they threw off, rejected, or preserved selective aspects of the supposed legacies of the old. This too gave a unique generational dynamic to the course of German lives, as people variously challenged, trumpeted, or bemoaned what they saw as the actions and omissions of their forebears. This book is, then, not a 'history of Germany' in the twentieth century, nor even a 'history of Germans', but rather, through exploration of the striking patterning of individual lives in the context of world historical events, an attempt to make more intelligible these extraordinary times, and to understand in greater depth how people perceived, were shaped by, and variously contributed to the turbulent times in which they lived.

2

Violence abroad: Generations and the legacies of imperialism

I consider the accused [Hans Paasche] to be a person who is energetic, dashing, but not adequately brought up, which is doubtless why any inhibitions seem to have been switched off...; I believe that his pacifist inclinations were rooted in his participation in the East African turmoil, where he distinguished himself in his part in it, but later, as he more than once reported, found the killing of people painful.[1]

There was no straightforward 'front generation', although there was a great deal of myth-mongering around this concept, claimed as it later was for political purposes. Nor did the escalation of genocidal violence in the African colonies of Imperial Germany, or the atrocities committed during the Great War, stand in any direct line of continuity with the brutality and genocide carried out under Nazi auspices, on a far more extensive scale, some thirty or forty years later. But these early experiences of colonial violence and European war did have a massive impact, with reverberations across the century. The Great War destroyed structures and un-leashed forces that destabilized the continent for decades, the ensuing tensions arguably only resolved with the end of the Cold War in 1989–90.

Far more insidious than any alleged front generation for the course of history in the following decades was the development of the war-youth generation: those whose lives were marked by what they saw as the consequences of the Great War, and by their self-imposed missions. Yet even here, matters are more complex than might at first appear. There was no single, simple understanding of what the 'mission' might be: even the war-youth generation, which has been singled out as a 'generation of the unbound' fighting for the radical right, was a deeply divided generation.[2] Radicalism and the use of violence for political purposes were common to many parts of both the far left and the extreme right in the Weimar years. Which strand ultimately became dominant was not a matter of particular 'formative experiences', but rather of power politics—and of the eventual domination of the radical right, with state monopoliza-tion of the means of violence, and brutal repression of political alternatives.

---

[1] Bundesarchiv Berlin (BAB), R 3003 / C 153 / 17, Vol. 2, Affidavit of Korvettenkapitän Walter Goethe, fol. 38.
[2] See particularly Michael Wildt, *Generation des Unbedingten* (Hamburg: Hamburger Edition, 2002).

Growing up in the shadow of the war-youth generation were those a few years younger, who were in the 1930s to become the 'first Hitler Youth generation': people who as youngsters had witnessed at first hand what the crises of the Weimar years had meant for their own parents and families. Depending on their political and moral background and inclinations, a substantial proportion of this generation was readily available for mobilization in the Nazi cause and prepared to engage in the use of violence in the course of the 1930s.

All of these comments with respect to the activities of distinctive generations merely refer to splinters: to those who stand out in the historical record as particularly active, particularly visible in spearheading or providing the troops in the many battles for the soul and future of Germany in a highly unstable age. Millions of others, less evident in the historical record, witnessed and were marked by the turbulent times through which they lived, and sought in far quieter ways to conform to the norms of the age or to make their own more wayward paths through the thickets of convention and constraint.

Through exploration of individual lives—in this case, particularly that of Hans Paasche—we can begin to understand some of the patterns and the costs of different kinds of individual responses to age-related challenges through imperialism, war, and crises bordering on civil war.

I. HANS PAASCHE AND COLONIAL VIOLENCE

In August 1905 Hans Paasche, still in his early twenties and in charge of a small group of European sailors and African *Askari*, or native soldiers, had to participate in a hastily assembled military tribunal in the small colonial outpost of Mohoro, on the River Mufiji in the then German colony of Tanganyika.[3] Paasche was roped in at the last minute as one of the military judges listening to the cases of four Africans who had allegedly been involved as rebel leaders in the Maji-Maji uprising. Paasche was unusual among the Europeans in the area in having taken the trouble to learn the native language, Kiswahili, and could more or less follow the proceedings. The four undernourished and semi-clad Africans whose cases were heard did not look to Paasche like dangerous rebels, unlike those whose armed combat he had faced in the bush. The assertions and counter-assertions presented that hot morning did not amount to anything that could be called a compelling legal case; the linguistic difficulties, and the speed of the hearing, did not inspire any confidence in the judgment. Following pleas of innocence on the part of the accused, and wild accusations on the part of witnesses for the prosecution, the four Africans were duly sentenced to death and hanged in front of a large group of local people who

---

[3] On Hans Paasche's life, including a selection of his works, see: Magnus Schwantje, *Hans Paasche: Sein Leben und Wirken* (Berlin: Verlag Neues Vaterland, E. Berger and Co., 1921); *Flugschriften des Bundes Neues Vaterland* Nr. 26/27, pp. 1–28; Helmut Donat (ed.) in collaboration with Wilfried Knauer, with an Introduction by Helga Paasche, *'Auf der Flucht' erschossen . . . Schriften und Beiträge von und über Hans Paasche. Zum hundertsten Geburtstag von Hans Paasche* (Bremen/Zeven: Schriftenreihe das andere Deutschland, 1981).

had been assembled to witness and learn from this demonstration of German 'justice'. The bodies of the alleged ringleaders of rebellion were left dangling from the trees in the square outside the administration building of this tiny outpost of European 'civilization', their stench increasingly unpalatable in the midday sun, but were not removed for hours as a 'lesson' for the native population.

This incident was to trouble Paasche for the rest of his life, radically affecting his attitudes towards war and the use of violence. He became an active member of the pre-war German youth movement, an outspoken critic of the pervasive military culture and political leadership of Imperial Germany, and eventually, following two years of increasingly disaffected service in the Great War, he became what one biographer has termed a 'militant pacifist'.[4] Paasche had drawn his own lessons from his experiences of violence in the German colonies which were very different from those of many others in his generation. Moreover, as the bourgeois son of the vice-president of the Reichstag, Hermann Paasche, Hans Paasche was drawn from precisely that class of society which had been socialized to uphold the dominant norms of Imperial Germany. His case, then, is all the more surprising—and highly revealing, both in the waywardness of his life and in the eventual manner of his passing, of the kinds of norms, pressures, and challenges facing young men of his background at these times. In a perverse kind of way, Paasche's idiosyncratic challenging of the boundaries of the dominant moral universe of Imperial Germany serves to highlight some of its key elements—and to illuminate aspects of the violent birth of Weimar democracy, a democracy that was truly less than democratic as far as radical politics were concerned.

Hans Paasche was born in 1881 in the Baltic port of Rostock.[5] His father, Hermann Paasche, was a committed National Liberal who first entered the Reichstag in the year of his son's birth; he was a landowner of comfortable means, as well as an academic economist who authored tracts on the devaluation of money, the East African economy, and the worldwide sugar trade. In the course of all this he also travelled very widely, including in Africa, the Far East, and North and Central America. Most importantly for his son Hans, he was an emotionally cold, authoritarian *pater familias* who came to stand, for Paasche junior, for all that was wrong with Imperial Germany and its notions of 'civilization'. The personal conflict between father and son embodied and reflected the wider generational and political conflicts in which Hans Paasche became so deeply engaged.

When Hans was three the family moved to Marburg, where his father held a position at the university; and when he was twelve, they moved again, this time to Berlin, so that his father could commit himself more fully to parliamentary activities while retaining his academic interests. Hans Paasche was gifted musically—encouraged by his mother Elise—but did not enjoy the strict, elite

---

[4] Werner Lange, *Hans Paasche: Militant pacifist in Imperial Germany* (Trafford Publishing, 2005).
[5] For biographical accounts, see: Helmut Donat, 'Vom preussischen Militär zum deutschen Pazifisten und Revolutionär—Zum hundertsten Geburtstag von Hans Paasche' in Donat (ed.), *'Auf der Flucht' erschossen...*, pp. 13–27; Lange, *Hans Paasche*; Magnus Schwantje, 'Hans Paasche: Sein Leben und Wirken', *Flugschriften des Bundes Neues Vaterland* Nr. 26/27 (Berlin: Verlag Neues Vaterland, E. Berger and Co., 1921), pp. 1–28.

secondary school he attended in Berlin, the Joachimsthal Grammar School (*Gymnasium*). With his strong dislike of the school atmosphere and discipline apparently compounded by poor health and inappropriate medical treatment, Paasche left school a year early, not following in his father's academic footsteps— a matter no doubt of some disappointment to his parents. But an acceptable alternative career was rapidly organized. With some assistance from his father's close friend Admiral Alfred Tirpitz, who was in charge of the Naval Office of Imperial Germany, Hans Paasche became a Naval Cadet in 1899 and, by virtue of ability as well as social background, rapidly rose to a position of some responsibility at a relatively young age.

By 1905, at the time of the colonial rebellion in German East Africa, Hans Paasche was a well-established young marine whose ship, the *Bussard*, had been conveniently cruising in the Indian Ocean off the coast of Tanganyika following a year-long trip starting in Bremerhaven in May 1904, and including a stint in Ceylon and the Seychelles. Paasche felt himself to be at the very dawn of his own life, enthusiastic and invigorated by the as yet unfamiliar world which still awaited him, as he proclaimed in his autobiographical account, penned and published a mere two years later, entitled *Im Morgenlicht* ('In the light of dawn').[6] But in August 1905 the course of his life was dramatically altered when he was called in to help suppress the Maji-Maji rebellion that had begun to trouble the German colonial administration over the previous few weeks.

This anti-colonial uprising was in some respects a simple rebellion against German economic exploitation and political repression.[7] But it had unique features, notably the belief in the protective powers of a 'magic water' which would allegedly protect wearers of certain charms against the lethal impact of German bullets. A number of 'ordinary magicians', versed in fertility medicines for both crops and human health, had been persuaded of the additional powers of the 'magic water' discovered by one particular magician. This belief, combined with successful techniques of peer-group pressure and somewhat coercive methods of forcibly persuading reluctant villagers to join the uprising through threatening those who refused, meant that the forces of rebellion spread rapidly across the whole of the southern area of German East Africa, beyond the initial location where small incidents among cotton-pickers had initially sparked unrest. Given the combination of magical beliefs and economic and political unrest, as well as incipient civil war among the rebelling and non-rebelling native populations (with plundering and burning of villages that had refused to join the rebels), and heightened movement across the area behind the European outposts for some weeks, there had been rising concern among the very thin and inadequately protected layer

---

[6] Hans Paasche, *'Im Morgenlicht'. Kriegs-, Jagd- und Reise-Erlebnisse in Ostafrika* (Berlin: Verlag von C. A. Schwedtke und Sohn, 1907).
[7] For general accounts, see: John Iliffe, *A Modern History of Tanganyika* (Cambridge: Cambridge University Press, 1979); and Thomas Pakenham, *The Scramble for Africa 1876–1912* (London: Weidenfeld and Nicolson, 1991).

of European authorities.[8] Moreover, African discontent with the European suppression led to violent incidents against what were otherwise seen as relatively harmless missionaries, with the murder of a bishop, two nuns, and three others connected with the mission precipitating particular disquiet among Europeans.[9] The uprising itself was relatively rapidly contained. It started in the early summer of 1905, reached a peak in August and was finally brought under control in the ensuing months of the autumn, winter and spring of 1905–6. Its longer-term consequences for the local population in terms of decimation through disease and mass starvation were, however, horrendous. Paasche's role in the immediate suppression of the uprising was but one part of the wider colonial effort, but by no means an insignificant part; and his ruminations on the use of violence are highly revealing.[10]

Paasche's first task was to guard the small colonial outpost of Mohoro on the Rufiji delta, but then news reached him that the rebellion was spreading and rebels were quite close at hand.[11] For fear that even more natives would feel they had little choice but to join the rebels if Europeans did not rapidly demonstrate decisive strength and restore order, and in the absence of clear orders from the colonial government in Dar es Salaam beyond the need to protect Mohoro, Paasche persuaded himself that it was best to go out and make a display of military superiority:

> Refugees reported that the rebels, an hour and a half away from Mohorro, were burning, plundering and shooting . . . The agitation of the people in face of the danger so close by gave cause for thought . . . Above all, since the rebels were ransacking and killing anyone who did not come over to their cause, the black people living in the surrounding areas had to decide whether to join the uprising in order to save their property and the harvest which they had just brought in, if they could not rely on protection by the Europeans.[12]

---

[8] There were conflicting contemporary accounts of how the uprising was precipitated, whether or how long there had been prior organization among those intending to rebel, how long those who were put to death had been detained, and why their punishment had been rapidly changed from relatively lenient sentences to the death penalty. See for one perspective of a local administrative official, Otto Stollowsky, 'Ein Beitrag zur Vorgeschichte des Aufstandes in Deutsch-Ostafrika im Jahre 1905/06', *Die deutschen Kolonien*, Bd. XI, 1912, 138–43, 170–3, 204–7, 237–9, 263–6; also available for download from <http://www.mhudi.de/maji/Anno25.html> (accessed 4 Oct. 2009).

[9] See Pater Cyrillus Wehrmeister, *Vor dem Sturm: Eine Reise durch Deutsch Ostafrika vor und bei dem Aufstande 1905* (St. Ottilien: Missionsverlag, 1906).

[10] A closer examination of Paasche's views reveals a more complex situation than that sketched in briefly by Isabel Hull, *Absolute Destruction: Military culture and the practices of war in Imperial Germany* (Ithaca and London: Cornell University Press, 2005) (who also mistakenly gives Paasche an undeserved 'von' before his surname).

[11] An anonymous official account may be found in 'Die Tätigkeit der Marine während der Niederwerfung des Eingeborenen-Aufstandes in Ostafrika 1905/06', *Beiheft zur Marinerundschau* (Mai Heft), Berlin 1907; also available for download from <http://www.mhudi.de/maji/Anno62.html> (accessed 5 Oct. 2009). Mohoro is variously written as Mohorro; I have retained the spelling within quotations as given in each source.

[12] Hans Paasche, *'Im Morgenlicht'*, pp. 80–1.

Thus convinced that he was actually also acting in the native people's cause, Paasche took a group of eleven sailors and thirty Askaris to find the rebelling natives or 'Schenzis'. A day in the bush of skirmishing and shooting ended with the deaths of several natives.

Even despite his earlier reasoning about the importance of a rapid and effective display of force, Paasche's first experience of causing death in military combat left him shaken and uncertain:

> That was, then, the first encounter with the enemy. Blood had been spilled. The first corpses lay there, shot by our guns. It touched me wondrously; who gave us the right to shoot people?—Why did precisely these ones die while others got away?[13]

Paasche was even more shaken following a subsequent battle—again 'successful', but which had left one of his own men killed—when he took the decision not to take prisoners of war, but instead ordered shootings on the spot. His reasoning was that he did not have the spare manpower required to march any prisoners of war back through the bush to a place where they could be securely held, but there was no superior at hand with whom he could discuss this decision. Paasche managed eventually to come to terms with what he had done, but remained somewhat ill at ease:

> The impressions of the morning, the battle, the death of a comrade and the decisions that led me to the death sentence for the rebels, overwhelmed me. And again and again the feeling of responsibility came to the fore: would it be recognized that I did the right thing in following the enemy into his hiding place and that I kept on pushing onwards? Would the sacrifice demanded by this morning's battle be understood?[14]

Paasche later managed, on a subsequent day when a prisoner was brought in and the Askari wanted him shot on the spot, to formulate a general rule that he considered an acceptable guide to future behaviour. Refusing to have this particular prisoner shot, Paasche reflected:

> Perhaps he simply joined the rebellion out of stupidity . . . You can't hold it against any of these heroes if they take up arms, and instinct leads them astray in the belief that through a common struggle they could get rid of disagreeable conditions.
>
>   So let that be our principle: we have to protect ourselves, whether or not through bloodshed—if we want to remain the masters, when after all we only have the right of the stronger party and the privilege of cultured beings . . .
>
>   Who would shoot his horse, that works for him, because it kicks out? Was not the rope perhaps too short; and the whip was supposed to help?[15]

While demonstrating some understanding and empathy for the plight of the Africans who were protesting against the conditions imposed on them by the German colonizers, Paasche's reflections still betray the assumptions of his time about European 'cultural superiority'; nevertheless, he supported only the use of

---

[13] *Ibid.*, p. 83.   [14] *Ibid.*, p. 102.
[15] Paasche, *'Im Morgenlicht'*, p. 121.

defensive violence to protect the German position, not the penalizing violence of making an example by having a prisoner put to death.

But the 'legal' hanging in the town square of Mohoro on that late August day left Paasche increasingly troubled; he was later even more troubled by his own failure to speak out against it at the time, and his failure, as he saw it, to 'tell the truth' about warfare in the years immediately following, allowing a mythology of the glory of military combat and violence to be sustained among those Germans at home who had not directly experienced it at first hand. In his account of this incident, written some three years later and first published in 1909, at a time when he was still trying to conform to the expected attitudes and mores of Imperial Germany, Paasche already registered a palpable degree of disquiet about his participation in this event: he felt uneasy about the cold 'justice' of this kind of killing, in contrast to the apparently more legitimate slaughter incurred in what he could consider as defensive field battles against the militant and threatening rebels.

The experience of colonial violence in German East Africa was a key turning point, or what Germans like to call a '*Schlüsselerlebnis*', for Hans Paasche.[16] He returned to Germany committed to reform, and over the following years energetically threw himself into movements serving a variety of causes: vegetarianism, protection of animals and birds (he was among the first to campaign against a trade in feathers from rare species of birds), the youth life reform movements critiquing the militarism and general mores of Imperial Germany, and pacifism. It is by no means the case that exposure to violence must always have 'brutalizing' consequences; and although Paasche was certainly a highly unusual character, he was far from unique in his responses to violence.

Did the suppression of the Maji-Maji rebellion in German East Africa also play a role in heralding, by contrast, the beginnings of a 'military culture' of violence that was to pave the way, eventually, to the genocidal policies pursued by Hitler?[17] This case has been raised, more directly, in relation to earlier developments in German South-West Africa. In the summer of 1904 General Lothar von Trotha had taken command of the suppression of the Herero rebellion against German rule, a task he pursued by ever more forceful measures. On 2 October 1904 von Trotha issued orders to shoot all adult males, and to expel women and children into the desert where, given the lack of food and water, they would soon die. Of the original Herero population of around 80,000, only 15,130 survived, according to a census carried out in 1911.[18] Von Trotha even sought to legitimize these effectively genocidal measures by reference to a 'race war'.[19] These policies, draconian and drastic in terms of their immediate consequences, found however little support at home; on 8 December the Kaiser issued orders to cancel von Trotha's policies, and

---

[16] See also P. Werner Lange, 'Die Toten im Maisfeld. Hans Paasches Erkenntnisse aus dem Maji-Maji-Krieg' in Felicitas Becker and Jigal Beez (eds.), *Der Maji-Maji-Krieg in Deutsch-Ostafrika 1905–1907* (Berlin: Ch. Links Verlag 2005), pp. 154–67.

[17] See Hull, *Absolute Destruction*.

[18] John Iliffe, *Africans: The history of a continent* (Cambridge: Cambridge University Press, 1995), p. 208.

[19] Quoted in Hull, *Absolute Destruction*, p. 59.

von Trotha himself was ousted from his position in 1905. Although he was received back in Germany to some acclaim, being awarded high honours and military medals, his policies had at the time aroused fierce debates and were successfully contested and repealed. Von Trotha had also in some respects broken a taboo by recognizing that the result of his policies would be mass death, and explicitly, if somewhat retrospectively, arguing that such genocide was justified.

This was a line which the Imperial Governor of German East Africa, Gustav Adolf Graf von Götzen, was not prepared explicitly to cross, although the implications of his policies were not dissimilar, and on a far greater scale in practice. The suppression of the Maji-Maji rising also caused massive loss of life, far greater in terms of absolute numbers than in South-West Africa, and not limited to one tribe. While estimates vary, perhaps somewhere between 250,000 to 300,000 people—between one half and three-quarters of the Vidundi, Matumbi, and Pangwa tribes—lost their lives either as a result of the fighting or the wilful destruction of agriculture and purposefully unleashed famine caused by German policies in the area, a death toll perhaps four times that experienced in South-West Africa.[20] In German East Africa, too, given the destruction of farming and habitation there were long-term consequences for a generation or more, as a once settled and profitably cultivated area returned to wilderness, and as fertility rates dropped by around one-quarter and mortality rates from diseases soared.[21] Given the relatively tiny losses on the German side—totalling perhaps 15 Europeans, as well as 73 of their Askari soldiers and 316 native auxiliaries—there was a general unwillingness to treat this as a 'war' worthy of the name.[22] But for those who suffered from German policies, the hangings and famine through which the Germans reasserted their authority were not so easily downplayed.[23]

Using hunger as a weapon in the suppression of the Maji-Maji rebellion was a conscious decision on the part of the German authorities. Although von Götzen had himself mooted it earlier, the 'policy' is generally attributed to one Captain Freiherr von Wangenheim, who on 22 October 1905 sent in a report from his base in Kilossa to von Götzen in Dar es Salaam claiming an urgent need for military reinforcements. Wangenheim cited the difficulties of fighting rebels whose fanaticism was sustained by belief in the magical powers of their special water, turning

---

[20] These figures are given in Iliffe, *A Modern History of Tanganyika*, p. 200; and Pakenham, *Scramble for Africa*, p. 622. A lower figure of around 100,000 is given by Felicitas Becker and Jigal Beez, 'Ein nahezu vergessener Krieg' in Becker and Beez (eds.), *Der Maji-Maji-Krieg*, pp. 11–13, although this is likely to refer primarily to the immediate deaths from scorched-earth policies and not the three-year famine which ensued. It is somewhat surprising that this area has not received greater attention to date.

[21] Iliffe, *Africans*, p. 208.

[22] Iliffe, *A Modern History of Tanganyika*, p. 200; also Becker and Beez, 'Ein nahezu vergessener Krieg'.

[23] For African perspectives given in eye-witness accounts and oral history testimonies, see G. C. K. Gwassa and John Iliffe (eds.), *Records of the Maji Maji Rising* (Nairobi, Kenya: East African Publishing House, 1968: Historical Association of Tanzania, Paper no. 4); for the arguable longer-term consequences in terms of the formation of a Tanzanian 'national identity', see Karl-Martin Seeberg, *Der Maji-Maji-Krieg gegen die deutsche Kolonialherrschaft. Historische Ursprünge nationaler Identität in Tanzania* (Berlin: Dietrich Reimer Verlag, 1989).

them into invincible 'soldiers of God'; moreover, their tactics of dispersion across terrain which was difficult and unfamiliar for the Germans were rendering traditional military methods ineffective, particularly with inadequate numbers of troops. In the meantime, while waiting for military reinforcements to arrive from Germany, von Wangenheim argued that:

> only hunger and want [can] bring about final submission; military actions alone will remain more or less drops in the water. Only when currently available food supplies have been totally consumed, yet people's homes have been destroyed by perpetual military expeditions and the opportunity of planting new fields has been taken away from them, only then will they finally have to give up their resistance.[24]

By the following spring, despite difficulties with the German military campaign during the rainy season that had made the terrain even more problematic, hunger was taking its predicted toll. As Graf von Götzen put it:

> The population of these areas had for the most part either fled or had gone under. The troop leader's report said about this, 'the numerous corpses of those who had starved to death revealed the conditions we primarily have to thank for people's inclination, here too, to submit'.[25]

By April 1906, the uprising was more or less over. In his account of the episode, published some two years later, von Götzen expressed regrets about the policy of suppression through starvation, particularly in terms of its long-term economic consequences:

> Peace had been restored in the district of Mahenge. But it was bought through a heavy sacrifice. Even if the period of starvation itself was not of long duration, since bounteous African nature lent a helping hand here, and even if the burnt-down dwellings were rapidly rebuilt, given their simple manner of construction, nevertheless the loss of population entailed a degree of damage that would inevitably have significant adverse consequences for years to come for the lowered economic productivity of an anyway thinly populated country.[26]

But even von Götzen recognized and regretted the awful consequences of the war, in some places far worse than others, including deaths not only from hunger but also from disease and heightened infant mortality rates; and registered the difficulties experienced in seeking to repopulate particularly badly affected areas.[27] The intention had been the suppression of the uprising, not the eradication of a people.

Perhaps these were 'standard military practices' in some sense. They were not uniformly applied across the different areas of suppression: Paasche, for example, preferred to 'reward' those villagers who refused to support the uprising by ensuring they were settled in places of safety and able to cultivate crops.[28] Even von Götzen

---

[24] Freiherr von Wangenheim's report quoted in G. A. Graf von Götzen, *Deutsch-Ostafrika Afrika im Aufstand 1905/06* (Berlin: Dietrich Reimer (Ernst Vohsen) 1909), p. 149.
[25] *Ibid.*, p. 178.   [26] *Ibid.*, p. 179.
[27] *Ibid.*, pp. 233–5.   [28] Paasche, *'Im Morgenlicht'*, pp. 125–42.

spoke of a '*Konzentrationslager*' (concentration camp) in a sense very different from the later use of the term: in this case the term referred to a camp designed to protect and feed the population of women and children, so long as they recognized German authority and did not support the rebels:

> In Kibata, next to the Boma [village compound] a large concentration camp had been established in which hundreds of women and children were accommodated. Here, those who were prepared to submit were collected and settled, so that, under the protection of guards, they could cultivate foodstuffs.[29]

Certainly the forcible means of imposing German authority on an occupied territory against a rebellious population—public hangings, starvation—were to be found again and again, with ever greater frequency, on an infinitely larger scale and with massively greater brutality during the Second World War. But to link developments in the suppression of colonial rebellions in Germany's African colonies in the 1900s with Hitler's policies and practices in Eastern Europe after 1939 is highly problematic. It was to be a long, twisting path, in which changing political constellations, shifts in the character of the state, and the location of power played a crucial role in determining which views and policies should predominate and which be suppressed. For the time being, everything remained open; and policies were continually contested.

II. 'CIVILIZED SOCIETY'

For a few Germans, the experience of violence exercised against 'inferiors' in Africa was readily transposed to the home front, and replayed with pleasure on the domestic scene. Dr Friedrich R:, a lawyer who had been born in 1905 into a well-to-do Berlin family—his father was a judge—recalled, for example, his childhood memories of one of the family's neighbours, a captain who had just served in South West Africa:

> He always had a hippopotamus whip and used it to hit his wife and children and servants . . . He often told me how good things were in Africa, because one could beat up the blacks, and if they defended themselves 'then I just always say: "against the wall!"' He was on 'leave' and the leave was really long, but then in 1915 he was sent to Belgium.[30]

---

[29] Von Götzen, *Deutsch-Ostafrika Afrika im Aufstand*, p. 133.

[30] HHL b MS Ger 91 (184), Dr. F. R., p. 3. This is one case from an extraordinary manuscript collection, held in the Harvard Houghton Library, of more than 260 essays written between the summer of 1939 and the spring of 1940 under the title 'My life in Germany before and after 1933' for an essay competition announced by three Harvard professors, Gordon Allport, Edward Y. Hartshorne, and Sydney B. Fay. This competition was designed to gain substantial first-hand accounts of the social and psychological consequences of Nazism, and offered a first prize of $500. The essay competition was announced in various German-speaking and exile newspapers, and elicited responses not only from émigrés, refugees, and victims of the regime, but also from some Nazi sympathizers and supporters who at that time had few hesitations about trying to proselytize for, or at least recounting, what they still tended to see as a legitimate cause; such frank testimony would be almost impossible to elicit after

But for others, the context, atmosphere, and issues in Imperial Germany were quite different. Life stories, expectations, and aspirations differed radically according to class, region, religion, gender, and milieu, within a wider framework of dominant norms sustained by political institutions and cultural traditions.

Military values had long pervaded Imperial Germany. Kaiser Wilhelm II set the tone himself, with his determination that Germany should have a 'place in the sun'. The traditional Prussian emphasis on militarism, a legacy of both the much-praised Frederick the Great and of Bismarck's wars of unification, was augmented by a more recent bourgeois emphasis on competitions for command of the world's seas in rivalry with Britain. The popularity of the growing navy was evident in innumerable ways, from Navy League Associations through to postcards, and even in a craze for the 'sailors' suits' (*Matrosenanzüge*) which were the height of children's fashion for a decade or more. A period characterized by rapid social change and a foreign policy of aggrandizement was pervaded also by a widespread sense among the dominant and articulate classes of the superiority of German 'Kultur'—an assumed national cultural superiority which even intelligent individuals of a liberal persuasion, such as Max Weber, held worthy of defence by military might. Such a framework provided the setting for the aspirations and value systems internalized, expressed, and played out in many families from the more affluent or influential classes, providing, in peacetime, more than adequate fodder for training for the leadership of a German army and navy.

The sons of the aristocracy were traditionally destined for a career in one of three areas: if they were from the landed nobility, and in line for the inheritance, they would of course have responsibility for tending the family estates; if they were a later born son, or from less well-endowed families, they would very likely be groomed to a life in service of the state, through the civil service, the law, politics, or diplomacy; and, of course, they could become an officer of the army.[31] While none of these careers were in any sense predetermined—having command over resources and a network of good connections always meant that a range of options were open—these careers formed the shapes of their lives, defined the patterns into which they were born; they informed the aspirations of parents and determined the

---

1945. The minimum word count of essays was supposed to be 20,000 words; most are substantially longer (a few very much longer) while a minority fall far short of the expected word count and some are effectively simply pleas for help in awful circumstances. They all have in common that they do not yet know that there will be the organized mass killing of millions in the 'final solution' which unfolded from 1941; for these writers, the key turning point was 1933, or 1938 in the case of residents of Austria. For a copy of the covering letter of 17 Sep. 1940 from the committee (Allport, Fay, Hartshorne) outlining the essay criteria, see HHL, b MS Ger 91 (179), Lotte P. Most were written in German, but some were written in English; where this is the case, I have made no attempt to correct infelicities of style in the quotations, but have on occasion corrected obvious typographical and spelling errors; I have also respected anonymity throughout by using only the first initial of surnames, and in some cases, where anonymity was already preferred by the writer, also using a pseudonym for the first name.

[31] For recent developments in research on the German aristocracy in European perspective, see e.g. Eckart Conze and Monika Wienfort (eds.), *Adel und Moderne. Deutschland im europäischen Vergleich im 19. und 20. Jahrhundert* (Köln: Böhlau Verlag, 2004); and Monika Wienfort *Adel in der Moderne* (Göttingen: Vandenhoeck and Ruprecht, 2006).

educational experiences and social networks of the noble young. Arnold Vieth von Golßenau, for example, was born into an old aristocratic family in Saxony, based in the court town of Dresden. In his later memoirs of his childhood and youth, sketching a detailed record of pre-war court life, he records his military training and experiences in some detail; like so many others of his class, at this time he aspired to be an officer, a station to which his birth more or less automatically entitled him irrespective of personal merit.[32] Women born into these circles had rather different assumptions about the course their lives would take, largely focusing around marriages and family connections.[33] Common to all upper-class Germans in the pre-war period, arguably, was the assumption and hope that, despite evidence of the rapid social and political changes associated with industrialization and urbanization, things would continue in much the ordered course they felt had been customary across generations of aristocratic domination of the social order.

Some of these aspirations also coloured the views of non-aristocratic circles in Imperial Germany.[34] Many bourgeois families were affected by the military fervour of the '*Gründerzeit*', the early years after the foundation of the German Empire following Prussia's successful war against France in 1870. Militarism pervades later memoirs of periods of childhood and young adulthood in Imperial Germany among the middle classes. James B., for example, who was born in 1867 in Perleberg, a small town in the Priegnitz area north of Berlin, later recalled the enthusiasm of the *Gründerzeit* which coloured his childhood and overrode differences of religion. His mother had come from Hamburg, where her Jewish family had interacted comfortably with north German and Danish Protestants; his father, the son of a rabbi, had come from Łódź, the 'edge of civilization' where 'eastern Jews' (*Ostjuden*) had fled from persecution in Tsarist Russia. In Perleberg, class differences predominated over differences of religious confession or background:

> Those of us who were students at the modern grammar school were the sons of the propertied class. The new epoch sharpened the contrasts between the classes. Lower class wives were at that time just beginning to go to work in the newly founded factories in large numbers. Increasingly frequently now working class children no longer had a hot midday meal . . . [35]

Militarism was part of the implicit class tensions even among the young, and pervaded all areas of life for those growing up in the shadow of the wars of unification:

> We grammar school students were also perpetually engaged in fights with the pupils going to the ordinary school . . . It was a pale reflection of the prevailing militarism. There was after all no greater honour in bourgeois families than when their adult sons

[32] Ludwig Renn, *Adel im Untergang* (Berlin: Das neue Berlin, 2001).

[33] See e.g. the depiction of childhood atmosphere and family connections in Tisa von der Schulenburg, *Ich hab's gewagt. Bildhauerin und Ordensfrau—ein unkonventionelles Leben* (Freiburg im Breisgau: Verlag Herder, 1995). For a biography of her brother, see e.g. Ulrich Heinemann, *Ein konservativer Rebell. Fritz-Dietlof Graf von der Schulenburg und der 20. Juli* (Berlin: Siedler Verlag, 1990).

[34] For the now rather dated debates over an alleged 'feudalization of the bourgeoisie', see David Blackbourn and Geoff Eley, *The Peculiarities of German History* (Oxford: Oxford University Press, 1984).

[35] HHL, b MS Ger 91 (39), James B., (1867) 'Memoiren eines deutschen Juden und Sozialisten', p. 8.

were appointed as lieutenants of the reserve. Anyone who did not attain this grade suffered perpetually from a loss of esteem and above all of self-esteem. But anyone who had become a Reserve Officer sought arrogantly to look down his nose in the same way as other officers and thus to distinguish himself clearly from ordinary burghers.[36]

Class and status were thus literally embodied, as inequalities of nutrition and opportunity in youth were echoed in inequalities of aspiration and status as adults, and different gradations of hierarchy were repeatedly aped, enacted, and practised in order to reproduce the militarized social order. The influence of rank and uniform was extended even to the flirtatious activities of young women:

> In our town there was, as in most towns of this great military state, a garrison . . . If the regiment came out early in the morning for an exercise, then every young woman would rush to the window to catch a glimpse of her beloved.[37]

And as James B. later recalled:

> In this way, youth too gained some experience of the great war. On the principal wall in the living room would hang two pictures: one of King William, as Emperor Napoleon surrendered his sword as a prisoner after the battle of Sedan, the other the declaration of the German Empire by Bismarck in the hall of the Palace of Versailles.[38]

Militarism, in this manner of representation, was a matter both of social status and national glory, not of violent death and futile destruction. The more recent experiences of colonialism compounded the legacies of longer-term Prussian military traditions and Bismarck's forceful manner of unification, and on occasion perhaps exacerbated patterns of familial authoritarianism.

Class and class conflicts were increasingly important, and play a far greater role than any whiff of militarism in the life stories of those from poorer backgrounds. Otto B., for example, recalled primarily the acute poverty of his youth. Although Otto B.'s memoirs were written in East Berlin in 1960, for the purposes of an East German Communist Party (SED) archive of working-class experiences, the rather jumbled, detailed, and ill-educated way in which they were penned suggests there was little artifice to his account of his early years, very likely reflecting rather accurately the way Otto B. recalled his experiences of childhood; only once he reached the stage of recalling young adulthood did the teleology of party-belonging kick in to help shape the account.[39] Otto B.'s father was a tailor; the six-person family lived in two rooms in a building next to what was known as the 'louse park' (*Lausepark*) due to the prevalence of lice among those who frequented it. He recalled never having enough to eat; and his schooling was limited to attendance at what was popularly known as the 'rags school' (*Klamottenschule*), presumably because of the pupils' apparel. The class teacher had a habit of taking regular sips from a schnapps bottle conveniently kept in his pocket. At the age of fifteen,

---

[36] HHL, b MS Ger 91 (39), James B., (1867) 'Memoiren eines deutschen Juden und Sozialisten', p. 9.
[37] *Ibid.*   [38] *Ibid.*, p. 10.
[39] LAB, C Rep 902-02-04, Nr. 65, Otto B. (1880), Erinnerungen, 20. Okt. 1960.

Otto B. became an apprentice machine-tool maker and from then on was constantly trying to improve his position and earn higher wages. His memoirs provide immense detail on how much he was paid in which job; apparently total and astonishingly detailed (presumably more or less accurate) recall of the precise wages received in each position suggests this was a constant, overriding concern at the time. The memoirs also, hardly surprisingly in view of the later context of writing, increasingly highlight the 'class struggle'. Otto B. joined the Social Democratic Party (SPD) in 1902, and was from then on a party and union activist, playing a leading role in various strikes; he was frequently either fired for his activities, or gave notice. He continued working in extraordinarily bad conditions, never—because of his political views—being able to be promoted to '*Meister*' (master of the trade) status, since he could then not be a member of a union, and in any event for him 'being a master was equivalent to being a capitalist lackey'.[40] Claiming that he had little respect for his bosses, Otto B. reports that he often just left his work and looked for another job.

The era of Emperor Wilhelm II was characterized by inherent instability for a variety of reasons. Changes in both social structure and the international system played a growing role in the destabilization of domestic politics. Unprecedented and rapid population growth, industrialization and urbanization, accompanied a rise in social tensions and posed a challenge to received status hierarchies. New interest groups and shifting political alignments, as well as the apparently inexorable growth of a social democratic movement which was more revolutionary in theory than practice, appeared to challenge the capacity to balance diverging interests of the system devised by Bismarck. In the international sphere, growing tensions and competition between the European powers both in the colonies and at home were exacerbated by an arms race which led almost inevitably to the expectation of war—a war which would, it was widely assumed, be of the old style: short, decisive, contained. The cataclysmic, long-drawn out and destructive war which actually came in 1914–18 was not the war for which German militarism was prepared and which old regime Europe had been expecting.

And perhaps for this reason, for the all tensions and speed of social change, in retrospect the pre-war era was seen as an idyllic and tranquil moment when expectations and life courses were a purely personal matter, not determined by the intrusion of external forces beyond an individual's control. The following third of a century or more was to be very different indeed.

Class, while highly significant in shaping political affiliations and configurations, by no means predetermined politics in an age where religious confession and regional backgrounds still played a major role. And for some, concerns with challenging traditional gender roles evolved as a significant issue of the turn of the century, heralding the better-known emancipatory movements of the 1920s.[41] The personal was, to prefigure a feminist rallying cry of the later twentieth century,

---

[40] *Ibid.*, p. 13.
[41] See e.g. Lillian Fadermann and Brigitte Eriksson (eds.), *Lesbians in Germany: 1890s–1920s* (NP: The Naiad Press, 1990).

already seen as highly political. Emergent generational conflicts also to some degree cross-cut class considerations, particularly in the last few years before the outbreak of the Great War—and particularly among the relatively well-off sons and daughters of the bourgeoisie who did not need to worry quite as much, on a day-to-day basis, as Otto B. did about the precise rate of pay for each job.

Among those seeing generation as a key fault line running across other social divisions, there was growing enthusiasm for cultural trends and views emphasizing the possibility of individual spiritual and physical renewal, as well as societal and political reform, through the energies of 'youth' against age, irrespective of class; and a growing desire to break with what were increasingly seen as the authoritarian shackles of a parental generation characterized by stern and dominant patriarchal values.[42] The *Wandervogel* (literally, 'wandering bird') movement, in which young people went hiking together and sought, in closer communion with nature, solace and answers to the complex problems of what later became known as the 'asphalt society', was far from the only youth movement at this period; there were inevitable differences in political views and priorities across different, often inchoate and constantly shifting, groupings.[43] What was common across these movements was confidence, curiously, in the energy and insights allegedly to be found from a life stage that was, by definition, doomed to be ephemeral.

Different youth movements came together on the Hohe Meißner mountain in 1913 for intense discussion of the ways in which the younger generation could transform not only politics but also, through 'life reform' movements, the world and themselves.[44] Present on the Hohe Meißner was Hans Paasche, who by this time was involved, along with the lawyer and writer Hermann Popert, in publication of a newsletter entitled *Der Vortrupp* (Vanguard) for the *Deutscher Vortruppbund* which they had founded in 1912. Paasche claimed that this newspaper 'sets itself the task of bringing together, as though in a mirror reflecting heat and light, all the conditions for lifestyle reform in Germany that can make every single member of the community [*Volksgenossen*] healthier, more competent, of stronger resolve, and thus to create better living conditions for descendants yet to come'.[45] Hans Paasche, now describing himself as a writer as well as an officer of the marines, had in the meantime written significant tracts critiquing Imperial Germany, one collection of which—echoing Montesquieu's *Lettres Persanes*—was a brilliant parody couched in the form of letters home by an African visiting Germany on behalf of his African sovereign, the letters dating from 1 May 1912 through to the ninth and last letter allegedly penned on the Hohe Meißner on 15 October 1913.[46] Shifting the perspective to that of the

---

[42] See the overview in Robert Wohl, *The Generation of 1914* (Cambridge, MA: Harvard University Press, 1979), pp. 42–7.

[43] See for an overview of varieties, shifts, and changes Peter Stachura, *The German Youth Movement 1900–1945* (London: Macmillan, 1981), who however resolutely uses the singular noun.

[44] See e.g. Winfried Mogge and Jürgen Reulecke (eds.), *Hohe Meißner 1913. Der Erste Freideutsche Jugendtag in Dokumenten, Deutungen und Bildern* (Köln: Verlag Wissenschaft und Politik, 1988).

[45] Reprinted *ibid.*, p. 108.

[46] Hans Paasche, *Lukanga Mukara. Die Forschungsreise des Afrikaners Lukanga Mukara ins innerste Deutschland* (Berlin: Verlag Eduard Jacobson, 1980; letters first published in *Der Vortrupp* from 1912–13).

surprised visiting African, Paasche—who had, following his marriage to Ellen Witting, spent a lengthy honeymoon in Africa and been ever more impressed by life beyond the constricting norms of Imperial 'civilization'—succeeded in critiquing all manner of German traditions and customs, from constraining clothes (including corsets for women who were thus actively turned into the 'weaker sex', barely able to breathe), gestures, social greetings, the 'performance' of social status through the wearing of certain clothes and adoption of patterns of bearing, through to excessive alcohol consumption and smoking, constantly being in a hurry, and living in a meaningless cycle of rushing to work, ricocheting between employment, transport, coal, schnapps, and prostitutes, marked out by incessant counting of money and time, in a society seen as constantly in motion but to no overall purpose. While such a lifestyle had become so ingrained and habitual as to appear 'normal' to the Germans—with traditional feast days, for example, being characteristically 'celebrated' by an ever more revolting inebriation—to the visiting African this lifestyle of perpetual haste, social and physical constraint, and repeated intoxication was both absurd and unintelligible; about the only aspects that gave cause for hope were the soothing powers of music, and the potential promise of the youth movement.

By mid-1913 the Vortrupp League had over 4,000 members in 140 different local groups; its newsletter had somewhere in the region of 8,000 subscribers, a quite considerable figure. At the meeting on 12 October 1913 on the Hohe Meißner, around 500 to 600 members were present, alongside members of perhaps fourteen different youth groups of various sorts in gathering totalling around 3,000 'young' people (including Max Weber, at this time in his late forties and perhaps no longer quite so young, though certainly struggling with significant problems relating to his own personal rebellion against an overbearing, authoritarian father).[47] Also present was one Alexander Schwab, born in 1887 in Stuttgart, the son of the composer and *Opernkapellmeister* Karl Julius Schwab.[48] Schwab was at this time closely associated with Gustav Wyneken, an influential youth activist and major proponent of educational reform, who played a leading role in creating a loose federation of the 'Free German Youth'. Together—less than a year before the outbreak of the Great War—these predominantly young people hoped, enthused by the companionship, fresh mountain air and beautiful surroundings, to be able to change both the world and themselves. Very soon many would be dead—and others in bitter conflict about which way to deal with the very real political issues of a society riven both by war and class tensions. Politics was by no means so easily resolved by appealing to the energies of youth and the virtues of a 'return to nature'.

[47] Winfried Mogge, 'Der Freideutsche Jugendtag 1913: Vorgeschichte, Verlauf, Wirkungen' in Mogge and Reulecke, *Hohe Meißner 1913*, pp. 33–66.
[48] Hans-Harald Müller, *Intellektueller Linksradikalismus in der Weimarer Republik. Seine Entstehung, Geschichte und Literatur – dargestellt am Beispiel der Berliner Gründergruppe der Kommunistischen Arbeiter-Partei Deutschlands* (Kronberg/Ts: Scriptor Verlag, 1977).

III. THE IMPACT OF THE GREAT WAR

The Great War brought Germans into the sphere of national politics as never
before: the involvement in the eddies unleashed by the war, whether in active
service at the front, on the home front during years of upheaval and deprivation, or
in the post-war after-swirls of hunger, illness, and economic and political instability,
meant that no Germans were left entirely untouched. And the significance of the
legacies of the Great War, in terms of international instability, the radicalization of
domestic politics, and transformations of German society, can hardly be overestimated. Considerable attention has been focussed on a few key issues: the
allegedly widespread enthusiasm for war among Germans in August 1914; the
commission of atrocities against civilians following the German invasion of Belgium
and France; the supposed formation of a 'front generation' formed by experiences in
the trenches, particularly on the western front; and, less well-explored, the possible
longer-term consequences of experiences on the eastern front. In all respects, the
realities were more complex and multifaceted than earlier myths might suggest; but
that the Great War had a massive impact on people's consciousness, and constituted
a major rupture in their personal lives, is beyond question.[49]

Whole cohorts of adult males were exposed to the experiences of slaughter on the
battlefields, maiming and death from wounds behind the front, captivity as prisoners of war, and the short- and long-term psychological consequences of prolonged
industrial warfare. The casualties were not on the scale of those later to be
experienced in the Second World War; but at this time, and particularly in
comparison with the relatively short and decisive battles of the nineteenth century
or recent colonial experiences of combat, the Great War amounted to an experience
of death and devastation on a previously unprecedented scale. Over 2 million
Germans were killed in the war, a far higher rate of death than experienced by
the British or French; of those Germans mobilized to fight, around 15 per cent
were killed and more than half were injured in some way.[50] Far higher rates of
physical casualties were experienced on the eastern front than in the trenches in

---

[49] These and related questions have given rise to a massive literature. See e.g. Rüdiger Bergien,
'Vorspiel des "Vernichtungskrieges"? Die Ostfront des ersten Weltkrieges und das Kontinuitätsproblem'
in Gerhard P. Groß (ed.), *Der vergessene Front. Der Osten 1914/15. Ereignis, Wirkung, Nachwirkung*
(Paderborn: Ferdinand Schöningh, 2006), pp. 393–408; Roger Chickering, *Imperial Germany and the
Great War, 1914–1918* (Cambridge: Cambridge University Press, 1998); Roger Chickering, *The Great
War and Urban Life in Germany: Freiburg, 1914–1918* (Cambridge: Cambridge University Press, 2007);
John Horne and Alan Kramer, *German Atrocities: A history of denial* (New Haven and London: Yale
University Press, 2001); Alan Kramer, *Dynamic of Destruction: Culture and mass killing in the First World
War* (Oxford: Oxford University Press, 2007); Jeffrey Verhey, *The Spirit of 1914* (Cambridge: Cambridge
University Press, 2000); Benzamin Ziemann, *Front und Heimat. Ländliche Kriegserfahrungen im südlichen
Bayern, 1914–1923* (Essen: Klartext, 1997); Bernd Ulrich and Benjamin Ziemann (eds.), *Frontalltag im
ersten Weltkrieg* (Essen: Klartext, 2008).

[50] German losses were 2,037,000; British deaths amounted to 723,000; and the corresponding
figure for France was 1,398,000. The British death rate was 11.8% of those mobilized. Figures taken
from Alexander Watson, *Enduring the Great War: Combat, morale and collapse in the German and
British armies, 1914–1918* (Cambridge: Cambridge University Press, 2008), pp. 11, 20–1.

the west, with around two and a half times the likelihood of dying in battle in the east than the west; but the trench warfare, the stalemate, the sense of a lack of control, as well as the experience of mutilated body parts of former comrades being scattered widely across the trenches and devastated landscapes of war, appears to have made the experience more horrific on the western front than in the east. Around one in twenty soldiers were recorded as psychiatric casualties, with the emergence of 'shell shock' as a new term to describe a syndrome of nervous and physical disorder following the traumatic experiences of war (in the later twentieth century, after the Vietnam War, displaced by the more generic notion of post-traumatic stress disorder).[51]

The impact of war was experienced also on the German home front in ways which were arguably unprecedented (at least since the devastating impact of the Thirty Years War in some areas, nearly three centuries earlier), although again not to the extent or in the manner of bombing, invasion, and occupation by enemy armies that was to characterize the Second World War. During the Great War, birth rates in Germany dropped massively: from the pre-war, slightly declining rates of between 30.7 and 28.3 per thousand of the population (figures for 1910 and 1913) to dramatic lows of 15.7 in 1916 and 14.4 in 1917—less than half the birth rate of five years earlier.[52] Rephrasing this: in some senses, what would potentially have been 'half a generation' was at this time not being born. For those who were children during the Great War, malnutrition and relative neglect had a major impact both physically and socially: with fathers away at the front or killed, mothers often called in to work in factories, schoolteachers away at war, younger children experienced a lack of the traditional authority figures that had loomed so large in pre-war years; shortages of food, fuel, and soap contributed to ill-health and a very real degree of widespread material distress.[53] A sense of 'moral panic' particularly about working-class youngsters who had grown up in these circumstances, and who appeared to be engaging in criminal activities in youth gangs, was later exacerbated by post-war conditions.[54]

More generally, as conditions worsened on the home front it appeared to many astute observers of the day that a sense of lawlessness in order to survive was widespread across classes and age groups, accompanied by 'demoralization' and a sense of inevitability, even hopelessness, as James B., by now a civil servant and lawyer well into his forties, observed:

> But not only the old and the new rich were gripped by this loss of morality through war: the whole nation was diseased . . . Since the lower classes saw how the upper classes were going about things, so gradually all hesitation about engaging in illegality was shed. Since they did not have enough to eat, they stole. They stole potatoes out of lodgings, vegetables from the fields, chickens and geese from their coops. They falsified

---

[51] Watson, *Enduring the Great War*, pp. 25, 22 ff., 43. The figures for psychiatric casualties were 4.58% of German soldiers, and 5.7% of those serving in the British forces.
[52] *Statistisches Jahrbuch für das deutsche Reich, 1924–25*, p. 41.
[53] See Chickering, *Imperial Germany and the Great War*, esp. pp. 120–5.
[54] See also Richard Bessel, *Germany after the First World War* (Oxford: Oxford University Press, 1993).

bread and meat cards and sold them. As metals became increasingly scarce, they stole them in order to sell them, handles from doors, even from railway carriages. With an increasing shortage of fabrics, they stole carpets from staircases and curtains and upholstery from railway carriages. Not just one or two cases, but rather there was scarcely a house or a train where one could not see signs of such devastation. Very often children could be seen running around in hardwearing trousers, the source of which was revealed by sections of print betraying the fact that they were made from stolen upholstery.

In offices, previously bulwarks of conscientiousness in the German lands, bribery had become a general practice. Everyone who had anything to do with bureaucracy, and that was the majority of people because of the thousands of orders being issued, would take with them an envelope containing a bank note, in order to leave it lying on the desk of the bureaucrat . . .

To this dissolution of all moral values was associated that of family bonds . . .

The worst of it all was not so much that disloyalty, profiteering, stealing, receiving stolen goods, bribery, swindling, had become general practice, but rather that the destruction of popular morality was experienced as something self-evident, beyond alteration. It was after all war. That was a force against which no-one could do anything.[55]

The extent to which such observations were 'true', in the sense for example of statistics on different types of crime (or relative success rates in prosecutions), is less important than the perception of contemporaries that the previous certainties of their social and moral world were being radically shattered.

The Great War and the turmoil which followed proved such a watershed that the relative peace and tranquillity of the preceding decades could only be seen in a rosy light, the pre-1914 years remembered or portrayed as a sort of golden age. Albert D., for example, was a Jewish doctor whose family had lived for generations on the French–German border on the right bank of the Rhine; he could trace his family's residence there as far back as 1743. The small town in which he had lived, with a population of around 12,000, was mixed in religious affiliation: while the majority were Protestant, around 33% were Catholic, and around three per cent Jewish. Albert D. later recollected that:

The way in which members of different religious confessions and various levels of society—not only economic but also social—were able to live together was at that time virtually ideal. It was not least this fact that caused me to choose this town as the place in which to base my existence.[56]

He married happily, and in due course had a son and daughter; his medical practice flourished, he had a wide circle of good friends and enjoyed an active and varied cultural life. But then, as for so many other Germans, everything changed: 'In the summer of 1914 I was, as every year, on holiday with my family in the mountains which I so loved' when the news of the assassination of Archduke Franz Ferdinand in Sarajevo and the eventual declaration of war came through.

[55] HHL, b MS Ger 91 (39), James B., (1867) 'Memoiren eines deutschen Juden und Sozialisten', p. 50.
[56] HHL b MS Ger 91 (54), Albert D., p. 2.

Albert D. was, like so many others, called up. The family were far from military enthusiasts, but rapidly came to terms with it: 'But my wife bore the inevitable as the consequence of patriotic duty.'[57] Albert D. became a troop doctor on the western front, where he earned the Iron Cross and other honours; and, despite suffering from serious illness in the course of the war, he offered himself back into service even before he had made a full recovery. As the war continued, he described the increasing unpopularity and poor discipline and poor nutrition:

> Reports in the strongly censored newspapers had not been believed for a long while, discipline was very lax, the food situation was desperate, and we doctors knew ahead of time far better than most people what the bitter end would be, because we were right there amongst the population. Then happened, what had to happen: collapse, revolution, and the ceasefire.[58]

A similar picture of a peaceful, almost 'golden age' before the Great War is given by Maria K. Born in 1893, she was a young woman when the war broke out; she trained to become a school teacher, and in 1917 she married a Professor of Oriental Languages at Giessen University. She summarizes the effects of the war quite succinctly:

> Before the Great War (1914–1918) we had a very peaceful, cheerful life . . . The war caught us totally unprepared . . . Everyone was caught up in the enthusiasm for war . . .

But very soon disillusion began to set in:

> The first great wave of enthusiasm for the war ebbed with the arrival of the first lists of casualties. For example, of all the officers of the Giessen Regiment who had gone to war in August, only two were still alive in mid-September . . . By around the summer of 1916 the war had become a great burden. The reasons were probably for the most part the never-ending casualty lists and the scarcity of food. Schoolteaching was made more difficult through the shortage of coal, malnutrition, and the way children were running wild.[59]

These accounts, written in 1940, like many other retrospective autobiographical texts, register some difficulty in seeing the period before 1914 as in continuity with what came later. Far from prefiguring the rise of Nazism, the pre-1914 period is seen as radically disconnected.

The disconnection was registered not merely at the political level but at the deeply personal level, in terms of a discontinuity even in the sense of self. This sense of difference, of even lack of recognition of a former self, is registered explicitly by a highly intelligent German whose now published diaries have illuminated the experiences of some of those who were within a matter of decades to be outcast and indeed headed for the gas chambers. Viktor Klemperer, a distinguished philologist whose Jewish origins lost him his academic position, his home, and very nearly his life in the Third Reich, took upon himself the mission of

---

[57] *Ibid.*, p. 2.   [58] *Ibid.*, p. 3.
[59] HHL b MS Ger 91 (101), Maria K., p. 1.

documenting the developments of his times in a diary where the personal was, inevitably, the political. Attempting in 1940 to write an autobiographical account of his own childhood and youth, Klemperer found it well-nigh impossible to think himself back into the self who had greeted war in August 1914 with a combination of the general enthusiasm and yet simultaneous doubts.

Explaining why he felt it necessary to reproduce old diary entries instead of rewriting as autobiography, as he had done with rest of his account of his youth, Klemperer first gave some general reasons: in his opinion, Germans generally faced war in 1914, after forty-three years of peace, much as fresh eighteen-year-olds discuss God and the meaning of existence but then later, 'with increasing maturity, become ashamed of time-wasting, triviality and self-revelations, and content themselves with the narrowly defined tasks and problems of their own existence'.[60] The same could be said of the meaning of war, which had been much discussed at first, but later forgotten as people were swept up in the process and consequences of war and simply had to get on with it. But secondly, and more importantly, there were personal reasons:

> But to these general reasons that are applicable to 'everyone' must be added more important personal reasons for the retention of the diary, applicable to 'me'. Today, how could the self-evidence of the 'we' and of the patriotic enthusiasm and of the absolute conviction about Germany's snow-white innocence, about Germany's justified claim to primacy in Europe, flow from my pen? I simply cannot manage to reproduce this in a new narrative, I can only copy it as though from a foreign text. And there is also something else that forces me to leave the text of the following weeks untouched. Today, in the autumn of 1940, when I am living among my former fellow citizens in more restricted conditions and with even fewer rights than a prisoner of war, emotionally my memory is overflowing with that united enthusiasm of the summer of 1914. Yet now, in reading through the old notes, I see with astonishment how even then, for all my absolutely unquestionable sense of being German, for all my enthusiasm and absolute certainty of those basic convictions, even so, virtually right from the very start I nevertheless had moments of self-reflection and doubt. And even these critical outpourings I can't recreate; otherwise I would never be rid of the fear that I was in some way falsely adding into my feelings of that time my thoughts of today.[61]

Klemperer thus abandoned his attempt to rewrite his experiences of 1914 as autobiography, and simply reproduced the diary entries of the time.[62] In one passage in particular, he clearly registered far wider views of the day, identifying:

> a popular lust for sensationalism . . . an urge to experience the extraordinary. War is the highest sensation and the only remaining catharsis for a civilized person [*Kulturmenschen*]. That is why war cannot be totally banned from any peaceful society.

---

[60] Victor Klemperer, *Curriculum Vitae. Erinnerungen eines Philologen, 1881–1918. Zweites Buch: 1912–1918* (Berlin: Rütten and Loening, 1989), p. 173.

[61] Klemperer, *Curriculum Vitae*, II, pp. 173–4.

[62] *Ibid.*, pp. 176–212.

War, the great historical event, can render whole nations immortal . . . War is therefore the mass surrogate for individual fame.[63]

This may perhaps have been what many felt in 1914; it certainly had little to do with what was to come. War changed German society in ways that, in 1914—let alone in the colonial wars a decade or so earlier—were entirely unpredictable. It also changed the people who lived through the war, whether at the home or at the front. In their own later self-perceptions, the period before 1914 came to seem like a golden age; in face of the challenges of war and the continuing turmoil of the period after defeat, nothing could ever be the same again.

IV. THE TRIALS OF HANS PAASCHE

Increasingly, Hans Paasche—who had initially tried to 'do his duty' as a good German citizen—came to oppose the war and the government which seemed only bent on prolonging it. By 1916–17, having been relieved from his marine command for failure to obey orders over a disciplinary offence, Paasche was more and more involved in activities designed to bring the war to an early end. He distributed pacifist and anti-war literature, and built up a network of contacts across Germany. By 1917, Paasche was of the view that: 'There is no point in raising youth in full health only so that they can later be used up as cannon fodder.'[64] In late 1917, Paasche was arrested on his estate of Waldfrieden, and put on trial on charges of high treason for his activities in opposition to the war. Given Paasche's social position, his defence lawyer was ultimately successful in getting a verdict amounting to 'mad, not bad', and rather than facing the death penalty for high treason Paasche was incarcerated in a 'mental hospital' wing in Moabit prison.

Paasche himself was absolutely clear that there were direct connections between the experience of violence in the African colonies, and the Great War. Both during his period of imprisonment and after the end of the war, which brought about his sudden release (or rather, liberation by mutinying troops) in November 1918, Paasche berated himself for not having spoken out more honestly and forcefully from 1905 onwards about what the experience of violence and killing really meant; he felt that, had he done so, more people might have been opposed to the Great War and perhaps even prevented it from starting.

The materials collated for the investigation of Paasche's mental state in the legal proceedings against him for high treason are highly revealing. The immediate generational conflict was clearly acute, as Dr Leppmann, the senior medical specialist, observed after one parental visit:

Unfortunately a few days ago, as my reliable Chief Warder reported to me, on the occasion of a visit paid to his son by Privy Councillor [*Geheimrat*] Paasche, the latter became so vehement and hurtful without any obvious cause such that, should Paasche

---

[63] *Ibid.*, p. 175.
[64] BAB, R 3003 / C 153 / 17, Vol. 1, fol. 135.

remain in this mental institution, I would on medical grounds refuse permission for any further visit for at least the next six weeks.[65]

Following six weeks of close observation of Hans Paasche as a patient, and after reading all ten volumes of the files of witness testimony and other evidence collated for the legal proceedings instituted against Paasche in 1917, Dr Leppmann summarized the situation as he saw it. According to Dr Leppmann's report, even Paasche's rather well-meaning parents-in-law were ever more convinced, not least on the basis of their acquaintance with him over many years:

> that this so gifted and many-sided man is totally unsuited to real life, that he could never really come to terms with life, just as they had witnessed how, in every position and in every occupation, he had immediately come into sharp conflict with those around him. The manner of his life style was already at that time highly peculiar. He often slept during daytime, and was not in a position to partake regularly in ordinary meals, although he actually never really exercised any kind of demanding job. He was always busy, without any regularity and without any disposition: more or less without any kind of plan or goal, he filled his life with correspondence and writing, with conferences and further discussions. In that period he read a lot and demonstrated in general a very strong desire for knowledge.[66]

However much such a lifestyle might seem understandable to those born into an era of creative freelancers, at this time and in this context Paasche, on this and the balance of much other evidence, clearly could not be 'normal'—an aberration which could, according to many of those giving evidence, be dated back to his experiences in the colonies.

It is worth quoting in full the indictment of the lifestyle of an individual who did not conform to the norms of Imperial German society in the ways expected of someone of Paasche's social station at that time:

> Experiences while in the colonies had precipitated his support for unconditional abstinence, following which came one after another the battle for vegetarianism, for animal protection, particularly for the protection of birds, for opposition to inoculation, and related causes. He worked with the Teetotallers and the Knights of the Templar, he fought on behalf of vegetarianism and in every case belonged to the most radical and fanatic representatives of this tendency. There were times when he nourished himself solely on herbs, roots, and all sorts of raw fruit . . . On top of this then came a concern with ethical movements. He joined the Associations for Ethics and Radical Ethics. For months he threw himself into so-called culture of the body and spent whole days sunbathing or in the open air . . . His father-in-law recalls having met him twice on the street dressed in such a manner that he had to be ashamed: with hair growing too long, not wearing a hat, carelessly dressed, and with a briefcase under his arm he looked more like a Baptist itinerant preacher than a former military officer who was after all living in good and secure circumstances.

---

[65] BAB, R 3003 / C 153 / 17, Vol. 1, Letter from Geh. Dr A. Leppmann, 9 May 1918, fol. 56.

[66] BAB, R 3003 / C 153 / 17, Vol. 1, 'Schriftliches Gutachten' by Geh. Medizinalrat Dr A. Leppmann, fols. 100–57, here fol. 108.

Then came the time when he threw himself into the youth movement, again of course also immediately making very radical demands, and where, in the Wandervogel and similar movements, he perceived the salvation of the world. He wrote about all these things and always in such a manner that his articles ever more frequently irritated someone and wounded their feelings, so that he was actually always feuding with someone or other.[67]

It seems a shame that Paasche had not lived some half a century or more later: from perhaps the late 1960s onwards such beliefs, causes, and apparel, particularly in a Western European or North American university city, would hardly have given cause even for passing comment, let alone passed as definitive proof of 'abnormality' bordering on 'insanity'.

Much of the 'evidence' for Paasche's 'madness', or at least 'not being quite normal', was thus garnered from behavioural observations, combined with comments about his apparently inadequate internalization of the rules of social discipline, allegedly compounded by his African experiences. A colleague from the marines, one *Korvettenkapitän* Walter Goethe, commented that: 'As long as I have known him personally (the last time [we met] was in the course of 1915), his personality was intellectually extremely stimulating, but erratic and sometimes self-contradictory.'[68] Walter Goethe sought to give key examples to strengthen the case:

The following two examples should serve as an indication of his exaggerated style: once, as I heard from a third party, as the leader of the company holding watch for the II. Torpedo Division he supposedly made an entry in the record book to the effect that several people had been drunk; then he added in writing: as long as the people in charge here set such a bad example it's not going to get any better, or some such comment. This his superior would inevitably read. Then another time because he missed church he was punished by being grounded; shortly afterwards he was supposed to serve as a judge. This role he refused on the grounds that as someone who had himself been punished he had no right to sit in judgement over others.[69]

Not merely did Paasche evidence signs of independent thoughts and actions (clearly symptoms of 'madness' in the naval circles of Imperial Germany); he also kept irregular hours, as Walter Goethe had recently learnt from a couple who had reported, following a visit to his wife:

that recently Hans Paasche had lived an extremely irregular life. So for example sometimes he arose at 12 o'clock midday, sometimes at 4 o'clock in the morning, and roamed around in the woods. He must therefore, through lack of any intensive occupation, partial loss of inhibitions and unsatisfied ambitions, have strayed into a peculiar cast of mind.[70]

Others too commented unfavourably on Paasche's irregular life style, which functioned as clear evidence of 'madness'. Ludwig Assmann, for example, whose sister

---

[67] *Ibid.*, fols. 108–10.
[68] BAB, R 3003 / C 153 / 17, Vol. 2, Affidavit of Korvettenkapitän Walter Goethe, fol. 38.
[69] *Ibid.*   [70] *Ibid.*, fol. 39.

had married into the estate neighbouring the Paasches' home, reported on an incident when he had visited his sister in 1917:

> I found myself one day in the front garden and was busying myself with a fishing net. I saw a man and woman on bicycles coming towards the house, they placed their bicycles behind the house and entered the same...On this occasion I made the acquaintance of the two cyclists. It was the accused and his wife...I heard at that time...that he was a somewhat strange person, who for example in summertime went around the garden with his family almost without any clothes on. I personally noticed that the accused came to see my relatives in a rather dishevelled state. He was without a hat and totally unshaven. If he had not been wearing a decent suit, he could have been taken for a tramp.[71]

Yet again, failure to wear a hat, and a dishevelled appearance provided supposedly clear evidence of Paasche's alleged 'madness'. This was compounded by having anti-monarchical attitudes, even if here the evidence was only based on hearsay: at Christmas 1917 Assmann's sister had talked to her brother about Hans Paasche, saying that his writings 'were directed against the Imperial house, against the Hohenzollern dynasty and also against the government...On the other hand my sister also revealed that she did not consider the accused to be normal...'[72] And the case for 'abnormality' was of course strengthened by repetitive corroboration, however apparently unfounded. As Emilia Assmann, the mother of this neighbour, put it to the court: 'I want to add that I heard, while staying with my daughter, but I cannot now remember who said it, that the accused was supposedly not normal.'[73]

Not being 'normal' was thus a constantly reiterated refrain among those who could not deal with Paasche's nonconformist lifestyle. But there was certainly a little more to his behaviour in the later war years than simply a clash of outlooks on regular sleeping and eating habits as well as conventions on when to wear a hat. Whatever Paasche's previous ideas and outlook, he does seem to have been made 'mad'—or rather, angry, chaotic, insomniac—by the combination of war worries, economic stress, and both personal and political conflicts with his father. The perceived effects of the Great War on ordinary people also seems to have played a major role in what did appear to be something of a breakdown on Paasche's part, even on the evidence of those who wanted to claim a degree of inherent madness all along. Bruno Deuss, the 26-year-old son of a local shopkeeper in the village of Filehne and at that time a lieutenant in the war, reported that:

> In June 1917...when I was on leave on Filehne and happened to be in my father's shop, the accused came into the shop and asked me about the mood of the people in the field. He then expressed the view to me that the people had to suffer most in war and the higher officers did not really feel much of the war since they were always

---

[71] BAB, R 3003 / C 153 / 17, Vol. 2, statement of Ingenieur Ludwig Assmann, 15 April 1918, fols. 256–7.
[72] *Ibid.*, fol. 257.
[73] BAB, R 3003 / C 153 / 17, Vol. 2, fol. 162.

behind the lines in safe locations; he was no longer comfortable with this and that was why he quit his service.[74]

Another local from Filehne, *Landsturmmann* Karl Huth, born in 1899 and still a teenager at the time of giving testimony, also prioritized Paasche's views on the war but felt he was perhaps overreacting:

> The accused often expressed himself to me in derogatory terms about the current constitutional position. He was of the opinion that much had been done wrongly, to which the war could be traced back, and he also said that only nationalism was to blame for the war and that the war would not have come about if people could govern themselves. I agree with these views of the accused.
> ... We spoke about the war and the great unhappiness that it had brought about. Suddenly Paasche threw himself to the ground and behaved like someone in despair, and then stood up again immediately and walked on with me. I gained the impression that the accused suffered greatly from the fact that the war demanded so much by way of sacrifice, particularly in terms of human beings. In my view Paasche concerned himself too one-sidedly with this. On the matter of losses, on one occasion when we were talking Paasche painted the following picture: If we were to estimate the total human losses in this war at 5 million people, then, if one stood these people up side by side, fully dressed for battle, and each man took up perhaps one metre of space, then it would produce a row of the dead that would be five times as long as the distance from Posen to Calais.[75]

A twenty-year-old who had got to know Paasche in the summer of 1915 through family connections claimed that everyone 'held him to be a hugely gifted man of great knowledge and idealistic views, who only wanted the best for his fellow human beings':

> At that time Herr Paasche was in my view mentally absolutely normal, although physically he sometimes appeared rather overworked. But I can imagine that through pondering on the war in particular, as well as the rift with his parents, he has now had a nervous breakdown.[76]

There can be little doubt that the family, as well as the war, played a considerable role in Paasche's 'madness', both in terms of his violent disagreements with his father's views and associated outbursts of rage, and also in terms of their own attempts to dominate the definition and diagnosis of his 'symptoms'.

The family was clearly concerned to establish Hans Paasche's 'madness', and its roots in his experiences in Africa. Paasche's sister claimed that his later experiences compounded an inherent instability:

> My brother ... is as far as I know mentally not normal and also from his youth onwards has always been highly strung ... When he came back and temporarily stayed with us, before he took leave of Africa, we had the impression that he was no longer to be taken seriously. He was extraordinarily agitated, liked to debate all manner of reformist ideas and would allow no other opinion on these matters.

---

[74] *Ibid.*, fol. 50.   [75] *Ibid.*, fol. 174.   [76] *Ibid.*, fol. 22.

She was for a long time of the opinion:

> that my brother was not mentally normal. As evidence were his external appearance, his unsteady gaze and restless existence, was well as his constant prowling around like a tiger [*Umhertigern*] during an agitated conversation.

But according to his sister, Paasche's personal experience of bereavement during the Great War appear to have exacerbated his problems and politicized his views:

> I particularly noticed this in February 1917, when I visited my brother on the estate that he had acquired from my parents. While my brother had earlier never concerned himself with politics and in general also thought like a soldier, after the death of his brother-in-law, who had died in action against the enemy, he was a changed person, swore about war, praised Grey and his colleagues, who he declared to be the only sensible people, and through this sort of talk succeeded in making us distance ourselves from him completely.

Paasche's sister had never been happy with his marriage to Ellen, the daughter of the *Oberbürgermeister* (Mayor) of Posen, *Geheimrat* Richard Witting, who came from a Jewish family with well-known left-wing intellectuals among the close relatives:

> I attribute this turn-around for the most part, besides his mental hypertension, to the influence of his parents-in-law Witting and his uncle, the well-known unpatriotic writer Maximilian Harden.[77]

Paasche's parents too emphasized the significance first of the African experience and claimed 'that Hans Paasche had after 1906 become someone quite different. After his return from the source of the Nile, his relationship with his parents, which had earlier been very touching, had also changed.'[78]

In his summary testimony, Dr Leppmann placed great emphasis on the significance for Paasche of the long-lasting break with his parents, and all that the upstanding members of their generation appeared to stand for, that had been first occasioned by the African experience. Leppmann suggested that only now could be seen:

> how deeply the rift with his parents agitated him inside and he was shocked and dismayed when, on the occasion of a recent visit to the prison he [Paasche] admitted how he had, half mad, had done innumerable injustices to his father only then, utterly distraught, to have on the following day burst into tears about being too weak to go openly to his parents and beg for their love. Terrifying and typical for his state of mind was the end of this confession, when, in tears and with his face distorted by grief, he suddenly remarked: 'Yes, if only I had at that time not let the negro hang, then we

---

[77] BAB, R 3003 / C 153 / 17, Vol. 5, statement made by Frau Major Paul Kritsler, geb. Paasche, 7 January 1918, fols. 61–2.

[78] BAB, R 3003 / C 153 / 17, Vol. 1, 'Schriftliches Gutachten' by Geh. Medizinalrat Dr A. Leppmann, fol. 112.

would not have had war'. That was why he had so much sympathy for all those unhappy people who were now suffering from it.[79]

Paasche himself laid some of the blame for his behaviour on his father. When asked how a former officer could possibly behave in the way he had done, he replied:

> It really doesn't matter a bit what one used to be. Since at that time I was in the proximity of a father who, by virtue of his whole attitude, put me into such a state that I really could not think about what I should be taking into consideration.

He commented further:

> I meant by that, that the fact of my earlier occupation in no way binds me to retain any particular prejudices that I recognize as such, and, if the intellectual development of the times leads that way, also to hold new thoughts and views that have not as yet become the property of the officer classes.[80]

Hans Paasche's behaviour included fasting until he felt quite faint, running around naked, and apparently attempting to identify with Africans he had come to know while in the colonies both in his behavioural experiments and more explicitly with *Lukanga Mukara*; he sought, in short, to critique both in words and practice his own society and all his parents, and particularly his authoritarian, overbearing father, seemed to stand for. But in the context of Imperial Germany it proved impossible either to express these views fully, or to live out the personal and political conflicts he was experiencing. Because Paasche did not fit in, and tried to 'reform' not only himself but also others, he was held to be 'not quite normal'. He was fortunate in having a doctor who treated him with a degree of sensitivity and understanding; but it was also clear that without a father in high places, Paasche would not have had the benefit of such an investigation. His 'treason' would have simply resulted in a death sentence. At this point, however, he was merely committed to an asylum for the insane; it took the collapse of Imperial Germany and the abdication of the Kaiser to secure his release from incarceration—but the turmoil which followed also sealed his own fate.

Hans Paasche was far from typical of the alleged and indeed highly diverse 'front generation' of Imperial Germany. But his case throws into sharp relief some of the possible 'lessons' of violence in the colonies, and the massive institutional, cultural, social, and even familial constraints that limited the freedom of those who, fired by a sense of the mission of youth, sought other ways forward against the views of those elites who dominated politics at this time. Paasche's fate after 1918 was again to highlight quite dramatically the changed constellation of forces after the fall of the monarchy and German defeat.

---

[79] BAB, R 3003 / C 153 / 17, Vol. 1, 'Schriftliches Gutachten' by Geh. Medizinalrat Dr A. Leppmann, fol. 134.
[80] BAB, R 3003 / C 153 / 17, Vol. 4, statement by Hans Paasche, 1 February 1918, fol. 80.

3

Uncomfortable compatriots: Societal violence and the crises of Weimar

I had acquired a pile of newspapers for myself and sat opposite Wuth in the waiting room and read. Wuth did not know who Kapp was, but there were even more names there, [von] Jagow and [von] Wangenheim and Pastor Traub. A few too many old men and old names, I opined to Wuth. [Von] Lüttwitz too is an old General . . .

'Couldn't give a fig if there are old names there', said Wuth, 'this is after all a matter for young people.' And thought for a bit and said: 'We have to turn back the revolution.'

'We have to carry on the revolution!' I said and looked at Wuth and thought, what a chasm even a difference of just five years in age makes between us.[1]

The concept of a 'front generation' was popularized by the radical right in the 1920s, deploying selectively reinterpreted experiences and the alleged 'lessons' of the lost war in the service of revisionist political causes. The legend of the supposed 'stab in the back' by Jews and Marxists (often combined in the notion of 'Judeo-Bolshevism'), while the German heroes at the front supposedly remained undefeated, was of course a central element in political myth-mongering; and the concept of the front generation was, for certain right-wingers—not least Adolf Hitler himself—of immense significance as a claim rather than a description. But this does not mean that historians have to tread in the tracks of those contemporaries. The impact of the Great War was by no means limited to that very broad and highly diverse cohort of males—one can actually hardly speak of a 'generation'—who were, at one stage or another, called up into military service. The 'front generation' was a convenient political myth, which served a certain purpose among right-wing circles; but as far as the disproportionate involvement of particular age cohorts in the later Nazi regime was concerned, it was in fact those who were too young to fight in the Great War, the 'war-youth generation', who proved to be of major historical significance.

What we see in this period is a rather interesting phenomenon, in which the diverse and often conflicting claims of contemporaries and the later findings of

---

[1] Ernst von Salomon, *Fünf Jahre Unterschied*, reprinted in Bert Roth (ed.), *Kampf. Lebensdokumente deutscher Jugend von 1914–1934* (Leipzig: Philipp Reklam jun., 1934), pp. 81–2.

historians are somewhat at odds. The concept of 'generation' perhaps became culturally salient as never before, but in practice pulled in all manner of different directions. On the one hand, the myth of the 'front generation' was a powerful rallying cry among leaders of the Free Corps movements and right-wing ethnic-nationalist (*völkisch*) groups, appealing to notions such as the alleged 'comradeship of the trenches', arguing the need to take issue with the Treaty of Versailles, and promoting the use of violence as a political weapon even in peacetime. There was also, however, arguably a far wider sense among former soldiers, however pacifist or otherwise in inclination, that they could never really transmit the full horror of their experiences at the front to those at home. In terms of relatively highbrow literary production in Germany this view was well-known through Erich Maria Remarques' *Im Westen nichts Neues* ('All Quiet on the western front') or in different ways in the semi-autobiographical account of *Krieg* (War) by the now communist Ludwig Renn (the literary pseudonym adopted by the aristocratic Arnold Vieth von Golßenau); yet, in the wider context of popular war literature, such views arguably remained in the minority. In these circumstances, 'generation' became in some senses a flag which could be waved by people of a wide variety of persuasions: age, and particularly 'youth' appeared suddenly highly relevant at this time, for whatever cause.[2] Some have suggested that the notion of generation failed to appeal as much to the left as the right: while particularly intellectuals on the right might think that generation promoted 'values' above material interests, the overriding concern of socialists and communists remained focused on questions of class irrespective of age.[3] But even among left-wing circles—and not only those taking their cue from Marx, but also religiously motivated and pacifist socialists—the youth movements of the day had an impact on thinking about 'generational' tasks for reshaping the future. Many of those involved in both the pre- and post-war youth movements were highly critical of those older Germans whom they saw as responsible for war. Interestingly, those involved in radical left-wing causes appeared, on average, to be a decade or so older than those drawn to the right: largely born in the 1890s, rather than the first decade of the twentieth century, many of the activists on the left were more likely actually to have been members of the much-vaunted 'front generation' than were the younger right-wingers to whom

---

[2] See e.g. E. Günther Gründel, *Die Sendung der jungen Generation. Versuch einer umfassenden revolutionären Sinndeutung der Krise* (München: C. H. Beck'sche Verlagsbuchhandlung, 1933; orig. 1932), which is dedicated: 'Den Alten zum Trost; Den Jungen zum Ansporn.' See for a key historical analysis and argument, Michael Wildt, *Generation des Unbedingten. Das Führungskorps des Reichssicherheitshauptamtes* (Hamburg: Hamburger Edition, 2002); English summary in Michael Wildt, *Generation of the Unbound: The Leadership Corps of the Reich Security Main Office* (Jerusalem: Yad Vashem, 2002), particularly the summary of the argument on pp. 11–13. Lutz Niethammer has suggested that appealing to 'youth' as a claim to reshape the world and prepare the future is basically a twentieth-century phenomenon; see his suggestive (but empirically less than entirely well-founded) essay, 'Sind Generationen identisch?' in Jürgen Reulecke (ed.), with Elisabeth Müller-Lückner, *Generationalität und Lebensgeschichte im 20. Jahrhundert* (München: R. Oldenbourg Verlag, 2003), pp. 1–16, here p. 2.

[3] Robert Wohl, *The Generation of 1914* (Cambridge, MA: Harvard University Press, 1979), pp. 82–4.

this label appealed so strongly.[4] Put differently, perhaps: the 'long front generation' (which included Hitler) was deeply divided, whereas among the war-youth genera- tion there was a highly active, visible, right-wing tendency, not echoed in similar proportions on the left. Common to all these strands, however, was the sense that 'generation' was a future-oriented vehicle for change: working towards the production for a better future, whether through revision of the past or completion of an unfinished revolution.

When the attitudes and actions of specific age cohorts defined by year of birth are analysed, rather than the self-constructions in the writings of articulate males, the concept of the 'front generation' begins to dissolve.[5] While the Great War left inescapable traces on all who lived through it as adults, the impact was too broad in terms of age groups, too class-, gender-, and region-specific to warrant the construction of such a label; this was simply not a coherent social or cultural group, let alone any kind of collective historical actor, even in part. By contrast, significant minorities among those born slightly later do stand out as 'sore-thumb generations'. Substantial numbers drawn from the war-youth generation (born roughly in the first decade or so of the twentieth century) and the 'first Hitler Youth generation' (born during and in the early years after the Great War) were in fact eventually to prove disproportionately the most ardent carriers of the new Nazi institutions, and most active participants in the exercise of state violence against newly defined outcasts in the 1930s, in contrast to older Germans who by and large disapproved of wanton violence in a peacetime society. In different ways, the experiences of the war-youth generation and the first Hitler Youth generation at key life stages arguably predisposed some active minorities among them to be disproportionately supportive of the Nazi cause; and those who were inclined to conform and be mobilized were by the 1930s at a key life stage, ready to launch and hitch their own careers to the Nazi regime, once this had come to power under quite specific historical circumstances. Generationally specific experiences during their childhood and youth thus rendered significant numbers of young people 'available for mobilization', both culturally and structurally, for extremist political movements both in the 1920s (among the older ones) and in the Nazi regime once it was in power, thus making a difference, ultimately, to the kinds of policies that Hitler could put into effect.

Even so, this analysis must be set in a broader political context: the availability of young people for mobilization does not itself explain the rise of the NSDAP to government.[6] Moreover, it is important to recognize that these were also deeply

---

[4] Cf. the generational analysis in Detlev Siegfried, *Das radikale Milieu. Kieler Novemberrevolution, Sozialwissenschaft und Linksradikalismus, 1917–1922* (Wiesbaden: Deutscher Universitäts-Verlag, 2004), particularly pp. 14 ff.

[5] See e.g. Richard Bessel, *Germany after the First World War* (Oxford: Oxford University Press, 1993); and on the writings of 'intellectuals', generally male, in comparative European perspective, Robert Wohl, *The Generation of 1914* (Cambridge, MA: Harvard University Press, 1979), Ch. 2.

[6] It cannot be emphasized too strongly that here, as throughout the book, I am not seeking to explain the course of events; I am, rather, trying to understand the differential impact of key events and periods on people of different ages who lived through them. For a standard analysis of the Nazis' rise to power, see e.g. the narrative and further references in Richard J. Evans, *The Coming of the Third Reich:*

internally divided generations; it was politics, rather than any alleged generationally specific 'formative experiences', which determined which currents became dominant, which were challenged and which suppressed—and thus whose voices could be heard, later proclaiming a 'generational status'. What different claimants to generational status sought to achieve was bitterly contested. It was a question of shifting constellations of power, not of inherited cultural traditions or easy transmission of experiences, which led from colonialism to Nazism. There may at first glance appear to be apparent 'continuities' between the acts of violence and atrocities evident in the German colonies in South-West and East Africa in 1904–7, the German invasion of Belgium and France in 1914, the invasion and occupation of Poland in 1939, and the invasion of the Soviet Union in 1941. But these apparent similarities (with key contrasts, too) are not simple continuities; they do not lie in any straightforward heritage and transmission of a supposed 'German military culture', as though this were some essential legacy of Imperial Germany in a direct descent towards Nazism.

Generationally specific experiences did however, within a broader and ever changing field of forces, play a key role in degrees of preparedness (or otherwise) to listen to a given message, fight for a particular cause. Thus experiences of Imperial Germany, of the Great War, and of the troubled Weimar years, differed not only by class, status, gender, region, and religious and political views, but also according to the ages and life stages of particular cohorts at the time of major historical developments. War, for example, was experienced very differently not only with respect to whether one was male or female, but also whether one was aged eleven, twenty or sixty at the time. And structurally given opportunities, or life chances, as well as culturally informed aspirations, were radically affected by the time as well as the place—social and geographical—of one's birth. But ultimately it was politics that made the difference: which political forces were able to achieve positions of dominance, and which were suppressed; which groups were able to extend their influence over and mobilize the young, and which were not; whose views were heard, and whose silenced.

I. THE PARTIAL RUPTURE OF 1918

The loss of the will to continue fighting played a central role in bringing the war to a close in the autumn of 1918, initiated by the sailors' mutiny and the subsequent setting up, all over Germany, of soldiers' and sailors' councils. The mutiny of the armed forces precipitated the collapse of monarchical government in Germany, with the abdication of the Kaiser and the announcement of a Republic on 9 November 1918, and the signature of the Armistice two days later, on

---

How the Nazis destroyed democracy and seized power in Germany (London: Penguin 2004); and for an exploration of far broader aspects of Weimar culture, particularly in terms of the ferment of creativity and modernity emanating in left-wing circles, see e.g. Eric Weitz, *Weimar Germany: Promise and tragedy* (Princeton: Princeton University Press, 2007).

11 November. But the end of violence as a political weapon was not merely not in sight; the collapse of the imperial regime appeared to have exacerbated, not alleviated, the internal tensions which the Kaiser had so proudly announced, in the summer of 1914, to be a thing of the past. What is more, the post-war cult of violence appeared to glorify the 'hero's death' in new ways, ways which were, among a radical minority, even then not a matter only of myth but also of deadly practice. But this was continually—and violently—contested; and contested under appallingly difficult and unstable conditions.

In the short-term, the forces of moderation took control. An interim government was formed under the initial leadership of Friedrich Ebert (who in 1919 became Weimar's first president) and colleagues from the Social Democratic Party (SPD), along with representatives of those further left in the Independent Social Democratic Party (USPD). Ebert soon entered into an agreement with the leadership of the army, leaving the military effectively outside parliamentary control—a situation which became increasingly problematic for the stability of the fledgling democracy in the following months and years. Military force in cooperation with the police and with the assistance of Free Corps units was used from the outset by Ebert's government to suppress radical uprisings: the murder of the Spartacist (communist) leaders Karl Liebknecht and Rosa Luxemburg in January 1919 provoked particular bitterness on the part of the more radical left-wingers, with the newly formed German Communist Party (KPD) now turned against the moderate Social Democrats of the SPD who had supported this forceful suppression of communist leaders. The left was from now on emotionally as well as politically divided.

Despite the climate of violence, elections were held, producing what at first seemed like a workable coalition dominated by the SPD. In the course of 1919, a new democratic and in some respects highly progressive constitution was adopted in Weimar (hence the name of the new Republic), given that the streets of Berlin were too unsafe for parliamentarians to meet in the capital city. But adoption of a constitution did not mean that parliamentary party politics would work smoothly in practice. This was not only an effect of the apparently punitive provisions of the Treaty of Versailles, revealed later in 1919, but was integral to the contested character of Weimar right from the very start.

With the continuation of fundamental disagreements over the shape that politics should take, and the rapid proliferation of paramilitary groupings, the early years of Weimar were beset by political violence. Everywhere, but particularly in areas such as Berlin or Munich at the times of putsch attempts, there were street battles between left and right, inflicting scores and at times hundreds of casualties. Photographs from the time reveal the extraordinary levels of violence in Berlin streets and at flashpoints elsewhere across Germany, with periodic explosions; destruction of housing, trees, and lamp-posts; the deployment of tanks and soldiers on streets; and signs that civilians should stay indoors because of the dangers on the streets.[7] Violence was

---

[7] Despite the Nazi orientation of the text and the clearly tendentious selection of photographs, an intriguing collection of visual material can be found in Hans Roden (ed.), *Deutsche Soldaten, Vom Frontheer und Freikorps über die Reichswehr zur neuen Wehrmacht* (Berlin: Paul Franke Verlag, 1935).

routinely deployed by both left and right in the course of assorted attempts to wrest control of local or national government. Free Corps units were deployed at first with and increasingly also well beyond the authority and guidelines of the Weimar government in attempts to influence the course of events in the provinces and border regions of a Germany which had lost not only its colonies overseas but also territory at home, creating in particular the hated 'Polish corridor' separating off East Prussia from the rest of the reduced state of Germany. Those influenced by the climate of conspiracy and clandestine organization also constructed their own sense of 'justice' through political assassinations and random murders of political opponents, some-times 'justified' by ad hoc decisions and post hoc attempts at legitimation.[8] But this was all within a climate which was, in a sense, given an aura of respectability from above: courts rarely prosecuted or gave lenient sentences to right-wing political offenders for violent acts, including murder, in contrast to the far more severe sentences meted out to those infringing the law from the left. Moreover, the radical reduction in the size of the armed forces following the Versailles settlement led to secret attempts at rearmament and clandestine military training. After Ebert's un-timely death from appendicitis in 1925, the aging hero of the Great War and veteran of the nineteenth-century wars of unification, General Paul von Hindenburg was elected in his place. Born in Posen in 1847, and in his own person representing all the old Prussian, militaristic, and aristocratic virtues of an age which was soon to disappear entirely, the anti-republican new president conspired with the army leadership to undermine the Weimar constitution which they had been empowered to uphold—and this even before the economic troubles of the years after the 1929 Wall Street crash precipitated a governmental crisis eventuating, within a few short years, in Hindenburg's appointment of Hitler as Chancellor. Thus from 1925 onwards, in the midst of Weimar's most stable and productive years, a predominantly anti-democratic political culture at the helm of the state more than counterbalanced the modernist experiments which were flourishing in the arts, architecture, design, and scientific and intellectual life of the time.

Equally if not rather more problematic from the point of view of the stability of the new Republic were the economic consequences of the ways in which the Great War had been financed through loans, combined with the ways in which the governments of the early 1920s chose to deal with apparently punitive reparations payments. The short-term outcome was the exacerbation of pre-existing inflation, which rapidly spiralled out of control, peaking in the summer of 1923 in a manner which left a searing mark on those who lived through this experience. In the medium term the introduction of the Dawes Plan in 1924 appeared to give some stability to the Weimar economy, while the statesmanship of Germany's foreign minister, Gustav Stresemann, assisted in restoring Germany's place in the interna-tional system. But the political party system remained inherently unstable, with coalitions among the relatively large number of political parties fragile and short-lived, bringing what was derogatorily known as 'the system' into some disrepute.

---

[8] A literary insight into this 'scene' can be found in Joseph Roth's first novel, *The Spider's Web*, trans. John Hoare (London: Granta Books, 2004).

Moreover, the relatively weak German economy crashed further and faster than any other European economy following the Wall Street Crash of 1929, which pre-cipitated the withdrawal of the American short-term loans on which Germany had heavily depended. If inflation had been the major economic catastrophe of the early years of Weimar, recession, depression, and mass unemployment—exacerbated by government policies—characterized its closing years. These developments were, inevitably, accompanied by political radicalization and renewed violence on the streets, even as democracy itself was undermined at the top by the replacement of parliamentary government by authoritarian rule by presidential decree already from 1930 onwards.

The short-lived Weimar period was, then, one of extremes and of inherent instability. Hypothetically, it might perhaps have stabilized had the economy enjoyed the same kind of developments as characterized West German transforma-tion after 1945 (and particularly after the introduction of the Marshall Plan, injecting money and expertise into Western Europe on a massive scale following the currency reform of 1948, a plan designed precisely in order to ward off the very real threat of political radicalization and instability). But it did not; and the broader conditions, individual decisions and detailed sequence of events that together help to explain the ultimate rise of the NSDAP and the appointment of Adolf Hitler as German Chancellor in January 1933 need little further rehearsal here. Less clear, however, are the ways in which members of different generations experienced this period of upheaval and instability, and the consequences of their experiences at particular life stages not only for their own life stories at the time but also for the ways in which they became entangled in the later development of the Third Reich and, in some cases, also the succeeding East German dictatorship.[9]

For the vast majority of adult Germans, the Great War and its ending appeared at the time to signify a major life rupture. It was not only Thomas Mann, who at the start of his magisterial *Magic Mountain* (*Der Zauberberg*), first published in late 1924, registered a sense that the pre-war world was in some sense a dream, a recent but now vanished country. Millions were afflicted by a sense that an old world had come to an end, and that they were having in some way to start anew. This was, arguably, the first great rupture of twentieth-century Germany; and it played out not only in the faltering, inadequate, but ultimately cataclysmic regime-change at the top of the political system in 1918, but also in repeated ways, multiplied a millionfold, in the everyday lives of ordinary people.

At this point, however, the rupture for those who were already adults at the end of the war was primarily one of dealing with changes as they affected lived experience in the present, rather than requiring also a fundamental questioning and indeed frequently radical rejection of previous personal identities, as was to be the case after 1945. There was after 1918 no equivalent of post-1945 'denazifica-tion' or fundamental critique of people's roles in the previous regime—far from it.

---

[9] See Detlev Peukert, *The Weimar Republic: The crisis of classical modernity* (New York: Hill and Wang, 1993), Ch. 4, for suggestive discussion of the experiences of different generations within the Weimar years.

And although the monarchical regime of Imperial Germany had been brought down by an internal revolution, it was not rejected and replaced quite as radically as was to be the case not only after defeat in war in 1945 but also after the 'gentle revolution' and eventual demise of the GDR in 1989–90. After 1918, there was both widespread yearning for what had been before, and also large continuity in the structures of social, economic, and military power, for all the changes in political regime and the diversification and flowering of new strands of culture, particularly in the growing metropolitan centre of Berlin.

Thus there was in 1918, despite the fundamental changes to the political system, no radical turnover of elites; and no radical critique of the past. The challenges for most people were primarily to do with how the post-war world affected their lives in the new conditions of the present; and not—as was the case after 1945, and in different ways after 1989–90—with (also) having to account for one's own past life. The shock of transition was thus principally a shock of dealing with new challenges and with the practical and emotional legacies of war, and generally very much less a matter of seeking to 'overcome the past' in terms of recasting one's own life story. Even so, the upheavals that history threw into personal lives necessarily also affected people's sense of self, although experiences and responses differed from one individual to another, depending on a variety of factors, as a few examples readily demonstrate.

II. TRANSITIONS

Released from his incarceration in a mental institution by revolutionary sailors on 9 November 1918, Hans Paasche went straight to the Reichstag and was rapidly elected a member of the Executive Committee of the Workers' and Soldiers' Councils (*Vollzugsrat der Arbeiter- und Soldatenräte*).[10] In the following few weeks, in which momentarily everything seemed possible during the very early period of the provisional, newly formed democratic government under Friedrich Ebert, Paasche was highly active in Berlin. Although on the left, he was no supporter of anti-democratic politics, and determined to discuss and debate as openly as possible without taking personal offence at those with whom he had political disagreements. He was, in many respects, uncomfortable with the emergent party political landscape of the winter of 1918–19, while writing agonized moral tracts about what had gone wrong with German politics over the preceding years. But, whichever direction his political activities might have led him, his private life dramatically intervened. Paasche took time out from politics in November to visit his wife Ellen, whom he had only been able to see on rare and intermittent visits during his period of imprisonment, and their four children at their home on the estate of Waldfrieden (near what is now Przesieki in Poland). Ellen had, like so many at this time, fallen prey to the post-war influenza pandemic, but seemed to be on the road to recovery. Following a short visit,

[10] Magnus Schwantje, 'Hans Paasche: Sein Leben und Wirken', *Flugschriften des Bundes Neues Vaterland* Nr. 26(4), 1921, p. 20.

Paasche went back to Berlin to resume his political activities, planning to return to Waldfrieden and his family very soon. But on 10 December 1918, the news reached him that his beloved wife had died, fatally weakened by her bout of influenza, at the age of twenty-nine. Paasche never fully recovered from this blow, and retreated from the national political arena as best he could, basing himself in Waldfrieden with his children, although still embroiled in numerous political controversies and continually plagued by distressing and threatening enmities.

The influenza pandemic was worldwide, not restricted to the post-war countries of Europe; but, given the exhaustion and malnutrition of so many in Germany in the later war years and immediately after the war, it had particularly virulent consequences in this context. Combined with the loss of around 2 million soldiers in military combat, the much lower birth rate during the war, and the increase in civilian deaths from other causes, the pandemic of 1918–19 left post-war German society demographically extremely skewed.[11] War widows; fatherless children; a disproportionate percentage of teenagers compared not only to younger children but also, more crucially from the perspective of generational tensions, to adult males who could exert some authority over them; all contributed to a sense of a deeply disrupted society, in which an attempt had to be made to build anew—but in which the age which had passed was retrospectively widely cast as neither fully rejected, nor entirely without merit. This was indeed a major rupture, but not an absolute rupture combined with absolute rejection. It was therefore open for some to combine a new revolutionary fervour with a wild twist of revisionist rhetoric. But this remained a minority; most simply tried to pick up the pieces of their 'private' lives and construct some sense of 'normality', despite all that seemed to be continuing to plague them even after the end of the war. And influenza was far from the only problem of the post-war period.

Albert D., like so many other adult males, had been called up and served on the front as a medical doctor, earning the Iron Cross.[12] Finally demobilized in spring 1919, Albert D. returned to try rebuild his practice, which at first appeared as if it would once again flourish. He was initially surprised at 'how rapidly my clientele reappeared and the relationship of trust between patients and doctor had not suffered as a result of the frequent and long breaks' in contact. But the psychological and physical consequences at home were infinitely worse than anything he had expected. Worse, then, came in the wake of war:

> But now . . . a new and weighty concern fell on me: my wife's state of health had suffered badly. The sudden death of her father not long before, the heroic death of her younger sister's husband, who had fought as a volunteer with the German troops in Palestine, the sudden death due to a lung infection of her sister, now a war widow, leaving behind two little boys, and not least the fact that her mother went blind at virtually the same time, all this coming on top of the worry and agitation about me so wore the poor woman down that in a fit of melancholy in the winter of 1919 she took her own life.[13]

---

[11] See Bessel, *Germany after the First World War*, pp. 224 ff.
[12] See Ch. 2 above, pp. 42–3.
[13] HHL b MS Ger 91 (54), Albert D., p. 3.

Both Albert D.'s own parents also died in 1918, within six months of each other. In face of these multiple family tragedies, which put a total end to the relative tranquillity and secure life plans he had been developing before the Great War and shattered his world, Albert D. tried to survive by throwing himself into work. A favourite cousin of his wife came to help take care of the children, and—like many widowers with small children—Albert D. ended up marrying the new housewife and mother substitute, and tried to rebuild his life. This attempt, which even in face of massive emotional upheavals was at least apparently based on secure economic foundations, was in the event short-lived. In 1922–3 came the inflation:

> Accumulated savings melted away, years of the hardest labour, both mental and physical, had been in vain, the solid foundations of the family began to shake. And once again the German people were highly agitated, in part in deep despair.[14]

Doctors were particularly affected by the inflation because of the relatively long delay between treating a patient and being paid from the sickness insurance funds (*Krankenkasse*), such that the fees were more or less worthless by the time they received them; Albert D. at one point found that when he was eventually paid for treating 500 patients he was able to buy only two loaves of bread. In his view, workers who were paid weekly were better off than professionals such as doctors, because workers could buy wares almost immediately at a price they could still afford with their frequently paid wages.

The Great War was thus but the first part of more than a decade of upheaval, a period in which history and personal life were closely enmeshed in ways which altered the course of people's lives. As Albert D. summarized his own experience, and its inevitable implications for his sense of self:

> If in 1920 the reconstruction of my family and of my own self [*des eigenen Ich*] had begun, with the end of the inflation in 1923 this was followed by financial reconstruction. War and the privations of war, shortages of food during this period, the revolution of 1918, general strikes, the attempt to establish a soviet-style republic [*Räterepublik*] precisely in the area of Franconia where I worked, and not least certain conditions and restraints of the Versailles Treaty and rapidly rising unemployment in the whole Reich repeatedly shook the faith of the German people in a better future. And in addition, people were the object of political agitation and divided among countless parties and party political groups.[15]

The experiences of illness and familial disruption were common to Germans of all religious confessions. Historical, social, economic, and political events in the widest sense affected the lives of virtually all Germans; life courses were massively affected by trends on a broad, societal scale, rather than displaying the random variations with vicissitudes rooted in personal decisions, fortunes, and misfortunes, that people felt they should have been able to expect and which they read back into the contrasting golden age before the war.

---

[14] *Ibid.*, p. 4.
[15] *Ibid.*, p. 4.

All Germans were in one way or another affected. Maria K. too recalled the post-war period as one of immense suffering, losing both her mother and her first baby in the influenza epidemic:

> I also experienced the devastating consequences of the hunger blockade. A huge number of people died in the influenza epidemics of 1918 and 1920. A body suffering from malnutrition has only weak resistance. So in February I lost both my mother and my eldest son in the flu epidemic.
>
> Hunger and privation had a demoralising effect on all of us; many laws were, if at all possible, circumvented. 'Hamstering' [foraging and storing up food], for example, was strictly forbidden.[16]

As after 1945, the overwhelming need for personal survival took precedence over the traditionally law-abiding conventions of the German educated bourgeoisie. Maria K. and her academic husband, along with another professor from Giessen University, went out to the countryside to engage in the foraging and illicit storing up of food ('hamstering') that was both forbidden and yet essential to the survival and well-being of their families. She also recalled—like many others—that the humanitarian aid given by Quakers was crucial: 'The nutrition of school children was very much improved by the Quaker food programme.'[17] But, a drop in the ocean of suffering on the home front, such aid would not prove sufficient to deal with the hunger and epidemic illnesses of the early post-war period.

Some Germans found additional problems emerging more forcefully at this time. Notably absent from Albert D.'s account up to this point was the further fact that he was Jewish. This played, in his recollections, absolutely no role whatsoever in his patriotic experiences of and involvement in the Great War and its tragic immediate aftermath. But very soon Albert D. was to experience the rising antisemitism and racially defined nationalist radicalism that was whipped up in certain quarters in the early post-war years. Albert D. became increasingly aware that Jews were being singled out as a 'whipping boy' or scapegoat (*Prügelknabe*), with antisemitism rapidly on the rise in the early 1920s. He noted further that right-wing groups were beginning to appropriate the word 'German' for their side only, for example calling their demonstrations a 'German Day' (*Deutscher Tag*), 'as though the right-wing parties and above all the Nazis were the only ones who could lay any claim to patriotic love'. And their methods, too, were more than clear: 'Right from the very start terror dominated the field.'[18]

This field was one that was, however, highly contested, and at this point there were many who were vehemently opposed to the extremist ructions on the right. Carl P. (born in 1895), was perhaps somewhat unusual in a variety of ways before the Great War broke out. Like many of his generation and background, Carl had been brought up in what were held to be strict Prussian virtues: in his own words, he was 'from the earliest age held to the tenets that one should have no "moods"

---

[16] HHL b MS Ger 91 (101), Maria K., p. 2.
[17] *Ibid.*, p. 2.
[18] HHL b MS Ger 91 (54), Albert D., pp. 5–6.

and should disguise one's feelings. Maintaining one's composure [*Haltung*] in every situation, that was the highest principle of education in our house.' Yet, now more in common with that minority of his generation and background drawn to the life reform youth movements, Carl rebelled:

> Just imagine: I refused to smoke and drink like other young people, because I thought it stupid and undignified! I generally ran around without wearing a hat, which at that time was still held to be unseemly, and wore shirts with the so-called 'Schiller collar', that is with an open neck. All that 'was simply not done'. For my part, I found my environment to be narrow-minded and petty [*spießig*], dumb and superficial, and I sought to 'get back to nature'.[19]

When the Great War broke out, Carl had refused to volunteer, unlike many other young men in his environment. He was, however, eventually called up in 1916 and worked in a paramedical capacity, having earlier trained in the Red Cross. Invalided out with tuberculosis in 1917, Carl P. remained ambivalent about his war experiences. But he was quite clear that, whatever lessons his cohort gained from this period, there were wider generational conflicts at play:

> We, the so-called generation of war volunteers, had something of the revolutionary about us. We protested against the burdensome social conventions inherited from the feudal era in Prussia, we no longer wanted to be led by the nose but believed instead in our own capacity to determine our own fates. It did not matter whether someone of my generation was a child of a working class family, a son of a bourgeois, or an aristocrat, all basically felt the same: but all had to fight against an inner resistance grounded in respect for one's elders or 'betters', rooted in our upbringing. Most of us succeeded only partially on this front. Some got stuck along the way. Others exploded and became radical fighters, only later to sink quietly into oblivion. Only a few were able to blend together the old and the new era in a harmonious union that would make it possible to them to be a valuable mediator of the old to the up-and-coming generation, and to lead the way into the new which held so much promise.[20]

Interestingly, although Carl P. saw 'generation' here as in some respects transcending class differences, he was acutely aware that the challenges facing those a few years younger could be responded to in very different ways, as radical solutions were increasingly sought to the tensions of the age. In the 1920s Carl P., now a committed Social Democrat living in Germany's eastern provinces—first in the Posen region, then in Silesia—became increasingly worried about the rise of extreme nationalist forces, which became ever more threatening as far as his own life was concerned. He threw himself into political work, primarily as a journalist on behalf of the SPD, commenting on the increasingly violent state of a country that, although technically at peace, was embroiled in conditions verging at times on outright civil war.

By 1919, Hans Paasche was also highly critical of the post-war situation. He too saw deep generational conflicts that overlaid political divisions and added an almost

---

[19] HHL, b MS Ger 91 (174), Carl P., pp. 8–9.
[20] *Ibid.*, p. 10.

irresolvable emotional complexity to the state of Germany at the outset of the first attempt at democracy:

> A double rift runs through our people. Free spirits irreconcilably oppose reactionaries; and between young people and their fathers yawns a chasm larger than ever before between two generations. If parents only knew how revolutionary the active youth of today feels, and particularly the offspring of aristocratic, militaristic, capitalist families, they would shudder. Below these there is then another youth, the hopeless war product of bigoted high-school teachers. In this stratum the concepts of violence, hereditary enemies, the Fatherland, will become completely ridiculous.[21]

In large measure these problems were rooted, not only in the institutional and political arrangements of the day, but also in what Paasche saw as the deeply authoritarian upbringing which had been so common in Imperial Germany, and which, in his view, was designed to bring about unconditional obedience and preparedness for death:

> Be aware, you German, that you have been brought up in a mentality of servitude . . . You are to obey anyone claiming authority over you: father, mother, policeman, conductor, you have to honour all of these, even if they are the least free and therefore the most criminal of people, cutting you off from friendship, love, happiness, and making this life a misery for you. This crime begins with your parents. Typical German parents are the most servile creatures the earth has ever produced. They do not want their children to be able to lead their own lives, and in this they succeed. The child's will must be broken . . . But, you obedient children, honour your parents who, out of heartfelt love, prepare you for all of this, for the school bench, the barracks yard, and a mass grave.[22]

Hans Paasche's remarks, bringing together the psychological and the broad political conflicts of his day, were rooted in bitter personal experience. He might have been in a small minority, but he was far from alone in his views or perceptions. Nevertheless, his contribution to the struggle for a better future remained some-what muted, following the death of his wife and his retreat to his country estate to live quietly with his four children. All the same, he continued writing, thinking, and liaising with others in search for solutions to the state of Germany, not only political and economic, but also social, moral, and deeply personal.

Wider responses to the new conditions were highly various, as members of different religious denominations and political persuasions sought to come to terms with the new conditions of the post-war regime. Some continued to struggle for left-wing causes, whether through the use of violence—as on the extreme left— or by exploring moderate or even pacifist routes. The German Quaker movement was even born in the 1920s, as the combination of the material relief provided by American and British Quakers and the wider message of principled non-violence fell on the receptive ears of young people who were shattered by the violence of war

---

[21] Hans Paasche, *Das verlorene Afrika* (Berlin: Verlag Neues Vaterland, E. Berger and Co., 1919; *Flugschriften des Bundes Neues Vaterland* Nr. 16), p. 7.
[22] *Ibid.*, p. 9.

and disturbed by their own Protestant Churches' support of the military action.[23] But this was a tiny handful of individuals. Other members of the front generation, who were what might be called 'social casualties of the peace', moved into the penumbra of rapidly proliferating right-wing circles. Despite Hitler's heightened visibility—and indeed excellent exploitation of national publicity—in the trial following the unsuccessful Munich Beer Hall putsch of 1923, the party with which he associated himself and then took over as leader was only one of many such right-wing groupings at the time.[24] Many people at this time became involved with one or other of many right-wing circles, including the emergent Nazi movement, only later to leave again. About the only generalization which can be made is that the vast majority of adults at this point were deeply unsettled, unsure of the shape the future would take, or in which direction—beyond personal material survival—they should devote their energies.

One such 'casualty of the peace' was Willy B. (born in the later 1880s), who was initially retained in the army after the end of the war but left it in 1919 because of his dislike of the new Republic.[25] Coming from a well-to-do family, Willy B. at first switched to the study of art history at Berlin University, rapidly gaining a doctorate in the subject, supported by his father. But his family's fortunes were ruined by the inflation (as was his father's health: he died in 1923), and Willy B. was forced to become a travelling salesman to make ends meet. Although achieving some modest success in this capacity, which he put down to his austere lifestyle in contrast to that of many contemporaries, Willy B. was deeply unhappy:

> For about ten years I could not get over the painful loss of a career as an officer . . . Anyone who knows what it was like to grow up in the Prussian Officer Corps will understand that, as a monarchist, it was impossible to muster any affection for the German Republic. And what high hopes were raised when a small opportunity arose somewhere to don once again the beloved military uniform.[26]

Willy B. thus became involved with radical circles involving individuals such as Graefe, Wulle, Ludendorff, Hitler, and was also a participant in the Kapp putsch of 1920, as well as an enthusiastic supporter of Hitler's 1923 Beer Hall putsch. As he put it:

> With incomparable enthusiasm I took my place alongside younger comrades from all possible nationalist associations, in the EHER publishing house in Munich's Schelling Street, in order to get revenge for the 'Jewish inflation' and the Jewish revolution. The failure and the thousandfold betrayals of those November days of 1923 in Munich threw us all back into deep despondency.[27]

---

[23] See further Ch. 10 below, pp. 423–5. See more generally Hans A. Schmitt, *Quakers and Nazis: Inner light in outer darkness* (Columbia and London: University of Missouri Press, 1997).
[24] See further Ian Kershaw, *Hitler: Hubris* (Harmondsworth: Penguin, 1998).
[25] HHL, b MS Ger 91 (22), Willy B.
[26] *Ibid.*, pp. 2–3.
[27] *Ibid.*, p. 3.

Willy B. explained how the loose groupings were held together by perpetual and constantly shifting enmities: one 'became an opponent of everything and everyone. There was barely anyone we did we not fight: Stresemann, the League of Nations, the Jews, the Marxists, we had become "perpetual fighters" [*ewige Kämpfer*].' He swung back and forth between different movements in the radical circles, and ended up slightly uneasily with the group around Hitler rather than Ludendorff, explaining that 'the desire to speed things up a bit drove one into the arms of the National Socialists'. Despite a slight sense of unease, he clung to the wider right-wing cause:

> When I had to take my SA group to stir things up in working-class areas, I was never quite able to rid myself of a feeling of injustice. But the prevalence of the Jews was enough to keep you in line. You would be pulled into the swirl of party activities and slowly a person does after all get used to things that one would at first have instinctively refused.[28]

Even the shifting language in this account—switching back and forth between the first person pronoun and the more distanced and general '*man*' ('one' or 'you') and '*der Mensch*' ('person') indicates Willy B's continuing slight sense of unease about actions he could not seem even in retrospect to take full ownership of or render compatible with a personal sense of authentic self. Clearly his character changed in the perceptions of people who knew him at the time, too. A former comrade, of rather different political persuasions, was quite shocked when he met Willy B. again; this man, Willy B. reports, 'shot himself when Hitler came to power'.[29] It is clear that, at least initially, the peculiar combination of persuasive pressure and collective action exercised by right-wing radical circles on a person of similar inclinations in principle was sufficient to overcome initial distaste for the implications of the programme in practice. But eventually Willy B., too, developed more serious doubts and even began to feel repelled by the circles in which he found himself.

Willy B.'s break with Nazism was at first somewhat ambivalent, but eventually sufficient to cause him to flee the country. The collapse of his business, however hard he worked, in the recession after 1929, he continued to blame on 'Jews'; his antisemitism clearly remained relatively untouched by his growing pangs of conscience. And yet, while he agreed on the alleged 'problem', he began to doubt the capacity of the Nazis either to provide appropriate answers or to deal effectively with the issues they were trumpeting as problems; and he increasingly came to criticize the violence of Nazi methods:

> Already in 1929 I was noticing a continuous decline in the income of my business, one could work and work but no longer get ahead at all. Trade and commerce had virtually completely gone over into the hands of Jewish people, and they would not tolerate a former officer as a representative there. So pressure built on pressure and produced hatred against all who were not Nazis. From them one expected salvation. But there was a muffled beat coming from the heart and the conscience . . . I allowed myself to

---

[28] HHL, b MS Ger 91 (22), Willy B.   [29] *Ibid.*

criticize, to harbour scruples, to raise doubts as to whether the party could rip us out from Versailles and the Dawes [reparation] payments.—In the deepest recesses of the soul, one became a defector.[30]

Interestingly, again the style of Willy B.'s account, with its oscillation between the first and third person, and occasionally even almost absent subject, reflects his vacillations, hesitations, and sense of unease and self-doubt. Unable to make a profitable living or feel at ease with himself, he eventually decided to emigrate, and left initially for Memel (a contested territory taken from Germany by the Treaty of Versailles, and later taken over by Lithuania); here, after Hitler had come to power, he felt he was being spied upon by Nazis. His final break with the cause came, however, only when his growing disquiet about Nazi methods was confirmed by the issues surrounding the burning of the Reichstag shortly before the elections of 1933:

> This served to break the last internal bond with these bandits. My instinctual feeling that crime would be raised to a state maxim had not deceived me. I have never been able to engage in hypocrisy and lying, just as little as cutting my coat to suit the prevailing wind.[31]

In his transition from willing antisemitic nationalist to principled refusal to engage in accommodation with a criminal regime, Willy B. was unusual. But the inner struggles between his sense of self and the demands of the cause, between the internalized aspirations and moral codes of his pre-war youth and the changed demands of his adult life, reveal particularly clearly just how much was at stake on a personal as well as public level even for those swept up in the right-wing movements of the day.

Willy B. wrote his autobiographical sketch while in Sweden in 1940, and concluded it with an oddly nationalist paean of praise to pacifism (now incorporating even use of the second person as he engages in injunctions to his future self):

> It was time to break camp here too. The fiftieth year of my life had been reached. Homeless, searching for freedom, you must wander in the world you little human vessel [*Menschenschifflein*]!—Everything has been taken from you that you used to consider noble and good. What are your medals? A farce. What is the Fatherland under the heel of these mad criminals? A hell-hole. Where is the free German spirit? Disappeared, and in its place a slave mentality and a desire for a place at the bigwigs' feeding trough.—Loudmouths, instead of quiet capable people!...Away, away from this plague of the spirit...A new world war is raging, and here, off the beaten tracks, stands a German man whose life has led him from the Prussian cadet corps to a humanistic pacifism![32]

Willy B.'s life course, as he recounts it, demonstrates perhaps a particularly striking trajectory. But he was far from alone in his earlier pattern of movement into and out of a variety of right-wing circles through the chaotic 1920s. And he was also not alone in having difficulty in trying to make sense of the post-1918 world in which

---

[30] *Ibid.*, p. 4.   [31] *Ibid.*, p. 5.   [32] *Ibid.*, pp. 5–6.

he found himself, in the light of principles, aspirations, and deeply rooted expectations inherited from a previous era. The difference in his life from those of millions of others was that, after 1933, despite being in broad agreement with many Nazi prejudices and aims, he found it harder than most on the right to swallow acknowledgement of the criminality of Nazi methods, and did, ultimately, recover some sense of autonomous self (even addressing himself as a 'little ship' which by definition only he could steer) outside the confines of a state which had given way to a regime of madness. His Fatherland, as he had conceived of it before 1918, had already effectively been taken away from him; removal from the geographical but no longer emotional homeland was then less of a step when Willy B. finally took it.

Experiences were very different among those who only reached adulthood after the end of the war, and were children or teenagers during the war: the war-youth generation. They had barely known anything but a condition of warfare; many had almost dream-like memories of what seemed to have been an idyllic childhood, broken suddenly by news that the country was at war—generally remembered as being problematic mainly for having cut short what should have been a seemingly unending summer holiday in the country, the mountains, or at the Baltic coast. The distinctive experience of this generation has been well-described by Sebastian Haffner (born 1907), who while in exile in Britain in the late 1930s penned what he conceived of as memoirs of a rather typical childhood and youth. For Haffner's generation, the stability of the mid-Weimar years was, experientially, an exception, and one to which many of his age group found it hard to accustom themselves after a decade (1914–24) of rapid and violent change during the formative years of their young lives. Haffner's account is highly suggestive in a number of respects. As he presciently commented when writing in 1939:

> Perhaps people will not think it worth making the effort to represent in such detail the inadequate reactions of a child to the World War. It certainly would not be worth the effort if this were just an isolated case. But it is not an isolated case. A whole German generation experienced the war in this or similar ways, as children or youngsters—and much more significantly, this is precisely the generation which today is preparing for a repeat performance.[33]

Equally presciently, Haffner went on to comment that:

> There was a lot which later assisted Nazism and modified its character. But its roots lie here: not in the 'experience of the trenches' (*Fronterlebnis*), but in the German schoolboys' experience of war. The front generation in general actually delivered relatively few genuine Nazis... The real generation of Nazism is rather those born in the decade from 1900 to 1910, who experienced the war, quite untroubled by its reality, as one big game.[34]

But the story of how a generation exposed to war as play became the carriers of the Third Reich was a complex one; and it is only a small part of this generation who

---

[33] Sebastian Haffner, *Geschichte eines Deutschen. Die Erinnerungen 1914–1933* (Munich: Deutscher Taschenbuch Verlag, 2002), p. 22.
[34] *Ibid.*, p. 23.

were to rise to historical prominence as the 'sore-thumb cohort' spearheading the expansion, through military aggression and oppressive civilian administration, of the Third Reich. The mechanism of transmission deserves somewhat closer attention. The details vary from case to case, but certain groups were very unlikely to become prey to right-wing radicalization.

Common to all of those who were still children at the time of the war was the officially transmitted atmosphere of war adulation, propagated not only through schools and newspapers, but also in the prevalence of war games in the playground and after school. As Haffner rightly emphasized, for his generation war was essentially a game, not a matter of exposure to real violence and real suffering. What counted for them was 'the fascination of the game of war: a game in which, according to secret rules, numbers of prisoners, territories gained, strongholds seized and ships that were sunk played roughly the role of goals in football or "points" in boxing'.[35] Such experiences were common more or less wherever children went to school. In Vienna, Stephen J., the son of a Jewish father whose family originally came from Hungary and a mother who was descended from a stream of Austrian state officials and members of the lesser nobility, recalled:

> As an eight-year-old boy I naturally saw only the glory of war and not the misery and suffering behind the gigantic, screaming headlines of the newspapers . . . I avidly read the war books that were appearing by the dozen at the time . . . In the park in front of our house I passionately played 'soldiers'.[36]

There are many similar recollections from amongst those who were children at this time.

Yet the lessons subsequently drawn from defeat were highly varied. In the course of the 1920s Haffner increasingly disassociated himself from those who remained absorbed in nationalist activities. He observed with interest but again some considerable critical distance those young people who had made dizzying economic gains during the early period of inflation and then could hardly deal with the stabilization of the economy that followed. By the time he was a young law student, Haffner had very clear and well-developed political opinions of his own which conflicted sharply, and in principle, with the possibility of making compromises with the new regime. Even so, it took him quite a while to realize this and draw conclusions about how he should respond in practice.

There were other reasons too for varying responses among members of this generation. Class, region, milieu, all played a role, as did, in part, differences of religious confession, particularly where individuals were increasingly aware that they were seen as partial outsiders, and as questions of 'race' began to become more salient.[37]

---

[35] *Ibid.*, p. 21.

[36] HHL, b MS Ger 91 (100), Stephen J., pp. 5, 6.

[37] In his detailed and insightful study of Breslau, Till van Rahden argues that the 'decisive turning point . . . came in the last years of the First World War and early in the Weimar Republic, when relations between Jews and other Breslauers deteriorated dramatically. Against the backdrop of experiences during the war and the army's "Jew count" of 1916, the postwar crises and inflation, the high degree of Jewish integration eroded. While the socioeconomic situation of Breslau Jews worsened

Wolfgang Y., for example, was born in 1908, in the Silesian industrial town of Kattowitz, of a Catholic father and a Jewish mother—a quite typical 'inter-faith' marriage at a time when this was both increasingly common, and not seen as in any way incompatible with commitment to German national identity. For personal reasons his parents divorced when Wolfgang was one year old, and he lived with his Jewish mother and her parents. His maternal grandfather:

> was a pious Jew, well respected in town, belonging to the better bourgeois circles . . .
> He was a stern, deeply religious man, who got along very well with the Catholic priests
> of the area and socialized with them on a friendship basis.[38]

At this stage, given his commitment to a notion of German and Prussian identity, Wolfgang, like so many living in this borderland region of Silesia, was as a young person attracted to a military career. Writing in 1940, Wolfgang recalled that:

> The population in border areas probably succumbs rather readily to chauvinistic
> influences, in these border areas there is a seamless transition from national to
> nationalistic . . . [I] wanted to become a soldier, an officer, a Prussian officer.[39]

Nevertheless, he was already somewhat put off this choice of career by the sight of his wounded cousin, who had been serving on the eastern front during the Great War:

> My mother and I received permission to visit him in a field hospital behind the front.
> We found lying on a straw bed a groaning being, and as a youngster I was badly
> shattered by this sight. Then we drove across a field of slaughter, it was winter, the
> wagon of the Polish farmer taking us to the station threw up great trails of blood in the
> snow.[40]

Subsequently Wolfgang's cousin died of his wounds, still in his mid-twenties, 'a handsome, highly gifted man'.[41] Yet even this direct personal witnessing, as a child, of the tragedies of war did not keep Wolfgang from active and enthusiastic participation in the standard war games of his generation while at school, by now living with his grandparents in Berlin, where he attended the Werner Siemens Realgymnasium. His account echoes that of Sebastian Haffner: 'There was a lot of talk of the Emperor, of Germany, of German-ness [*Deutschtum*], of German heroes . . . during school breaks we played war in the schoolyard. I was often the leader of the German troops . . . At that time I learned very little, I just read war stories, my life was completely filled up by talk of war.'[42]

Unlike many others of his cohort who had been caught up in the excitement of war while playing games at school, however, Wolfgang Y.'s views became clearer

---

after 1918, anti-Semitism increased and gained in significance in many spheres of social life in the city.'
Till van Rahden, *Jews and Other Germans: civil society, religious diversity and urban politics in Breslau, 1860–1925*, trans. Marcus Brainard (Madison: University of Wisconsin Press, 2008), p. 4.

[38] HHL, b MS Ger 91 (251), Wolfgang Y., p. 1.
[39] *Ibid.*, p. 2.
[40] *Ibid.*, p. 3.
[41] *Ibid.*
[42] *Ibid.*, p. 9.

and he distanced himself from unthinking adulation of all things military as he grew older. One uncle, who was married to a Catholic Hungarian, lived in a villa in the well-to-do Berlin suburb of Grunewald, quite near to the house of the German foreign minister, Walther Rathenau (who was Jewish, and assassinated by right-wing extremists in 1922). The uncle, whom Wolfgang visited frequently, talked endlessly about the Kaiser; he also 'wore a moustache like the Emperor, also held himself in a very military posture'.[43] In the course of the early 1920s, when Wolfgang visited some of his Christian relatives by marriage (the parents-in-law of an uncle) who lived in Weimar, he became increasingly critical of the petty bourgeois attitudes and adulation of authority evident in these circles:

> I would like to adduce one phenomenon that seems to me typical of the outlook of this bourgeois stratum: every senior teacher, every burgher in Weimar was not only proud that Goethe had belonged to the same people as he himself, but also behaved as though something of Goethe's genius had been passed on to him. When these people talked of the poet, they then grew in their own self-esteem and in their own eyes became great minds.

Adulation of Goethe was quite compatible with a combination of ultra-militaristic tendencies, anti-republican sentiments, and heavy emphasis on the maintenance of conventional social roles and the appearance of morality, while the superficial guise of social order could readily mask a total lack of moral considerations in practice:

> Everyone talked of war, of the Emperor, of Generals, not a single one supported the Republic. One always conducted oneself in a dignified and measured way, and laid great value on everything being in order. Later I learned, through my aunt, how fragile morality really was in this stuffy bourgeois nest [*Spießernest*], what sorts of things went on behind the mask of honour in the best families in town. My hatred of everything smacking of petty bourgeois stuffiness [*alles Verspießerte*] arises not least from this trip to Weimar.[44]

At this time, Wolfgang Y. simply felt a degree of distaste; but within a matter of a decade, it was from precisely such circles as these that support for far more radical policies came, ultimately ousting people like Wolfgang Y. from their homeland—and worse.

Some members of the war-youth generation were, in the context of the crises of both the early and the late years of the Weimar Republic, highly ideologically mobilized—but in a variety of directions, both left and right. It was again *politics* that determined which elements would be fostered, be offered particular opportunities and chances, and 'rise to the surface' of the historical stage at different times. Members of the war-youth generation subsequently played a role in *both* German dictatorships, and not just the Third Reich: they disproportionately provided the carrier classes of the Nazi regime, but also some of the leaders and long-lasting functionaries of the GDR. The splits that were visible between members of this generation already in the 1920s and 1930s continued to be played out under the

---

[43] *Ibid.*, p. 9.   [44] *Ibid.*, pp. 21–2.

Cold War conditions of the 1950s and 1960s. But it was those on the radical right who eventually won the battle for domination in the course of the 1920s and 1930s.

III. THE FREE CORPS AS TRANSMISSION BELT OF VIOLENCE

Why did some young people in the period after 1918 particularly glorify violence? Why did not the experience of death, and the apparent senselessness of the destruction not merely of so many lives all around but of whole landscapes laid waste, not have the universal effect on mentalities that might have been promoted by the well-known (anti-)war literature of the later 1920s? A part of the answer must lie not only in the prevalence of popular literature glorifying war, but also, more importantly perhaps, in the lack of personal experience of violence for most of these young people during the war itself, which was witnessed only at a distance, vicariously, and largely in terms of exaggerated reports of German successes; for the war-youth generation, it was news of unexpected defeat, rather than exposure to real violence, that came as the major shock. This stood in marked contrast to the later experiences of many young people at the end of the Second World War, when massive bombing of the home front, experience of flight and mass dislocation, and exposure to violence all around in the chaos of the closing months, served to render eventual defeat not only very real but in some respects also a relief. Added to the only distant knowledge rather than direct first-hand experience of physical front-line brutality in the Great War were, for the war-youth generation, the difficulties of the early Weimar years, with economic and political chaos providing the context for some to look for more radical solutions to persisting problems. Finally, the political situation both permitted and indeed fostered the flourishing of groups ready to mobilize youth in service of violent causes. It is this last, perhaps, which provided the key to the transmission of traditions of violence as a political weapon, although without willing partici-pants and followers such leadership would have remained on the meaningless fringes of history.

It is in the politics of the Free Corps movements and the right-wing *völkisch* groups—first in a small way, but sanctioned from above and with backing in high places—that certain members of the war-youth generation were initially mobilized in service of right-wing causes, at a time when the army was officially reduced to a rump of a mere 100,000 men for purely defensive purposes (and some of those who had been demobilized were still searching for a military cause). The Free Corps were self-styled representatives of the 'front generation' in conjunction with what they claimed to be the nation's youth.[45] The more significant groups—which were often named after their leaders—developed songs which contributed to the sense of

---

[45] See e.g. Ernst von Salomon, *Das Buch vom deutschen Freikorpskämpfer* (Berlin: Wilhelm-Limpert Verlag, 1938).

comradeship and belonging, such as the 'Ehrhardt-Song' of the Ehrhardt Brigade: 'Comrade, give me your hand / together we will stand . . . Swastika on the helmet / Black-white-red band / The Ehrhardt Brigade / is our name . . . Comrade give me your hand / As we once swore to each other . . . / The Ehrhardt Brigade / will one day rise again!'[46] The last phrase, with its connotations of the Christian concept of resurrection (*wird einst aufersteh'n*), conveys some sense of the quasi-religious mystic community of struggle and ultimate redemption that was being enacted here.

Much of the Free Corps legacy was significant precisely by virtue of its capacity for myth-making, both at the time and in retrospect. A purple passage from a pro-Nazi rendering of Free Corps history, published in praise of Hitler in 1936, for example, provides something of the general ideological flavour and construction of history. First its author, Edgar von Schmidt-Pauli, praises the heroism of German soldiers in the Great War, hitting all the key phrases:

> In the face of death only that remains which possess eternal value, and out here this is above all comradeship and leadership.
>
> So at the front a new world is formed . . . A new homeland [*Heimat*] is born, one that inevitably rejects everything not worthy of it, but in return knits together all the more closely those who are sworn to this community.[47]

Soldiers on returning to Germany in 1918, on this account, saw the decline and decay of the home front with new eyes; they felt they were having to return, actually 'un-defeated' but called back purely because they had been 'betrayed', and were supposedly shocked by the Germany to which they returned:

> Because it was impossible that the meaning of four years of fighting and struggling could be [reduced to] what was happening all around: this chaos, this cowardly revolution, this downfall of a nation that had been held to be immortal.[48]

On this view the Free Corps had but one aim:

> They only had the one goal, to save their Fatherland. From decline, chaos and bolshevism within. From the enemy at the bleeding borders and the attacks of Bolshevism from abroad. For them it was about Germany. Only about Germany![49]

In support of his arguments, Schmidt-Pauli included a quotation from Erich F. Berendt's *Soldaten der Freiheit*:

> 'The front generation, along with a nation's greatest treasure, its youth, has come together in strong determination to change German fate. Not because of the anxious calls for help on the part of a government to which they were opposed, but rather out of recognition of an ineluctable duty towards people and Fatherland. And it was not

---

[46] Excerpts taken from the full version as reproduced in Manfred von Killinger, *Kampf um Oberschlesien 1921* (Leipzig: v. Hase und Koehler Verlag, 1934), pp. 51–2.

[47] Edgar von Schmidt-Pauli, *Geschichte der Freikorps 1918–1924* (Stuttgart: Robert Lutz Nachfolger Otto Schramm, 1936), p. 17.

[48] *Ibid.*, p. 23.

[49] *Ibid.*, p. 27.

only a battle for German borders and the existence of the Reich. The battle they were waging was also a battle for the German soul.'[50]

This quotation nicely brought together the front generation and the nation's youth in a common fight for the people and the Fatherland, and even, to conclude the potent mixture, the 'German soul'. Von Schmidt-Pauli sought to come to an equally neat and persuasive conclusion:

> So we see here, after the lost Heimat of the front and the estranged Heimat of the Fatherland after Versailles, a new Heimat arising for the best Germans . . . the Heimat of the Free Corps.
>   From this Heimat the path then leads up to the final great Heimat that we are today happily experiencing, the Heimat of the New Germany.[51]

Many similar accounts were produced in the first years of the Third Reich. In fact, however, the lineage from the front-generation experience through the violence of the Free Corps, in the early years after 1918, to the violence first of the storm troopers and then of the established Nazi state was far from as simple or direct as portrayed in this sort of propaganda. Even so, these groups and related acts of violence had a major effect on the lives of those involved.

The Free Corps groups were predominantly led by men who had indeed fought at the front. Like the 'front generation' more generally, the leaders' ages spanned more than four decades: of thirty-nine Free Corps leaders whose birth dates are known (out of a list of forty-one), the oldest was born in 1859; eight were born in the 1860s, eight in the 1870s, thirteen in the 1880s, and nine in the 1890s.[52] Well over a third of these leaders (sixteen of the forty-one) had the aristocratic 'von' in their name. Only four of the Free Corps leaders, including one of the two youngest, born in 1899, appeared not to have had any active experience in the Great War. This was, then, a small group of older men who were in large part motivated by the fact that they could not accept that Germany had been defeated. And there were many continuing causes after the cessation of hostilities and particularly after the Treaty of Versailles which seemed to them to demand violent solutions. These ranged from combating left-wing movements, rebellions or putsch attempts, as in Berlin, Munich, and the Ruhr, to skirmishes on Germany's contested post-Versailles borders in the east, particularly in the Baltic and in Silesia.

But if the leaders were drawn from the very wide and amorphous cohorts of the front generation, spanning four decades, their followers were a far more tightly knit generational group, apparently crossing differences of class rather than age. Young men who had just left school or who were of student age appear to have been particularly drawn to military activism in these groups. One idealized account,

---

[50] Edgar von Schmidt-Pauli, *Geschichte der Freikorps 1918–1924* (Stuttgart: Robert Lutz Nachfolger Otto Schramm, 1936), p. 29.
  [51] *Ibid.*, p. 30.
  [52] Analysis compiled on the basis of material in Robert Thoms and Stefan Pochanke, *Handbuch zur Geschichte der deutschen Freikorps* (MTM Verlag, 2001), 'Kurzbiographien berühmter Freikorpsführer', pp. 153–8.

published in 1934, depicted the frustration of secondary-school boys in the Great War wanting to be old enough to join the war:

> Fear of being too late made many sixteen- or barely seventeen-year-olds begin to think about volunteering for military service. Why still hang about in this grammar school phoney existence, in the summer doing labour service in agriculture and in winter having 'coal [shortage] holidays'? In September 1918 the first of them volunteered. Before they were deployed in active service, there came—the Revolution.[53]

Some of those who had been too young to see military action even in the closing months of the Great War now seized the chance to be part of a wider movement, a cause, experiencing the much-vaunted 'cameraderie', committing their lives to what they saw as defence of the Fatherland, and willingly facing the chance of dying a 'sacrificial' or 'hero's death'.

The highly educated young recruits were joined by men of a similar age drawn, it would appear, from across the social range: young aristocrats fought alongside men from bourgeois, peasant, and working-class backgrounds, a much publicized pre-quel to later Nazi claims of a 'classless' national-ethnic community (*Volksge-meinschaft*) coming together in service of the Fatherland. As one account of the battles of 1921, published in 1934 after the Nazis had already come to power, put it when recounting the funeral of three 'comrades':

> The priest then said something about the peace that everyone yearns for. Senior Lieutenant von Jagow held a better funeral speech: 'Here rest in peace an aristocrat, a bourgeois and a worker. The representatives of the different strata of our society, that are always in conflict with each other, here died together for the common Fatherland, for the common Heimat. A people finds itself in deepest distress, and in death it finds its unity.' Three salvos are fired across the graves, and we head off to our quarters. We sing: 'I once had a comrade' and 'The Ehrhardt Brigade will one day rise again'.[54]

Whatever such heavily ideological accounts might have wanted to suggest by way of painting the Free Corps as precursors of a classless society, with more than a whiff of the *Volksgemeinschaft* ideology about it, it is quite clear that some of the men who were initially attracted to these groups were simply poor and desperate. Once the Free Corps were officially disbanded, many continued a more shadowy under-ground existence: the Ehrhardt Brigade, for example, had a long after-life as the 'Organisation Consul'. And many of those who had been drawn into this penum-bra of violence and life as part of illicit bands simply continued their activities under the guise of 'work commandos' on rural estates, particularly in Germany's troubled eastern provinces.

The disturbing atmosphere and the continuing underground activities of these groups was well captured by Carl P., a witness of secret rearmament and

---

[53] Johannes Jobel, *Zwischen Krieg und Frieden. Schüler als Freiwillige in Genzschutz und Freikorps*, 3rd edn (Berlin: R. Kittlers Verlag, 1934), p. 23.

[54] Manfred von Killinger, *Kampf um Oberschlesien 1921* (Leipzig: v. Hase und Koehler Verlag, 1934), p. 67.

paramilitary training. In his view, the great inflation had not only brought about 'the most disagreeable manifestations of corruption' but the nationalists were also:

> energetically engaged in spreading the word that the Republic was a Jewish Republic and that one should finally do away with the 'filthy swine economy'...
>
> Anyway, I can't say that it was very cosy [*gemütlich*] in the eastern areas of Germany from the autumn of 1920 onwards... People in fantastic garb and with reckless expressions could be seen carrying flags that generally bore a death's head symbol. On the streets and in hostelries there was talk of 'work commandos' that were supposedly steering those in need of work towards the large estates. Since I had remained true to my habit of occasionally roaming through the woods at night, I often saw night-time exercises and secret transports of weapons. We—my friends and I—took considerable trouble to observe the perpetual shifting of weapons. There is no denying it: after the Kapp Putsch we German republicans had been pushed back onto the defensive...[55]

While posing as part of the 'Black Army' (*schwarze Reichswehr*), and presenting themselves as a means of defending Germany, the reality of these groups was, in the view of Carl P., both more mundane and more murderous and inherently threatening:

> The leaders of these work commandos were menial farm labourers of the worst sort. They were work-shy, rootless people hoping to use the adventure of perpetual civil war to battle their way through life. The national slogan was just a reframing of the question of bread.[56]

But they were doing more: they were seeking also to 'win the peace' by assassinating their enemies, real and imagined. Carl P. noted that:

> As a result of the brutality of this light-shy rabble many people disappeared without a trace... The secret leadership of the 'work commandos' set up its own system of justice and this with the knowledge and tacit approval of the Ministry of the Armed Forces. The formula according to which this 'court' passed sentence was short and to the point: 'Traitor, condemned by summary justice [*Feme*]!'—Anyone was a 'traitor' who was suspected of being one. At the behest of the Ministry of the Armed Forces, a handful of wild characters travelled around Germany putting the sentences passed by these kangaroo courts into effect.[57]

There were literally hundreds of casualties of these gangs, with their imposition of the 'justice' of the *Fememorde* on perfectly ordinary citizens, as well as assassinations of better-known political figures.[58] The Minister of Justice (under-)estimated a total

---

[55] HHL, b MS Ger 91 (174), Carl P., p. 14.
[56] *Ibid.*, p. 17.
[57] *Ibid.*, p. 17.
[58] Bernhard Sauer, *Schwarze Reichswehr und Fememorde* (Berlin: Metropol Verlag, 2004), claims that such murders were primarily targeted against people within their own ranks with whom they had fallen out, and not against political opponents. This was clearly not the case: see R. G. L. Waite, *Vanguard of Nazism* (Cambridge, MA: Harvard Historical Studies, Vol. LX, 1952), pp. 216–27; see also Irmela Nagel, *Fememorde und Fememordprozesse in der Weimarer Republik* (Köln u. Wien: Böhlau Verlag, 1991).

of 354 individual political murders committed by the Free Corps during the short period from 1919 to June 1922, when Rathenau was assassinated; and one of the leaders of shock troop units, Heinz Oskar Hauenstein, later estimated that his own troops had killed around 200 people in Upper Silesia alone.[59]

More significantly for the borderlands of Germany, there were specific battles over territory, particularly in the Baltic and in the Silesian borderlands with Poland at the time of the plebiscites seeking to finalize the boundaries in this strongly contested area.[60] A key, and perhaps final great battle as far as the mythology of the Free Corps was concerned was that of the Annaberg hill in Silesia. The local landed nobility appear to have provided considerable logistical support in terms of food and lodgings for the Germans fighting against Polish insurgents; and there were many with aristocratic names among the active German leaders of the fight.[61] A decisive day of concerted attack by groups from different directions secured the Annaberg hill for the Germans by the evening. In the flowery but rather typical account of one former Free Corps member, at the end of the fighting on the historic day of 21 May 1921:

> And as the rays of sunshine fall across the hillside, they light up the German flag on the highest point of the hill, proclaiming far and wide the glory of the Germans.
>
> Great was the victory, great the volunteers' joy, now beaming from every face.
>
> The brave self-defence force had to lament twenty dead and one hundred and twenty wounded. But the sacrifice had not been in vain. The Pole had been chased away as though driven by a storm wind.
>
> …The spirit of German faith, German courage to make sacrifices, German honour, had set up a brightly shining beacon here too, on which the hopes of all Germans for a new future were firmly pinned.[62]

The disagreeable sweat and blood of the day, the reality of young lives cut down brutally in face-to-face skirmishing on the side of a nondescript little hill in the Upper Silesian countryside, significant for nothing more than a disputed border, was thus transformed into some kind of transcendental experience in which the rays of the sun and the spirit of the few dozen volunteers were fused into a symbol of

---

[59] Waite, *Vanguard of Nazism*, pp. 216, 226–7.

[60] For an extremely clear account of the Silesian case, see T. Hunt Tooley, *National Identity and Weimar Germany: Upper Silesia and the eastern border, 1918–1922* (Lincoln and London: University of Nebraska Press, 1997). Hagen Schulze has suggested that there were colonial elements to some of the struggles in the Baltic and Silesia, and that it was 'no accident' that some of the Free Corps leaders had backgrounds including colonial experience: see Hagen Schulze, *Freikorps und Republik, 1918–1920* (Boppard am Rhein: Harald Boldt Verlag, 1969), p. 329.

[61] See the detailed, highly partisan account by Manfred von Killinger, *Kampf um Oberschlesien 1921* (Leipzig: v. Hase und Koehler Verlag, 1934).

[62] Jobel, *Zwischen Krieg und Frieden*, pp. 139–40. See also e.g. the accounts in Bert Roth (ed.), *Kampf: Lebensdokumente deutscher Jugend von 1914–1934* (Leipzig: Philipp Reklam jun., 1934): 'Wir stürmen den Annaberg. Berichte von Freikorpskämpfern', pp. 85 ff.; 'Von einem Kämpfer des Korps Roßbach. Bei der Sturmabteilung Heinz', pp. 85–7; 'Das Freikorps Oberland greift an', pp. 87–9. See also Generalleutnant a. D. von Hülsen, 'Freikorps im Osten' and Rittmeister a. D. von Schaper, 'Freikorpsgeist—Annaberg', in Roden (ed.), *Deutsche Soldaten*, pp. 110–16, 161–9; and F. W. von Oertzen, *Kamerad reich mir die Hände. Freikorps und Grenzschutz Baltikum und Heimat* (Berlin: Im Verlag Ullstein, 1933), 'Das Ringen um O. S.', pp. 202–43.

national renewal. Given the significance of this victory for right-wing violence, a huge memorial to alleged German bravery and national pride, containing the bodies of fifty-one Free Corps fighters who had died in the cause (rather more than recounted by Jobel) was built on the site, acting as a shrine, a 'site of memory' and even tourist attraction during the Third Reich. As Dr Walter K., the *Landrat* (roughly, chief executive) of the county in which the Annaberg was located put it in the 1936 edition of the *Heimatkalender Groß Strehlitz*:

> In our midst rises up the Annaberg, the landmark of Upper Silesia. It provides protection to this peaceful country. Its slopes are consecrated by the blood of the sons of all German regions [*Gaue*] who battled here for the freedom of our Upper Silesian Heimat.[63]

And an article on 'the Annaberg and its surroundings' by one Ernst Mücke in the 1937 edition of the *Heimatkalender Groß Strehlitz* reiterated its importance, raising it now from regional to national significance:

> In 1921 the Annaberg became the flaming symbol of the German spirit of heroism. Here it was that, on 21 May of that significant year, the first German armed victory since the Revolution and collapse was achieved. Since those days the *Annaberg has become the national shrine of the German people*, which recently has found visible expression through the construction of a memorial and a site for celebration.[64]

The shrine to German national greatness achieved through the use of armed force was however pulled down by the new Polish government once it had taken over this territory after the Second World War.[65]

Despite suggestive elements, not least the use of swastikas on the helmets of the Ehrhardt Brigade, there were no direct or simple lines of personal transmission, no compelling individual or organizational continuities, between the Free Corps and successor movements of the early 1920s and the violence of the Third Reich. Many individuals did indeed move from violence in the Free Corps through to membership of the SA and/or NSDAP; but many did not. Even among those who supported Nazism initially, some were casualties of Hitler's imposition of a new order once the army appeared to Hitler to be more significant than the radical violence of the rabble in achieving his goals in power. A significant number of former Free Corps members who had joined the SA and were close to the SA leader Ernst Röhm were later among those who were casualties of the slaughter of June 1934 in the so-called 'Night of the Long Knives'.[66] Yet there can be no doubt that the experiences and myths glorifying violence to which some young men were exposed at this time played a formative role, from which they learned lessons that

---

[63] *Heimatkalender Groß Strehlitz* no.161, 1936, p. 31.

[64] *Ibid.* no.162, 1937, pp. 56–8, here p. 56 (emphasis in original).

[65] Thoms and Pochanke, *Handbuch zur Geschichte der deutschen Freikorps*, pp. 39–45, 169–70; See also James Bjork and Robert Gerwarth, 'The Annaberg as a German-Polish Lieu de Mémoire', *German History* 2007, 25(3), 372–400.

[66] Schulze, *Freikorps und Republik*, p. 333. See also, approaching these issues from a rather different angle, Richard Bessel, *Political Violence and the Rise of Nazism: The storm troopers in eastern Germany 1925–1934* (New Haven and London: Yale University Press, 1984).

would shape their responses when violence had been appropriated and monopolized by the state under Hitler's regime.

This was a repertoire of experience and rhetoric that could be drawn upon selectively at a later date, garnished and reshaped as required. In the mid-1930s a number of accounts of the Free Corps activities were published which glorified their deeds and outlooks as precursors to Hitler's Third Reich, which was presented as the culmination of all they had struggled for.[67] Von Schmidt-Pauli even claimed in 1936 that what he was writing was:

> an overview in time and place of the emergence, struggle and dissolution of the Free Corps, an encapsulation of the Free Corps idea in its first light, its blazing and heroic zenith, and its sinking beneath the ashes of its own bitterness in times of adversity,— until it could rise again from these ashes, a resurrected Phoenix, to bathe its glorious plumage in the sun of the new Germany . . . For the blood sacrifices of that time are redeemed and crowned only now, when Adolf Hitler has achieved that for which we fought and suffered: a well fortified, secure, free and proud Fatherland.[68]

Less easy to document, however, are the influences which the Free Corps and the wider atmosphere of paramilitary violence had over the climate in which people lived at the time.

Some members of the war-youth generation were still too young to join the Free Corps actively, but were greatly influenced in their formative years by the use of violence as a political weapon. Dr Walter K.'s son, Udo K. (born 1910) was still only a schoolboy at the time of the famous storming of the Annaberg by Free Corps units in 1921, but was strongly influenced by the wider significance of this event. The Annaberg was not only geographically not far away from where he lived; his father, Walter K., at that time held the role of *Landrat* of Leobschütz, very close to the new post-war border with Poland, and was intrinsically affected both by the immediate violence of the clashes between German nationalists and Polish insurgents, and the larger concerns about territorial losses in this border region. Udo K.'s father, as *Landrat* at this troubled time, played a key role—or so his staff later claimed on the occasion of his retirement—in dealing with the threat of Polish and Czech renegades at the borders.[69] Although too young to be actively involved himself at this stage, Udo K. was hugely impressed by the Annaberg success, as he later recalled:

> The most significant and very moving event at that time was the storming of the Annaberg, the landmark of Upper Silesia, the highest peak on the edge of the industrial

---

[67] See e.g. Roden (ed.), *Deutsche Soldaten*.

[68] Von Schmidt-Pauli, *Geschichte der Freikorps*, p. 10. See also e.g. Friedrich Glombowski, *Organisation Heinz (O.H.). Das Schicksal der Kameraden Schlageters* (Berlin: Verlag von Reimar Hobbing, 1934).

[69] Landschaftsverband Rheinland, Rheinisches Archiv- und Museumsamt, Archiv des LVR, Nachlaß K., 185, Dr Walter K., Seine Tätigkeit im Zusammenhang mit der Volksabstimmung in Oberschlesien [1920], 1930. Udo K.'s father, Dr Walter K., later became *Landrat* of the nearby *Kreis* of Groß-Strehlitz, and, in the mid-1930s, adorned the *Heimatkalender Groß Strehlitz* with small celebratory articles and praise for the Annaberg incident: see e.g. issue 161, 1936, p. 31 quoted above, p. 78; and issue 162, 1937, p. 29.

region, on which a much-visited pilgrimage chapel had stood for centuries. This conquest did really put things to rights again as far as power relations in Upper Silesia were concerned.[70]

From the mid-1920s—by then in his mid- to later teenage years—Udo K. was increasingly involved in paramilitary activities.[71] The organizational arrangements were at this time somewhat fluid: in part related to the increasingly militaristic interests of the local Scouts, but soon going well beyond these. Eventually, it was clear that those willing members of the youth in the area were to be secretly trained up in the use of weapons and strategic manoeuvres through former army officers and former Free Corps activists. One such youth group, in which Udo K. and a close friend, Hans K., were very actively involved, was known as the 'Following' (*Gefolgschaft*), assisted and trained by members of the so-called 'Black Army' (*schwarze Reichswehr*). Udo K. recalled with pleasure the camp fires where:

> we swore to one another that we would remain faithful to the Fatherland . . . Then there were the tales of the Free Corps from the Baltic, where the last knights were fighting against Bolshevism . . . A time of idealism, a sense of sacrifice, having to rise to a challenge, a time in memory that I would not like to have missed, since we felt duty bound to a task that we saw as right and good: the protection of our borders.[72]

In May 1932, on the occasion of the tenth anniversary of the referendum in Upper Silesia, Udo K.—by now a law student at Breslau University, somewhat further west in Silesia—and his father went along together to a ceremony on the Annaberg commemorating the significance of this location for the German nation. This turned out to be an occasion on which oppositional forces tried to heckle and shout down the nationalist speech, a commotion only ended by the singing of the national anthem.[73] And in late 1932, when Udo K. wanted to speed up his application for membership in the SA, he was able to call on his by now extensive experience of paramilitary training sessions—many of which he had personally led—as part of his application, appending a certificate of honour [*Ehrenurkunde*] detailing his service in nationalist causes in the borderlands:

> The certificate of honour expresses recognition for my service since 1925 for the border protection of Silesia. First of all I was trained in weaponry and field exercises, later I served as an assistant trainer and was seen as a future leader of border defence troops. In the period from 1925 to 1933 I have taken part in around 120 training programmes of this sort.[74]

---

[70] LVR, Nachlaß K., I. 208 'Erlebt—Davongekommen. Erinnerungen. Erlebt—überlebt. Erster Teil 1910–1948', p. 16.

[71] See *ibid.*, pp. 26–36.

[72] *Ibid.*, p. 34.

[73] *Ibid*, p. 71.

[74] BAB ZA VI 265. A. 14, Akten betr. den Regierungs-Referendar Udo K., letter of 4 January 1941, from Udo K. to the Reich Interior Ministry in Berlin, '*Zur Ergänzung meiner Personalakten*', claiming that since 1925 he was very active in a paramilitary group called the '*Gefolgschaft*' which was a disguised school organization for the military protection and defence of Silesia; on his own account, membership of this effectively fast-tracked his SA application (it got him out of the 'usual application waiting period'—'*üblichen Anwärterzeit*').

Such paramilitary activities were in his case, as for so many others from this generation, perfectly compatible with a seamless switch into a career in the civil service and, in due course, in the regular army.

The long-term significance of the war-youth generation was not confined to the right-wing youth in support of the rising Nazi tide, however; it was to see a later, second blossoming in the communist dictatorship that succeeded the Third Reich in one part of defeated Germany, the Soviet zone of occupation which became the GDR. In the shorter term, the willingness to countenance violence among members of the war-youth generation during the Weimar years was not only a phenomenon of the right. The tendency to seek radical solutions, deploying violence as a political means if necessary, was to be found on the left too, with consequences for the ways in which all those growing up in this period perceived the present and their hopes for changes in the future. We should therefore not simply read backwards from the striking preponderance of members of the war-youth generation who became carriers of the Nazi regime, appealing to some 'generational experience' which allegedly mobilized significant numbers to the right-wing cause. Rather, it was the specific historical constellation of 1933 which determined that those who had been mobilized for radical causes and who now took a disproportionate role in the historical record were on the right rather than the left. For in the short term, it was the forces of the right who won out, under the particular historical circumstances of the late Weimar years; after 1945, in the Soviet-controlled zone of defeated Germany, it would be a left-wing minority who were able to take a leading role.

IV. WEIMAR CRISES AND INDIVIDUAL LIFE STORIES

On a warm early summer day, 21 May 1920—exactly one year to the day before the storming of the Annaberg—Hans Paasche was bathing with his four children in the lake of their country home of Waldfrieden. At about three o'clock in the afternoon he was suddenly summonsed by the local gendarme, one Wendtland, to come back up to the house, as supposedly he wanted to talk with him about some matter. As Paasche, wearing only his swim trunks and a jacket, walked up the garden from the lake accompanied by the local gendarme, with a couple of his children following behind, he became aware of large numbers of armed men waiting half-hidden among the bushes and trees surrounding the open lawn. He was surrounded by somewhere in the region of sixty soldiers. Turning around suddenly, apparently in some anxiety, Paasche was unable to flee. Three shots were fired, and Hans Paasche was instantly dead.[75]

No case was ever brought against those who had assassinated Hans Paasche. The local authorities in charge of police and justice had presumably already been

---

[75] Based on the account compiled by his closest friends and the children's governess, Frau Hadwig Lahrs-Dorsch, who was at home and witnessed the tragedy, as recounted in the Berlin daily newspaper *Freiheit*, 25 May 1920, No. 191, and reprinted in Magnus Schwantje, 'Hans Paasche: Sein Leben und Wirken', *Flugschriften des Bundes Neues Vaterland* Nr. 26(4), 1921, pp. 23–4.

irritated by the outcome of the case they had largely unsuccessfully brought against him in 1917, and saw little reason to investigate this one too closely. Moreover, the accusation was made that Paasche—a well-known pacifist!—had been collecting weapons in preparation for an armed communist uprising or even civil war, and that therefore a search of the house by sixty fully armed soldiers was clearly justified. In the event, all the search turned up by way of 'incriminating' material were a couple of left-wing newspapers and a list prepared for the impending local elections. Nevertheless extensive precautions and preparations for this search had been taken by the state authorities in the preceding days, including cutting off telephone wires in the neighbouring area and preventing access to the Paasche estate on the part of locals. The suggestion has been made that the group of five dozen soldiers who surrounded the house were members of the *Reichswehr Schutzregiment* 4, and had previously belonged to a Free Corps unit commanded by the military hero of German East Africa, Paul von Lettow-Vorbeck. After murdering Paasche, soldiers in the courtyard of his house were heard singing the 'Ehrhardt song' of the eponymous Free Corps unit: 'Swastika on the helmet / Black-white-red band / The Ehrhardt Brigade / is our name'.[76] Paasche, too, had fallen victim to a targeted political murder; his case once again reveals the complex constraints of the time, in which violence, backed by the authority of the state, was repeatedly used to silence 'those who thought differently' (to adopt a phrase from Rosa Luxemburg, at whose funeral Paasche had acted as a wreath-bearer).

Paasche's death was the cause of great mourning among friends and neighbours who knew him well. As the children's governess, Frau Lahrs-Dohrsch, commented at his funeral, one of the reasons why locals held him to be 'soft in the head' was because of his remarkable goodness and generosity towards them, which must clearly be the mark of a fool. The other symptom of his 'madness' was held to be his 'paranoia', the fear that his life was in danger because of the cause for which he stood up; this anxiety now proved only too well justified.[77] There was briefly some outrage in the left-wing press of the day, and homages to Paasche were penned by Kurt Tucholsky and Carl von Ossietzky, among others.[78] The legal investigation, such as it was, into Paasche's murder closed with the remark that 'the death of Paasche was caused by a combination of unhappy circumstances which could not have been foreseen, and for which no-one is to be held criminally responsible'.[79] James B., who had cooperated with Paasche during his period in the Council

---

[76] P. Werner Lange, 'Die Toten im Maisfeld. Hans Paasches Erkenntnisse aus dem Maji-Maji-Krieg' in Felicitas Becker and Jigal Beez (eds.), *Der Maji-Maji-Krieg in Deutsch-Ostafrika 1905–1907* (Berlin: Ch. Links Verlag, 2005), pp. 154–67, here p. 161.

[77] Schwantje, 'Hans Paasche', pp. 24–5.

[78] See Werner Lange, *Hans Paasche: Militant pacifist in Imperial Germany* (Oxford: Trafford Publishing, 2005), pp. 252 ff.; also Helmut Donat, 'Hans Paasche—ein deutscher Revolutionär' in Helmut Donat and Helga Paasche (eds.), *Hans Paasche, Ändert eueren Sinn! Schriften eines Revolutionärs* (Bremen: Donat Verlag, 1992), pp. 10–51.

[79] Decision of the Oberstaatsanwalt, November 1920, quoted by P. Werner Lange, 'Die Toten im Maisfeld. Hans Paasches Erkenntnisse aus dem Maji-Maji-Krieg' in Felicitas Becker and Jigal Beez (eds.), *Der Maji-Maji-Krieg in Deutsch-Ostafrika 1905–1907* (Berlin: Ch. Links Verlag, 2005), pp. 154–67, here p. 161.

Executive of the revolutionary weeks after the armistice, recalled in his own memoirs, written in 1940:

> On the Executive Council [*Vollzugsrat*] I particularly valued my party comrade Marine Lieutenant Hans Paasche. He was a well-known pacifist, one of the most prominent characters of those times . . . Then he soon withdrew completely from the Executive Council, although he remained faithful to the movement. Reason enough for the General Staff to have him murdered by the Army while he was in his idyllic property, just as he was fishing . . . In the Weimar Republic, this officially ordered murder was the most outrageous of all its scandalous deeds. As though the Third Reich had already begun, not even judicial or other proceedings were opened, as had after all still happened, at least pro forma, against the murderers of Karl Liebknecht. The murderer was supposedly not to be found! But it was quite clear: precisely because Paasche himself came from the circles claiming the sole right to rule in Germany, to them he appeared a particularly dangerous traitor to his class.[80]

But Paasche's case and the causes for which he had fought were soon to be forgotten, submerged under the turmoil of the coming years. And James B., who was not only a committed socialist but of Jewish descent, penned these lines while in exile in Paris in March 1940. The last note in James B.'s file, dated 13 December 1940, was a letter from the American Friends Service Committee in Philadelphia, trying to make contact with him in France, but in vain. James B., born and brought up in the Prussian military virtues of Imperial Germany, a fully assimilated German patriot and lawyer, was to be one of the millions of casualties of that later use of political violence on a far greater scale.

Paasche's death was not so easily forgotten by his daughter, Helga, who was four years old at the time. When questioned about her life and asked about her experiences as a young person some eighty-seven years later, her memory of her youth was patchy apart from that one traumatic moment: she could not get over the image of her father lying dead on the lawn in the garden of her home.[81] Who had looked after her in the following years, where she had gone to live, with which relatives, how she later came to attend the Staatliche Augusta Schule in Berlin, were all blanked or hazy in her failing memory. But the image of her father, and his words and appearance as enshrined in books and a few photographs displayed on her bedside table, were very present in old age; the troubles and legacies of Imperial Germany and its immediate aftermath were still highly emotive in the first decade of the twenty-first century. The penalty for the lessons drawn by Paasche from the hanging of four Africans in Mohoro in 1905 still distantly reverberated in a small room in an old peoples' home in the affluent Federal Republic of Germany more than a century later.[82]

---

[80] HHL, b MS Ger 91 (39), James B., (1867) 'Memoiren eines deutschen Juden und Sozialisten', pp. 57–8.

[81] Discussion with Helga Paasche, Bavaria, August 2007.

[82] I in fact broke off trying to talking to Helga Paasche about her youth and later life precisely because she became so upset at the vivid memory of her father's death, and it seemed more appropriate to switch the conversation to entirely non-personal, more comforting topics.

Those of Helga Paasche's generation, who were subsequently to become the 'first Hitler Youth generation', born during or shortly after the Great War, too young to have consciously experienced or able to remember the war itself, were nevertheless mightily marked by its longer-term consequences. For all those born during or in the early years after the war, the historical context of their childhoods and youth was simply inescapable, even if not always as violent as in Helga Paasche's case. But their reactions to this context, and the longer-term 'lessons' they took from the experiences of these years, varied considerably according to location and social belonging as well as individual personality. This was also a relatively broad age range, spanning those who experienced the Weimar years as a period of early childhood to those who were already teenagers and on the verge of adulthood by the time the Republic came to its eventual chaotic end. For many, at least in the short term, personal awareness of Weimar's problems rendered them peculiarly available for mobilization. While those a few years older, the war-youth generation, were mobilized in the 1920s and were to become key carriers at the forefront of the Nazi project once in power, much of the energy behind the violence of youth in the 1930s would be drawn from these younger cohorts who had a greater or lesser degree of conscious exposure to a period 'before Hitler'.

At the older end of the age range of the first Hitler Youth generation were those born shortly before or during the Great War, shading over from the last cohorts of the war-youth generation. Their experiences of violence in the Weimar years were as people who were teenagers, verging on young adulthood by the time Hitler came to power. For them, in diverse ways, even vicarious experiences of violence could make a major difference in the development of attitudes, with individual variations in response.

Particularly for those young middle-class Germans whose households were still marked by patriarchal authority, the father figure was one to be reckoned with— whether as a powerful continuing influence, or one against whom young people would eventually, in one way or another, rebel. The political stance of the fathers thus carried over indirectly into the developing attitudes and actions of the younger generation. Ruth L., for example, was born in 1914, hence on the older cusp of what was to become the 'first Hitler Youth generation'. She came from a relatively well-to-do bourgeois family in Danzig, in the geopolitical borderlands of Germany where the perceived problems of the Weimar Republic were experienced most acutely. In her autobiographical account written in 1940, Ruth L. allotted a relatively central role to her father, and clearly suggests his formative influence on her own views. After the Great War her father, who worked in civil service administration, was posted first briefly to Magdeburg, and then to Marienwerder in East Prussia. Ruth L. recalled with horror the early years after the War, which she experienced during her father's stint working in Magdeburg:

> The short period in Magdeburg fell in the frightful months of the revolution. The Spartacists were abroad in the town, plundering the shops and warehouses and rendering the streets unsafe. We children were not allowed out alone on the streets, and yet even so, often enough we were witnesses to street battles and assaults carried

out by the wild hordes against officers or people from the middle classes. There were scenes that, in their horrific brutality, made a deep impression on me, even though at that time I could barely understand the connections. I heard how my parents talked, how my father stood on the 'black list' of the Spartacists, and my mother was at that time constantly in a state of anxiety, fearing for his life.[83]

Following the family's move to Marienwerder, Ruth claimed that she and her five siblings 'spent a perfectly carefree youth here'. Yet the political lessons of this borderland area of East Prussia were not lost on her. Her father took her with him on many of his travels in the course of his work as a state official and, on trips to villages on Polish border, sought to rub in the injustice of the loss of German territory to Poland, as well as to make clear his views on the alleged inferiority of the Poles. These views were conveyed in terms which Ruth L. repeated, quite uncritically, in her own descriptions of these trips. She depicted in some detail, for example, a farmstead that had been forced to lose some of its orchard to Poland on the territorial reorganization, and the farmer's family had not been not allowed to pick up the apples that had fallen from the tree on the wrong side of the border. The Polish side, on her account, gave ample symbolic evidence of the classical stereotype of Polish 'sloppiness' (*Schlamperei*): 'A barrier closed off the road beyond the village of Gutsch. On the other [Polish] side of the barrier grew grass and weeds . . .'[84]

By the later 1920s, Ruth's family was beginning to be adversely affected by the economic problems of East Prussian agriculture. In the recession following the economic crash of 1929, one of her family's estates was subjected to enforced sale, and was ultimately bought by Poles. Her father expressed the fear that 'Poland is just waiting for the moment to swallow up East Prussia'; he was also of the view that 'in the Reich' most Germans did not understand conditions in the eastern territories.[85] Ruth L. reported on a cycle trip that she undertook with school friends through East Prussia in the summer of 1931, in which farmers allegedly told her of the border protection troops (*Grenzschutz*)—'border protection or, rather, an advance warning service'—and the fear that Poland would invade and overwhelm East Prussia. Allegedly there were frequent Polish manoeuvres at the border, with particularly widespread rumours in 1932, accompanied by fears that 'an army of 100,000 men, as stipulated by the Versailles Treaty' was not going to be enough to defend German territory. Because of the growing economic crisis Ruth L.'s family had to sell up their 'beautiful house with the glorious park' in Marienwerder and move to a more modest house in Königsberg; they also had to cut down from 'several maidservants' to 'just one' and eventually to merely 'a cleaning lady twice a week'.[86]

Ruth herself now moved to live with an aunt in Hamburg pending a delayed start to her studies (which her father could at this time not afford to support). The

---

[83] HHL, b MS 91 (128), Ruth L., p. 1.
[84] *Ibid.*, p. 3.
[85] *Ibid.*, p. 7.
[86] *Ibid.*, pp. 7–12.

aunt had benefited from a rich inheritance and was apparently devoting herself to doing good: she took Ruth to visit members of the unemployed and poor in Hamburg, opening up Ruth's eyes to poverty in a large city in a way she had never witnessed before. Ruth threw herself into trying to help a family of eight where the father was unemployed, and was aghast at the misery and need all around her, putting her own family background into some perspective. Yet at the same time she was horrified by the political representations on the part of the left. On witnessing 'clashes between Communists and National Socialists', she was most frightened by the former, describing a KPD demonstration in the following terms:

> They were very badly dressed, their faces were stubborn, often brutal . . . I always felt a boundless sympathy for poor people . . . But when the communist mobs gathered together I was flooded with fear. You could almost feel the destructive hatred pouring out from these people, hatred against me as well as everyone else who was better off than them . . . Their greeting, the raised fist, seemed to me an expression of primitive force, and quite instinctively I realized with certainty that the fate of my Fatherland should never be allowed to fall into the hands of these people.
>
> Among the communists there were also many people who came from circles other than the working class. There were many educated people among them, women too, who threw themselves into working for a Communist Party victory. I could understand these people least of all. The groundless hatred of a workers' movement without any rights, their bitterness, their desire for revenge, all of that I could understand among those living in need and misery. But the educated had, in my opinion, no reason to put the future of Germany into the hands of primitive violence.[87]

Interestingly, Ruth saw the violence of the communists as 'primitive', against which the imposition of some form of civilizing order was required. The competing right-wing radicals, the National Socialist Party, by contrast, appeared to have given Ruth an impression of forceful security: the National Socialists potentially offered protection against the 'primitive violence' of the communists, and some hope of salvation of Germany from the present troubles:

> From their marches and speeches one gained the impression of a strong will and a united power that wanted not to tear down but rather to build up . . . At the same time it was necessary to move with absolute ruthlessness against those elements who carried the seeds of destruction and who had led to the downfall of the German people.[88]

Ruth's comments echoed the views of many people who turned to the violence of the Nazis as a form of 'protection' against something even worse—in line with the Nazis' own self-portrayal and claim to exercising merely 'defensive' violence, both then and later. Very many, but far from all members of Ruth's generation experienced the Nazi movement in terms of the promise of the restoration of 'order' by meeting violence with violence.

In part, of course, differences in political, cultural, and religious milieu played a major role in how people responded to the turbulence of the Weimar period. But

---

[87] HHL, b MS 91 (128), Ruth L., pp. 22, 23–4.
[88] *Ibid.*, pp. 22, 25–6.

individual reactions even within one family could be very different; so too could be the ways in which children from the same family continued or broke with their patriarchal home background.

A somewhat contrasting case is that of Hildegard B., who was one year older than Ruth L, having been born in 1913, and whose fascinating and ultimately tragic story reveals much about the tensions of the time and the ways in which broader historical forces could play out in individual lives. The daughter of a respectable Berlin professor, Hildegard B. grew up in a highly ordered household. Her mother died prematurely during the war, when she was two; her father was deeply committed to his work, and out of what she describes as modest means—the legacy from her mother was lost in the inflation of 1923—they were able to afford one maidservant (*Dienstmädchen*) and a separate study for her father, who was to be undisturbed during his work. He was very a much a man of the imperial period: he never moved or talked outside the narrow status group of those he considered his equals, and was given to uttering his views or supporting his own position in brief aphorisms: 'The woman belongs in the home'; 'I am a Prussian state servant'; 'I have sworn my oath to the Kaiser.'[89] Looking back at her 1920s childhood from the vantage point of 1940, Hildegard was only too aware that later far worse was to come; but at the time, the prevailing view in her family home was that of strong critique of Weimar conditions and a yearning for the restoration of order on imperial lines:

> Neither the Republic nor the Kaiser meddled in peacetime in people's private lives to the extent that the Nazi [*sic*] did. But at that time I did not know that, and was genuinely outraged about the evil people who had robbed us of the Kaiser and the pomp and power of the German Empire in favour of some dark criminals who had consorted with their foreign counterparts and had concluded the Versailles Treaty, which was why we were having such a hard life. Most younger people in Germany at that time believed something along those lines, since they heard this at home and in school and never got around to checking whether or not such assertions were right.[90]

Hildegard's father was so deeply convinced of the old status order that he found it well-nigh impossible to accept the reversals of authority brought by the new Republic. On one occasion, his sense of the 'right ordering' of the social world even overcame his equally strong sense of duty, as Hildegard recalled:

> Once, I still remember, some Minister of the Interior was supposed to turn up to an academic ceremony, and my father, who happened at that time to hold a senior position in the faculty, was supposed to greet him; but, against his usual sense of duty, he took sick leave and arranged for a deputy to take his place. The Minister was formerly a working class man who had made a career with the Social Democrats—I can't now remember his name—and my father simply could not comprehend that this man was now supposed to be his superior. He didn't know how to talk to him. For him, a Minister was only ever an aristocrat, superior to him by virtue of birth, since in

---

[89] HHL, b MS 91 (33), 'Hildegard B.' (pseudonym), p. 2.
[90] *Ibid.*

Prussia in former times only aristocrats became Ministers. This little episode has stuck in my memory so because it was one of the few occasions on which I saw my father in a conflict of conscience. He was otherwise always a person who simply followed a direct course of action, for whom in any given situation there was no other course. This simple and perhaps rather schematic and militaristic way of thinking, as it was seen, of which these circles were so proud, belongs to those characteristics that were drummed into the Prussian people by their kings across the centuries. I simply could not understand that Father could ever dither and have doubts about anything. But that began to occur ever more frequently from 1932 onwards.[91]

In Hildegard's view—looking back on her teenage years in the Weimar Republic, from the perspective of a 27-year-old in 1940—her father's experiences were fairly typical of his generation and social milieu. In the case of her family, and for those of many in similar situations, parental disapproval of the new order was not merely rooted in one's own social discomfiture, but compounded by the closure of previously traditional career routes for less than gifted male offspring:

For all these status groups that were so influential in Germany, all these officers, officials, teachers, now felt that their prestige was under threat. For the first time they faced existential problems that they had never previously known. My own brother was after all not the only one who in earlier times would have been put into a Cadet School, and who would certainly have become a competent officer rather than running around in dubious company.[92]

Rather than being whisked off to a cadet school to be groomed as an officer, a route more or less closed off by the reduced size of the army after the Versailles settlement, Hildegard's brother 'Fritz' (as she called him, to preserve the anonymity of her account) had drifted on at school, and fallen in with a group of heavy-drinking SA members; he duly himself became a member of a storm-trooper section.

In contrast to Ruth L.'s perceptions in Hamburg, Hildegard did not see the violent activities of the National Socialist movement on the streets of Berlin as in any sense a potential path to the 'restoration of order'. Nevertheless, given his conservative nationalist critiques of Weimar, Hildegard's father found it difficult to discipline or condemn his son:

Fritz went as a sixteen-year-old to the group of storm troopers now called S.A. Father was not at all happy about this, but the troops were at that time nationalist, and that meant, so it was believed, that they wanted to restore the old monarchy, and so Father couldn't say anything against it.[93]

Moreover, in Hildegard's perception her father held the somewhat sexist view that, while his daughter should behave 'appropriately' to her status, it was possible for a boy to 'sow his wild oats':

Although he [Fritz] had not yet finished with school, he was always running around agitating and electioneering, he always wore the brown uniform although it didn't suit

---

[91] HHL, b MS 91 (33), 'Hildegard B.' (pseudonym), p. 10.   [92] *Ibid.*, p. 9.   [93] *Ibid.*, p. 9.

him at all, and he came home at ever more irregular hours. He was involved in all sorts of brawls and held the wildest speeches. This annoyed me far more than it did Father, since he was of the view that boys could be allowed to get away with all manner of things as long as the core was not rotten.[94]

Hildegard's perceptive comments draw attention also to the conflicting issues and problematic sense of social status on the part of her father. On the one hand, the disorderly behaviour of the brownshirts was anathema to her father, whose political and gender views overrode, in this case, his social distaste; but on the other hand, it was precisely this semi-legitimate transgressing of the boundaries, this officially sanctioned relief from previously weighty social taboos, which in part attracted Fritz and many others to the rowdy, youthful, Nazi movement. Hildegard recalled that her father also did not approve, but failed to enforce his objections, when Fritz brought his new SA comrades home with him:

> Most of them were older than him, and all of them drank a great deal and held wild speeches. It was not at all the sort of society that should have belonged in our house. Listening to them, it sounded as if they did nothing else all day except slaughter Jews and rape girls. I am convinced that it only sounded like this, since most of them did not look nearly so dangerous. They puffed themselves up, as boys like to do, and for them National Socialism meant that the state and respectable society allowed them to. I believe that in general a major role was played by the fact that National Socialism let so many people to do things they wanted to do, and that otherwise were not actually allowed.[95]

Hildegard herself, however, experienced increasing estrangement from her brother and the company he was now keeping, an estrangement exacerbated by her own social distaste for the rough speech and apparently crude expressions current among these circles, which clashed with her own sense of decency and orderly behaviour:

> But at that time I was frightened by the way these boys talked, and I did not like being together with them. Perhaps I am not very shy by nature, rather by upbringing, but I had a very clear feeling that these people were not right for me, and I was uncomfortable with them. When I was then alone with my brother, Fritz used to ridicule me, asking whether I was too cowardly to trust myself among German youngsters, or whether perhaps I was even going with a Jewish boy. I don't want to repeat the original expressions that he always liked to use in this context—and anyway they are in the slang of Berlin [lower class] districts, and I would have first to try to translate them into respectable German [*ins Hochdeutsche*], which I simply can't do—but to him they probably sounded very impressive and grown-up.[96]

Within one household, then, there were three different reactions to the 'new times'. While the father was exceedingly discomfited, but rendered incapable of strategic action—retreating into feigned illness rather than shaking the hand of a socially inferior but officially superior functionary, looking on but unable to exert any discipline over his son—the teenage brother threw himself into the enthusiasms of

---

[94] *Ibid.*, p. 10. [95] *Ibid.*, p. 9. [96] *Ibid.*, pp. 9–10.

a movement which seemed to promise adventure, a purpose in life, and a new 'adult' status through exaggerated claims of sexual prowess and violent deeds. Hildegard, caught in the constrained and tense atmosphere between these two poles, felt acutely discomfited. Yet she was also in some respects herself briefly a beneficiary of the new age, being able to enrol as a student in Berlin University and to a small degree rebel—or at least assert herself—against her father's wishes. Nevertheless, not long after Hitler came to power, despite—indeed even because of—this particular household configuration, Hildegard was soon to find herself a victim of the new regime, first betrayed and denounced by her own brother and then callously cast out by her father.[97]

Those at the younger end of what was to become the first Hitler Youth generation often only had a somewhat derivative sense of the problems of the period, which were nevertheless very directly transmitted to them through their parents' actions and strategies. Their very existence and family structure was often connected directly to the historical conditions of the time even in their own much later accounts of their lives. Amalie H. (born 1922), for example, even when interviewed in her eighties in 2005, chose to introduce herself precisely in terms of the historical circumstances: 'I was born in 1922 in the inflation, that's already when it all started, didn't it.'[98] Similarly, Brigitte D. (born 1924), interviewed also in 2005, on being asked if she had any brothers and sisters, responded:

> No, I had—was a single child, had no brothers or sisters, it was after all bad times then, my year of birth falls in the time of the inflation, you know, women went to collect the men at the factory gate in order to take the money and go shopping immediately because the next day it would already be worth even less. And so you didn't want any more children, that, well, that was after all the world economic crisis, in the twenties, that's why I remained an only child.[99]

Clearly in this case the anxiety of parents about their capacity to feed additional children did not end with the inflation itself, and affected their reproductive behaviour even in the years when things started to improve. Many also recalled the difficulties their parents experienced in making ends meet, and continuing uncertainties even in the few 'good years'. Parental authority was constrained by economic crises as well as by ailing, psychologically or physically wounded fathers. For those members of the first Hitler Youth generation born in the early to mid-1920s, then, there was a direct, often even bodily, awareness of what were the problems to which, for some, Hitler seemed in the first instance to offer 'solutions' while for others redemption was later sought in left-wing causes. They were thus perhaps peculiarly receptive to messages of redemption offered in the coming years; and many of them, from whichever class background, experienced as teenagers the ways in which the return to full employment in the 1930s affected their own

---

[97] See further Ch. 4 below, pp. 104–6.
[98] Interview with 'Amalie H.' (not her real name), August 2005.
[99] Interview with 'Brigitte D.' (not her real name), August 2005.

family's fortunes, even if at the very basic level of the father having a regular income again after years of difficulty.

In this direct personal awareness of the crises of Weimar, however much this was gained from a child's-eye perspective, these cohorts differed crucially from those who were born in the closing years of Weimar, the '1929ers'. Most of the latter generation, who were to prove so vital in the attempts to build a new and better Germany after 1945, had conscious awareness of little or nothing before their socialization under Hitler; in this sense, the 1929ers, who were effectively a 'second Hitler Youth generation', not only had different experiences of the Hitler Youth organization itself in the later stages of the Third Reich when membership became compulsory for them, but also had from the outset, from the conditions in which their lives began, a rather different degree of receptiveness to the Nazi message. Although none of this was as yet preordained in the later Weimar years, the timing of birth during this short period did make a quite significant difference to the impact and longer-term significance of later experiences.

Experiences in the 1920s, in the long shadows of the Great War and in the later context of economic depression and political strife, predisposed Germans by the later 1920s and early 1930s to sharply polarized political positions. Which segments rose to the surface, and how people in different positions were constrained or chose to act and lead their lives, was very much a matter of politics. It was, then, subsequent circumstances—the character of the two succeeding dictatorial regimes—that determined which strands would rise to prominence, which social types would achieve historical visibility under different conditions, and who would be marginalized, suppressed or cast out. Meanwhile, the political and economic instability of the Weimar years provided key background experiences for those who were young at this time, predisposing at least a significant proportion of them to be more ardent and enthusiastic followers of Nazism during the subsequent decade than many of those who were already adults well before Hitler came to power.

However important age at the time may have been for later predispositions and susceptibility to the Nazi message, the tidal wave which swept Weimar Germany as its political system collapsed in face of severe economic and constitutional crises cannot be reduced to generational shifts. Carl P. was, as ever, a perceptive observer. He commented on his impressions as he travelled between Silesia and the Posen area in 1930 on SPD business:

> In the summer of 1930 things looked sad in the German provinces. When I went to Vietz I saw that my party colleagues, but also my opponents, had changed . . . Businessmen stood with concern in front of the doors of their enterprises and asked me anxiously if things would soon get better. Former competitors . . . had been badly affected by the crisis; they complained to me about what they were suffering, and many broke down. Somewhat uncertainly Jewish tradespeople inquired whether there were swastikas elsewhere too; after 1924, they had only recently popped up again in this area. The unemployed stood around on the streets and in the squares, also in front of the employment office. They had a different expression from other people, their comportment too was different, and when I passed by I could feel how they

were looking at me and I felt a sense of shame that I was well dressed and not downtrodden.[100]

As the depression deepened, so the Nazi movement grew, with a degree of status and a place in the world playing a role for some of those in social distress.

Across the country as a whole it was not primarily those who were actually unemployed, but predominantly those in fear of unemployment and loss of social status—the lower middle classes in small towns and rural areas, particularly in the Protestant, northern and eastern provinces of Germany—who disproportionately flocked to support the Nazi movement. Catholics generally tended to remain loyal to their own Catholic Centre Party. Much of the urban working class remained left-wing in orientation and voting behaviour, although, given the sheer size of the working class in this by now highly industrialized society, even a relatively small percentage of working class votes could yield quite high absolute numbers as far as electoral support for the NSDAP was concerned. But even among the dispossessed, the Nazis made inroads, and among what were perceived as the 'rougher' classes of youth—a fact which was particularly significant as far as their capacity for violent action was concerned, as Carl. P. observed in the provinces of eastern Germany:

> Fresh-baked National Socialists admitted to me personally why they had turned their backs on the KP [Communist Party]; they were unemployed, family life had been destroyed by having to live in want, and now the Nazis were coming as the saviours and offering them an SA uniform, 50 Marks and service in the SA barracks with free food and one Mark pocket money daily! It is interesting that, along with other properties, houses that belonged to the I.G. Farben industry have been turned into this sort of SA barracks. Anyway it is only this sort of conversion to National Socialism among a considerable portion of the working class that has for the first time given Adolf Hitler the punch that he needs to maintain his position on the streets. Up till then we had taken pleasure in chasing the grammar school and petty cash kids with swastika decorations into fear and terror, if they started to become too cheeky; but from now on it looked rather different.[101]

And historians would concur with Carl P.'s further observation that Hitler seemed to be offering something for everyone, and hence did to an extent succeed in garnering support across a relatively broad social spectrum, even if disproportionately more among some social groups than others. There was inevitably something of a snowball effect. As Carl P. commented:

> Everyone now ran around with a party badge and declared himself already from a distance. The whole people seemed to be in some way wearing uniform and fell little by little into a frenzy of political passion. I had at that time the feeling that I was living through times similar to people in the Middle Ages when the plague raged. At that time, so the Chroniclers report, it happened that the still living danced upon the

---

[100] HHL, b MS Ger 91 (174), Carl P., p. 30.
[101] *Ibid.*, pp. 41–2.

dead. Here a despairing and starving people was dancing on the corpse of German prosperity.[102]

The landscape was transformed as people flocked to the cause in terms simply of visual signs of belonging:

> Now I had the impression that Germany consisted only at all any more in swastika flags, brown and black uniforms and grotesque, murderous faces, of the same ugly colour as the trousers of the SA . . .
>
> These people were so easy to steer! Their need was great, so great that there was no-one who could at this moment give them anything more than words of consolation. So they became enthusiastic about appearances: a uniform gave a man the value that daily life could not give him, the 'watch' in the SA barracks or in the Reichsbanner hostelry lent him the appearance of importance, the political mottos of the day called him to their defence or implementation and gave him a sense of being valued in action. And just like the man, so also the woman. Her own ragged dress, old-fashioned hat, down-at-heel shoes, are covered up by the party badge, and the bright flags shining out of the windows throws a cheering light into her poverty . . . Whoever can offer more in terms of external appearances works more strongly on the undecided, who let themselves be captivated by the sheer quantity of what is on offer. Oh, it was so very simple, so simple, that the conquest of power was only a question of the propagandistic penetration of the country, but not a question of reason and reflection.[103]

But Carl P. was not merely an observer of events; he was also highly politically active and increasingly in trouble for his work on behalf of the SPD.

However much aspects of the political and economic chaos affected all age groups, it was again young adults, particularly those of the war-youth generation, who were most readily mobilized into the active exercise of violence in conditions verging on civil war of this time. Udo K., for example, who was a student in Breslau from 1930, describes the way in which young people were drawn increasingly into street brawls following political arguments which got out of hand, and were mobilized to join one or another of the array of paramilitary groupings: the communist *Rote Frontkämpferbund* (Red Veterans League), the overwhelmingly social democratic *Reichsbanner Schwarz-rot-gold* (Reich Banner black-red-gold), and the right-wing nationalist *Stahlhelm* (Steel Helmet), as well as the Nazi SA.[104] On the nationalist end of the spectrum, Udo K. also continued his paramilitary training under the secret guidance of the 'Black Army', supported by local weighty individuals and the civilian authorities nationally and regionally.[105] In a period of rising unemployment, effective political deadlock and rule by presidential decree under the increasingly senile Hindenburg, it was the right-ring groupings that appeared to have the upper hand as far as support in high places was concerned.

---

[102] *Ibid.*, p. 43.
[103] *Ibid.*, p. 44.
[104] LVR, Nachlaß K., I. 208 'Erlebt—Davongekommen. Erinnerungen. Erlebt—überlebt. Erster Teil 1910–1948', pp. 66–7.
[105] *Ibid.*, pp. 35–6, 60–1.

In the summer of 1930, Carl P. came into possession of materials concerning the paramilitary organization of right-wing youth in Silesia. The local state authorities were determined that he should not make this material public:

> When I came into possession of material concerning the secret training of young people in nationalist circles, I was ceremoniously informed by Count Degenfeld, the German nationalist Landrat of Reichenbach, who was instructed by the Commandant of the Fortress of Glatz on behalf of the Social Democratic President, that I was to desist from publication, otherwise the charge of national treason would be brought against me.
>
> When it is a matter of the dear, good Army, the ponderous and cumbersome Prussian-German administrative apparatus could work surprisingly quickly. In this case the Landrat rang me up before I had even opened the letter containing the material, since it was of course very important that the Army, with the support of the Prussian administration, should secretly be training nationalist youth, especially as it was graciously allowing a few Reichsbanner people to participate too.[106]

Paramilitary organization of youth was not the only issue in the area, and once Carl P. came into possession of compromising material over corruption in high places among the Silesian aristocracy his life came under threat. Further incidents led both to court proceedings and to right-wing attempts to assassinate him.

Carl P.'s account of the attack on him, planned for 8 August 1932, suggests a degree of continuity with earlier troubles in this area, only a few years beforehand. One Kurt J. had been given the task of disposing of him, using a bomb from army stocks:

> He himself was the 'Press Advisor of the SA subdivision Middle Silesia-South'; in other words, he was the leader of Cell G., that was the Feme-Organisation [summary justice organization] of the NSDAP in this area . . . My murder . . . had been ordered by the party leadership.
>
> . . . In general it turned out that the Silesian aristocracy did not have entirely clean fingers in this affair. Figures like Count Pückler-Burghaus and Count Hochburg made a less than pleasant impression in the Special Court in Schweidnitz. However: I had received from the wife of a Silesian magnate material about malpractices concerning the use of the moneys which had been made available through the 'Help for the East' programme; that was embarrassing, since my publications threatened to compromise further circles. And in the question of saving their own skins the feudal overlords were never very picky and choosy.[107]

By the time the NSDAP actually came into power in January 1933, Carl P. had to flee for his life. He succeeded in crossing the border to Switzerland on 21 March 1933 calculating, correctly, the precise moment on the infamous 'Day of Potsdam'—the day of the celebratory opening and swearing in of Hitler's new government by President Hindenburg at Potsdam's garrison church—when border officials would have their mind on other matters:

---

[106] HHL, b MS Ger 91 (174), Carl P., p. 40.
[107] *Ibid.*, p. 50.

It went quite smoothly; for in Germany at this precise time, as my friends—women, of course—had calculated, everyone was standing to attention to mark the moment that General Field Marshall von Hindenburg stood at the grave of Frederick the Great with his 'Bohemian corporal' [Hitler] and engaged in a national tearjerker. So of course the border guards had neither the time nor desire to take a closer look at the man with a brief case—I had taken nothing else with me—and dressed in traditional green Alpine clothing.

That was my farewell to Germany.

. . . I hardly need to say . . . that I was happy . . . to be finally among normal people again.[108]

Millions of others remained, however, within the borders of a state that was now to be ruled with an extraordinary combination of violence, terror, and adulation, the consequences of which would throw a shadow far longer than the twelve-year existence of the 'Thousand Year Reich' itself.

Speaking of 'the German as compliant and cheap cannon fodder', Carl P. had suggested that: 'Adolf Hitler offered him hope for a golden future; he dangled before him paradise on earth. The despairing had faith in him and faith can move mountains.'[109] In June 1932, Friedrich M., a theologian, teacher, and professor, wrote a little position paper purely to clarify his own thoughts, entitled 'My position on National Socialism'. Having explored the reasons why he himself would never fall for National Socialism—dislike of racism and antisemitism, disapproval of the use of force rather than discussion as a means of resolving differences—he commented on the way in which young people were flocking to the cause:

> That young people fall for Hitler, I understand; for youth always runs after resounding words. But I fear for the time when their honest faith ends in disenchantment. And this time must come, since the Party is promising the impossible. Those who are disenchanted either become dulled or throw themselves into the opposite cause.[110]

The views of this committed Christian, who viewed the rise of Nazism with some horror, as well as those of Carl P., who was lucky enough to get out in time, were to prove only too prescient.

---

[108] *Ibid.*, p. 57.
[109] *Ibid.*, p. 43.
[110] Kempowski BIO, 5482, Friedrich M. (1875–1947) 'Meine Stellung zum Nationalsozialismus'.

4

Divided generations: State violence and the formation of 'two worlds' in Nazi Germany

Shortly after Hitler's appointment as Chancellor of Germany, the by now upcoming and young lawyer Dr F.R. moved lodgings in Berlin. He came home one day in February 1933 to find his landlady's daughter, then aged fourteen, in a terrible state. While at school that day, she had participated in bullying one of her classmates, a girl by the name of Helga. According to the girl's account, Helga had been wrestled to the floor, beaten and jumped on, simply for being Jewish, a newly relevant point of stigmatization. Thus trampled by her classmates, Helga had cried and screamed with pain, and eventually the girls decided it was time to release her. But at this point a teacher, who had been observing the fracas, intervened and asked: 'Whose side are my German girls on?' Thus encouraged—indeed effectively told by a person in authority to continue tormenting their friend—the schoolgirls resumed jumping up and down on Helga. Eventually Helga stopped screaming and fell silent. She had then been taken to hospital, where she died. That evening, back at home, the landlady's daughter was utterly distraught about what had happened, crying and repeating over and over again 'How could we do such a thing!'[1]

This was a phrase which was to echo a millionfold over the decades after 1945—although often accompanied by the self-exculpatory plea that one had 'known nothing about it'. But up until the military defeat of the Nazi regime in May 1945, such behaviour, such violence, and such acquiescence in the sponsoring voice of authority, sufficient to suppress any rising qualms, was to be repeated over and over and over again.

This small and deeply tragic incident epitomizes so much of the way in which Nazism was 'possible', and illustrates at a very early date the ways in which Nazism was so often enacted and experienced: the designation and stigmatization of victims; unleashing of violence as a means of dominant-group identification and expression of superiority; enactment by people who would arguably never, on their own, have been capable of becoming 'perpetrators'; active encouragement by authorities, who gave some form of official 'legitimation', sanctioned from above; and often, too, a degree of individual disquiet, even horror, when, too late, those involved realized the full consequences of their actions.

---

[1] Harvard Houghton Library (henceforth HHL), b MS Ger 91 (184), Dr F. R., pp. 37–8.

Violence was all around from the very outset of the Nazi regime, experienced by innumerable opponents and victims, and visible for everyone with eyes to see. Even if the Third Reich had unexpectedly come to an end in the summer of 1939, before the wartime atrocities of the *Einsatzgruppen* (special execution squads) and the mass murders of the extermination camps, acts of violence and killing on an almost unthinkable scale had already been committed and innumerable suicides had been precipitated among victims who despaired and saw no other way out.[2] As one German-American businesswoman, of mixed Jewish and non-Jewish background, later commented:

> The brutality of the Nazis beggars description and is hard to believe. In 1933, in Epstein im Taunus, a small town near Frankfurt, the Nazis tied an opponent to a cart, dragged him thru [*sic*] the streets until he was dead. The culprits were slightly punished for this deed.[3]

It is indeed almost remarkable, in view of later developments, that the 'culprits' were 'punished' at all; within a rather short time, such atrocities would be beyond the law entirely, indeed would become the desired practices of Hitler's Third Reich.

Hitler's programme for the so-called 'Final Solution to the Jewish Question'—the attempted mass murder of all Jews in Nazi-dominated Europe, alongside many other 'racial' and political victims of Nazism—has, for very good reasons, over-shadowed the history of the Third Reich. Given later patterns of self-exculpations among Germans who claimed they 'never knew', it is worth first making the effort to understand the period before the war in its own terms, to see how radically those living through even the peacetime years of the 1930s were affected by the progressive nazification of German society.

While some were able to sustain their blinkered view of Nazi Germany's alleged achievements in the peacetime years, murderous violence was built into the regime from the outset. What was new after 30 January 1933 was not the sheer existence, nor even the massively increased prevalence of violence as a political tool, but rather the rapid monopolization of force by the Nazi authorities, with the continuing but by no means instant or straightforward demotion of countervailing institutions of law and order, the progressive capitulation to Nazi rule on the part of traditional conservative nationalists, and the radical suppression of opposition. The trail of events in the spring and early summer of 1933—the Reichstag fire of 27 February, the mass arrests and clampdown on political opponents, the less-than-free elections of 5 March, the strategies of intimidation, cooption or suppression of political rivals, the famous 'Day of Potsdam' and the Enabling Law of late March, the abolition of trade unions in May, and the creation of a one-party state in June—is well known. So too is the chronology of the progressive concentration of the institutions of coercion through the 1930s, with renegotiations of the roles of the SA and the SS after the so-called 'Röhm Putsch' or 'Night of the Long Knives' in

---

[2] On suicides in Nazi Germany more generally, see Christian Goeschel, *Suicide in Nazi Germany* (Oxford: Oxford University Press, 2009).
[3] HHL, b MS Ger 91 (3) Erna A., English original, p. 9.

late June 1934, the cooption of the Army culminating in its oath of personal obedience to Hitler following the death of President Hindenburg in early August 1934, and the rise of Heinrich Himmler as effective leader of an increasingly centralized and coordinated system of terror, including the regular police forces and Gestapo, from 1936 onwards, achieving its most murderous form in the activities coordinated by the Reich Security Head Office (*Reichssicherheitshauptamt*, RSHA) from 1939.[4]

Yet, for all the familiarity of the chronology of terror, debates continue to rage over the ways in which 'ordinary Germans' related to this system. Such debates have often been framed in terms of rather simple dichotomies: coercion and consent, repression and support, terror and commitment, resistance and conformity, although historians, whatever their positions on these debates, generally acknowledge the ambiguities of behaviour and attitudes across a wide and ever changing spectrum.[5] Once explored in more depth, it becomes clear that we are dealing not with binary oppositions, but with a far more complex picture entirely, in which outward behaviours and inner states of mind were to varying degrees, and often entirely, at odds with each other. While outward patterns of behaviour can relatively readily be extrapolated from the sources, the real difficulty lies in getting at the 'inner states'—and at the ways in which people's perceptions, strategies, and sense of self changed over time.

Here, it would seem that an alternative approach is needed. Rather than—or perhaps in addition to—focusing on the distinctive combinations of terror and obedience, or congruence of interests and commitment to ideology, or social backgrounds and personal motives, it may be helpful to explore the Third Reich (and indeed other dictatorships, and not only dictatorships) with an eye as to how people adopted and learned how to play new roles; and how they developed the newly appropriate 'manners of speaking and acting' required of them under the new circumstances. For some, these were never lightly worn; for others, they were readily assimilated into an enhanced repertoire of standard attitudes, stock phrases, and routinized behaviour patterns, all of which could be selectively drawn upon as the occasion demanded; for a few, such patterns could become more or less second nature, with relatively unthinking commitment encouraged and confirmed by informal repetition among salient peer groups, enforced participation in mass rallies, party and state organizations and activities, and officially endorsed emotional

---

[4] This is not the place to provide references to even a small selection of the relevant secondary literature. But see for recent overviews of relevant areas and guides to further reading: Jane Caplan (ed.), *Nazi Germany* (Oxford: Oxford University Press, 2008); Richard J. Evans, *The Third Reich in Power* (London: Penguin, 2006); Dietmar Süß and Winfried Süß (eds.), *Das 'Dritte Reich': Eine Einführung* (Munich: Pantheon, 2008).

[5] For differing approaches to this area, see e.g. Eric Johnson, *The Nazi Terror: Gestapo, Jews and ordinary Germans* (London: John Murray, 2000); and Robert Gellately, *Backing Hitler: Consent and coercion in Nazi Germany* (Oxford: Oxford University Press, 2001). A still classic early contribution to the debates, emphasizing dissonance and ambivalence, is Ian Kershaw, *Popular Opinion and Political Dissent in the Third Reich. Bavaria, 1933–45* (Oxford: Oxford University Press, 1983); see also, for the role of the charismatic *Führer* as a key integrative factor, Kershaw, *The 'Hitler Myth': Image and reality in the Third Reich* (Oxford: Oxford University Press, 1987).

reactions to public events. It is always extremely difficult, under any regime, for ordinary people to 'speak truth to power', or even to step out against what peer group pressures dictate by way of the acceptable spectrum of attitudes and fashions at any given time; under the Third Reich, such attempts could be literally suicidal. 'Enactment', rather than commitment, may be at least one of the keys to understanding the avalanche that rolled over Germany from the very beginning of 1933, carrying with it not only those buried and crushed by the snow and ice but also those floating on the surface and riding high on the crest of the new wave, until the absolute destruction of the landscape eventually engulfed them all, leaving many victims and only a few dazed survivors.

Thus what was also new, and far less well conceptualized by historians to date, are the ways in which the Nazi project was assimilated and enacted by extraordinarily large numbers of people.[6] Many Germans were relatively rapidly mobilized—for whatever combinations of reasons—to behave as though they believed in the cause, whatever their individual disagreements over particular issues or residual sense of inner distance from the ideology may have been. And these widespread patterns of conformist behaviour and mass mobilization—without necessarily any accompanying individual motivation—had massive consequences, not only for the conformists and careerists who rode the Nazi tide, but also, more fundamentally and eventually for millions fatally, for those on the receiving end of Nazi oppression. While the former found ways of developing a new 'social self', whatever their degrees of inner distance from their behaviour, the sheer physical survival of the latter was existentially threatened. No one could live through this period of history unaffected by world historical developments; and there was a relationship between capitulation and proactive conformity, on the one hand, and the capacity of the regime to put into effect the machinery of murder, on the other. The notion of 'bystander' is, with very few exceptions, predicated on a fundamental misapprehension of the way in which Nazism was not merely imposed by force on, but also pre-emptively carried by, millions of those living through these times.

The Third Reich was a regime which was imposed and sustained by force; but it was also one which succeeded in mobilizing significant sections of the population in such a way that, with startling speed, German society was fundamentally transformed from within: there was a rapid, progressive, 'racialization' and brutalization of German society from which no one could stand aside. While traditional distinctions of class and status did not disappear, new lines of stratification on 'racial' lines were introduced, not merely as an 'official' matter of law, policy, and ideology, but also as a matter of everyday behaviour in situations well beyond the sight of any authorities, within a matter of months. 'Politics' thus not only penetrated every last area of German society during this time through the

---

[6] But see recently Peter Fritzsche, *Life and Death in the Third Reich* (Cambridge, MA: Harvard University Press, 2008), which on the basis of a comparable attempt to evaluate subjective material from diaries, letters, and autobiographical writings, frequently comes to somewhat similar interpretations to those suggested here, but tends to cling to a notion of ideology rather than enactment.

monopolization of violence; it was also carried, enacted, and in part formed by the ways in which people internalized and proactively played, or at least 'mimed'—and in too few instances refused to play, or subverted—the parts officially scripted for them. This delicate balance is exceedingly complex to apprehend and describe, and underlies repeated debates among historians abut the balance between terror and consent in the Third Reich. Yet without understanding how the two were intrinsically linked, it is impossible to grasp the ways in which Nazi society fundamentally affected the lives of those who lived through it, and was also carried and sustained by the apparently spontaneous actions and behaviour of large numbers of people towards others—behaviour which, often unsupported by appropriate beliefs, many were later to disown.

Within this context, new opportunities were opened up for those young careerists who were willing to ride the tide; and in order to make a career at all within the new state, those on the brink of adulthood had to make the relevant compromises or show the right kinds of attitudes and attributes. Among younger cohorts, pools of enthusiasm for a better future could be whipped up into a frenzy in service of 'the cause'. The rise to prominence of the war-youth generation and the 'first Hitler Youth generation' as carriers of the Nazi system and readily mobilized troops for the exercise of violence was a by-product of the very nature of that system: both dynamic and constraining, fostering certain kinds of behaviour and subduing others, producing the very social types it needed and forcing the rest into a stultified silence, sometimes sullen, sometimes agonized, rarely capable of breaking out of the repressive mould. But no one, absolutely no one could in the long term escape being affected by the nature of this state. And it made a massive mark on the character of German society, only somewhat refracted by issues of generation. We therefore have to start with exploring the ways in which German society was 'nazified from within', before looking at some of the more startling generational features of the era.

I. 'HIDDEN VIOLENCE'? THE PROGRESSIVE 'NAZIFICATION' OF GERMAN SOCIETY

Within hours of Hitler's coming to power Germans were jostling to reposition themselves—a repositioning which involved a more or less far-reaching redefinition of political, social, and 'racial' identities. This process of regrouping, realigning of social selves according to the now inescapable criterion of 'race', was in fact a form of 'hidden violence', not merely hurting those newly defined outsiders who registered its effects at the time but also, insidiously, producing over a longer period one of the key preconditions which ultimately made mass murder possible. The nazification of German society from within accompanied, and often even pre-empted, the more familiar history of the imposition of antisemitic policies from above.

The major phases of racist legislation and policy of course provided the official framework and external impetus for this nazification of informal social relations. The boycott of Jewish shops and businesses on 1 April 1933, in which SA thugs stood menacingly beside shop windows smeared with antisemitic slogans and prevented 'Aryan' customers from entering, was the first major illustration of the kinds of brutal activism favoured by Goebbels and radical sections of the NSDAP; and it was far from popular.[7] The euphemistically entitled 'Law for the Restitution of a Professional Civil Service' which followed a few days later, on 7 April 1933, excluding those of Jewish descent or the 'wrong' political opinions (socialists, communists) from jobs in the professional areas of the German *Beamtentum*, a far wider category of those employed by the state than that connoted by the narrower sense of the term civil service in English, provided the classic illustration of an attempted 'legalization' of discrimination, following tactical retreat from antisemitic measures which, in their more nakedly brutal form, had not gone down well with the wider German public and threatened to have adverse effects on Hitler's popular standing. By the early summer of 1933 the programme of mass compulsory sterilization of those deemed, on spuriously 'scientific', 'eugenic' grounds, to be unfit to reproduce soon demonstrated the regime's broader agenda of producing a 'racially' defined 'healthy national community' (*gesunde Volksge-meinschaft*) with implications for communities well beyond those covered by the 'Jewish question'. By the mid-1930s, the classic swing of the pendulum between brutality on the streets, favoured by Nazi radicals but unpopular with the wider public, and the 'legalization' of discrimination which seemed more broadly accept-able, was evidenced again. Rising violence on the streets during the summer of 1935 was soon followed by the Nuremberg Laws announced at the Nazi Party Conference in September, distinguishing between fully Jewish and various 'mixed-race' categories, and awarding second-class status, with all the attendant disadvan-tages and discrimination, to those now ousted from full German citizenship. Antisemitic measures continued, escalating rapidly through 1938, cumulatively robbing Jews of their rights, their possessions, their livelihoods, and their freedom of movement, making it ever less possible for them to live on German soil, even, in some cases—as for those caught in the worst violence of November pogrom of 1938, or incarcerated in concentration camps in its wake—to live at all.[8] State-sponsored discrimination and violence was evident all around from the moment of Hitler's assumption of power in January 1933, even if, during this period of 'peacetime', it had not yet taken the ultimate form of the intended murder of every single person categorized as Jewish across Nazi-occupied Europe. Such was the broader context of political ideology and action in which informal social relations were radically transformed and personal identities renegotiated.

Antisemitism was, then, of course a matter of state policy. It was often also a matter of local authorities proactively introducing measures in advance of and

---

[7] See e.g. the contemporary comments in Bernd Stöver, *Berichte über die Lage in Deutschland. Die Meldungen der Gruppe Neu Beginnen aus dem Dritten Reich 1933–1936* (Bonn: Verlag J. H. W. Dietz Nachfolger, 1996), p. 575.

[8] There is neither space nor need here to recount these developments in detail, since there are many excellent accounts available; see particularly Saul Friedländer, *Nazi Germany and the Jews: The years of persecution, 1933–1939* (London: HarperCollins, 1998); and Marion Kaplan, *Between Dignity and Despair: Jewish life in Nazi Germany* (Oxford: Oxford University Press, 1998).

irrespective of dictates from above.[9] But the progressive enactment of the Nazi project of constructing what was deemed to be a racially defined *Volksgemeinschaft* was also effected through patterns of informal social relations, often proactively and frequently going way beyond what might have been 'purely' required by law.[10] Had this not been the case, the pattern of developments might have been very different; unfortunately this remains in the realm of the hypothetical, not that of the historian.

If the state had impinged on people's lives with ever greater intensity from the Great War onwards, it was now utterly inescapable; a renegotiation of identity was inevitable, whether one welcomed it or not. As Martha L., a working-class woman, married with one son, summarized the situation: up until 1933 she and her partly Jewish husband, both committed socialists, had been able to live

> purely in the service of the German workers' movement and our own family . . . [W]e were actually contented, despite frequent periods of unemployment, that is, we knew we were masters of our own fate and could make our own decisions about ourselves and our lives. But with one fell swoop all this changed. Namely from January 1933 life in Germany generally became less peaceful, and the life of every single citizen was no longer determined by himself but by the state.[11]

Hidden violence, at an informal level beyond state policies and open practices of physical violence, entailed, first of all, the 'recognition' of who was now to be an insider and who an outsider, and, secondly, the severance of social ties, often with the utmost politeness and accompanied by expression of regret.

'Recognition' and 'self-designation' was often a complicated business, entailing considerable readjustments of identity. In the decades before the Nazi assumption of power in 1933, German Jews had been highly integrated: being Jewish in Germany was (with obvious variations depending on degrees of orthodoxy or secularism, and degrees of assimilation) a matter of culture, religion, family background, and not of 'national' identity. Gerhard M., born in 1911, into a family which had owned and run mines in the industrial area around Kattowitz in Upper Silesia for three generations, found this enforced reconceptualization of identity almost impossible; as he put it, right at the opening of his autobiographical sketch written in 1940, his awkwardness of expression reflecting the difficulties of imposed recategorization:

---

[9] See e.g. Wolf Gruner, *Judenverfolgung in Berlin 1933–1945. Eine Chronologie der Behörden-massnahmen in der Reichshauptstadt* (Berlin: Stiftung Topographie des Terrors, 1996), pp. 17–25, for the extraordinarily comprehensive and wide-ranging exclusionary measures in the months February to May 1933, which were at this stage applied in respect of both '*Mischlinge*' and 'full Jews'.

[10] I use the word '*Volksgemeinschaft*' here purely in the sense of the Nazi claim, making no assumptions about the extent to which Nazi goals were or were not translated into practice, whether in 'reality' or 'ideology'. For debates about attempts to deploy this concept not merely as an object of study but also as a heuristic device and an analytic tool, see Michael Wildt, *Volksgemeinschaft als Selbstermächtigung. Gewalt gegen Juden in der deutschen Provinz, 1919 bis 1939* (Hamburg: Hamburger Edition, 2007); and Frank Bajohr and Michael Wildt (eds.), *Volksgemeinschaft. Neue Forschungen zur Gesellschaft des Nationalsozialismus* (Frankfurt am Main: S. Fischer Verlag, 2009).

[11] HHL, b MS Ger 91 (137), Martha L., p. 1.

My personal outlook is that of a Jew who is not religious and felt more German than— well, I cannot say: Jewish, because I do not believe in a Jewish people or race, but, perhaps, better—who felt German only.[12]

Others who did feel Jewish, whether in terms of religious commitment or in the more secular variants of cultural legacies and familial affiliations, often had comparable difficulties in accepting that the notion of 'Germanness' was now to be redefined so as to exclude Jewish Germans from a more narrow 'racial' conception of 'Germanness', forcing an unwanted exclusion from their homeland and identity. The by now well-known philologist Victor Klemperer was not alone in being forced to rethink his identity and renew his sense of Jewish identification.[13] Anna B., for example, was born in 1895 and lived in a small university town in southern Germany, where she and her husband ran a small factory and were the only Jewish family for miles around; they were well-integrated in the local community, and her children were happy, with many friends, at school. After 1933, things became progressively more difficult; but as she later put it:

We were so assimilated, that we replied to all religious Gentiles, who wondered, that we didn't consider to go to Palestine: 'We are Germans by nationality and Jews by religion, as you are Christian . . .'[14]

But unavoidably, from 1933 onwards 'race' and ancestry rapidly became highly salient; and the language of religious or cultural affiliation was displaced and overlain by the new terminology of 'racial science'.

Putting this into practice was not all that easy at first. There are many more or less humorous stories of misrecognition, as people rushed to try out their new 'knowledge', and teachers sought to impart the relevant distinctions to students, many of whom were not immediately inclined to take it all seriously. Erna A., a 'half-Jewish' businesswoman of American origins who ran a company in partnership with someone who was fully Jewish, recalled for example that:

In 1933 my [Jewish business] partner's daughter was a senior at school. She was eighteen, a tall, slim, blond girl with blue eyes. A new class in racial biology had been put on the curriculum. The teacher was new. She asked the girls to name one in their midst whom they thought would specify to the Nordic type. All, including the Nazis, suggested Liesel. The teacher beamed. She measured the circumference and the length of the skull, all the other measurements were taken, every one was perfect. Here was a case of the purest Aryan type. 'Where do your ancestors come from?' she asked. 'Palestine' was the answer amid the roar of the other girls.[15]

Such examples could readily be multiplied.

Yet as they began to learn who was 'in' and who 'out', many Germans seem, without a great deal of prompting or explicit threat of any specific penalties, to have

---

[12] HHL, b MS Ger 91 (158), Gerhard M., English original, p. 1.
[13] See e.g. Victor Klemperer, *Ich will Zeugnis ablegen bis zum letzten. Tagebücher 1933–1945* (Berlin: Aufbau Verlag, 1995), pp. 15, 209–10, 220.
[14] HHL, b MS Ger 91 (25), Anna B., English original, p. 32.
[15] HHL, b MS Ger 91 (3) Erna A., English original, p. 26.

more or less spontaneously 'regrouped' themselves, realigning their social networks in terms of the new racially defined criteria. In memoirs and contemporary writings there are numerous illustrations of friendships being explicitly broken off, social relations being dropped, and even avoidance of recognition when meeting accidentally on the street.[16] Somehow, 'Aryan' Germans became aware that it was no longer 'politic' even to know, let alone be friendly with, fellow-Germans of Jewish background. This apparently spontaneous breaking off of formerly close friendships is one of the most curious aspects of the spread of Nazism through German society.

Hildegard B., the daughter of the Berlin professor who was very much of the old guard, recalled how her father began to drop his Jewish colleagues at university.[17] His story is typical of the ways in which many on the conservative nationalist right responded to the new demands of the Nazi regime, and enacted the consequences in their own lives with few misgivings:

> I was very surprised when Father replied to me that at my age you have to make concessions to the times, and even he had gradually had to limit his contacts with Jewish colleagues or lecturers . . . Today I can well understand that Father was more influenced by the opinions of others than he himself really knew. He had been proud of his nationalist convictions all his life and so he could not bring himself to resist inwardly when a dominant movement like National Socialism went further along the road that he did. For him—and I believe this is also true for many others—the Hitler party was never really something hostile, but rather just an exaggeration or an unhealthy malformation of the same thing as he himself wanted. I experienced it this way myself at the time, after all I had been brought up to believe that there could be nothing more beautiful and magnificent than the old Reich, that had of course been destroyed by criminals in 1918 and that Hitler wanted to resurrect. But you only have to live abroad for a couple of years for things to look quite different.[18]

By now aged twenty, and herself a student, it dawned on Hildegard with ever greater clarity that her father was far from infallible. Just how deep-rooted his prejudices were, and quite what an irresolvable conflict in her own and the family's life the new regime was to bring, was not yet clear, but was to become so within a mere matter of weeks.

Hildegard unwittingly entered her brother's room one day and witnessed, to her amazement, that he was involved in a homosexual encounter with her father's trusted university assistant, Leonhard. Although shocked at Leonhard's apparent abuse of her father's trust, Hildegard thought nothing further of this incident, considering it a private matter between her brother and this man. But Leonhard or her brother—she was never sure who instigated the idea—decided to get some form of 'pre-emptive revenge' on her for having witnessed their behaviour. Hildegard had at the time a platonic friendship with a fellow university student, Wolfgang, of

---

[16] On street greetings, see also Andrew Stuart Bergerson, *Ordinary Germans in Extraordinary Times: The Nazi revolution in Hildesheim* (Bloomington and Indianapolis: Indiana University Press, 2004).

[17] See above, Ch. 3, pp. 87–90.

[18] HHL, b MS 91 (33), 'Hildegard B.' (pseudonym), pp. 22–3.

whose family background she was hardly aware; nor did it matter to her at all that, as it turned out, her friend was Jewish. But following an unfounded denunciation to the effect that he and Hildegard had been involved in a sexual relationship, Wolfgang was arrested in the middle of the night and taken to a concentration camp. Hildegard desperately tried to help, but all four lawyers whom she approached for assistance gave different reasons for why they had to refuse help. Then Hildegard's own house was subjected to a forcible search of the premises (*Haussuchung*) by SA members at night; she was torn out of her bed and taken to a makeshift jail, guarded by young thugs, with no evidence of either ordinary uniformed police or real officials; Hildegard noted that the man taking down her details was aged thirty at most, with the bureaucratic style but not the reality of law behind any of the decisions taken here. She did not dare to challenge what was happening but broke down in tears, alongside other women who were also the subject of rough handling. On a Sunday in April 1933, Hildegard was then made, with other women, to parade through the streets of Berlin bearing a placard saying 'Swine that I am, I gave myself to a Jew'. On her way from the jail to this public ritual of humiliation she saw Leonhard laughing cynically at the sight of her in this state ('Because of his mocking smile when I recognized him—he was a man who rarely smiled—I realized then for the first time that he saw me as his enemy and this day as his revenge').[19] During the two hours or so during which she was humiliated by being paraded through the streets, Hildegard was repeatedly photographed; she subsequently heard that the photographs had been published in the Nazi newspaper, *Der Stürmer,* although she never herself saw a copy.

This sort of individual denunciation for purposes of 'revenge' and then public humiliation was a familiar pattern in Nazi Germany, inscribing new norms and codes of behaviour onto an ever more frightened public but also giving people additional public tools to wield in private disputes. The twist that Hildegard's story then takes is what perhaps makes it more unusual than other similar stories; it encapsulates, indeed, all that was wrong with the old as well as the new in her family. When the day of her public humiliation was over, Hildegard's Uncle Wilhelm appeared at the prison in his officer's uniform and informed her that she had been ousted from the family; if she did not accept this verdict, the 'honour' of her father demanded that he should shoot himself. In Hildegard's words:

> He said to me . . . that I was a rejected creature, I had only brought shame on my father and my father wanted to hear no more of me. His voice sounded different from how it otherwise did in the family circle: he spoke harshly, in a clipped and militaristic style. I only cried and started to plead my innocence again. His answer was only that, after this incident, I could never return to my family. For my father as an Officer of the Reserve—I forgot to mention this earlier, that Father, like all people of a higher social status in Imperial Germany before 1918, had been an Officer in his youth—after this incident there were only two options, either he must immediately shoot a bullet into his head, or maintain the position that he had never had a daughter . . . Even if you suppose that my father really believed everything that people had probably said to him

[19] *Ibid.*, p. 33.

about me—without ever having talked to me about it—even then I find his approach, even according to the Prussian military code of morals, excessive.[20]

Hildegard's uncle Wilhelm brought her some money and her passport, and the next day she left Germany for ever. Her father died two years later, a fact which she only gleaned from the newspaper. Having started a new life under a new name in a new part of the world, Hildegard concluded her tale:

> Since then I have emigrated to another part of the world, have taken another name, and started a new life. I am only a small piece of world history; I know that things have gone far worse for others. I have survived this—it wasn't always easy to start with—and have become a different person. But I also know now that there are criminals and underworlds elsewhere too, and yet my experiences would never have been possible anywhere else. That is why I want to have nothing more to do with my family, that threw me out, and nothing more to do with the German people either. That is all that I have to say about my life in Germany.[21]

Hildegard's tale is perhaps extreme in every respect, encapsulating as it does so many aspects of the transition from the old Germany to the new; it is also extremely well-written, making the reader wonder momentarily whether it was not crafted with an eye to novelistic creativity rather than autobiographical writing. Yet, penned just a few years after the painful events it describes, without the historian's 'benefit of hindsight', and in the midst of a World War where infinitely worse was developing on all sides, this seems unlikely. It simply epitomized, in the small compass of one family's story, what was happening in different ways all over Germany from the moment the Nazis came into power, as people interpreted and deployed the new 'rules of the game' in the light of their personal interests, social considerations and cultural codes.

The breaking off of social relations with colleagues and friends occurred from very early on, and occurred across age groups; even teenagers and young adults appear to have somehow sensed that an invisible form of social ghettoization and spontaneous segregation was in order. Such separation and severing of the ties of friendship is recounted in numerous memoirs: after 1933, the introduction of 'racial' categories overrode emotional ties that had withstood even differences of class, status, and politics.

Before January 1933, within a relatively broad spectrum of similarity of social background, precise differences of status—aristocratic or bourgeois, Jewish or Christian—seem to have played little role in friendships among schoolchildren. Class was perhaps a more major barrier to mutual understanding and friendship; even so, the segregation of residential districts and schooling according to class meant that, given the relatively high degree of assimilation that had taken place in Germany over preceding decades, non-Jewish and Jewish children of similar social backgrounds were more likely to coexist than were children from different, bourgeois and working-class backgrounds. What were still seen as 'religious' distinctions

---

[20] HHL, b MS 91 (33), 'Hildegard B.' (pseudonym), pp. 34–5.   [21] *Ibid.*, p. 37.

could be readily overcome in the relatively neutral context of school playgrounds and classrooms within any particular social milieu. Margot L., for example, who was born in Posen in 1917, went to school in Königsberg, following her family's move there when Posen became Polish after the Great War. At Königsberg, she gained her first experiences of SA violence in 1924. Her schooldays in Königsberg were happy; in a class of around thirty-five, there were seven Jewish girls, including herself, and the question of whether or not one came from a Jewish family appeared totally irrelevant to the classmates. As Margot pointed out: 'We noticed nothing with respect to questions of race, any sort of discrimination or disregard. We were all brought up the same way as German.'[22] Particularly important for Margot after her entry into the grammar school (*Gymnasium*) in 1930 was her close friendship with an aristocratic girl: 'That this girl was not only Aryan but also aristocratic was completely irrelevant.'[23] Even major political differences, including support of Nazism, did not seem to make a great difference to Margot's friendships prior to the Nazi assumption of power. Following her family's subsequent move to Breslau, Margot's best friend became one Anneliese, daughter of a high state official, and Anneliese's political views reflected her family's support of Nazism; but the two girls did not talk about politics. As Margot summarized it: 'She did not count me among those Jews against whom the Nazis were fighting. For her I was just German and her friend Margot.'[24] In her later reflections, written in 1940, Margot suggested that most people in her acquaintance who were pro-Nazi before 1933 took from Nazism what they wanted and ignored the rest; virtually no one actually saw what was coming, whether the struggle with the churches or antisemitism, and for most of them the most relevant point, given the areas in which she lived, was that they thought that a Nazi government would assist in regaining the 'Polish corridor' for Germany, and in fighting communism. Insofar as Jews were seen as a potential target, it was the distinctively different 'Eastern Jews' (*Ostjuden*) but not the German Jews that they thought would be attacked.

Gerhard M. from Kattowitz had similar experiences. He attended a vocational high school (*Oberrealschule*), where one of his best friends was a boy called Heinz, son of one of their teachers; and in the early 1930s Heinz became a Nazi supporter. At first, this did not affect the boys' friendship: it was only in the course of the months after January 1933 that Heinz realized quite what Nazism should mean in practice, as Gerhard later recalled:

> Before Hitler came to power, the little controversy of race did not matter between Heinz and me. [At first] our friendship remained as firm as ever. On the boycott day, 1st April '33, he came to warn me in spite of the danger which it meant to him . . . Later he wrote in a long letter, explaining that 'our two peoples were locked in a desperate struggle and that we had no choice but to take sides'. He had become a party member . . . and was very active throwing bombs and making speeches.[25]

[22] HHL, b MS Ger 91(142), Margot L., p. 1.
[23] *Ibid.*, p. 2.
[24] *Ibid.*, p. 9.
[25] HHL, b MS Ger 91 (158), Gerhard M., English original, p. 3.

Gerhard proceeded to study at the Technical University in Breslau. While at university, he enjoyed a wide social life, as well as being deeply engaged with his studies; it was an excellent time for him, despite increasing restrictions on his movements and career prospects. But again, after 1933 Gerhard had the experience of the cordial ending of a formerly close friendship because of his Jewish background. One very good friend, according to Gerhard, collected old folksongs but was not really political. As Gerhard recalled:

> What he loved most was his freedom, and [I] cannot to this day understand his change into a Nazi. But in 1933 he came to see me, we had a long discussion and came to the conclusion, that our friendship was no longer possible. He told me about the 'call of his blood' and 'the marvellous transformation of the German Nation', and I had pains not to show my grin when I looked into his dreamy blue eyes behind strong glasses. Later he wrote me, again saying how he regretted, but that our ways had to part and we should not be sorry as our time together had been splendid.[26]

In these and countless other documents, it is clear how readily young people adopted the current slogans of the day and translated them into personal practice, thus 'legitimized'. In short, they learned, rehearsed, and enacted the new scripts.

Among adults, pragmatic considerations perhaps outweighed the ideological arguments adduced by newly convinced teenagers; or perhaps these were simply brought out more frequently in an attempt to rationalize break-ups in terms which the person breaking off the friendship thought might be more understandable, if not acceptable; adult friendships of some depth might also be sustained for somewhat longer, until the potential practical consequences became all too clear. Thus for example Hanna B., born in 1895, provides a lengthy description of a gentile friend who had tried to keep up the friendship with herself and her Jewish aunt, with increasing difficulty:

> But about 1936 she once came to my aunt to tell her with tears in her eyes, that she was now obliged to be more cautious, as her husband was a professor at a vocational college, although she still felt the same way towards my aunt and always will. She was no longer allowed to take a walk or meet my aunt in public during the day. But she promised to come to see her sometimes in the evening. She did no longer dare to invite my aunt to her house, nor to phone from there and begged her, not to call her at the phone by name, as the telephone conversations of Jews were sometimes overheard. My aunt was deeply concerned and begged her not to see her anymore, as she loved her too much to do her any harm by their relation. They sometimes met with a nonarian [sic] friend, whose husband was a Gentile, but in the evening only.[27]

At other times, it was the Jewish person who, out of consideration for his friends and the potentially deleterious consequences of a continued friendship which they appeared to be overlooking, initiated or first acted in such as way as to effect a break-up. Martin F., for example, was a Berlin lawyer born in 1875, who as a result of Nazi legislation lost his position and his clientele, and was forced to change jobs a

---

[26] HHL, b MS Ger 91 (158), Gerhard M., English original, p. 7.
[27] HHL, b MS Ger 91 (25), Hanna B., p. 35, English original.

couple of times and move to Charlottenburg, away from the well-to-do and prestigious so-called 'privy councillors' quarter' (*Geheimratviertel*, on the south-east of the Tiergarten and west of Potsdamer Platz, in an area now the home of cultural institutions such as the New National Gallery). He saw less and less of his friends as his circumstances deteriorated. He still, however, frequented chess cafés on the broad, tree-lined main street of the Kurfürstendamm, where he met 'Aryan' friends who were left-wing in their views and very unwilling to give up old friend-ships. But gradually Martin F. himself came to the view that he should protect even these friends by not seeing too much of them, seeking to retain a strict separation in his mind between the regime and the German people:

> It was only those currently in government who were bad—the German people was no worse than any other, despite the aberrations into which it had got itself, and not without some fault of its own. I soon began to avoid the little artists' pub, since I feared that I might cause difficulties for my good old acquaintances which they, in their light-hearted, outspoken way could for the time being not see.[28]

The price, of course, was increasing social isolation.

Gerhard M. recounted in some detail the way social life developed under these circumstances:

> Since 1933 a new era had begun. Social life was closed for the Jews. Former friends did not see and greet them, theaters or concerts were not safe places. So they retired behind their four walls, gave little parties, and had rather depressed conversations. Even that was not safe. The one or other house had been raided, and men led away without reason. The nervous strain was terrible. New friendships developed, Jews crept closer together. Alcohol consumption and playing cards for high stakes increased. My mother who had never before touched a cigarette started to smoke, talks centered around emigration, transfer of money abroad, new developments in anti-Jewish shops. Spe-cially trying the difference of atmosphere at home and at the T.H. [Technical University of Breslau], for instance, where life went on as before. On the one side people who had faith in an alteration, on the other men with the only wish to leave Germany as soon as possible. Even our family was divided: my stepfather for emigra-tion, me and my mother for waiting. But with the passing of time, even the most stubborn had to understand that remaining was not possible, that bonds had to be cut. Conditions became worse. Jews were no longer permitted to live in houses owned by Aryans, beer-gardens had signs with 'Jews not admitted', whole towns and villages bore these signboards, and nice paintings of a Jew driven out by a brawny SA man. Jews were virtually living in Ghettos.—And when speaking perchance to an Aryan he would say: 'Well, you know we do not like to be dictated and we don't like the antisemitic side and the foreign policy and the lack of good materials and the decline of decent art,—but business IS good.'[29]

Sometimes the increasing separation of Germans of Jewish backgrounds—whether or not they were religious, whether or not they believed in theories of biological descent (in either the Nazi or the orthodox Jewish variants), whether or not they

---

[28] HHL, b MS Ger 91 (68), Martin F., p. 72.
[29] HHL, b MS Ger 91 (158), Gerhard M., pp. 14–15, English original.

were held to be of 'mixed descent' ('*Mischlinge*') or 'fully Jewish'—from the social circles of their German compatriots was so gradual that the person barely noticed it at first, leaving no sediments in daily diaries of the time. As Inge C.-L., for example, recounted, she only registered after some considerable lapse of time that she was no longer invited to participate in social activities with her school classmates, and that her family was increasingly cut off from former circles; there was no one specific moment at which this assiduous diary-keeper noted this development in her records of daily events.[30] But other '*Mischlinge*'—perhaps because they were still rather younger at this time—found their social neighbourhoods and networks were highly supportive. Ilse J., for example, who was born in late November 1932, found that as a child in the 1930s her major difficulties were first of all, being refused permission to join the local sports group; and more generally, the regime discrimination against her mother, her aunt, and maternal grandmother, who were the Jewish side of the family.[31] She also noted that she was aware of being an only child for political reasons, since her parents, fearful of the new regime and the uncertainties of the future, had not dared have further children after Hitler came to power in 1933.

The position for those of 'mixed blood' was somewhat unpredictable throughout the Nazi regime. The 'Aryan Paragraph' of the April 1933 'Law for the Restoration of a Professional Civil Service' stipulated that those 'not of Aryan descent' should lose their positions (with some exceptions to do with length of service to the state, and military service in the Great War), affecting also people from mixed marriages. In the first two years after Hitler came to power, the tendency among those imbued with racist prejudice was generally to treat anyone of 'non-Aryan descent', 'mixed blood', who was 'half-Jewish', with as much contempt as if they were 'fully Jewish', but this remained a vexed question among racist circles.[32] Nazi policymakers sought to reach some compromise formulations in the Nuremberg Laws of 1935, with 'clarification' hinging on how many Jewish grandparents an individual had, and in cases where there were two 'Aryans' and two 'non-Aryans' bringing into play the questions of religious practice and affiliation through marriage; even so, the consequences in practice remained in some dispute as did the related issue of Jews in 'mixed marriages' with 'Aryans'. These questions were still being debated during

---

[30] Interview with Inge Cohn-Lampert, 3 Dec. 2006.
[31] Interview with Ilse J., Berlin, 26 Apr. 2007.
[32] On policy developments with respect to '*Mischlinge*', see Jeremy Noakes, 'The development of Nazi policy towards the German-Jewish "Mischlinge" 1933–1945', *Leo Baeck Institute Yearbook*, 34(1) 1989, 291–354; on subjective experiences as refracted through oral history interviews, see Beate Meyer, *Jüdische Mischlinge: Rassenpolitik und Verfolgungserfahrung 1933–1945* (Hamburg: Dölling & Galitz, 1999); James F. Tent, *In the Shadow of the Holocaust: Nazi persecution of Jewish-Christian Germans* (Lawrence, Kansas: University Press of Kansas, 2003). As a term which was already in use in the nineteenth century, but which was by this time deeply implicated in Nazi racial ideology, the word Mischling should in principle always be surrounded with scare quotes. The term should always be understood as a concept applied from a particular world view, and in one sense as 'unreal'; unfortunately, however, like every kind of stigmatization, this particular form of categorization in terms of 'mixed race' had a very real impact on those so labelled and personally affected, however little they shared the mental paradigm from which it emanated. In this sense, however untenable the underlying world view, the consequences were very real and use of the label is unavoidable.

and after the Wannsee Conference coordinating the 'Final Solution' in January 1942, with differing views on whether persons designated as being in one of these 'mixed' categories should be deported to be gassed, sterilized, or for the time being 'merely' restricted in movement and activity pending a more propitious moment for definitive action. Needless to say, from the early 1930s perspective, the notion that anyone at all might within a matter of a few years be headed for murder in specially designed gas chambers was of course unthinkable: not conceivable within the universe as they knew it. The 'worst' was on a continuum with what had been happening since 1933, not what was to come in an as yet unknown and unimaginable future. In the 1930s, both '*Mischlinge*' and others found it difficult to predict what their position might be, as indeed the endless debates over whether to emigrate or stay and sit it out in one's own homeland amply demonstrate.

Gerhard M. summarized the situation with respect to one of his close friends, 'the daughter of a professor of Breslau University, a jew [*sic*]. Her mother, Aryan, of noble birth':

> New laws were passed, most important the Aryan and Official Laws. The existence of ¼, ½, or ¾ Aryans was introduced to the German people and indeed to the whole world for the first time. The actual facts, I suppose, are known. Not known is the terrible unhappiness and the high number of suicides which were the result. 'Mischlinge', children of mixt [*sic*] parentage did not know where they stood, regarded as Jews by the nazis [*sic*] and with suspicion by the jews [*sic*]. They had no rights only duties, as paying fees to some organisation where they were allowed to stay or even forced to do so, 'Deutsche Arbeitsfront' for instance.—A girlfriend of mine was Marion R. was one of the most charming and intelligent girls I have ever met . . . Her father married again after his wife's death, again a baroness; she brought 2 children with her out of her first marriage, pure Aryans, and they had two more children. They all got on splendidly till Hitler came. Then the situation developed that brother Hans had to become member of the Hitler Youth, brother Karl, however was not allowed to join. Same thing with the sisters. The father, as good a German as any, officer in the army, bearer of a famous name, was deprived of his post on account of the new laws and had to leave Germany. The girl remained faithful to her country. I often tried to convince her to leave but in vain. She had friends, both under Aryans and Jews, but was terribly unhappy about the fate of her family. Her case, I dare say, was typical for half-aryans. Mixed marriages were forbidden, dissolving of such bonds encouraged. The idea of a 'Racial Disgrace', 'Rassenschande' was coined. Men, divorcing their wifes [*sic*], but still loving them and having intercourse, were punished under this law. Old affairs were unearthed and 70-year old people put in Concentration Camps for disgracing Aryan girls.[33]

'Legal' distinctions between 'full Jews' and people with varying degrees of 'mixed blood', introduced officially in the Decrees following the Nuremberg Laws of 1935 but never fully resolved, were not always clearly observed by members of the German population in the 1930s, more often to the disadvantage of the 'Mischling'

---

[33] HHL, b MS Ger 91 (158), Gerhard M., p. 15, English original.

than otherwise. The fully 'Aryan' working class socialist, Martha L., whose husband was a 'Mischling', reported for example that:

> My husband had been employed since June 1930 as an assembly operator in a large cigarette factory. Since he has a Jewish father, so is a half-Jew ['Mischling'], in July 33 he was dismissed as an 'enemy of the state', and this was not instigated by his managers but rather 'because of the state'.
>
> Since in March 33 every state employee [*Beamter*] in Germany had to swear on oath a statement about their family relations and race [*Rassezugehörigkeit*], my sister, who has 9 years experience working in associations, and has for 12 years lived in Berlin as a social worker in state employment, was immediately dismissed, since German law states that: anyone who is married to or is an in-law of a Jew cannot be a state employee in public service [*Staatsbeamter*]. For two years she had neither support nor work...[34]

Whether or not this working-class woman was quite accurate in her recall of details and dates—the letter was written in some anguish in 1940—the gist of her story continues in the same vein.

The story of the ways in which Martha L.'s teenage son, technically a 'quarter Jew', was also discriminated against, is highly revealing of the ways in which racism played out through institutions and everyday encounters and was systematically enacted by people across society, radically affecting the lives of those thus discriminated against. Before the Nazis came to power, Martha's son had attended a relatively progressive school, the Dürerschule.[35] In stark contrast to most of the academically oriented high schools (*Gymnasien*) in Germany, the Dürerschule had in the late 1920s drawn around one-third of its pupils from working-class backgrounds—in 1927 as many as 33 per cent, compared to only 3.2 per cent in the grammar schools. And, in contrast to the dominant ethos of many similarly academically oriented schools in the Weimar Republic, which played up the virtues of militarism and harked back to the lost monarchy, the Dürerschule emphasized the virtues of tolerance and pacifism. The school was accordingly closed down by the Nazis in 1933. Forced to leave this school, Martha L.'s son found difficulty in gaining a place at any other school. Once he did manage to re-enter formal education, despite his academic potential he was systematically given low grades by his teachers because of his background and specifically because of his obviously Jewish surname. Nor was his treatment any better on the streets, although here the brutality was more obvious and directly physical. At the age of sixteen, while pausing with his bicycle to chat to a female friend whom he met on the way home, he was subjected to an attack for alleged 'racial defilement' (*Rassenschande*). He arrived home, as his mother recalled:

> with black eyes and a smashed up face. It had happened this way. Two S.A.-men came up to him and said: 'Well, you swine of a Jew, what are you doing standing around on

[34] HHL, b MS Ger 91 (137), Martha L., p. 2.
[35] Burkhard Poste, *Schulreform in Sachsen 1918–1923. Eine vergessene Tradition deutscher Schulgeschichte* (Frankfurt-am-Main, Berlin, Bern, NY, Paris, Wien: Peter Lang, 1993), pp. 433–52.

the street here and committing racial defilement. We should beat the hell out of you!'
Then they had already started punching him and pushed the lad with his bicycle onto
the busy main road.

His mother, filled with a sense of outrage at this unprovoked and violent attack, still
at this point thought she should complain to the authorities to seek redress—an
indignation and a faith in legal procedures and justice which would not last long in
this state:

> So right away I went to the police and filed a charge against the 2 S.A.-men for physical
> assault. But the matter was dealt with already at the magistrate's level and I was
> informed in writing that: 'The two S.A.-men acted in the interests of the state!', in
> other words, the blows had been delivered with the backing of the law.[36]

It was not only physical assault backed by the state, but also more subtle discrimination on the part of fellow citizens that further affected the future of this 'quarter-
Jew'. Having decided to give up his ambition of being able to study to become a
doctor, now blocked by the problems with schooling, Martha's son took an
apprenticeship which he completed to a high standard; but, despite his clear
intelligence and accomplishments, he was not subsequently offered any employment. On inquiring on behalf of her son with the relevant municipal organization,
Martha L. was told: '"We can't force any firm to take on someone of Jewish
background!"'[37]

  Experiences of violence were frequent, but this was not merely a question of
'state' versus 'society': the interrelations were more complex. Violence was often
initiated and 'legitimated' by party, police, or judicial authorities, but exacerbated
or complicated by the responses of the population following an incident, many of
whom disapproved of physical violence while yet supporting the Nazi movement
and its leader.[38] Wolfgang Y., the son of a Catholic father and Jewish mother from
Kattowitz, who had moved to Berlin, went on the occasion of the boycott of 1 April
1933 to his mother's shop to keep her company on this difficult day.[39] He was
brutally beaten up by SA men, and in the course of the fight his jaw was broken.
The hospital in Berlin refused to admit him for treatment: 'I was told outside that a
Jew who gets beaten up on the Day of the Boycott is certainly a Communist.' He
was in the event relatively well looked after in a clinic somewhere outside Berlin by
a group of, ironically, Nazi health workers, who at this stage did not wish to
associate Hitler with the thuggish violence of the SA:

> A little swastika flag stands on the table, a picture of Hitler hangs on the wall. The
> women belong to the middling sorts of state employee. They talk very nicely to me.
> They are all very sorry about my misfortune. That was certainly not what the Führer
> would have wanted [*nicht im Sinne des Führers*], the attack on me.[40]

---

[36] HHL, b MS Ger 91 (137), Martha L., p. 4.
[37] *Ibid.*, p. 4.
[38] For this kind of complexity see also Kershaw, *Popular Opinion* and Kershaw, *The 'Hitler Myth'*.
[39] On his childhood and youth, see Ch. 3 above, pp. 69–71.
[40] HHL, b MS Ger 91 (251), Wolfgang Y., pp. 47–8.

Following this incident, he was advised not to return to his mother's shop for fear of endangering her; he was also advised to emigrate. Having taken the decision to leave the country, Wolfgang visited a former teacher in order to say goodbye. He found his former teacher—also at this very early moment in the regime—in a state of despair:

> [H]e is deeply unhappy. His wife is Jewish. His second oldest son comes home one day in an absolute rage. Why did he marry a Jew? Now the future had been ruined for him, the son, he couldn't join the SA, the father had committed a crime. I was told that [the father] hit the boy horribly. He gives him money, tells him to get out of the house for ever, and has his room walled up. He sits in his armchair, a broken-down, ruined man . . .
>
> Just as the train is reaching the border, tears roll down my face. I have lost my homeland. Why?[41]

For Germans of Jewish descent, then—whether practising Jews, Christians with a Jewish family background, or, to varying degrees, designated as people of 'mixed blood' (*Mischblütige* or '*Mischlinge*') and their relatives—from January 1933 onwards life became increasingly difficult, and in innumerable cases intolerable. And it became intolerable not merely on those occasions when the physical violence encouraged by the Nazi regime was unleashed—whether on 'official' and well-known occasions, such as the April 1933 boycott, or in the innumerable instances of thuggish behaviour on the streets—but also through the psychological pain wrought by the severing of ties of friendships, and the radical changes in informal social relations which Germans enacted, seemingly spontaneously, from below, and right from the very beginning of the regime.

Why did so many adults conform to the new regime? One rather a-historical answer which gained a wide popular hearing is that 'Germans' had allegedly always been antisemitic, that their brand of antisemitism was peculiarly radical, and that now Hitler and the Nazi regime served to sanction, support, and actively foster pre-existing tendencies towards an 'eliminationist antisemitism' which in other circumstances might be restrained.[42] But this generalization fails to deal adequately with the historical evidence.[43] Other prevalent approaches emphasize either the significance of force and repression, such that Germans were effectively constrained to conform; or, conversely, the role of both ideology and self-interest in ensuring that large numbers of Germans apparently willingly cooperated with the regime, with this interpretation tending to underplay both the extent of resistance and the role of

---

[41] HHL, b MS Ger 91 (251), Wolfgang Y., pp. 49–50.

[42] This is of course the thesis advanced by Daniel Jonah Goldhagen, *Hitler's Willing Executioners* (New York: Knopf, 1996).

[43] For critiques and further discussion, see e.g. Geoff Eley (ed.), *The Goldhagen Effect: History, memory, Nazism—facing the German past* (Ann Arbor: University of Michigan Press, 2000); Norman Finkelstein and Ruth Bettina Birn, *A Nation On Trial: The Goldhagen thesis and historical truth* (New York: Henry Holt, 1998); J. H. Schoeps (ed.), *Ein Volk von Mördern? Die Dokumentation zur Goldhagen-Kontroverse um die Rolle der Deutschen im Holocaust* (Hamburg: Hoffmann & Campe, 1996); Robert R. Shandley (ed.), *Unwilling Germans? The Goldhagen debate*, essays translated by Jeremiah Riemer (Minneapolis and London: University of Minnesota Press, 1998).

repression.[44] The historical realities are, as always, more complex, and no single summary will suffice—nor, indeed, is this the primary aim here, when the focus is rather on exploring the variety of ways in which people of different generations faced the challenges of living through the Nazi regime and the consequences of these experiences for outlooks and behaviour in later periods. However, it is important to emphasize that individual responses and processes of adaptation are not always well encapsulated in the dichotomies of coercion and consent, repression and ideology, fear and conviction, in which these issues have often been considered.

For many Germans, it was in large part a matter of following the herd as far as visible behaviour was concerned, with an eye both to peer-group pressure and considerations of personal advantage, without either great fear of repression or much by way of inner conviction on many matters—although this varied across different issues and times. In some respects, one could argue that many people behaved with apparent 'pre-emptive obedience' (*vorauseilende Gehorsam*), although the sanctions and strategies were rather different for 'Aryans' in relation to the Nazi regime than they were for those to whom this term has more usually been applied. The notion of 'pre-emptive obedience' has most frequently been applied to members of Jewish communities across the ages who, fearful of pogroms and enforced exile, allegedly developed a tendency to hurry to cooperate with whichever authorities were in power, in order to avert the worst potential catastrophes which might otherwise befall their people. It has frequently had pejorative overtones, as if 'passive victims' almost 'deserved' their fate (echoing some more recent debates on women and rape). The phrase has rarely been applied with respect to the German masses who cooperated so pre-emptively with Hitler's new racial order. Yet in some respects it is a highly apposite notion, at least in an amended form.

Contemporary accounts repeatedly give stories of the way in which people supported Nazism for all sorts of reasons and excuses. These included, for example, the former communist who told Albert D. that ' "Yes, outwardly I am brown, but inwardly I'm still as red as ever" '; another was later arrested because his young son reported that in the evening he would take off his uniform, lay it over the chair, and say ' "Right then, the Nazi is now lying on the chair and the Kozi is going to bed!" ' [*Kozi* = Communist]'.[45] Outer conformity was for many people clearly compatible with a sense of inner distance.

For some, the new regime did clearly touch chords of prior conviction, or seem to answer felt needs. Rare glimpses into the inner convictions and doubts of someone who acted out a full Nazi role in public are afforded by the diary of one

---

[44] The emphasis on force and lack of viable alternatives in a highly repressive state with severe sanctions for nonconformity was favoured by many Germans and became embedded in historical consciousness and popular representations of the Third Reich after 1945, helping in the process to exonerate the part played by many 'ordinary Germans', and was echoed in much of the historiography up until the 1980s. The latter view, emphasizing cooperation, was argued most prominently with respect to denunciations by civilians to the Gestapo by Robert Gellately in his book, *The Gestapo and German Society* (Oxford: Oxford University Press, 1990), and developed more generally in his work on *Backing Hitler*. Richard J. Evans has strongly critiqued Gellately's interpretation and re-emphasized the changing role of the repressive forces as the regime developed.

[45] HHL, b MS Ger 91 (54), Albert D., p. 6.

Wilhelm B.[46] Born in Duisberg in 1896, Wilhelm B. attended only elementary school (*Volksschule*), followed by apprenticeship as a locksmith. He went through the Great War without incurring either serious injury or military decoration, and, despite training as an engineer in the Weimar Republic, clearly only came fully into his own once the NSDAP had gained power. In the mid-1930s he threw himself into work for the NSDAP cause with great enthusiasm, holding political offices and travelling extensively in the service of 'educational' functions. He had few illusions about the difficulty of his work, as he commented following an apparently poorly attended meeting in November 1935:

> On the 8th I was in a nigger village (*Negerdorf*) in the Büren district, Niederntudorf. We have all of 3 party members there, and on top of it all they all come from the not much loved vintage of 1933 (March and May hares) [i.e. those who opportunistically jumped to join the NSDAP when it was possible to do so once in power]. The breed of this area is hereditarily burdened by religion. Otherwise the best of material. A shame. It will take another 10 years to achieve any improvement.[47]

For all the difficulties involved, Wilhelm B.'s new role was a source of great satisfaction and pride, and one which constantly spurred him on to try to achieve even greater things. His diary entries capture the characteristic flavour of constant 'movement' without much clarity about the ultimate outcomes—perhaps something of a prefiguration of the later *Götterdämmerung* (twilight of the gods) mentality of the closing war months—that remained prevalent among many ordinary followers of the 'Hitler movement' even in power:

> If you manage to battle your way out of the status of 'proletariat' and conquer the heights of education, knowledge and respect, if you become a leader [*Führer*] in your little circle and hold a leadership position within Adolf Hitler's movement, that is always gratifying. But I am always driven further forwards. I see a long path before me, I know not whether it will take me to heights or depths, but I shall certainly not remain on the same level.[48]

Something of an autodidact, despite his new rise to a clearly fulfilling position Wilhelm B. nevertheless plagued himself with private questions about his own 'biological inheritance'. Deploying poorly internalized Nazi concepts and rather weak grammar (omitting expected punctuation), he engaged in some revealing, if awkward, private philosophizing in his diary:

> This all has to be seen as determined by nature, if you even resist this thought, it shows you are an outsider! Perhaps I am one such. Since I reached maturity, I have had an inner urge for action. Viking blood wants to raise the world from ruins. Only one thing is always stopping me from doing this. That is the legacy of the warrior, putting oneself in a subordinate position. Like right now. And yet, you do what you have to. What drew me, as a seventeen-year-old volunteer in 1914, to join the German Army out

---

[46] Kempowski-BIO, 4842 / 1 + 2, Wilhelm B., (1896–1982).
[47] *Ibid.*, entry of 12 Nov. 1935, fol. 15.
[48] *Ibid.*, entry of 27 Jan. 1936 (perhaps he should have thought more carefully about potential 'depths'; this entry was written nine years to the day before the liberation of Auschwitz), fol. 22.

there, where there was want and misery, dead [*sic*] and destruction? What allowed me to hold out for four years. Was I, among the ranks, also an outsider who, treating death with contempt, sometimes went voluntarily into the heat of battle. One single thrust drove me onwards, my genetic inheritance! And then. Wailing and work in the pay of the Jew. And yet I managed to show them some teeth. Worked and made demands. Why did I break out again and create a new platform. Others made things comfortable for themselves, I had to learn . . . [49]

In this case, there seems to have been no ironic distance at all (however terrified rather than playful any such 'irony' could have been at that time) from the new 'racial' or 'biological' interpretation of an essential, biologically based 'character'.

Moreover, for perhaps the first time in his life, Wilhelm B. saw his own individual life and mood (not to mention that of his horse) and the fate of history as rolling together towards future greatness, predicated on 'revenge' on those held responsible for previous downfall:

Now the avalanche of meetings is rolling again over Germany. Our soldiers are marching in the Rhineland. I think back to 1918 when, hungry and freezing, I returned from France across the Rhine bridge near Koblenz. My horse, on which I cowered as anything but a 'proud rider', was in the same state as me. Now the time of revenge has come.[50]

Like many others, Wilhelm B. allotted a large role to Hitler in this scheme of personal and historical time. Having witnessed Hitler's birthday celebrations on 20 April 1936, the most extravagant yet in the short history of the Third Reich, Wilhelm B. committed to his diary the following comments:

The feelings that overwhelm an old soldier on this occasion cannot be described. I am glad that I always [was] with the Führer, and never battled against him. Some—including those previously 'non-party'—must be blushing with shame today.

Overall, what is the condition of Germany today: A single great Reich has developed out of an anarchistic state of political confusion. The sham Treaty of Versaillie [*sic*] has been torn to shreds. Both banks of the Rhine are free again. A strong army is protecting the national community [*Volksgemeinschaft*]. The people have work again.[51]

Wilhelm B. may have been in a relatively small minority as far as his own definition of self in terms of a combination of biological inheritance and personal commitment to the greater historical cause was concerned. He was certainly far from alone in applauding Germany's apparent return to a state of national greatness and economic security in the mid-1930s. Social, economic, and international developments garnered widespread enthusiasm, in view not only of the horrendous depression since 1929 out of which Germany had appeared to recover so rapidly but also in view of the wobbles and difficulties in consumer satisfaction as recently as 1935.

[49] *Ibid.*, fols. 20–1.
[50] *Ibid.*, entry of 17 Mar. 1936, fol. 32.
[51] *Ibid.*, entry of 5 May 1936, fol. 35.

But for many others, it was a matter of what appeared to be opportune in their situation: status maintenance, fear of losing one's position, conforming to what was held to be appropriate. Anna B., surprised that one of her children's teachers had become 'undecided and restless' when talking to her in the street, discussed this with a friend, who commented that 'it was rather compromising and even dangerous for officials to be seen "associating" with Jewish people'.[52] Quiescence included a combination of passive conformity accompanied by degrees of silent disagreement, as people appear to have shut down their critical faculties, allowed the propaganda to wash over them, and ceased to take issue with the daily drip and occasionally more vehement onslaught of ideology. The ways in which these processes affected behaviours are captured in many near contemporary accounts. Erna A., for example, recalled that:

> At one of those delightful garden restaurants that used to make life so fascinating in Germany, I ran into a typical Nazi couple. They sat at my table and a conversation with them could not be avoided . . . I tried to vere [*sic*] from politics but it could not be avoided. I tried to start a conversation with his wife, but she as a good German Hausfrau took no part in the conversation. Every word he uttered showed that he read his Nazi Paper very thoroughly . . . I thought it best to gulp down my dinner and go.
>
> Hitler was forever making speeches over the radio at that time. Everyone was forced to listen. The larger stores and factories had loudspeakers erected and everyone was forced to attend. The smaller stores were closed and sent their employees to cafes or street corners where they could listen. In private homes the servants were assembled to listen. They did not want to interrupt their work but the risk for the employer was too great if he did not see that Hitler's will was enforced. Not a word was ever spoken, one listened to the applause and the shouting, but not a muscle was moved. Later whispered comments could be made.[53]

The radio certainly had a major impact on the views of many German, even if the saturation was greatest in cities, and some areas, such as rural Württemberg villages, remained virtually untouched.[54] From radio broadcasts, those who were so inclined could acquire stock phrases and ready explanations to be trotted out where relevant as 'their own' opinions on matters of the day—a point which became even more important during the war, when interpretive frameworks were so desperately needed.

By no means all adult Germans were taken in by or prepared to conform to the new patterns of social relations which were spreading with such pathological speed through the rapidly nazified German society. But the penalties for refusing to conform, or for actively working against the Hitler regime, were severe. The active socialist Martha L., for example, recalled that 'Up to 10 April 37 we managed to live in Germany, hounded and hungry.' But then her husband was arrested and 'taken

[52] HHL, b MS Ger 91 (25), Anna B., p. 31, English original.
[53] HHL, b MS Ger 91 (3), Erna A., p. 23, English original.
[54] A point made forcefully by Jill Stephenson in debate with Peter Fritzsche at a conference on the Nazi *Volksgemeinschaft*, German Historical Institute London, 25–7 March 2010. See also Fritzsche, *Life and Death in the Third Reich*, and Jill Stephenson, *Hitler's Home Front: Württemberg under the Nazis* (London: Hambledon Press, 2006).

into so-called "protective custody for re-education"': he was first incarcerated in Sachsenhausen, and then in Dachau. On 20 July of that year, he managed to obtain his release through the help of Quakers—who are again mentioned frequently in these reports for their very proactive assistance, which in cases such as this made all the difference between the possibility of release and subsequent emigration, or continued incarceration and possibly death.[55] Help on a smaller scale could make a significant difference too. Käthe Tacke, who was born in 1909 and brought up a Catholic, was in the 1930s working with children in Berlin.[56] She later recalled how her disagreement with the Nazi authorities, and her close relationships with a number of Jewish neighbours and friends, brought her ever closer to Quakers; she later converted to Quakerism. Now only in her twenties and an assistant in children's care centres, Käthe Tacke's scope for helping people persecuted by the regime was limited; but she did whatever she could on an individual level (bringing milk and food to Jews who were malnourished, hiding a suitcase for a communist friend), and also played a small role in the work of the Quaker office in sending food parcels to people who were imprisoned, and seeking to get individuals out of Germany at this time. The work, which included personal involvement on the part of American and British Quakers, was largely secretive: 'they worked completely in secret, the whole group did not know what was going on there'. As Tacke later put it, 'naturally as a young person I did not get to hear very much about these things, I only knew that many contacts were made with the authorities, were made with government, and were made with leading personalities'.[57] However small her own role, Käthe Tacke did not feel, after the war, any sense of a guilty conscience—with the sole exception of the night she failed to leave her apartment, where she had a visitor, and get to the Bahnhof Zoo in response to an urgent call from a Jewish couple whom she had been helping. Viewing her whole life in terms of a process of spiritual searching, she also did not, apparently, have the 'zero hour' need to rewrite her notion of her self; the inner dissonance had not been compromised by outer conformity with which she would have felt uncomfortable, even though, as she put it, 'it always seemed to me in my work and also in my personal life as if I was always standing with one foot in the KZ'.[58] Other very committed members of the Christian Churches who are far more well known, such as Dietrich Bonhoeffer, were not in the end lucky enough to survive.

It was not only that tiny minority of Quakers and others motivated by religious faith to oppose Nazism, or socialists, communists, and others motivated by political convictions, or those who by virtue of sexual orientation or for other reasons were the subject of discrimination, who held to their principles, refused to conform, and stood up against the Nazi regime or tried to alleviate its consequences for those individuals whom they could help. Others too, in far less influential positions, not

---

[55] HHL, b MS Ger 91 (137), Martha L., p. 2; see also Hans Schmitt, *Quakers and Nazis: Inner light in outer darkness* (Columbia: University of Missouri Press, 1997).
[56] Käthe Tacke, interview with Roswitha Jarman, (East) Berlin, 7 August 1985, transcript pp. 6–7. I am very grateful to Roswitha Jarman for making a copy of this and other interviews available to me.
[57] *Ibid.*, pp. 12–13.
[58] *Ibid.*, p. 7.

apparently part of any organization or group, and for no apparent personal reason whatsoever—indeed often in face of considerable risk—nevertheless were simply, as individual human beings, also prepared to do what they could to alleviate suffering. Following her husband's return from his imprisonment, Martha L. recounted that 'my husband does not talk to me about what he experienced in both concentration camps'. But he did report that on his return journey, having been released from Dachau, he did not have enough money both to get home and also to eat while on the journey; he did not even have enough money for a ticket for the fast express train, prolonging the period of hunger. While he was sitting with another released prisoner on a bench, waiting for the cheaper stopping train, according to his wife's account:

> A railway official went up to them and said: 'Well well, where do you come from, from Dachau?' When both of them said yes, he went with them into the waiting room, bought them something to eat and drink, and gave each of them 1 RM [*Reichs Mark*] as well. That was a very big thing for him to do, particularly since in Germany you get imprisoned for giving this kind of help.[59]

Such assistance on an individual basis could make a world of difference to those thus helped; but it did little even to divert, let alone destroy, the broader course on which the regime was embarked.

The experience of creeping racialization and growing violence in Nazi society was experienced rather differently by those who were younger at this time. Even within a relatively homogeneous milieu, the imposition of the new order through the means of socialization could have devastating consequences. While it tore apart what might otherwise have been a relatively cohesive group, in the longer term it also, in some sense, held them together by virtue of the challenges to which they had been exposed.

II. THE CLASS OF 1935

Hans Paasche's daughter Helga, who had lost her mother in the influenza pandemic of 1918, and who had been a mere four years old when her father was murdered in 1920, was subsequently brought up by relatives in Berlin. The secondary school which she attended in the later 1920s and early 1930s was at that time called 'Staatliche Augusta Schule'; it was formerly the Königliche Augusta Schule, with the state displacing the imperial reference in 1919. In Helga's class, very close friendships were soon forged. The story of this group of friends, and their wider school class, reflects in microcosm the forces tearing German society apart in the 1930s—and holding the generational group together, although with considerable emotional tension and physically scattered across the world, through to the deaths of the majority of them several decades later.

---

[59] HHL, b MS Ger 91 (137), Martha L., pp. 2–3.

The Augusta Schule catered particularly for well-to-do Berlin families who believed that not only their sons but even their daughters deserved to follow a classical education, with Greek and Latin, and to take the academic school-leaving examination, the *Abitur*, which gave entry to university studies. Attendance at such a school would bring with it not only the obvious consequences—academic achievements and the prospect of professional careers at a time and place when this was highly unusual for women—but also a degree of underlying self-confidence, intelligent energy and individual assertiveness in a male-dominated world. Alongside such attributes fostered by an academic, progressive education were common features of the Berlin social landscape from which many of the girls came: the notorious '*Berliner Witz*', or wit; an enjoyment of the regional Berlinese dialect (with its own verb, '*berlinern*'); a liveliness and commitment to a distinctive cultural and social life.

Beyond commonalities derived from shared social backgrounds, the school had a major impact on those who studied there in the first half of the twentieth century.[60] Helene Lange (1848–1930), one of the early leading lights of the women's movement in Imperial Germany and a constant campaigner for women's education on a par with that offered to men, spent a year teaching there, and her pedagogic ideals became something of a model for the school. Significant directors included the redoubtable Lina Mayer-Kulenkampff, who lost her job in spring 1933 because she refused to swear an oath of obedience to Hitler or to raise the swastika in the school grounds. Girls who attended often went on to take up prominent positions in their own right. Well-known alumnae included Winifried Wagner, daughter-in-law of Richard Wagner, who throughout the Nazi period ran the Bayreuth festival and was a personal friend of Adolf Hitler; and, at the other end of the political spectrum, Annemarie Renger, who after the war became a Social Democratic member of the West German Parliament (*Bundestag*) from 1953 to 1990, and not only held leading roles within her own party but was the first female president of the *Bundestag* (1972–6) and as the SPD candidate in 1979 narrowly missed becoming the first female president of the Federal Republic of Germany.[61]

The drive and initiative shared by such very different characters appeared to have been common to a large proportion of far less prominent alumnae. Even a cursory survey of those former pupils of the school, or '*ehemalige Augustanerinnen*', who kept in touch with the Old Girls' Association throughout the post-war years, reveals an extraordinarily high number who had not merely pursued a university degree but had gone on to do postgraduate degrees and were active in a very wide range of professional fields, scattered all over the world.[62] A certain shared style and outlook on life—educated in the broadest sense and valuing this education; articulate, inquisitive, humorous; proactive, determined to use one's talents and do good in

---

[60] I am very grateful to Bodo Förster, a senior teacher at the school, for letting me have a copy of his history of the school written for its 175th anniversary in September 2007.

[61] Annemarie Renger, *Ein politisches Leben* (Stuttgart: Deutsche Verlags-Anstalt, 1993).

[62] The letters to the Old Girls' Association (*Verein der ehemaligen Augustanerinnen*) are collected in the Schöneberg Heimatarchiv, Berlin.

the world—is evident in letters from former pupils from across the globe, from New York to Tel Aviv, from Switzerland to Australia, from the Federal Republic of Germany to the German Democratic Republic.

Commitment to education and learning certainly seemed to be a life-long endeavour for these women. One 90-year-old resident in a care home for the elderly in East Berlin in the later 1980s, for example, was taking pleasure in trying to teach Greek to a 21-year-old who had come to repair the hinges on her wardrobe door: as a conscientious objector to compulsory military service in the GDR, this young man had been first briefly imprisoned and then refused entry to university, but was determined to study archaeology and felt knowledge of Greek would be good preparation, despite currently having to work as a handyman undertaking repairs of all kinds.[63] Another pensioner, this time in West Germany, had always wanted to be a medical doctor in the mission field 'working like Albert Schweitzer', but had been thwarted at a crucial period in pursuing her professional goals by Hitler's policies; now, in retirement, she was able to visit 'a totally primitive hospital in Ruanda' and was trying both to give practical help in the field and to raise awareness and funding at home.[64] Many similar examples could be given from the letters of these highly educated and active alumnae. The school certainly seemed to have stamped a characteristic mark on pupils who had attended it in the 1920s and early 1930s and were still corresponding amongst each other and attending (or, fortunately for the historian, writing lengthy letters updating fellow alumnae on the details of their lives and apologizing for not being able to attend) class reunions in the 1960s, 1970s, and 1980s.

There is however another, more particular angle binding former pupils together, which has to do with the experiences of those who attended the school when the Nazis came to power, and who were subsequently scattered less by personal choice than by the exigencies of Nazi racial policy and genocide. Hans Paasche's daughter, Helga, joined the class from which a much reduced number were still able to take the *Abitur* exam in 1935. This class did not participate in the Old Girls' Association, but kept together as an extremely close informal group, meeting at regular intervals in a collective *Klassentag* (class reunion) and corresponding with each other from the early post-war years, when news started circulating about who was living where and how they had spent the war years, right through to the period of their decline and deaths in the later twentieth and even into the twenty-first century.[65] The last time all members of this group were together at school was the term before Easter 1933, after which some of them did not return to school. Among members of this group, there formed a very close set of emotively laden and generationally specific bonds, rooted in what were actually highly diverse experiences of Nazism and genocide.

---

[63] Schöneberg Heimatarchiv, Letter of Hildegard B., 27 Nov. 1987.
[64] Schöneberg Heimatarchiv, Letter of Dr Irmgard K., 16 Nov. 1979.
[65] I am extremely grateful to members of the respective families for both talking to me and allowing me to use letters and diaries held in private family archives.

Members of the group to which Helga Paasche belonged were born in 1916–17: in the midst of the Great War, and on the cusp between significant generational cohorts. Those a few years older, members of the war-youth generation who witnessed but did not actively participate in the Great War, later provided the active functionaries of Nazi Germany: their socialization through the turmoil of the Weimar Republic, and their coming to maturity at a time of rising unemployment and political instability, led many to be susceptible to claims that Germany 'needed' a strong leader; their experiences as young adults in the 1930s often served to cement their faith in the *Führer* state. Those a decade or so younger, by contrast, born from the mid-1920s to the early 1930s, were able to claim a degree of 'innocence by virtue of late birth': they disproportionately became the committed 'builders' of the two new German states founded in 1949. This particular cohort however, born in the middle years of the Great War, were not left untainted by their diverse experiences of the Third Reich; whatever they did, they could not fully escape the legacies or personal damage caused by their experiences of Nazism; they could not quite shake off questions concerning their very diverse roles and the marks left on them.

The girls in this group were in one respect typical of pre-1933 Berlin: drawn from a range of bourgeois, professional and upper-class backgrounds, the question of whether one was Jewish, partly Jewish, or Christian mattered, until January 1933, not much, if at all as far as friendships among the young people themselves were concerned (although of course such issues mattered a great deal in their families with respect to later marriage partners); and nor did parental politics, as long as there was the money to pay the school fees. Among Helga Paasche's group of close friends, and seen by her teachers as someone with 'leadership' qualities, was one Alexandra von S., whose conservative-nationalist upbringing emphasizing the 'Prussian' virtues of 'duty' and militarism, was in stark contrast to the idealistic outlook and reformist lifestyle of Helga's father Hans Paasche. Alexandra was a Prussian aristocrat related to the distinguished Boitzenburg line of von Arnims and the zu Eulenburgs; her grandfather had been a diplomat in St Petersburg on behalf of Bismarck's Germany; and she had herself been born in 1917 in the former aristocratic palace and then ministerial building owned by the royal family on Wilhelmstrasse, in the grand centre of the government quarter. Following the Revolution of 1918, the family had been forced to make way for the new president, Friedrich Ebert, and moved to the nearby Tiergarten area to live in a wing of Schloss Bellevue (a former palace which is now the seat of the President of the Federal Republic of Germany). Helga Paasche had perhaps more in common with Franziska, whose left-wing father, Alexander Schwab, had like Hans Paasche been involved in the pre-war youth movement, had been an active participant in the meeting on the Hohe Meißner in 1913, was a founding member of the Independent Social Democratic Party (USPD) in 1917, and remained very active in left-wing circles throughout the Weimar period and early years of the Third Reich. Many girls came from Jewish or mixed backgrounds, which were generally entirely irrelevant to them at the time. But massive changes were inaugurated with the accession of Hitler to the chancellorship, as 'race' and 'politics' displaced 'class' as key overriding distinctions of status.

The moment when Hitler came to power signalled instantly a massive change for the school. Annemarie Renger (who was slightly younger than the 'class of 1935', being born in October 1919 and aged thirteen when Hitler came to power) vividly recalled the change of atmosphere:

> The day when Hitler took over in power was a Monday, on which, as at the start of every week, students and the teaching staff gathered together in the school hall. On this 30th January there was a very singular atmosphere. Apparently in the morning it had already somehow leaked out that Paul von Hindenburg was going to name Adolf Hitler as Chancellor of the Reich. I had a sense of foreboding. Before the Director, Frau Dr. Mayer Kulenkampff, could start to speak, my long-term German teacher, with his NSDAP-Party badge on his collar, jumped up onto the stage and held a glowing impromptu speech about the 'Saviour of his Fatherland', which is what he thought his 'Führer' to be. And this was the very same teacher who in lessons had always talked a lot about humanism.
>
> By contrast, I think with great admiration and gratitude of Frau Dr. Mayer-Kulenkampff, who following this outpouring from the German teacher calmly went up to the microphone, wearing a simple black silk dress and read out a poem by Rainer Maria Rilke as though all this had nothing to do with her.
>
> I can't now remember if this was on the same day, but I have a very clear memory that when the Nazis wanted to raise the swastika flag in place of the black-red-gold flag, our Director refused to take down the flag of the Weimar Republic. It was not long before the school got first an acting Head and then a Director who was acceptable to the Prussian Minister for Cultural Affairs, [Bernhard] Rust. Frau Mayer-Kulenkampff was demoted to a job in another school.[66]

Mayer-Kulenkampff was in fact replaced by two strongly Nazi Directors in rapid succession, who took a far more radical line with respect to the pupils and the curriculum. Many girls were soon 'forcefully persuaded' to leave school, for both 'racial' and political reasons.

Renger came from a social democratic background: her father, Fritz Wildung, was active in the workers' sports movement and from 1907 was editor of the Workers' Gymnastics Magazine (*Arbeiter-Turnzeitung*). But like so many, he lost his job in the course of the Nazi takeover of the press and exclusion of Social Democrats from influential positions; and Renger's family was no longer able to afford the Augusta Schule school fees. Renger recalls that for other Augusta Schule girls whose families found themselves in straitened financial circumstances, a scholarship would readily have been found; but this was not the case for someone

---

[66] Annemarie Renger, *Ein politisches Leben* (Stuttgart: Deutsche Verlags-Anstalt, 1993), pp. 33–4. In an undated letter to Inge Cohn-Lampert, Renger recalled that the teacher who held 'eine glühende Rede auf Hitler' was Dr Schochow, the class teacher of the 'class of 1935' that is under particular focus here. I am very grateful to Bodo Förster for passing this on to me. Bernhard Rust's two daughters also attended this school, so that he had a personal interest in who was in charge of it and the character of the student body.

of her political background. What was perhaps even worse for her, as a young teenager at the time, were the responses of classmates:

> I had to leave the grammar school because I was refused a scholarship. We could not pay the fees. Probably they would otherwise have found some other way to make me leave the school. But I did not let myself get discouraged, not even by the way my fellow students took their leave of me. I will probably not forget their snide advice: 'So Annemarie, now you will have to wash floors nicely. You have to get a bucket of water and first sprinkle the floor with it so the dust doesn't rise.' I was fuming with rage and injured pride.[67]

Not all of Renger's fellow students were quite so harsh, however; and it was quite clear within the school that the reasons for her exclusion were primarily political. One former classmate, Gertraud S., later recalled:

> I can recall quite clearly that [Renger] had to leave school early—'for reasons of state'—. That affected me as a *c.*12- or 13-year-old schoolgirl quite closely, because our English teacher told us about her leaving with particular regret and sympathy. [She said] the reason was the social-socialist attitude of the father . . .
>
> At that time I had a class teacher who was fired with enthusiasm for National Socialism. That didn't really influence me, because I was bothered by this fantastic raving. That was the same with all the external brouhaha at the school: having to walk along the corridor with your arm raised in the Hitler greeting, etc., and loads of marching music. I also didn't like hearing Göbbels' [*sic*] voice . . . At home: just music and painting and creative writing.[68]

Renger had clearly fallen foul of the political consequences of the Nazi takeover of power for her father's employment, and hence his income, which in combination with the school's now dominant Nazi attitudes forced her out. Many more were adversely affected by the rapid translation of racism into practice. This was again either 'indirectly', as a result of what were often represented as 'purely financial' reasons—which were of course caused politically, by loss of employment following the April 7 Law for the Restoration of a Professional Civil Service; or blatantly and directly, through the proactive policies of the schools themselves.

As early as Easter 1933 and continuing through 1934, in an energetic pre-emption of exclusionary policies which only became a matter of official legislation years later, girls with a Jewish background (including not only those who were fully Jewish but also those of 'mixed descent', the so-called '*Mischlinge*') in the Augusta Schule and neighbouring schools were being forcefully eased out of school. The 'Aryan Paragraph' of the April 1933 Law for the Restoration of a Professional Civil Service had already made it clear that no person with a Jewish grandparent (even only one) would be able to take up a professional position which came under the very broad German category of state employees (*Beamten*). Given the limitations on their children's chances of university study, and the denial of future professional careers imposed by this ban—as well as, in many cases, their own immediate loss of

[67] Renger, *Ein politisches Leben*, p. 37.
[68] Letter from Gertraud S., 17 Sep. 2006, to Bodo Förster.

livelihood through being ousted from professional positions—many parents were 'persuaded' that their children 'had no future' in any event, and that it was therefore no longer worth paying school fees for the coveted school-leaving exam, the *Abitur*, if they could no longer aspire to university studies or a professional career.

The figures in the annual reports from the neighbouring Chamisso Schule, also located in the 'Bavarian quarter' of Schöneberg with its relatively high Jewish population, reveals how pupils with any kind of Jewish background were removed from school already from the very start of the Third Reich.[69] In 1933 the Chamisso Schule had 513 pupils, including 162 who were counted in a column labelled 'Jews' (31.6 per cent), with as yet no distinction between 'full' Jews and those of 'mixed descent'; by 1936, the columns in the Annual Report revealed that the school was down to 364 pupils, with only 25 'Jewish' and 11 'Jewish-mixed blood' (*jüdisch-mischblütige*) pupils remaining on roll. Of the 330 pupils remaining at this school in 1939, there were none in the 'Jewish' column, and a mere three clinging on in the '*jüdisch-mischblütige*' column. One of these three had earlier been forced out of the highly academic Augusta Schule, but was taken on eagerly and held by the neighbouring Chamisso Schule because she was a champion swimmer, capable of winning all the cups in inter-school sports competitions.[70]

Sudden departures from school could come as a shock to schoolmates who remained. Alexandra von S., who over the Easter break in 1933 was away attending her uncle's funeral at Boitzenburg, in the Brandenburg countryside outside Berlin, could hardly believe the news when she heard that one of her best friends would not be returning to the Augusta Schule on its belated reopening under the new director after Easter. As she wrote:

> But, you know, I'm shattered, I really never would have thought it! I probably always hoped you would stay at the school . . . But that now you really are at the Lettehaus [secretarial college] is simply unbelievable! As for me, which really takes second place here, I will now have to mourn away my life in school all alone . . . O-o-o-o-ooooh! Frightful,— *frightful!!!* . . . Well—but I'll just have to get used to it—Nothing will help![71]

But, as it turned out, it proved hard to sustain the innocent friendships of childhood and early adolescence under the new circumstances of Nazi Germany. Within a matter of less than a decade, when her former friend was already in exile, Alexandra was living in an area just twenty-five miles north of Auschwitz, married to a member of the Nazi civilian administration of this occupied Polish territory; and further members of the Berlin circle of young people who had played as children together in the 1920s and friends in the early 1930s were in fear of their lives and had emigrated without ever having wanted to leave their homeland, or had already been murdered.

When in December 1934 the 'class of 1935'—or rather the much shrunken group of thirteen girls who had remained in school to take the final school leaving

---

[69] Schöneberg Heimatarchiv, file entitled 'Chamisso-Schule 1900–1941'.

[70] Interview on 3 Dec. 2006 with Inge Cohn-Lampert, whose sister was the champion swimmer in the Chamisso School.

[71] Letter from Alexandra von S., 23 Apr. 1933, private family archive. I am very grateful to her son for allowing me use of these letters.

exams—finally came towards the end of their time at the Augusta Schule and were preparing to take the *Abitur*, they had to write brief autobiographical sketches, which were neatly filed alongside their teachers' reports and records of their grades. This collection provides a glimpse of what a handful of Berlin girls, born into professional and socially privileged families in the midst of the Great War, thought important, or at least what they thought should be mentioned for the purposes of being allowed to take the *Abitur*, about their lives to date and their enthusiasms and aspirations nearly two years into Nazi Germany. It also shows just how their life paths prepared them—or not—for what was yet to come.

It is striking, when reading through this collection, to notice just how many of them mentioned how they were affected by having been 'war children' (*Kriegskinder*) with respect to the Great War. Most had spent the first years of their lives in temporary accommodation, with their mother and perhaps with grandparents or other relatives, while their fathers were away in military service; several had lost their fathers in the war, while others could recall the first time they consciously 'met' their father on his return from the front or following a period as a prisoner of war. A significant proportion had experienced lengthy periods of ill-health as a child, necessitating long absences from school, or periods sent for recuperation in the country. The war and its impact was clearly sufficiently 'present' in their minds to be considered worthy of mention in these brief autobiographical essays of the mid-1930s.

They were also quite consciously young women 'caught in the middle' with respect to emancipatory trends. Virtually all mention, in one way or another, how their own well-educated, professional parents had brought them up with a love of learning and a desire for a humanistic education. Several then go on to mention what it was that they would ideally have liked to study, or what profession they would in principle have liked to follow. But several then rather sadly go on to qualify this, saying that now, as a young woman, this was no longer possible for them; so they would instead like to follow what the new regime had designated as an occupation more appropriate to women, such as baby- or child-care of some sort. What is interesting here is the way in which the recent restrictions on opportunities about which they had earlier been enthusiastic seem to have been quite simply internalized and accepted as constrained horizons and reduced aspirations.[72]

---

[72] For broader discussion of controversies over women and gender in Nazi Germany, see e.g. Gisela Bock, 'Antinatalism, maternity and paternity in National Socialist racism' in Ian Kershaw and Moshe Lewin (eds.), *Stalinism and Nazism* (Cambridge: Cambridge University Press, 1997); Claudia Koonz, *Mothers in the Fatherland* (London: Jonathan Cape, 1987); Mary Nolan, 'Work, gender and everyday life: Reflections on continuity, normality and agency in twentieth-century Germany' in Ian Kershaw and Moshe Lewin (eds.), *Stalinism and Nazism* (Cambridge: Cambridge University Press, 1997); Dagmar Reese, *Growing up Female in Nazi Germany*, trans. William Templer (University of Michigan Press, 2006; orig. 1989); Eve Rosenhaft, 'Women in modern Germany' in Gordon Martel (ed.), *Modern Germany Reconsidered* (London: Routledge, 1992); Adelheid von Saldern, 'Victims or perpetrators? Controversies about the role of women in the Nazi state' in David Crew (ed.), *Nazism and German Society, 1933–45* (London: Routledge, 1994); Jill Stephenson, *Women in Nazi Society* (London: Croom Helm, 1975); Stephenson, *The Nazi Organisation of Women* (London: Croom Helm, 1981); and Stephenson, *Women in Nazi Germany* (London: Pearson, 2001).

Most striking is, perhaps, the way in which so many of them speak about the German lands and people in an incipiently nationalist way, talking of 'Germanness' (*Deutschtum*) and the ways in which German borderlands require protection against neighbours who are portrayed as both inferior and threatening. Many speak from the personal experiences of their families and with a real sense of place, having visited some of the border regions or having family backgrounds which had been affected by the redrawing of boundaries in the Versailles settlement. This is a compelling combination of 'lived experience' and family traditions as related in the home, on the one hand, and the significations, vocabulary and aspirations of the Nazi state, on the other.

Ulrike B., for example, the daughter of a senior teacher in the school, was born in 1916 to parents who both came from Pomeranian pastors' houses 'in which Prussian tradition and understanding for German-Protestant culture as well as for humanistic education was cultivated'. She recalls that her parents' families 'had already been living for generations on this eastern German colonial territory. And even in my earliest childhood I had heard from my father about the historical development and the national significance of this area.' Her love of her Fatherland, and its eastern provinces and lost territories, had been further strengthened by school trips:

> Other class trips in recent years took us to the wonderful brick buildings in the Altmark, to East Prussia, and to the Harz area. We came to understand the singular historical and national significance of the German lands in the east that are threatened by the Poles and Lithuanians. Here, for the first time, I gained an impression of the frightful danger in which the Germans in border regions [*Grenzlanddeutschtum*] have to live, and of our duty to stand by them. In the same way we experienced the great affection and friendliness there with which they greet anyone coming from the innermost part of the Reich.

Although she was too young to remember the Great War and Revolution, she claims: 'I experienced the national renewal with full consciousness and great enthusiasm, since it was for me the first time that political developments of such incredible significance for the fate of our people had swept me up.'[73]

Many took the opportunity not merely to profess their values, but also to claim active engagement in service of the German national cause. Hildegaard H., the daughter of a lawyer, reported that:

> Right at the start of my schooldays in the Augusta School I joined the V.D.A. [Association for Germans Abroad, *Verein für das Deutschtum im Ausland*, which in 1933 was renamed the *Volksbund für das Deutschtum im Ausland*, National League for Germans Abroad]. Since already before that I had cultivated a lively interest for German communities abroad [*Auslandsdeutschtum*], this gave me the opportunity to engage in practical work. I worked a lot in the V.D.A. Later my work was made easier by many visits to the border regions. Particularly in Czechoslovakia I got to know many members of German communities abroad and could convince myself of the difficulties they experienced in these foreign countries; situated close to their mother

---

[73] Schöneberg Heimatarchiv, 'Lebenslauf der Oberprimanerin Ulrike B.', 1 Dec. 1934.

country and yet exposed without any protection to every kind of capricious action just because of a senseless drawing of the borders. In October I joined the Eastern Section [*Oststaffel*] of the V.D.A. and after that was dissolved I went over to the B.D.M. [*Bund deutscher Mädel*, the girls' section of the Hitler Youth organization].[74]

Irmtraut D., who introduces herself as the daughter of a ministerial official (*Ministerialrat*) in the Ministry for Science, Art and Education (*Ministerium für Wissenschaft, Kunst und Volksbildung*), also professes her concern for lost territories and borderlands: 'I belong to the Association for Germans Abroad. My interest in this Association had been particularly stimulated by the fact that my family on my father's side had for generations up to the World War been resident as owners of a landed estate in an area which has now been given up to Poland.'[75]

That such professions of commitment to the German national cause were not essential for permission to enter the *Abitur* exam is evident from other cases where there are no such mentions of commitment to Nazi political goals and ideology. Dorothea F., for example, the daughter of a single mother—her father had been killed by a British tank attack at Cambrai on 20 November 1917—wrote only of her love of books from an early age, her difficulties in making the transition in October 1929 'from the little town of Kreuznach to the big city' when she and her mother moved to Berlin, a city rendered attractive for her only through 'the possibility of a grammar school education', and, following a gesture towards the need to extend her 'knowledge of housework through half a year of [domestic] labour service or training on a landed estate', her long-term goal and desire to study medicine.[76]

The differences among these girls soon began to become evident, as racism was, even in this small and socially close-knit group, translated into practice in interpersonal relations. Despite her initial reaction of shock, Alexandra von S.—like so many other Germans—soon began to drift away from former friends with a Jewish background; views on the crucial events of the year in which Hitler came to power, particularly the burning of the books on Unter den Linden, just across the road from what is now the Humboldt University (at that time called the Friedrich-Wilhelms-Universität), on 10 May 1933, were simply too far apart for friendships to be sustained in the earlier carefree and un-political manner. Alexandra von S. also appears to have had to work hard on overcoming hesitations about being close friends with anyone who was in Nazi terms 'racially impure'. In a letter to one of her formerly closest friends, while continuing to assert her friendship, the nearly seventeen-year-old aristocrat sought to explain the theoretical background for a growing distance and cooling of relations—arguably precipitated by political differences, which were of course now impossible to separate from questions of 'race':

As long as the Jews in Germany lived apart, that means, consciously as a foreign people, everything went alright. But as soon as they began to mix themselves with the Germans

---

[74] Schöneberg Heimatarchiv, Hildegard H., 'Lebenslauf', 1 Dec. 1934.
[75] Schöneberg Heimatarchiv, Irmtraut D., 'Gesuch um Zulassung zur Reifeprüfung. Anlage: Lebenslauf', Berlin, 1 Dec. 1934.
[76] Schöneberg Heimatarchiv, Dorothea F., Lebenslauf.

biologically, and later even came into leadership positions, then it was all over, then they brought only trouble to our people. Democratic, materialist ideas, etc., that are in essence Jewish and not German . . . It took a Hitler to show the people again what was German and what was foreign, and that the foreign element must be removed. The conservatives always fought against Jewish ideas, but precisely only against the ideas, and did not grasp the evil by its roots. Therefore they <u>had</u> to fail. Only Hitler, who saw the right path, could be successful. If we now seek to cleanse the people from everything Jewish, then that is not directed against the individual Jew; we simply want to be German and not a mixed race.[77]

This is an extraordinarily striking example of the translation of Hitlerite ideology into everyday practice—all the more appalling because there is no evidence here of 'working towards the *Führer*' (that is, pre-emptively or proactively carrying out what people thought the *Führer* would like to see accomplished), or seeking personal advancement or gain. This is simply the unthinking wholesale adoption of an ideological outlook of biological racism, building on and expanding a pre-existing and less well-articulated climate of racism that was widely prevalent and socially enacted in many circles, with lifetime consequences for subsequent pathways and self-perceptions in each case.

These two may be unique only in the survival of the documents; their story was repeated a thousand fold in 1930s Germany. Breaking up of friendships and beginning to think of each other as 'different', no longer in the category of those with whom one could be friends, was moreover institutionally furthered by the excessively rapid and proactive translation of regime ideals into everyday practices.

What happened to other close friendships that had been forged while at school? Slowly, people with the 'wrong' background became increasingly isolated, excluded from social invitations and the round of social events associated with the Hitler Youth organizations. Inge Cohn-Lampert describes this process of social exclusion as sufficiently gradual as to be barely perceptible at first; but there then came a moment, in the later 1930s, when she suddenly realized she probably would never be able to marry: as a Christian but of 'racially mixed descent', she could marry neither a Jewish boy, nor an 'Aryan' one.[78] Others, of 'Aryan' descent but political opponents of the regime, survived through 'half-lives', outwardly conforming— making the gestures demanded of them by way of *Heil Hitler* salutes and appropriate appearances on different occasions, but inwardly sensing a vast gulf between their thoughts and their actions. Franziska, for example, whose father Alexander Schwab was active in a left-wing opposition group and was incarcerated by the Nazis from 1935 until his death in prison some eight years later, subsequently confessed that she felt guilty that she had tried to lead an outwardly 'normal' life at this time. So did many others who inwardly felt opposed to the regime, but could see little way of actively mounting any effective resistance. Some left the country entirely. Others, conforming to the new demands of the regime, settled into the lives scripted for them: doing their Reich Labour Service, marrying, taking up

---

[77] Letter from Alexandra von S., 11 Jul. 1934, private family archive; her emphasis.
[78] Interview with Inge Cohn-Lampert, 3 Dec. 2006.

positions in, for example, charity work as befitting their status as wives, and in the process losing touch with those of their former class mates who were not to be part of the racially and politically defined '*Volksgemeinschaft*'.

Some of those who were scattered across the racial ravines of Nazi Germany sought to retain some form of contact, even during the war years. Even a fleeting gesture of recognition and greeting to an old schoolmate now dressed in rags and wearing the yellow star could mean an awful lot in those circumstances. As one alumna, a Jewish survivor of the concentration camps who subsequently emigrated to the USA, wrote more than two decades later to the convenor of the Old Girls Association:

> Many thanks for sending me Renata R.'s address. I'm very pleased that I can now write to her. She happened to meet me in 1941, when I was wearing the Jewish star, and times were hard for us in Berlin, and she had the heart and the courage to greet me in a friendly way on the open street. Since at that moment I was very ragged and because of that very impolite, but because it also at that moment meant a great deal to me, I always wanted to thank her for this action, I am very grateful to you for now giving me the opportunity for this.[79]

It is a sad irony that it was the victim of racist policies who, more than two decades later, felt the need to apologize for lack of politeness in returning a greeting.

But among others, the newly introduced racial divides of the Third Reich ran sufficiently deep for a quite different trajectory to be possible.

III. THE MOBILIZATION OF THE WAR-YOUTH GENERATION AND THE FIRST HITLER YOUTH GENERATION

Once the state had channelled and made only certain kinds and directions of violence possible, there was a progressive and rapid narrowing of what voices could be heard, with the silencing of others, legitimating and instigating certain sorts of violence and seeking to disarm others. After 1933 the picture of the 'violent society' inherited from the 1920s was quite different: one side alone had a virtual monopoly on the deployment of physical force. There nevertheless continued to be tensions and strains between different factions after 1933, and even well into the wartime years, with shifts in the balance of power among different elements within the radical and conservative right, and in the character and issues involved over time.

In the early years of the Third Reich, there continued to be disputes between different elements of the judiciary and civil service—though already from April 1933 pruned of socialist and Jewish lawyers—and the new Nazi *loci* of brutish and overt violence. Even as any notion of 'decency' should have been seen to be slipping away under the guise of state-sanctioned discrimination, distinctions between 'legal' measures and 'terroristic' violence continued to be made, with a fine line

---

[79] Schöneberg Heimatarchiv, letter from Hedwig K., New York, 28 Sep. 1962.

drawn between what were held to be 'decent' and legally sanctioned acts of discrimination, stigmatization, and exclusion—which in practice amounted to robbery, degradation, and denial of human rights—and acts of overt physical violence or thuggery on the streets. Yet at the same time many educated young men, those of the war-youth generation born in the first decade of the century, were just embarking on careers within the civil service, broadly defined. Many of these saw political violence and the legal profession as perfectly compatible. It is remarkable just how many of those who later made careers in the Nazi apparatus of military occupation and genocide were undergoing legal and professional training and experiencing rapid rises in their careers in the course of the 1930s, riding on the tide of the new political wave, fostered by the new elites. For some, then, the dynamism of the Third Reich appeared to offer unprecedented opportunities for rising in a career, receiving recognition and distinctions.

Sebastian Haffner was one of the very few who could not make peace with the new regime, and, although not in any obvious category to be persecuted by the regime—of impeccable 'Aryan' descent, not homosexual, not disabled, not 'asocial', not even particularly active as far as politics was concerned—nevertheless felt an uneasy conscience however they behaved under the new circumstances.[80] Haffner himself left for Britain. But his scruples, doubts, and determination at an early stage to make no compromises in facing the challenges of the new Nazi regime were highly unusual for young up-and-coming professionals of his generation. The vast majority of those in this generation, just making career choices and entering positions of responsibility in young adulthood, simply conformed to the demands of the time and made their way through the various rungs of the career ladder. Many seamlessly switched from the radical violence of the Weimar years to the 'legal violence' entailed by service to the Nazi state, whether in civilian administration or through the newly compliant army.

One such was Udo K., who in 1938 married the former Augusta Schule pupil, Alexandra von S. Born in 1910, and growing up in the troubled Silesian borderlands with paramilitary violence all around, Udo K.'s career provided a classic example of the ways in which the Nazi regime affected the lives of those who in other times might have developed in quite different directions. Following his successful application of late 1932 for membership of the SA, building on his previous experience in the paramilitary organization of the 'Gefolgschaft' in the Silesian–Polish borderlands, in February 1933, three weeks after Hitler's appointment as chancellor, Udo K. applied to join the NSDAP, receiving the party membership number 1,9411,466.[81] By the summer of 1938 he was still a member of the SA—despite the dwindling national membership figures at this time—but

---

[80] Haffner, *Geschichte eines Deutschen*.
[81] Bundesarchiv 1050088525, letter from Udo K. to the Reichsschatzmeister der NSDAP München, Berlin, 31 Jan. 1935, claiming that 'Am 22.II.33 beantragte ich in Breslau meine Aufnahme in die NSDAP'; Bundesarchiv ZA VI 265. A. 14, Letter from Udo K, Bendzin, 4 Jan. 1941, to RMI Berlin 'Zur Ergänzung meiner Personalakten', and 'Abschrift' of an affidavit from a functionary of the Nationalsozialistischer Deutscher Studentenbund München, 15 Dec. 1932, in support of his application to join the SA. See also Ch. 3 above, pp 79–81.

his activities had definitively shifted towards the more central activities of the army and his own chosen profession as a legally trained local government official.[82] His career in the course of the 1930s was relatively typical for men of his background and generation, if perhaps somewhat accelerated in light of his relative acuity, energy and intellectual gifts, which he demonstrated in apparently exemplary service of the new state. A reference by Dr Bode, a senior government official (*Oberregierungsrat*), supporting Udo K.'s promotion in 1937 highlights what were deemed to be virtues among young civil servants of his generation, drawing attention to the close links between paramilitary, military and state service even within one person's career. Udo K. had proved himself to be 'a particularly capable civil servant';

> K. is a government civil servant [*Regierungsreferendar*] of good appearance, combining natural confidence and elegant bearing with good etiquette. He has the gift of being able to understand things quickly, has a feel for practical matters, demonstrates healthy ambition and great assiduity, and works fast. There is no doubt that he has a great interest in making a career as an administrative civil servant, yet without this preference making him one-sided. Alongside his actual professional training K. has, for years, dedicated himself with great interest to military matters, and during the period 1925–1933 was active in the border protection troops of Upper Silesia. Later he happily took up the opportunity of doing military service, so that by 1936 he was already a Lieutenant of the Reserve in the I.R.9 [Potsdam Infantry Regiment 9]. His interest in military matters has also found expression in his writings . . . He is the author of a pamphlet on 'Race and Military Law' which appeared with Kohlhammer in 1936. And on other matters too K. has occasionally written essays for publication. He is the Reich Group Organizer for mid-level government civil servants in the National Socialist League of Jurists [*Reichsgruppenverwalter für Regierungsreferendare im nationalsozialistischen Rechtswahrerbund*] and has published in the journal of the 'Youth and Law' publishing house. It should also be mentioned here that K. has belonged to the NSDAP since 22.2.33 and is also a member of the SA and here holds the post of a Senior Assault Group Leader [*Obersturmführer*].[83]

This positive evaluation of Udo K.'s ability and track record was supported by others. The *Landrat* of Teltow (a district bordering on the southern fringes of Berlin, where Udo K. had done some of his practical training), for example, 'evaluates him in words of high praise as reliable by character and naturally cut out for a leadership role, and counts him "among the best of the up-and-coming generation"'. Additionally, Udo K. had devoted his legal talents to the racial cause in a rather difficult case:

> Even in carrying out a special task that was not entirely easy, sifting material from the Foreign Office for the Cairo Jews' Case [*Kairoer Judenprozess*] on the instructions of the Reich Minister for Enlightenment and Propaganda, K. worked with great assiduity and ability as well as success.[84]

---

[82] Bundesarchiv SA / 4000002271.
[83] Bundesarchiv ZA VI 265. A. 14, Akten betr. den Regierungs-Referendar Udo K. vom 16. Oktober 1933 bis—, p. 1.
[84] *Ibid.*, p. 2.

It is worth for a moment considering what was involved in this particular demonstration of commitment to the racist cause, even (perhaps especially) within an international spotlight.

The '*Kairoer Judenprozess*' in which Udo K. had demonstrated his skills was a court case held in Egypt following accusations of antisemitism made by one Léon Castro and the 'Egyptian League for fighting antisemitism' (*Ägyptische Liga zur Bekämpfung des Antisemitismus*) against a German publication. According to Wolfgang Diewerge, the Nazi journalist covering the case, the publication in question was 'guilty' merely of factual and accurate reporting: 'The unduly large influence of Jews in Germany was demonstrated through the use of impeccable statistics' and the publication had demonstrated that Jews 'had exercised a corrosive influence on the economic and cultural life of Germany ... [and] also were beginning to show symptoms of degeneration'.[85] But the results of this legal action were by no means foreordained, so far outside Germany's borders, with the eyes of the world on the trial, which was reported on across Europe, including by *The Times* in London. A success for the Nazi cause was only pulled off by fast legal footwork and the extensive preparation of materials in Berlin to support the case, in which task Udo K. had assisted to such notable effect. According to Diewerge, the seventy-page long brief sent by the German lawyers demonstrated 'with German thoroughness and scientific precision' that 'Jews in Germany were active as parasites, that they had exerted a destructive influence on cultural life, that Jewish business morality was expressed in the crime statistics and that they finally showed symptoms of degeneration'.[86] Diewerge was of the opinion that this was decisive in the case:

> Using this analysis, the Jewish interpretation of the political and legal bases for the complaint was illuminated and opposed with scientific precision, superior knowledge and subtle humour.[87]

Yet Castro mounted a highly convincing response, which made the further turn of events even more surprising:

> In the most careful examination all possibilities of a Jewish response were thought through and ways of arguing against them worked out. Thus it was possible—and this was seen in legal circles as a sensation—for the German side to produce, within a matter of a few days, an additional piece, the so-called 'Note additionelle', which was handed over to the court and the opponent. This 'Note additionelle' was also, following the practices of large trials, printed and amounted to the impressive total of 94 pages. This piece of work too demonstrated such mental superiority on the part of the German side, and at the same time ... presented outstanding arguments for dealing with the Jewish Question ...[88]

---

[85] Wolfgang Diewerge, *Als Sonderberichterstatter zum Kairoer Judenprozeß. Gerichtlich erhärtetes Material zur Judenfrage* (München: Zentralverlag der NSDAP. Franz Eher Nachf., 1935), pp. 18–19.
[86] *Ibid.*, p. 29.
[87] *Ibid.*, p. 31.
[88] *Ibid.*, p. 53.

Whatever Udo K.'s own, possibly only modest, contribution to this legal 'sensation' might have been, given the early stage of his career, even to have received an explicit mention in this connection certainly assisted his promotion; and the fact that he assisted at all in what was clearly an explicit construction of a detailed case against what was seen as 'undue Jewish influence' in Germany suggests that Udo K. was not merely willing to support the Nazi cause, but could have had no illusions whatsoever about its intrinsically racist character. This was not, then, a case of supporting Nazism primarily for reasons of the revision of the Versailles settlement, apparently dealing with 'chaos' on the streets, or achieving a return to full employment, factors which were widely popular among many who later professed they had barely noticed evidence of racism in the 1930s or that it had played little or no role in their support for the regime.

This incident also provides ample demonstration of the fact that lawyers of this generation could readily combine deployment of their intellectual skills with offering their physical strength to the Nazi state. Udo K. was far from alone among the cohort who came to maturity in the 1930s and, more importantly, were 'culturally available' for mobilization, willing and eager to put both their minds and bodies at the service of the Nazi cause, however accompanied by momentary qualms and doubts about precisely which direction they should take. In the course of the mid- and later 1930s, Udo K. combined a rapidly rising career in the civil service with periodic stints of military training in the Potsdam Infantry Regiment Number 9—through which he met one of the girls from the Augusta Schule class, Alexandra von S., whose brother Viktor was active in the same regiment. Like so many others of his generation, Udo K. continuously oscillated between service to the Nazi state in the army and in civilian administration.

At the same time, a far more radical system of brutality and physical violence was being built up—again drawing from the war-youth generation, although from rather different elements and with rather different responsibilities in what became a division of labour between 'legal' repression and physical violence. From 1936 onwards, Himmler and his SS empire were increasingly set loose from the inherited legal system, increasingly independent, although still operating under some restraint. Such restraints only truly began to be dissolved after the start of the war in 1939, and even then there was both a stepwise progression towards cold-blooded mass murder and a degree of working in tandem with civilian administration in ways which have not as yet been adequately explicated.

Who was at the forefront of the apparatus of internal repression, charged with carrying out new state-sanctioned violence which escalated in the course of the mid to later 1930s? Here, there is a major generational divide to be observed: younger Germans were charged with locking up and controlling older Germans. Physical violence was predominantly exercised by those drawn from slightly younger cohorts than the war-youth generation: the 'first Hitler youth generation', those born during and shortly after the Great War and who were too young to remember the war but who experienced its legacies in the 1920s and were only too well aware of the crises of the late Weimar years.

Table 4.1 Analysis of *SS-Totenkopfverbände* membership by year of birth

Birth cohorts	Number	Comments
1899 and before	58	
1900–4	61	
1905–9	237	
1910–14	1,554	
1915–19	3,839	
1920–22	3,370	Of which:
		1920: 1,705
		1921: 1,286
		1922: 389

The generational aspect of the Third Reich is evident in startling clarity in the personnel of the SS groups guarding the concentration camps of the peacetime years.[89] With the expansion of Himmler's control over the repressive forces of the Third Reich in 1936 came a shift in the character of these forces. From 29 March 1936 the *SS-Wachverbände* were renamed *SS-Totenkopfverbände* on Himmler's orders. By 1938, with the escalation of violence and acquisition of new territories in Austria and the Sudetenland that year, considerable expansion of the repressive forces for the control of those imprisoned in concentration camps was planned. As Himmler put it in a speech on 8 November 1938 speech in Munich to *SS-Standarte 'Deutschland'*, clarifying Hitler's Decree of August 1938: in the next ten years the regime would 'certainly enter into as yet unheard-of conflicts'; a struggle of world views was developing in which the 'whole of the Jewry, Freemasonry, Marxists and Churches of the world' would be 'annihilated'.[90] The *SS-Totenkopfverbände* accordingly recruited predominantly young men, born during or in the first years after the Great War. Of the 9,126 men in the *SS-Totenkopfverbände* in 1938, 6,820 were born in the years 1915–1921; including the 389 born in 1922 fully 7,209 of the total of 9,119 were drawn from the 'first HJ generation'. (See Table 4.1.)

It might be argued that this striking age profile is simply an outcome of the SS recruitment policy, and of course there is an element of truth to this. Recruitment works best among those who have not yet settled into an established career pattern. But those recruited have also to be willing and 'psychologically available' for the tasks to which they are being recruited; and here the cohorts of 1915–21 stood out, not only within the organizational structure of the Third Reich, but also within the wider sphere of the exercise of violence on the streets.

[89] See further Karin Orth, *Die Konzentrationslager-SS. Sozialstrukturelle Analysen und biographische Studien* (Göttingen: Wallstein Verlag, 2000).
[90] The table and Himmler quotation in this paragraph are derived from: Klaus Drobisch and Günther Wieland, *System der NS-Konzentrationslager 1933–1939* (Berlin: Akademie Verlag, 1993), pp. 256–7, based on *Statistisches Jahrbuch 1937*, p. 51, and *Statistisches Jahrbuch 1938*, p. 79.

Young people of these cohorts were the most easily mobilized for the 'spontaneous' acts of violence which the Nazis periodically whipped up on the streets during the 1930s. But even for those who kept well away from brutality and affray on the streets, it was difficult to escape a degree of mobilization for the Nazi cause. The 'first Hitler Youth generation'—roughly, those who were teenagers in the 1930s—is often written about in terms of youth non-conformity. There were certainly significant numbers of young people who resisted all attempts by the Nazi organizations to co-opt them for the Nazi cause and who were impervious to attempts to instil Nazi ideology. Unofficial dissenting and oppositional youth groups, such as the 'Edelweiss Pirates', the Munich 'Blasen', and the Hamburg jazz fans, have received well-deserved places in history and memorialization.[91] However, viewed in terms of differences in relative support for Nazism across age cohorts, the very widespread conformity of most young people is far more striking than the dissent of a minority; and there is abundant evidence of active commitment to the Nazi cause among many young people, often with apparently very little sense of inner distance from the regime's demands, unlike those who were rather older and had already developed other positions. Even where it might be overstating matters to talk of active commitment, there is evidence of widespread conformity rooted not so much in any desire to realign oneself with newly dominant discourses and practices, but rather simply because of the absence of alternative frameworks of belief, or support for alternative patterns of behaviour. Young people were the most vulnerable, susceptible, and exposed to nazification, unless growing up in milieus which provided active and strong alternatives.

A wide range of sources, particularly those produced by left-wing opponents of Nazism who viewed the enthusiasm of the young with growing concern, repeatedly comment that young people in the 1930s were much more positive about National Socialism than those a few years older.[92] One socialist in Munich, for example, reporting to the Social Democratic Party in exile (Sopade), claimed that

> it's the young people who bring real enthusiasm into the Nazi stable . . . I would almost say: the secret of Nazism is the secret of its youth. The fellows are simply so fanatical that they believe in nothing so much as their Hitler. Sometimes it seems to me as if only a war could bring them to their senses.[93]

He went on to complain on rather different grounds about those who were already adults in the 1930s—in the process predicting rather accurately the future course of German opinion: 'they sometimes just make me sick, these whiners. Just as they

---

[91] On dissenting youth subcultures, see e.g. Detlev Peukert, *Inside Nazi Germany* (London: Batsford, 1987), and Peukert, 'Youth in the Third Reich' in Richard Bessel (ed.), *Life in the Third Reich* (Oxford: Oxford University Press, 1987); see also the discussion in Johnson, *The Nazi Terror*.

[92] I discuss some of the following examples and further evidence of youth involvement in violence in an essay on 'Changing states, changing selves: Violence and social generations in the transition from Nazism to communism' in M. Fulbrook (ed.), *Un-Civilizing Processes? Excess and Transgression in German Culture and Society: Perspectives debating with Norbert Elias* (Amsterdam: Rodopi, 2007).

[93] *Deutschland-Berichte der Sozialdemokratischen Partei Deutschlands (Sopade) 1934–1940* (Frankfurt am Main: Verlag Petra Nettelbeck und Zweitausendeins, 1980), Vol. 1, No. 2, May–June 1934, p. 118.

earlier swore at the economic bigwigs, so today they are swearing at the Nazis and tomorrow they will swear at our socialist dictatorship.'[94] Members of the left-wing resistance group, *Neu Beginnen*, were equally clear about the way young people were disproportionately supporting the Nazi cause. As one put it:

> It would be mistaken to count on any victories or successes for opposition among young people. Given the very strong power of attraction that fascism exerts on youth, as shown by the Italian example, it must by contrast be expected that young people will deliver the strongest support for the regime.[95]

Similar comments were made by a Social Democrat:

> Let us not forget that fascism does not draw its strength solely from economic conditions, but that its power lies in its ideology. We have to overcome fascism ideologically. It is clear that it is precisely the young people, [who are] the nation's strength, who are still completely caught in the fascist way of thinking.[96]

Young people appear to have internalized Nazi ideology to a higher degree than did older Germans who had prior belief systems in the light of which to assess the Nazi onslaught. While adults who were less than happy about the course of events seem to have simply withdrawn into a more-or-less sullen silence, it was the young who showed active enthusiasm. As one radical left-winger commented:

> The labour front has been brought into line as far as organization goes, but not ideologically, particularly among older people. One could say that there is rather a depoliticization, a tendency towards indifference and passivity. Fascist activism is only among the younger ones.[97]

In the view of one worker: 'Old socialists' like him 'could not be won by the Nazis; they had been brought up in the spirit of socialism and had grown old with it and they were not to be parted from it.'[98] But the situation among the young, who had known little or nothing else, was very different.

Young people were in several respects the most susceptible members of Nazi society. For one thing, simply by virtue of age they had no prior experiences and fully developed views on which to draw, which could act as a counterbalance to what they were now being offered—and were being offered everywhere, in schools, in organized activities, in their free time, and in open spaces. There were, for many young people, ever fewer alternative points of view to which they could be authoritatively exposed. The young were also structurally more readily available for mobilization by persons in authority, and hence were more likely to be actively involved in the numerous Nazi-organized 'spontaneous' acts of violence against Jews in the 1930s.[99] Reports on the growing

[94] *Deutschland-Berichte der Sozialdemokratischen Partei Deutschlands (Sopade) 1934–1940* (Frankfurt am Main: Verlag Petra Nettelbeck und Zweitausendeins, 1980), Vol. 1, No. 2, May–June 1934, p. 117.
[95] Stöver, *Berichte über die Lage in Deutschland*, pp. 65–6.
[96] *Deutschland-Berichte*, Vol. 1, April–May 1934, p. 13.
[97] Stöver, *Bericht über die Lage in Deutschland*, Nr. 6, Feb. 1934, April 1934, pp. 102–3.
[98] *Ibid.*, p. 104.
[99] See also the generational distinctions showing up in interviews decades later, in Eric Johnson and Karl-Heinz Reuband, *What We Knew: Terror, mass murder and everyday life in Nazi Germany* (London:

number of violent incidents on the streets of Berlin in the summer of 1935, for example, repeatedly point out the prevalence of young people, as on the evening when, on the Kurfürstendamm, an elderly Jew was beaten up following which the 'to some extent very young demonstrators then charged after each other through various cafés, threw over tables and chairs, and shattered windows'.[100] On occasion, the violence of youth was not even condoned, let alone instigated, by their own Hitler Youth leaders, as in other incidents in the summer of 1935:

> Since around the end of June it may be observed that, at both Hermannsplatz and Kottbusser Damm, ice cream parlours owned by Jews have been systematically attacked by Hitler Youths...On 5 July at the Bayerischer Platz around twenty youngsters [*Halbwüchsigen*] gathered around in front of an ice cream stall and started chanting 'anyone who buys from a Jew is a traitor to the Volk'. Then the flying squad [*Überfallkommando*] arrived and the youths disappeared.[101]

But on other occasions, older Nazis criticized those of their number who were not prepared to get involved as actively as youth; one was reported as saying, for example, 'that they were "cowardly dogs" and should follow the example of youth'.[102] Glancing ahead, young people were again massively involved in the violence of the 1938 November pogrom, again accompanied by widespread disapproval among adults; and the experiences of war after 1939 were also quite distinctive for those cohorts who were teenagers in the 1930s and who, if they were male, were thrown into battle from the outset of the war. By this time, they had been well trained and indeed drenched in the violent ideology and practices of Nazism, in distinctive ways not shared by any other generation at this time.

More broadly, there were not merely pressures but also incentives to increased involvement in Nazi organizations and activities, as one social democratic observer commented:

> Youth is, now as before, in support of the system: the novelty; military drills, uniform, camp life, so that the youthful community comes above home and school, that's all wonderful. Big times without danger. Many believe that they have new economic opportunities as a result of the persecution of Jews and Marxists. The more enthusiastic they become, the easier are the exams, and so the easier it is to get a position, a job. Peasant youth in the HJ and the SA are for the first time incorporated in the state. Young workers are also going along with it . . . The young people of today have never had much interest in education and reading. Now nothing much is being asked of them, quite the contrary, knowledge is being openly condemned.
>
> Parents are also involved in this. One cannot forbid a child from doing what all children are doing, one cannot refuse him the uniform that the others have. One cannot forbid it, that would be dangerous.

Hodder, 2005). Note that participation in what were often collectively organized acts of violence is not the same thing as engaging in individual denunciations, which young people were less likely to do. On the prevalence of denunciations among adults, see Gellately, *Gestapo and German Society*.

[100] Stöver (ed.), *Berichte über die Lage in Deutschland*, Nr. 16, July 1935, p. 574.
[101] *Ibid.*, p. 577.
[102] *Ibid.*, p. 575.

> Children and young people, led on by the HJ, then demand of their parents that they should be good Nazis, that they should give up Marxism, Reaction, and dealings with Jews.[103]

The pressures to join the Hitler Youth organization were considerable, even before it became compulsory. As Erna A. put it:

> The Hitler boys and girls are caught in the same vise [sic] as the adults. A few years ago many parents did not wish to have their children join. I know of cases where boys could not find jobs when they left school because they were not in the Hitler Youth. The bosses would take them but their 'cell' men would veto the decision. The boys had to show their party papers to get the job. Of course they enlisted. Their friends heard about it and they joined. Now it is compulsory and no Aryan child is not a member.[104]

Remarkably, the Hitler Youth often managed to override any moral socialization within the family.

The proactive co-option of the young, along with the increased demands on the time of adults, taking time away from family life, thus led to new tensions and strains within families, particularly where parents held different views from those in which the young were being inculcated. As Miriam A. put it, reflecting on the situation in a family she had recently visited: 'What of the proud Catholic boast that given a child until his sixth year and he was theirs forever? The Nazi appeal to adolescence had prevailed . . . There were constant conflicts, recriminations and unhappy political discussions.'[105] Inevitably, then, the pressures of the wider world led either to splits within families, or to tensions between families which succeeded, against the odds, in sustaining an alternative vantage point, and the external world in which they had to operate. As one observer, Albert D.—a medical doctor who was, as a German of Jewish background, himself increasingly excluded from the '*Volksgemeinschaft*'—put it:

> The rift which the Nazi party cut through the German people, who were still suffering badly from the consequences of the war and the peace treaty, divided them ever more deeply and ominously. These clashes even broke into the final cell, the family at home. Often worried parents told me the following: ever since you began to hear and read of nothing but politics, whether at work, in free time, on the street, in society, on posters, our family too has become politicized. In not a few families the father was organized on the left, the adult son was however a right-wing radical. So even at the dinner table it often came to quarrels. Young people—always and everywhere inclined towards the radical and new—saw in the Hitler movement the 'renewal of Germany'. Every word of calculated propaganda seemed to become their argument.[106]

Albert D. was far from the only person to comment on the ways in which young people were often willing to denounce their teachers and even their own parents as

[103] *Deutschland-Berichte*, Vol. 1, No. 2, May–June 1934, p. 117.
[104] HHL, b MS Ger 91 (3) Erna A., p. 25, English original.
[105] HHL, b MS Ger 91 (9), Miriam A., p. 78.
[106] HHL, b MS Ger 91 (54), Albert D., pp. 8–9.

'opponents of Hitler' (*Hitlergegner*). One patient even—extraordinarily, in the circumstances—found that for once the situation of Jews was in this respect enviable. As he commented to Albert D.: '"You Jews have it good, at least in your families at home you have the opportunity to talk as you like and don't need to be wary even in front of your very own children!"'[107]

Even where parents were not necessarily opposed to the regime but simply passively conformed, increasing involvement in political activities and public meetings meant that there was ever less available to children by way of a countervailing balance to the influence of authority figures in schools and youth organizations, or peer-group pressure, exposure to public propaganda and so on. This was of course exacerbated in families where there were strong political disagreements and where dissenting parents felt ever less able to speak out in front of their children. Whichever way one looks at it, family life was extremely strained; even—or perhaps especially—where families held closely together and sought to maintain some kind of alternative reality, there were enormous strains and tensions arising from the necessity of sustaining a double life. At the same time, the spread of the Hitler Youth organizations and activities (weekly activities, weekend hikes, longer camps) and the for several months all-encompassing activities in virtually compulsory Labour Service (*Arbeitsdienst*) meant that young people were ever more exposed to the offerings of the National Socialist world view. Even when they were not in any real sense convinced, they were constrained to act 'as if' they were supporters of the cause.

Elisabeth B. was dubious about the real commitment of young people to Nazism; she comments that 'young people in today's Germany are far from all as reliable as the Nazi leadership would like to think'.[108] But Elisabeth B. also suggests that many young people were simply not exposed to alternative views, materials, and ways of thinking, so tended to go along with what was expected and demanded of them; and, when they felt uncomfortable, to resort to the pleasures of oblivion provided by excessive drinking. According to one young man to whom Elisabeth B. had talked: 'At a big "comradeship evening" of the regiment it became very apparent that young people didn't want to have to think, but rather they sought, by much loud bellowing and boozing, to create the kind of atmosphere that no Nazi "uplifting celebration" could produce.'[109] This was of course the same cohort of young males who resorted to similar means of seeking to survive, by this time as soldiers, the war into which they were sent just a few years later.

It took a very determined parent to withstand the demands of school and Nazi youth organizations and provide alternative support for the children. Maria K. (born 1893), a former schoolteacher, a mother and wife of a university professor, was not at first sight a woman of strong moral opinions or religious convictions— although she had experienced some qualms when she first overcame her traditional standards of obedience to authority to go 'hamstering' after the Great War.[110] But

---

[107] *Ibid.*, p. 12.
[108] HHL, b MS Ger 91 (18), Elisabeth B., p. 11.
[109] *Ibid.*, pp. 11–10.
[110] On Maria K.'s experience of the Great War and its aftermath, see above, pp. 43, 62.

the challenges of Nazi regime served to reveal extraordinary qualities in this, at first sight, ordinary middle-class woman; and her case illustrates not only the ways in which it was possible to stand out against Nazism but also, ultimately, the potential penalties and costs of maintaining common principles of humanity in this political context. Maria K. successfully resisted having any of her sons join the Hitler Youth for most of the 1930s, until, for the youngest who had turned ten in 1937, membership finally became compulsory. Maria K. firmly resisted the cajoling comments of neighbours and relatives:

> All my relatives and acquaintances tried to argue with me: 'You'll be thrown into prison. Your husband will lose his position. You can't take this kind of responsibility, it's ridiculous to try to oppose such a movement, your sons will later only reproach you for this', and so on.[111]

Despite constant pressure, Maria K. stood firm. She decided she had to devote a considerable amount of time to her sons, to ensure that she was giving them an active alternative to the activities and worldviews being propagated through school and, via their classmates, also indirectly rubbing off from the Hitler Youth organization: she organized cycle tours, swimming and boating outings, and weekend 'philosophizing' over an extended breakfast:

> In those hours everything came out that they had learnt in school in terms of Nazi wisdom. Everything was talked through and we owe it to these peaceful, harmonious and joyful times together that none of my sons fell victim to the influence of the Nazis.[112]

Even so, the attempt to combine authentically held views at home with survival through school meant a degree of duplicity and acquiescence in school demands, which too had its costs in terms of learning to lead something of a double life and disguising one's private opinions when at school. This learning to be somewhat dishonest—a demand rooted in the attempt to survive and stay in one's home and native country until the regime blew over—was in itself experienced by Maria K. as something of a moral compromise: 'The only thing that often bothered me was whether it is right to teach children quite consciously to engage in dissimulation; since at school and on the street they obviously had to go along with things . . .'[113]

Even despite Maria K.'s best efforts to provide, very proactively, an alternative base of belief and moral compass, she noticed that when her youngest son was forcibly joined up in the Hitler Youth he was relatively soon being subtly influenced in his moral views. She managed, after three months, to withdraw him from HJ outings and 'service' activities, 'because I could see that the boy was slowly falling prey to the influence of the HJ . . . One day he came home from the HJ filled with enthusiasm . . . Theft on orders!' But she could only withdraw him from labour service with the Hitler Youth on 'health' grounds, which had

[111] HHL, b MS Ger 91 (101), Maria K., p. 8.   [112] *Ibid.*   [113] *Ibid.*, p. 8.

then to be extended to withdrawal from school attendance too: 'On the basis of a doctor's note I was able to free him from service in the Hitler Youth and but at the same time I had to take him out of school.'[114]

During the course of 1937–8 her oldest two sons were unavoidably called up in the Labour Service. Again, Maria did everything she could to support them through this by regular visits and bringing in extra food. According to her description, conditions in the Labour Service camp were terrible, including very early rising, a great deal of sport and 'national-political education' (*nationalpolitische Schulung*) in between the periods of heavy manual labour, with virtually no time or space to themselves, and inadequate food of poor quality. When Maria's second son was in camp, one of his comrades died of meningitis, while twenty-five others suffered from scarlet fever or diphtheria and had to be hospitalized.[115] It turned out that in the same camp in the previous year there had been two deaths from diphtheria and one from meningitis, and a further batch of 250 young people had been sent to the camp without any attempt at disinfection. On this occasion, Maria's husband and a couple of other parents, including a lawyer, succeeded in having the camp closed, quarantined, and disinfected.

Even for this fully 'Aryan' family, disagreement with and disapproval of the regime led to progressive social isolation. This became even more the case from the autumn of 1938, when the developments became ever more radical. As Maria put it: 'After the disappointment of Munich for us, we tried as far as possible to cut ourselves off from the outside world.'[116] Very soon, Maria K. and her family were going to find themselves even more at odds with the Nazi regime and the surrounding society that appeared to have capitulated so easily to its demands; and cutting herself off while continuing to live in Germany were no longer viable options.

Children born from, roughly, the mid- or later 1920s into the early 1930s—the '1929ers'—were the most exposed to state propaganda, the most influenced and socialized within the framework of Nazi worldviews and organizations, and had the least by way of fall-backs, alternative bases, countervailing forces on which to draw—unless, of course, they had been born into families of the 'wrong race' or very strong alternative politics and ethics. Even the variations in individual experiences and responses to the nazification of German society did not entirely override a degree of homogenization (and later sense of generational belonging) among significant numbers of those who grew up and came to maturity at this time. As it turned out in the longer term, however, it was the responses to the experience of violence in war and the structure of their opportunities after the war that most moulded the paths they took in later life. All the apparent success of Nazi attempts to influence the 1929ers at this time was blown to the winds when they discovered just how deeply they had been, as so many of them later saw it, misled and 'betrayed'.

---

[114] Ibid., pp. 8–9.   [115] *Ibid.*, p. 10.   [116] *Ibid.*

IV. 'ASHAMED TO BE GERMAN'? THE RADICALIZATION OF VIOLENCE, 1938–9

The year 1938 was a turning point, in which brutality and violence escalated, and Nazi oppression was extended dramatically, both territorially and with respect to individuals. It changed many people's lives and their views of Nazism dramatically; and in the course of this year, the divisions between generations within the Nazi '*Volksgemeinschaft*', particularly with respect to the exercise of violence, became more apparent than previously.

The *Anschluss* of Austria in March 1938 brought significant extra territory into the Third Reich, precipitated initial reactions of apparent wild enthusiasm and support among many Austrians, and unleashed a reign of terror for those Austrians who were potential opponents or racial victims of Nazism—socialists, communists, people of Jewish descent. The reactions of the population in Austria provide almost a speeded-up version of what had taken place in the 'old Reich' areas of Germany during the preceding five years: from enthusiasm and fear, accommodation and resignation, conformity and fright, support, flight, and destruction. The invasion destroyed lives and split families; and the wild flag-waving of the early weeks was soon transformed into the dull acquiescence and enactment of the demands of the Nazi regime of the following years. All these elements played a role in the later problematic cultures of repression and remembrance in post-war Austria.

On 12 March 1938 Hitler's troops marched over the Austrian border, following a day of intense politicking culminating in the enforced resignation of Austrian Chancellor Schuschnigg, whose plans for a referendum to garner support for Austria as a separate, independent state were sabotaged even before the voting could begin. The outcome of this planned referendum had not been certain and the ballot papers had been constructed to elicit the most desired answer. The voting age had also been raised to twenty-four, as one perceptive observer, Stephen J. (son of an Austrian Christian mother and a non-practising Jewish father) put it, 'in order to cut youthful elements, who form a large part of the Nazi party following, out of having a vote'.[117] But there was in the event no chance to test Austrian opinion. Hitler's machinations ensured that Nazi supporters within Austria were able to take control of the government in the preceding hours, and the *Wehrmacht* troops were able to cross the borders into Austria uncontested. For many Austrian troops, who had been ready and waiting in their barracks to defend their country from what they saw as 'invasion', this situation was at first almost unbearable. Reactions over the following days and weeks varied dramatically—providing something of the basis for contesting representations of Austria as 'Hitler's first victim' and yet as having welcomed in the Austrian-born *Führer* with hysterical demonstrations of support, waving arms and bunches of flowers as his 'invasion' turned into more of a

---

[117] HHL, b MS Ger 91 (100), Stephen J., p. 67.

triumphal procession towards Austria's capital, Vienna, which he had left before the Great War as a failed art student, twice rejected from art courses.[118]

Terror and enthusiasm were two sides of the same coin, with a fairly rapid change in the atmosphere over the coming months. Henry A. was a 27-year-old Catholic who held a post as assistant lecturer at Vienna University; he was a patriotic Austrian who also served in the Austrian army and witnessed with horror the way in which the troops were commanded not to put up any resistance to the entry of the German troops in March 1938. He also, now more to the point, had a Jewish father, and was thus considered a 'Mischling'. Following his later escape from his homeland, Henry vividly recalled (in an account written in English) the first days after Hitler's entry into Vienna:

> In town were thousands of people. Reflectors illuminated enormous red swastika-banners. Pictures of Hitler were to be seen in many windows. Nazis in Uniforms [*sic*] or similar dresses marched around and cheered police and army…Women sobbed hysterically. Children cried and yelled. Youths climbed the monuments and columns around the place and waved swastika-banners, the air rung with roar.
>
> I succeeded in finding a taxi. When I sat in the dark cab and the driver speeded up, I felt like rescued [*sic*]. I had the feeling that now I was safe. When I reached home all the doors were locked carefully. I pulled down the shades to shut myself off from the world. When I had huddled on the studio couch, tightly wrapped in a blanket, and the deep quietness of my home surrounded me, I felt relieved. There was an idea that this was the only safe place now. The first 24 hours of the Nazi regime had already caused what might be called a serious psychic restriction. This certain state of mind, feeling secure only alone, at home, possibly covered up in a dark room, was like a psychotic disease. I met hundreds of people showing these symptoms. Fright and terrified nervousness were the first two reactions of the indifferent or anti-Nazi circles of the public.[119]

Similarly, Stephen J. expressed his initial shock at hearing the initial declaration of the takeover:

> At first I was as if struck dumb. My wife burst out in tears. One moment had served to ruin my existence, all the travails of twelve years, all the suffering and toiling had been in vain. It was clear that because of my ancestry I would not be able to remain a lawyer.[120]

Stephen J. too went on to describe the scenes of mass demonstrations with waving crowds of swastikas, Hitler's speech in Vienna, and the ways in which Jews were forced to get down on their knees and scrub the streets with little brushes. By the next morning, Vienna's appearance had changed radically: 'Over night the whole country had shrouded itself in swastika flags.' Any conventional notion of 'law and order' was radically pre-empted or displaced by the new state-ordained rule of force:

---

[118] See Ian Kershaw, *Hitler: Hubris* (London: Penguin, 1998).
[119] HHL, b MS Ger 91 (4), Henry A., no pagination, excerpts retyped as 'pp. 45–50', English original.
[120] HHL, b MS Ger 91 (100). Stephen J., p. 69.

Gangs of young SA people simply went into shops and stole the money from the cash-till . . . The Nazi gangs, drunk with victory and greedy for spoils, took the law into their own hands and stole wherever they could.[121]

The experiences of Austrian Jews encapsulated within a matter of weeks and months what had unfolded far more slowly and gradually in Germany over the preceding years, and indeed soon overtook anything as yet tried out within the previous borders of the German Reich.

Many male Austrian Jews were arrested and transported to the rapidly expanded concentration camp of Dachau, experiencing for the first time the sadism and disregard for law which was so characteristic of the Nazi state. Stephen J. was among those arrested, for some considerable time imprisoned—along with former socialist members of parliament, prominent intellectuals, and many others, all of whom still had at this point some faith in the due process of law—and then sent on a train to Dachau, maltreated, taunted, and assaulted by the SS guards along the way, experiences echoed in other accounts of the time.[122] Within Dachau, intolerable living and working conditions were rendered worse by their consequences for relationships among the prisoners:

> With this sort of life, it was no wonder that the nerves of many prisoners gave out, and in the mornings on more than one occasion someone was found in the washroom who had hanged himself. The mood among the prisoners was edgy, and there was continuous quarrelling and arguing. The dangers of war produce good and firm friendship, [but] imprisonment in a concentration camp creates hatred and mistrust among the individual prisoners.[123]

A few weeks later new transports of Jews arrived, 'who had simply been caught in the street or dragged out of their flats. There was never one of these transports without several people who were already dead [on arrival].'[124] But on being moved to the equally rapidly expanding concentration camp of Buchenwald, Stephen J. realized for the first time that things could actually be even worse than in Dachau:

> We had a shock when we saw the prisoners there. They looked pale and hollow-cheeked, like ghosts . . . They moved much more slowly and paused more frequently than would ever have been possible in Dachau.[125]

Conditions of overcrowding, lack of water and food, were all much worse in Buchenwald than in Dachau, further exacerbated by what Stephen J saw as the crazy, nonsensical commands and reprisals repeatedly being carried out, such as killing 200 Jews for the shooting of one SS guard by an 'Aryan' prisoner.[126] Stephen J. summarized his experiences thus: 'we were in a madhouse, in which those who were normal were being guarded by the mad'.[127]

---

[121] HHL, b MS Ger 91 (100). Stephen J., p. 72.
[122] See also e.g. the account in HHL, b MS Ger 91 (99), Ernst J., letter of 30 May 1939 describing his trip to Dachau in 1938.
[123] HHL, b MS Ger 91 (100). Stephen J., p. 90.
[124] *Ibid.*   [125] *Ibid.*, p. 98.   [126] *Ibid.*, p. 99.   [127] *Ibid.*, p. 100.

At this stage, it was still possible for a few—very few—to survive and be released from a concentration camp. Suddenly on 15 October 1938 Stephen J. was one of only eight men (out of the then 10,000 inmates) who were released. He had to sign a form with a 'gagging clause', promising 'not to say anything about what I had seen in the camp, neither in Germany nor abroad'.[128] On his return to Vienna, his father, his wife and his stepmother were at the station to meet him—but none of them recognized him. Moreover, for him, too, the altered mood made Vienna itself almost unrecognizable:

> The Vienna that I saw again was yet again just covered with flags to mark the incorporation of the Sudeten territories. But there was nothing to be seen of the clear enthusiasm of the March days. People were groaning under the burden of the Nazi yoke . . . Vienna was a conquered city.[129]

Managing to survive the following few weeks unscathed (including a period in hiding), Stephen J. and his family succeeded in emigrating to Australia, where his account was written. Unlike many other Germans and Austrians with a Jewish background, Stephen J. was able to end his account on a note which, while registering a severe sense of loss, expulsion, and radical change, nevertheless still contained a small element of self-confidence and hope:

> Here ends the story of my life, insofar as it concerns Germany, or more specifically my homeland of Austria. I have to start again from scratch and the further course of my life lies in darkness and has not as yet gained any firm contours. First I have to apply myself to building up a material basis for existence, but the spiritual world within me is not destroyed and one day must shape my life again in some discernible way.[130]

Millions of others were not to have even this small chance of starting anew.

Even for all the violence consequent on the annexation of Austria, the vast majority of Germans seem at the time to have registered even this only as a 'peaceful foreign policy triumph'. Perhaps the enforced silence over what was really happening to those Jews who disappeared from their homes, workplaces, and streets in the following months was readily ignored by the 'Aryan' majority.

But Germans could not so easily ignore the massive outburst of public violence on the streets that erupted with the 'November pogrom' of 1938, commonly known as '*Kristallnacht*' in view of the prevalence of broken glass on the pavements as the windows of Jewish shops and businesses were smashed.[131] This was, also, the moment when generational distinctions in reactions to violence perhaps became most apparent; and when the notion of being 'ashamed to be German' first became more widely uttered.

In the preceding weeks, the German government had sought to oust Jews of Polish origin; yet Poland as of late October 1938 refused to accept them. The plight of those deported was horrendous. One German Jew whose parents had been

---

[128] *Ibid.*, p. 101.   [129] *Ibid.*, p. 103.   [130] *Ibid.*, p. 108.
[131] This term has become something of a taboo in Germany, and is now widely no longer considered 'politically correct'.

expelled kept extracts of his mother's letters recounting their experiences. The Germans had taken their papers away so they were considered 'illegals' in Poland and roughly sent back to the German border; but there they were either attacked by Germans with bloodhounds—one woman had her baby torn to shreds (*zerrissen*) by dogs—or sent back to the Polish side of the frontier where they were again refused entry as being 'illegal'.[132] Some Polish peasants had helped by providing food and coffee, but this could not continue over the long run. They were left without money, papers, or identity passes; they could not arrange a postal address to pick up money from relatives if it could even be sent; they had only the clothes they had been arrested in, which were by now drenched and turning to rags. Others in their group had been even less fortunate: 'Some of the older people have already died, since the physical and emotional strain was too much for them.' Henry I.'s parents had been trying to obtain exit visas to emigrate before this had happened, and had even already paid half of the cost of their planned travel to Shanghai, but had found no one willing or able to pay the remaining half, which they could not muster themselves; they had encountered all manner of difficulties with the visa authorities. Henry I.'s father had tried all sources of potential help, as his mother explained: 'He spoke to Professor G., who said to him that he could do nothing for Germans who had been excluded from their country. When my husband asked him if we should poison ourselves, he shrugged his shoulders and said he did not know.'[133] The sad tale ended with Henry I.'s mother knowing all too well what sort of fate would soon befall them:

> There is no other country any more that would take us. If we are not now legalized by one or another side, it is to be feared that we will be deported again—to the German border.
>   WHAT THAT MEANS...[134]

The fate of Henry I.'s family was shared by perhaps 12,000 others, including the family of Herschel Grynszpan. Born in Germany to parents who had emigrated from Poland before the Great War and had taken on German citizenship, Grynszpan was incensed by the forced expulsion and brutal treatment of his family. Lacking in any means to give them practical assistance, Grynszpan resorted to an act which was not so much one of revenge but rather of attempting to draw the world's attention to the plight of these people: at that time resident in Paris, he simply walked into the German Embassy and shot into the abdomen of an embassy official in Paris, Ernst vom Rath, who died two days later from his wounds.

This incident was used as the pretext for an already planned orgy of violence (presented as the supposedly spontaneous reaction of the German people) largely incited by Goebbels. Although Hitler gave his blessing to the pogrom, on seeing the generally disapproving public response he was quick to distance himself from any responsibility for it; others in his entourage were also highly critical of Goebbels'

---

[132] HHL, b MS Ger 91 (98), Henry I., p. 2.   [133] *Ibid.*, p. 3.   [134] *Ibid.*

tactics.[135] Nazis—often members of the SA but in plain clothes—set fire to synagogues, while police and firefighters were instructed to desist from intervention, dousing only flames which threatened nearby non-Jewish buildings. Large numbers of Jews were beaten up on the night itself and scores murdered, while tens of thousands of adult males were subsequently arrested and taken to the concentration camps of Dachau, Buchenwald, and Sachsenhausen.

The exercise of violence, and expressions of repugnance, appear to have sharply divided the generations. Thuggish behaviour on the streets was particularly prevalent and carried out in the main by youngsters in their teens and early twenties—as would be expected given the involvement of the Hitler Youth, whether in or out of uniform. But perhaps more surprising than the relatively easy mobilization of young people was the rather widespread disapproval of violence among older Germans where, for more or less the first time since Hitler came to power, the phrase 'ashamed to be German' was widely used.

There is ample contemporary evidence of the ways in which acts of physical violence on the streets met with disapproval on the part of large numbers of adult Germans. Immediate reactions of disgust included, for example, an old lady in Saxony of high social status:

> There were a lot of jeers [*Pfuirufe*] as the Nazis came past. An older lady, supposedly a Baroness, who was going for a walk with her daughters and observed these events, cried out loud: 'It's a scandal to still be a German in these circumstances'. She was taken away, kept repeating her protest, and all attempts of the daughters to silence their mother foundered on the old lady's attitude. As she was being arrested, a group of people gathered around, who were then scattered by the police, and here too there was no lack of loud and very disparaging criticism.[136]

Similarly, in Silesia, there appears to have been initial public support for the attempt of a railway official to protect an elderly Jewish woman who was being attacked by members of the Hitler Youth:

> When during the November pogrom a railway worker in Hindenburg spoke out against these shameful actions and protected an elderly Jewish woman who had been attacked by the Hitler Youth, nothing happened to him at that time. But now, for defamation of the Hitler Youth, he was sentenced to 6 months in prison. At the same time he lost his job.[137]

A few months later, in February 1939, it remained clear 'just how deeply these incidents have affected people and how they will not so soon let the National Socialists forget this'.[138] Disapproval was widespread, as many reports of the time confirmed:

> The attitude of the population is unusually uniform. The reports that were coming in to us already in the first few days after the pogrom are repeatedly confirmed: the

---

[135] See e.g. the accounts in Kershaw, *Hitler*, and Friedländer, *Nazi Germany and the Jews: The years of persecution*.
[136] *Deutschland-Berichte*, Vol. 6, February 1939, p. 225.
[137] *Ibid.*   [138] *Ibid.*, p. 213.

overwhelming majority of the German people reject the antisemitic acts of violence, and are also outraged by the current wave of robbery.[139]

Even well into the summer of 1939, as the secret reports to the German Social Democrats in exile commented: 'This action has stirred up public opinion which will be laid to rest and it has also entailed a severe loss of prestige for the regime among the German people.'[140] In his account written in 1940, Albert D. recalled how, following the events of November 1938 (in which he narrowly escaped arrest and deportation to a concentration camp), he made arrangements to leave his home and managed to hand over the remaining rental agreement to a German aristocrat who had befriended him. Albert D. quotes this friend as saying to him: '"Doctor, I assure you, after what has happened I am ashamed to be a German".'[141] Similarly, Rudolf B., a former senior lawyer in Nuremberg had, along with his wife, narrowly escaped from their first floor flat on the night of the pogrom by throwing a mattress out of the window, making a sort of rope with sheets, jumping and breaking their fall on the mattress, and running through back yards until they finally found refuge in a barn storing Christmas trees. In the dawn hours they knocked on the door of a Christian house they could trust and were told that the mob had left their house. When they returned to their home, everything had been destroyed. The same sorts of sight were to be seen in all the Jewish houses and places of work across the whole town, accompanied by numerous reports of suicides, deaths, and brutalities. Rudolf B. commented on the way the events had affected the population:

> When, on the morning after this unholy night, the population who had not been involved as members of the police or SA forces woke up and saw the destruction that had been wrought, there were consequences that the instigators had not expected. Unmistakably a deep feeling of depression and shame overcame the public. For the first time circles of the remaining population dared to come out and demonstrate their sympathy. You could hear people saying 'I'm ashamed to be a German'. I know of a teacher in a higher public education institution who, because of the destruction of flats in his housing block, called in sick to his manager and then immediately sent in his application for retirement since he no longer wanted to serve such a state.[142]

'Ashamed to be a German' was, after such widespread physical violence against the lives and property of neighbours and compatriots, a phrase heard from many adults who had previously quite readily gone along with the insidious 'hidden violence' that was a logical consequence of adopting the new norms and behaviour patterns fostered by this deeply racist regime.[143] Even so, once violence against Jews and other victims of Nazi hatred was whipped up on a far greater scale in the east in the following wartime years, such shame was no longer on the public agenda.

At this time, it was highly striking that young people constituted an exception to such feelings of shame. They were apparently the most susceptible to Nazi

---

[139] *Deutschland-Berichte*, Vol. 6, February 1939, p. 223.   [140] *Ibid.*, Vol. 6, July 1939, p. 918.
[141] HHL, b MS Ger 91 (54), Albert D., p. 40.
[142] HHL, b MS Ger 91 (28), Rudolf B., p. 44.
[143] See also David Bankier, *The Germans and the Final Solution: Public opinion under Nazism* (Oxford: Blackwell, 1992), pp. 73, 77.

propaganda and the most willing to engage in or condone violence, as contemporary reports suggest:

> There is little that is new to be said about the inflammatory propaganda against the Jews, other than that this has remained constant and despite the complete 'victory' has in no way declined. The National Socialists know that, as far as their violence against the Jews is concerned, they have the population not with but against them, and their continued hate propaganda represents a constantly renewed attempt, despite this, still to produce the desired mass mood.
>
> As for young people, the constant barrage they are subjected to in school, in the Hitler Youth, on the street, in newspapers, naturally has a strong impact. Children and young people also distinguished themselves—as the following reports repeatedly confirm—by demonstrating particular brutality in the days of the pogrom.[144]

While it was only a minority of young people who were mobilized into violence on the streets, it is nevertheless notable that they could be so mobilized, in a way that most adults, it would appear, at this time could not. In part, this may have to do with the fact that those against whom violence was being directed were—still—in a sense part of the local community, however much they may have been excluded, with much or little by way of expressions of regret, from informal social circles as well as formal organizations and institutions. To see one's next door neighbours being beaten up, their possessions ransacked, and items thrown out of windows, was still shocking for adult Germans, as was the 'wanton' waste of goods in the destruction of shop windows and looting by people on the streets. These all occasioned disapproval among adults who upheld notions of a certain degree of law and order with respect to buildings and property, and disapproved of visible violence, even if they were prepared to cut off former friendships and banish former colleagues from their social and work spheres. Young people of 'Aryan' backgrounds had by this time perhaps less by way of a sense of belonging to the same community as their compatriots of Jewish descent.

The sense of shame among adults also had to do with the sheer visibility of this physical violence, in contrast to the 'hidden violence' of the social exclusion which had been enacted, one might almost want to say, in private between consenting adults ever since 1933. One of those who had herself been affected by both sorts of violence was sharply aware of this distinction. Erna A., the 'half-Jewish' businesswoman of American origins who had already remarked on the difficulties with introduction of 'racial' categories in the classroom, had noted in the summer of 1938 that local 'Aryans' barely seemed to notice what was happening to Jews, even when they were arrested, taken to concentration camps, and ten days or so later relatives were offered their ashes. Erna A.'s explanation for this apparent indifference was that the 'Aryan' population simply did not know how bad things were for Jews because their lives were by now so segregated:

> Aryans, not in contact with Jews, had not the faintest idea of what was going on. Those who did find out were generally shocked, but could do nothing. They would harm

---

[144] *Deutschland-Berichte*, Vol. 6, p. 211.

themselves and the Jews even more. That is one of the important reasons for keeping Aryans segregated from the Jews.[145]

Erna A. was herself injured while her store was smashed up in the November pogrom; as she pointed out, it was accomplished not by young thugs or hooligans, but by men drawn from the war-youth generation, 'all very well dressed in civilian clothes, between twenty-five and thirty-five years old—not riffraff off the streets'.[146] The owner of a neighbouring store, 'a very nice old Jewish gentleman', died three days later as a result of the violent attack on his premises. In the following days, Erna A. commented:

> For the first time I heard open criticism. The people were shocked and disgusted. Before that if they had no contact with Jews, they thought that they were being treated well; they saw them on the streets, in their stores. Some even thought that they were being treated with too much consideration. Now, their eyes were opened. If they made a remark, in public, they were arrested. You could hear more whispering than formerly.[147]

Somewhat later, Erna A. was shocked by the appearance of those Jews who returned from periods of incarceration, clearly having gone through experiences comparable to those of Stephen J., but unwilling—since they had not escaped from Germany to a place where they could speak or write freely about their experiences—to break their vow of silence for fear of the consequences. Erna A. described people returning from what she called 'Weimar' (Buchenwald):

> I could never find out what happened to them there. It must beggar all description. No one would tell me about it. They were not allowed to talk as it was. When they were discharged, they had to sign a paper on which was written that they would tell nothing of what had happened; they would state that they had just been to a health resort (*waren in einem Luftkurort*), otherwise, if it were found out that they had talked, they would be sent back to the concentration camp, never to be released. While in Germany, none of them said a word, just perhaps a remark dropped here or there. You could easily put two and two together, especially when you saw them—pale, a frightened look in their eyes, shorn heads, and hands and face usually swollen and sore by frostbite.[148]

For Erna A. and so many others, the events of November 1938 formed something of a turning point. Soon, she admits, she was 'on the brink of a nervous break-down'. But, with much difficulty about her passport, her papers, her company, her house, her property, her 'fully Jewish' daughter (having three Jewish grandparents), her passage, her tickets, Erna A. finally made it back to her native USA on 27 January 1939—six years to the day before the liberation of Auschwitz, a phenomenon as yet to come, and on a scale of violence and murder as yet undreamt of.[149] The nightmare seemed already, to people such as Erna A. and Stephen J., writing their autobiographical reflections in 1940, bad enough.

---

[145] HHL, b MS Ger 91 (3), Erna A., p. 42, English original.   [146] *Ibid.*, p. 57.
[147] *Ibid.*, pp. 59, 61.   [148] *Ibid.*, p. 62.   [149] *Ibid.*, p. 71.

The 1929ers were not the youths of the first Hitler Youth generation who were involved in acts of violence; they were a few years younger, still children or only just teenagers at this time. They often recall a sense of bafflement at witnessing these scenes of violence.[150] Fritz E., for example, was born in 1928 and was by 1938 an enthusiastic member of the younger children's section of the Hitler Youth, the *Jungvolk*. He later recalled the deep impression these events made on him as a child: 'as for me, what, what still looms very large in my memory, that was the Night of Broken Glass [*Kristallnacht*]'. But as a child he had been particular deeply impressed for what might seem a relatively trivial reason:

> There was in Teltow a shoe shop, where the owner was a Jew, and there all the shoes, brand new shoe boxes, just as they were, thrown onto the street, the windows of the shop were broken in, and the shoes, this heap of shoes with absolutely new shoes, was set on fire, petrol poured over it and set on fire. And we youngsters found that really terrible, well for us that really—the new shoes there!, and then I went over and pulled out a pair of shoes for myself, that I wanted to have, that weren't yet burnt, and then an SS man, or an SA man, hit my fingers and said, a German boy does not take things from a Jew and then threw the shoes back in the fire. That really was for me—well, that I still remember today, that he took the shoes away from me and then I cried. I was after all a child. I cried. The lovely shoes so brand new and they are throwing them into the fire because it, because it was from the Jew, and that I could not understand.[151]

Generally brought up to believe in the Nazi cause as something essentially good, the violence nevertheless shocked the 1929ers at an age where they were both impressionable and yet at the same time confused and effectively powerless. But it is notable that, whatever their initial reactions, they were nevertheless urged to conform to the regime ideals of 'a German child' who would 'take nothing from a Jew'.

If older Germans were 'ashamed', they also often seem to have felt that there was very little they could do about the situation. It was only very few among those who were unaffected personally by the Nazi attacks who had the courage to try to aid their Jewish fellow citizens. Maria K., who had earlier tried so hard to insulate her children from the influence of Hitler Youth, now found that not only she but also her sons, at first quite independently of each other, had come to the assistance of local Jewish shopkeepers whose stores had been ransacked.[152] On 10 November, as news reached them of two of Bonn's synagogues going up in flames, she had taken possession of a manuscript brought to her by the wife of one her husband's Jewish colleagues for safe-keeping. One of her sons rushed off to help a Jewish watchmaker's wife hide the valuables from their store, and then went to perform similar services for the Jewish owner of a chocolate shop. Over the following days and weeks, Maria and her sons helped these shopkeepers by secretly selling their wares for them and smuggling the money back to them, so that they still had some means

---

[150] See also, for generational differences in patterns of memory, Johnson, *Nazi Terror,* p. 257.
[151] Fritz E. (1928), interview, summer 2005.
[152] HHL, b MS Ger 91 (101), Maria K.

of livelihood. But on one of her visits, along with her eldest son, they were caught by the police.

Maria's husband was immediately dismissed from his university chair; her son, at that time a music student, was expelled from his university place; their house was attacked, and windows broken. On the street outside the house was written 'Traitor to the People! Friend of the Jews!' As German commandos approached with a car, Maria made a rapid escape on her bicycle, since, as she put it in her account written a little over a year later: 'I did not want to be beaten to death in the sight of my children and I was also, after all, just a danger for my family.'[153] For a time she was protected by nuns, who kept her in their convent well out of reach or sight; eventually she felt it was safe to return home again. But Maria was now given clear 'professional advice' that there was really only one way out for her, if she cared at all about her family: in January 1939 she was advised by a neurologist that the whole family was being endangered by her sheer existence:

> Particularly important in this whole period was a visit in January 1939 from a well-known neurologist, who as Reich Training Manager was knowledgeable about the Jewish Question. While we were alone over the course of two afternoons he told me what would happen to me and my family, according to the motto 'Jews and friends of Jews must be eradicated' [*ausgerottet*]. 'We eradicate friends of Jews and all their progeny.' Then he said that I was not to be saved, but my family might be. When I asked him what I should do, in answer he told me several stories in which the woman committed suicide and thus saved her family . . .

At this point the doctor gave Maria a prescription for Veronal, a barbiturate at that time often prescribed for insomnia but which in higher doses is fatal, and she went through one of the lowest points in her life before coming to a decision:

> I carried the Veronal around with me for several days but then I decided not to die but rather to try to flee abroad <u>with</u> my family.[154]

Only three colleagues visited Maria and her family during the four months they remained in Germany after the events of November 1938. But by a variety of routes the entire family managed, in different ways, to leave Germany, and on 2 April 1939 they left the European continent for Britain. Maria was a woman of no great religious or political convictions, but had steadfastly sought to maintain her own sense of morality throughout the 1930s; now for her sympathy with fellow Germans in times of trouble, she too had finally to leave her homeland.

Cases such as that of Maria are very rare. More representative was the comment of the wife of one of Maria's husband's colleagues, explaining why she was unable to visit or support Maria: 'It's not cowardice, we're just recognizing the way things are.'[155] Depressingly standard, too, were the responses of the university authorities. In expelling Maria's son, the disciplinary committee set up by his university explained that:

---

[153] HHL, b MS Ger 91 (101), Maria K., p. 11.   [154] *Ibid.*, pp. 11–12.   [155] *Ibid.*, p. 12.

the conduct of the student [is] thoroughly reprehensible. Because he thought it right after the well-known incidents to take himself into a Jewish shop, he has massively compromised the reputation and dignity of the university and thus contravened his academic duties.[156]

Nor were university colleagues any kinder to Maria's husband when he lost his university chair. As a former colleague from another university put it, perhaps not unkindly in intention but highly revealing of the widespread capitulation of the intelligentsia in face of the brute force of Nazism:

We younger colleagues all regret the fact that, because of the conduct of your lady wife, which was against all instincts, you have been denied an honourable departure from the university.[157]

There was merely one, tellingly anonymous, letter of support to Maria, which she received on 20 November 1938:

My dear lady,
Please allow me to express my heartfelt admiration for your magnanimous and courageous deed. All decent people would have liked to have done the same, but we lack the courage, as demonstrated by this letter with disguised handwriting and without signature.[158]

Some individuals were clearly deeply troubled by more than just the smashing of property on the night itself; but by this time they hardly dared to make themselves known and the consequences even for registering sympathy could be severe.

One of the oddest aspects of the November pogrom and its after-effects, however, is the way in which some adults seem to have failed even to register what was going on, let alone reflect explicitly on it. One searches in vain for any mention of the November pogrom in the diaries of the highly intelligent and well-educated Thea L. (born 1907), for example, who in November 1938 was back working in a medical clinic in Vienna, where she had previously studied medicine. Extremely lonely and dissatisfied with her life, Thea L. confided her many miseries to her diary; the entries of November 1938 all circle around her own problems and relationships, with no mention whatsoever of *Kristallnacht* or antisemitism or anything else in the wider social and political world. Her entry of 28 November 1938 is relatively typical:

I am restless, without happiness or friends. Work does not satisfy me or fulfil me. My inner loneliness drives me into infatuation with P. One cannot live by letters alone. My aggressive vivacity towards P. is loathsome even to me.[159]

Some relatively apolitical adults thus seem to form something of an exception in terms of the way in which they seem to have failed to register the enormity of the

---

[156] *Ibid.*, Appendix p. 2.
[157] *Ibid.*, Appendix p. 3, letter of 23 Nov. 1938 from Prof H., Göttingen.
[158] *Ibid.*, Appendix.
[159] Kempowski-BIO 2918, I-II, Diaries of Dr med. Thea L. (1907–90), entry of 28 Nov. 1938.

violence which was so publicly fomented and orchestrated that night—or, in retrospect, they play down their own perceptions of the time, in order to account for their continued support for Nazism.

In many accounts of committed Nazis too, there is little or no mention of *Kristallnacht*. It is as though it either never happened; or it did not impinge on their consciousness at the time, so they could be 'forgiven' for being unaware of the darker side of Nazism at this time; or they simply were oblivious to the sufferings of those they had already excluded from their moral universe as creatures for whom there need be no compassion. Ruth L., for example, who had earlier been so impressed by the Nazi use of violence to impose, as she saw it, law and order against the 'primitive violence' of the communists, makes no mention of *Kristallnacht*, nor indeed of the Nuremberg Laws or other major steps in the progressive antisemitic measures of the later 1930s, which she appears barely to have noticed.[160] In the case of Ruth L., perhaps the increasing segregation between the racially excluded and the now dominant '*Volksgemeinschaft*' could be held up as an excuse for her failing to register the events of November 1938, possibly compounded by living at some distance from any Jewish synagogues or affected communities—although even so, the general outcry and the official publicity surrounding the allegedly spontaneous 'actions' following vom Rath's death at the hands of a young Polish Jew in Paris render such an explanation implausible.

There is a similarly odd absence of full memory of the November pogrom in the memoirs of Udo K., whose later self-representations throw interesting light on the ways in which it was possible for members of his generation—the war-youth generation—to see their support to the system as in some sense justified, despite all that was going on all around them and despite the policies they were themselves upholding and enacting.[161] In September 1938 he had married Alexandra von S., who had left the Augusta Schule following her *Abitur* exam in 1935. By November 1938, he was an up-and-coming civil servant assisting in the administration of the newly occupied Sudetenland, based in the town of Aussig (now Usti nad Labem). Key to the occupation of this area—as in Austria earlier in the year—was the introduction, very rapidly, of Nazi policies against Jews.[162] Yet Udo appears here—as did so many other 'ordinary Nazis'—to have made a distinction between what were seen as in some sense 'legitimate' policies of conquest, occupation, repression, and exclusion, and more radical, sporadic acts of visible physical violence. Thus while on the one hand assisting in effecting racial policies in every area of life, on the other hand Udo subsequently distanced himself from support for, and to some considerable degree even any knowledge of, the pogrom of November 1938. In his memoirs written in 1980—by which time he must clearly have known far more of what the Nazi invasion and occupation of Austria and the Sudetenland had meant

---

[160] HHL, b MS Ger 91 (128), Ruth L. See also Ch. 3 above, pp. 84–6.

[161] For later developments in more detail, see Fulbrook, *A Small Town Near Auschwitz: Ordinary Nazis and the Holocaust* (Oxford: Oxford University Press, 2012).

[162] See generally Jörg Osterloh, *Nationalsozialistische Judenverfolgung im Reichsgau Sudetenland 1938–1945* (München: R. Oldenbourg Verlag, 2006).

for Jews, socialists, and others who were subjected to Nazi brutality, torture, enforced emigration or death—Udo seeks to convey a sense of how he felt at the time. He comments that 'the foreign policy successes of 1938 . . . conveyed the feeling that Hitler had after all done an enormous amount for the German people, which was also recognized abroad' (arguably illustrating continuing assumptions about both the existence, and the intrinsic value, of the 'German *Volk*', no matter at what cost to those excluded from this concept).[163] Reflecting more broadly on the Nazi 'successes' of the 1930s—not only in foreign policy, but also in the reduction of unemployment—Udo also recalls that '[a]part from the gutter press that was not to be taken seriously (*Der Stürmer*, produced by Julius Streicher, who was soon to fall into disgrace), as an outsider one noticed relatively little by way of antisemitic agitation'.[164] Such successes were only marred by the 'night of broken glass': 'The night from 8 to 9 November 1938 dealt a major blow to all such reflections!'[165] These juxtapositions are worthy of further reflection.

Udo K. claimed in his memoirs that the events of 9 November 1938 were dreadful. His wife, Alexandra, had allegedly been driven by taxi through Berlin's Friedrichstrasse shortly after *Kristallnacht*, and had emitted the cry of 'Oh my God!', whereupon she and the taxi driver—who had supposedly turned around 'with a serious expression on his face' and remarked, presumably with heavy irony, 'yes, yes, we Germans are the foremost cultural nation on earth!'—had exchanged glances and 'understood' each other. This was supposedly a turning point for Udo (who was, we should remember, by now a relatively long-standing member of both the SA and the NSDAP):

> And what one then heard from all round Germany was so catastrophic that you had to give up hope of any improvement in conditions. So whoever had not already registered this on 30 June 1934 [the 'night of the long knives' against the SA]: on 9 November 1938 there was nothing more to be done to whitewash the image of this state.

The only resort now, according to Udo K. in his memoirs, was to turn to the army: 'This was the only source of power that appeared to us to be capable of providing any redress. What an illusion!'[166] We see here already the typical pattern of a cautionary tale to indicate distance, and an appeal to what might be seen as the 'acceptable illusion' of retreat to the supposed 'decency' of the army, a topos repeated many times later in Udo's account of life under Nazism.

At the same time, however, Udo claimed that he personally had witnessed nothing of *Kristallnacht* in Aussig, a claim accompanied by a small concession to the possibility of psychologically beneficial failings of memory:

> I cannot remember anything at all as far as my own personal experience is concerned. I don't think or believe that the Jewish synagogue in Aussig was set on fire. It would be a bad case of repression if it turned out that this was indeed the case.[167]

---

[163] Archiv des Landesverband Rheinland (LVR), Nr. I-208: Udo K., *Erlebt–Überlebt*, p. 132a.
[164] *Ibid.*, p. 102.   [165] *Ibid.*, p. 132a.   [166] *Ibid.*   [167] *Ibid.*

What did in fact happen in Aussig on the night of the November pogrom? On closer inspection, Udo's story certainly requires some amendment.

The spacious and fairly new Aussig synagogue, built in 1880 and extended in the early twentieth century, was indeed set on fire on 9 November 1938. While the inside was entirely destroyed, including the holy scrolls and other objects, the walls, windows and roof were damaged but remained standing, witness to the Nazi-instigated atrocity. The Nazi-run municipal authorities duly complained to the Jewish religious community that: 'The roof which was destroyed by the heat of the fire and the broken windows, as well as the façade which was in part blackened by the smoke, form an eyesore not only for the immediate surroundings but also for the image of this part of the city.'[168] The organ, which had been purchased at the beginning of the twentieth century when the synagogue was extended, was then destroyed by the Nazis at the end of December 1938, and the outer shell of the building was handed over to a butcher for a sausage-production workshop and butcher's staff premises—presumably in deliberate affront to Jewish sensitivities.[169] In towns in the surrounding area for which Aussig was the administrative centre, it was—as elsewhere in the Reich—generally only those synagogues which might, if set ablaze, present a fire risk for neighbouring buildings which were spared from destruction. Again, as elsewhere in the Reich, the destruction was met with widespread popular disapproval, as noted, for example, by an anonymous writer for the émigré newspaper *Die Weltbühne*:

> It can be said without exaggeration that the ninth of November was not a day of success for the Nazis. The pogroms contributed significantly to driving forwards a process of disillusionment and disenchantment among the Sudeten German population. It is characteristic of the mood that in a gathering of tradespeople from Aussig the phrase was heard: 'Preferably more Jews and fewer taxes!'[170]

The erasure of any memory of personal exposure to these events, while acknowledging indirect knowledge and registering distance and personal distaste, on the part of a civil servant who was in the thick of administration of the debris, both physical and human, of Nazi policies of destruction, is not entirely plausible. Far from being overlooked, the events were actively monitored by the *Landrat*'s office in which Udo K. then worked. In February 1939, the Aussig *Landrat*'s office produced a list of figures, reporting that 'in the town of Aussig the Jewish temple was burned down or rather annihilated [*vernichtet*]'.[171] Oddly, it may be that this report was produced in a rather specific context which Udo K. does remember in some considerable detail, that of an official visitation from an inspection team; but whether or not it was for this particular occasion, it seems likely that very little of

---

[168] Quoted in Osterloh, *Nationalsozialistische Judenverfolgung im Reichsgau Sudetenland 1938–1945*, p. 212.

[169] <http://www.martinkrenn.net/projects/49.htm>, accessed on 20 Apr. 2008.

[170] Quoted in Osterloh, *Nationalsozialistische Judenverfolgung im Reichsgau Sudetenland*, p. 220.

[171] Quoted *Ibid.*, p. 213. See also the collection of documents in *Intoleranz: Tschechen, Deutsche und Juden in Aussig und Umgebung 1938–1948. Edition der Dokumente aus den Beständen des Archivs der Stadt Aussig*, 1998.

substance could have escaped the attention of these assiduous local government officials:

> The whole morning long the Landrat, I and the senior officials in the office were examined, files were presented for inspection, figures made available. At that time the administration was held on a very tight rein.[172]

And Udo can barely have overlooked the main tasks of the *Landrat*'s office over the following weeks, as a census was taken; registers of births, marriages, and deaths seized and collated; and the population monitored and divided into Jews, half-Jews, even quarter-Jews, and non-Jews, for treatment accordingly.[173] This was an exercise that was to be repeated in every succeeding occupation, including the Warthegau and Eastern Upper Silesia—with, ultimately, murderous consequences.

It appears, then, that it was possible for an intelligent Nazi civil servant to continue the business of racist administration as usual, while bracketing off the immediately visible signs of physical violence and ignoring the wider context and consequences of the administration of Nazi policies on the ground. It also appears to have been possible, at this stage, to have continued working with a strong sense of duty to a state the leadership of which had already visibly stepped beyond the limits of civilized conduct. A sense of 'inner decency' could, on this view, be preserved by distancing oneself from visible acts of physical violence while continuing to go through the outward motions of the state service that kept the regime functioning.

Others at this time had perhaps a far greater awareness of both the deadly nature of the regime and the general character of what was about to come—particularly those who were being persecuted and seeking, with increasingly difficulty, to flee for their lives. This was true not only across the great divides by which German society was now riven but also, in microcosm, in the little world of the Augusta Schule class of 1935, which had but a few years earlier seemed socially and culturally such a homogeneous group. Helga Paasche, the 'racially mixed' daughter of Hans Paasche and his Jewish wife Ellen, had by now fled to Mexico; many of her relatives on the Jewish side of the family were in Palestine.[174] A handful of others from the Augusta Schule too had gone into exile in the USA, the UK, or Switzerland; and one had been incarcerated, along with her partner, for left-wing political activities in opposition to the Nazi regime. Others who were internally opposed to the regime gritted their teeth and sought to live through it as best they could, as in the case of Franziska, whose father, Alexander Schwab, a former colleague of Hans Paasche in the pre-1914 youth movement, was by now in prison for his political activities. Within a matter of years he too would have died in imprisonment.[175]

---

[172] Archiv des Landesverband Rheinland (LVR), Nr. I-208: Udo K., *Erlebt—Überlebt*, pp. 130–1.

[173] See Osterloh, *Nationalsozialistische Judenverfolgung im Reichsgau Sudetenland*, pp. 231–51.

[174] I am very grateful for this information received by personal communication from a distant relative of Ellen Paasche by marriage, who was surprisingly present in the audience when I gave a lecture on this topic in Paris in October 2009.

[175] Based on personal letters; I am grateful to the respective families. It is likely that the majority of these young women from bourgeois and professional backgrounds, whom I have not discussed

The atmosphere perhaps changed most rapidly and dramatically in Austria, even within the first six months after having become part of the expanded German Reich. Henry A., who had been so shocked by the widespread flag-waving and apparent enthusiasm of his fellow Austrians at the entry of Hitler in March, noted how rapidly the atmosphere had changed within a matter of weeks:

> It was tragicomic to watch how everybody tried to change and to adapt to the situation...A muddy flood of hypocrisy, lie [*sic*] deceit and falsehood drowned every decent feeling [here spelt 'felling'] and behind all this was pale fright...[176]

Henry himself barely dared make notes in his diary:

> The leaves of diary [*sic*] of these days are blank. Who dared to make a note concerning general ideas? A few sentences express the pain of these days: 'Constricted. Bound up in oneself and struck dumb in self-contradictory experiences. Wanting to make a reckoning with oneself at the moment as painful as the most frightful overcoming [of this urge]. One wrestles with staying silent...'
> Even today I find it bold that I dared to write down these words.[177]

Oddly, given his own difficult situation as a 'Mischling' and that of the fully Jewish members of his immediate family, Henry was acutely perceptive about the mindset of fellow Austrians who were opposed to Nazism but not threatened on 'racial' grounds:

> It is hard to recollect or to describe this pandemonium of psychic confusion and subversive trends. The conflicts arose everywhere. They split families, parted lovers, and really made it difficult or even impossible to differ [*sic*] between right or wrong ...But the conditions made it impossible to decide, more impossible to carry out. There was the horror of being arrested, tortured or killed; there was the general hopelessness in social life and in professional regards. One was denied the basic suppositions of existence, one was eliminated as a human being. The most original forms of the struggle for existence revived. It was no more a question of honest or dishonest, of morally allowed or forbidden, of right or wrong; it was the very 'to be or not to be' that was at stake.[178]

Henry A. continued:

> Some people actually were at their wit's end. (This refers not only to Jews but to all who were not actually Nazis.) Many developed a certain dull rigidity which had something definitely dis-normal. For hours they sat and stared just into a corner, they had stopped worrying. 'I do not care any more. No matter what happens, I am through...' a friend said...A detailed description of the inner discussions every single one of us

explicitly here, simply conformed and went along with the new society, much like their aristocratic schoolmate Alexandra, while also distancing themselves from the physical thuggery of those Nazis who were in any case deemed to be far lower in the social spectrum.

[176] HHL, b MS Ger 91 (4), Henry A., pp. 52–3, English original, except for the embedded quotation which was in German.

[177] *Ibid.* Where I have typed 'pain', the word was actually spelt 'apin'; I assume this was simply a typographical error.

[178] *Ibid.*, p. 62.

went through, could fill pages . . . But I only want to emphasise that the average citizen, the indifferent, the less persecuted non-Aryans and similar large groups suffered more psychically than in any other respect.[179]

With help from some of his 'Aryan' former colleagues in the army, Henry A. managed to obtain the relevant emigration papers, just before 9 November 1938. This, to him, seemed like the last straw for both Jews and non-Jews alike:

> Just when I felt thankful for the serious comradeship of my former superiors this positive impression . . . was once more—and finally—dimmed by the horrifying happenings of those November days after the killing of Herr von Rath in Paris . . . A government under the regime of which such events are possible, not to speak of one which favors such atrocities, is sentenced from whichever angle one may look . . . I did not try to see more of the terror than I had to see. For a last time I went through all the psychic torture, the nervous shock of a terrified public. I will never forget the general sad expressions the pale faces showed. Everybody seemed concerned. Strange how brutality causes cast-down feelings even in those not directly concerned.[180]

But these feelings were shared only by those who were not in a position to affect how things would develop. Power lay elsewhere.

Not only those who were persecuted but other Nazis too had a better sense of the character and future of the regime than Udo K. later professed to have had, as did the wider public; Hitler's views were, after all, no secret, and some of his wilder goals were even turned into the status of a repeated 'prophecy', as was most notably the case with his January 1939 Reichstag speech announcing that any future war would bring about the 'extermination' of the 'Jewish race'. Wilhelm B., an infinitely less well-educated person than Udo K., and a relatively insignificant cog in the party machine, summarized in his diaries in the winter of 1938–9 where he saw Germany going. Looking back on the momentous events of the past years and his own life and role in the future, he commented that 1938 had been:

> The greatest year in history for Germany ever. All comparisons, all other times, pale in comparison with the year of 1938.
>
> I am glad that my healthy instincts led me in the right direction, so that I could help in leading this march into such a beautiful future. I am also glad, however, that the great God gave me gifts that, after the battles in the trenches and the street, as well as the speaker's platform in the times of struggle [*Kampfzeit*], also charged me with working towards the carrying out of the inner revolution.[181]

A month later, as Wilhelm B. looked forward to the future at the start of 1939, he commented, presciently:

> If 1938 was the great historical turning point and year of harvesting, so we are grateful for destiny. Many people believe that now there will be peace in the German lands. They will find they are mistaken. This generation will not reach this goal for a long

---

[179] *Ibid.*, pp. 65–7.   [180] *Ibid.*, p. 71.
[181] Kempowski-BIO, 4842 / 1 + 2, Wilhelm B., (1896–1982), entry of 10 Dec. 1938, fol. 53.

time yet, even the next generation not yet, perhaps not even in a hundred years. Greater Germany is ridiculously small in comparison with the strength beaming from its manhood . . . So new tasks lie before us. 1939 will therefore have to bring preparations in order to extend our currently too cramped space towards the east.[182]

In the diary of this insignificant Nazi, representative of probably only a small minority in the 1930s, the rantings of the national leader were faithfully reproduced as though they were his own thoughts. But while most adult Germans had arguably only conformed or partially supported Hitler's policies to date—maintaining their distance or expressing reservations when they were adversely affected, paying their dues where they could not avoid this, taking opportunities where these were presented if the personal costs were not too great, or suffering the consequences for seeking to uphold a sense of personal integrity against the grain—the situation would be very different with the coming of the war that was so inevitably built into Hitler's cause.

By 1939, vast numbers of Germany's Jewish population had fled for other shores; many non-Jewish Germans had been sentenced for 'political' offences, or incarcerated without trial. The character of the regime was not lost on them, nor on the millions of others in less obvious opposition but fearful of the consequences of nonconformist behaviour, such as those who knew but failed to support Maria K. or engage in comparable acts of kindness and support to their Jewish neighbours. At the same time, terror was being exported by apparently more traditional and quasi-legalistic means. The classic civil servant's separation between the 'unacceptable' face of wild terror, as evidenced in the events of the night of 9–10 November 1938, and the planned terror of invasion and occupation of foreign territory allowed members of the war-youth generation to march into and administer new areas of Europe on Nazi racial lines. Following the Munich Conference of September 1938, the expansion of the German Reich into first the Sudetenland and, the following spring, Bohemia and Moravia, inaugurated, the following autumn when the Allies finally took a firm stance with respect to Poland, what was to become the Second World War.

V. 'ORDINARY NAZIS' AND THE SOCIAL SELF IN THE LATE 1930s

A mere six years of Nazi rule had dramatically transformed not only the character of state and social organization in Germany, but also the nature of informal social relations, and hence the ways in which people constructed their sense of self. New distinctions had been introduced, creating chasms where previously there had been only minimal fault lines; suspicions, fears, enthusiasms, and commitments had turned Germans into sharply different directions. While the development of Nazi policies and their practical impact have been well and frequently

---

[182] *Ibid.*, entry of 11 Jan. 1939.

documented, it is far harder, for all sorts of reasons, to assess the ways in which these developments affected a sense of self. There can be no unmediated means of accessing this; but self-representations at the time and later, as well as the depictions of social context in autobiographical accounts, provide some glimpses and subjective insights into quite how much had changed, what compromises and constructions had developed, over this short period of time in which so much had happened.

Gradually, during the period since 1933, people had learned to form distinctions between what they saw as their 'private' and hence presumably 'authentic' selves, and their public behaviours. Albert D. describes, for example, how social relations changed in the relatively small Franconian town in which he had previously so successfully practised medicine, and where his practice effectively collapsed through loss of patients long before the introduction in 1938 of a law forbidding Jewish doctors to treat 'Aryan' patients. In private people remained pleasant towards him, but:

> In public by contrast people are cautious, short-sighted and constrained. In this sort of small town everyone knows everyone, everyone thinks himself under observation and spied upon and nothing is more feared than a denunciation to the Nazi authorities. Then you are rapidly branded in public as a 'Jewish lackey' [*Judenknecht*], as an 'enemy of the people' and similar.[183]

By the later 1930s, everyone was, in Albert D.'s view, terrified of expressing their true opinions. He was fortunate enough to have remained in contact with many decent Germans who refused to break off connections with him, and so perhaps he overestimated the extent of oppositional feeling and the significance of fear in preventing its expression, but his descriptions of the general atmosphere are nevertheless illuminating. Even on public transport people dared not express their opinions openly:

> In contrast to previous times it was now obvious to everyone on all sides how cautious, how reserved and even reticent the public had become, even when together over long periods of time. Apart from this one also noticed that during and after reading official pronouncements on posters no one even dared to make a face from which someone else nearby could draw any conclusions. Such posters were stuck up at virtually all places where there was considerable traffic.[184]

The twenty-year-old son of a close acquaintance of his must have laughed cynically while reading one such poster, for shortly afterwards he was arrested and sent to Dachau for 're-education'. Albert D. commented further:

> The fear of these concentration camps quite understandably dominated the masses and kept them quiet. Despite the secrecy with which these camps were surrounded and despite the fact that the press was naturally strictly forbidden to publish anything about life there, for a long time now it had become known how barbarically the unhappy and

---

[183] HHL, b MS Ger 91 (54), Albert D., p. 17.   [184] *Ibid.*, p. 32.

defenceless people in the camps were dealt with and what sorts of atrocities were taking place. In the meantime the whole wide world knows about this.[185]

This comment too, it must be remembered, was made well before the extermination sites in the east were set up and put into operation.

By the summer of 1936, Albert D.'s son had emigrated to the USA and his daughter was working in a distant town in the north of Germany. Albert D. moved into a smaller apartment and was for a while able to run a more or less viable private practice, including Christian patients who came via an entrance on a side road where they could not be seen. Through his patients, who simply by virtue of remaining loyal to a Jewish doctor were far from representative of the broader population, Albert D. heard a lot about the mood of people who were not entirely enamoured of the regime. These included a man in good health who came to Albert D. to request a sick note in order to get out of compulsory attendance at demonstrations; participants were now being issued with numbered tickets, so the party could control who had stayed away, and then inflict unwanted consequences; so the appearance of 'gigantic marches, gigantic gatherings, gigantic demonstrations' was being forcefully created against the will of at least some people.[186] Meanwhile, the effect it had on those who did attend was often precisely as intended by the Nazi authorities; a sense of excitement and willingness to be part, even if for only a few hours, of a wider community; behaviour signifying wild enthusiasm, and hence complicit in enacting precisely the sort of 'national community' the Nazis sought to evoke.

Albert D. finally decided to give up his practice just a few months before he would have been forced out, and moved to live with his daughter, her husband, and their small baby in a large city in the north. He immediately registered the contrast in atmosphere, sensing that there was far less evidence of Nazi propaganda and oppression. As he commented on the experiences of the first few months after leaving Franconia for the north: 'When we now came to rest here, we felt for the first time how highly strung our nerves had become in the previous few years.'[187] But this sense of some relief and relaxation of tension did not last long. Within a few months the 'Jews not wanted here' [*Juden unerwünscht*] type of placard began to appear everywhere, even in what Albert D. had hoped would be a last bastion of apparent non-Nazism, and optimists realized worse was coming after all. His daughter and son-in-law, with their baby, managed to emigrate to the USA in the summer of 1938, and Albert D. too prepared to get out. Following the Sudeten crisis, many 'Aryan' Germans said to them that they were the lucky ones to be leaving, the Aryans remaining in Germany would eventually be worse off. As Albert D. summarized it:

Just how much the people generally already reckoned with war as the consequence of Hitler's politics of violence is apparent from a remark that we heard again and again as a form of speech in a range of variations . . . They are taking away your property from

---

[185] HHL, b MS Ger 91 (54), Albert D.
[186] *Ibid.*, p. 33.   [187] *Ibid.*, p. 35.

you Jews, it is true, but the dear God will still get you out in time—whereas they will certainly take away from us Christians our children in the next war![188]

Other repeatedly heard comments included variations on: 'Be glad that you are getting out, nothing good awaits us lot. Our beautiful Germany has just turned into nothing but a prison.'[189]

Can one generalize at all about reactions and responses to the challenges faced by Germans in the peacetime years of the 1930s? In view of the myriad stories told by contemporaries of daily incidents of abuse, maltreatment, denigration, and denunciation by their fellow citizens, and the tragic tales of those who were forced to abandon their lives and homes, were murdered, or who ultimately took their own lives when they could no longer bear a situation in which there seemed no other way out, it seems almost beyond the capacity of historians to summarize, even to select illustrations, on any sensible basis. The subjective experiences of contemporaries seem, moreover, more complex, on occasion more ambiguous, than the later debates of historians about the respective weighting to be given to 'consent' and 'coercion', to support and terror, can encapsulate. Participation and behavioural evidence of commitment to the regime was always accompanied by a very real sense of peer-group pressure and the possible penalties for failing to conform, as even the request to obtain a sick note in order to avoid a demonstration indicated. But that the character of social relations had changed dramatically under six years of Nazi rule in Germany is beyond doubt. And it was not only fear, but also the more or less willing cooperation—ranging from genuine enthusiasm to an oppressed sense of capitulation—of ordinary Germans, who put into daily effect the new 'rules of the game' and enacted the new 'racial' identity scripts, that played a major role in this transformation. At the same time, large numbers (precision here is simply impossible) did not at the same time necessarily identify with the roles they felt required to play in public. A sense of at least some degree of dissonance as people's private lives were so dramatically constrained, shaped, and channelled by national policies, pressures, and norms was inevitable.

There are many ways of looking at patterns of response beyond the level of individual choices—according to class, religion, region, gender, prior political commitments, all of which shaped not only which options were open but which options were perceived to be acceptable. For all Germans, the penalties for transgressing the newly imposed boundaries of the racial state were severe, and any attempt to go against the dominant norms, any aspect of 'difference' on racial or political grounds, could lead to the most horrendous consequences. The capacity for repression in a state ultimately ruled by force even while it still maintained a façade of the rule of law should never be underestimated, least of all when that state was the Third Reich. Yet the capacity for this state also to mobilize those who were, for whatever reasons, susceptible to its lures should also not be overlooked. And here, there were distinctive generational differences.

---

[188] *Ibid.*, p. 37.   [189] *Ibid.*

One further factor was important, in addition to the obvious questions of class, politics, religious affiliation, and the like: for those born in the early years of the twentieth century, anyone who wanted to make a career would have to hitch their star to that of the state. Members of the war-youth generation were, then, particularly susceptible to the lures and compromises which were necessary to make their way up the social scale and realize ambitions which might well have been formed in rather different times. Many had also been socialized at a time, and in particular areas, where violence not only appeared in some way to be acceptable as a political tool, but where the 'hero's death' was glorified, and revenge for Versailles a major priority. Furthermore, those a few years younger, the 'first Hitler Youth generation', were also particularly susceptible. They had experienced as youngsters the crises of the later Weimar years and were open to the search for a 'solution'; and, once Hitler was in power, they were perhaps uniquely exposed to the full onslaught of Nazi propaganda. It is clear that the influence of Nazi youth organizations was never complete, and that many failed to heed the Nazi message or indeed risked their own lives and well-being through overt acts of non-conformity. But it is equally clear that young people were highly vulnerable, over-exposed, and hence more readily mobilized, and ultimately disproportionately willing to go along with the Nazi cause. They had least by way of prior experience or firm convictions; the support of the family was dented, while educational and religious institutions by and large capitulated to the demands of the regime and exerted further pressure on the choices of young people.

This does not mean that all those who appeared to be mobilized, in terms of their outward behaviours, also actually agreed with every aspect of Hitler's policies or had individual motives for action which were rooted in principled commitment to Nazi ideology rather than pragmatic considerations about conformity and survival. The Nazi party activist Wilhelm B. was arguably a rare individual (certainly as far as willingness of family members to deposit such materials in archives are concerned), one whose whole identity seemed to be defined within the framework of Nazi discourse and whose personal fulfilment and sense of self-worth was confirmed by his participation, in however small a role, in the national cause. Far more prevalent, perhaps, were those who metaphorically hung their Nazi uniforms over the back of the chair when they got home and reverted to other identities, retaining a sense of distance between themselves and the 'real' Nazis—and having to bear the consequences later, if denounced by their children or others during the Third Reich, or when being forced after 1945 to account for their previous participation in Nazi organizations. 'Real Nazis', particularly after the war, were conventionally defined in rather narrow terms, with a particular focus on the SS and Gestapo; a sense of dissonance could allow many who had actually upheld the Nazi state to believe in their own personal morality and their inner distance from the regime, however much their outward behaviours may have belied their alleged private convictions.

Up until 1939, in some areas and among some groups—those who were not forcibly excluded, or in opposition for whatever reason—the demands of the state could frequently be ignored, although at the price of also ignoring the fates of fellow citizens in less fortunate positions. However bad some contemporaries may have felt at the time, it was still easy for others to support the state and its policies without, apparently, experiencing anything by way of a guilty conscience. The mobilization of the people was a very different matter when it was a question of the national conscription of bodies for warfare and not merely of outward behaviours on a periodic basis. It was perhaps as the war reached its worst stages that the social self was most deeply defined in terms of its 'racial' belonging and participation in a 'national' cause.

5

The escalation of violence: War and genocide

Death and brutality were hallmarks of National Socialist rule throughout Hitler's period in office as chancellor and *Führer*. The claim that 'we did not know' is, if one pauses only for a moment, quite absurd in view of the highly visible violence perpetrated by the party in power from the very outset—violence that was condoned and tolerated by wide sections of German society, including the army and the (continually pruned and selected) civil service. The army leadership indeed swore a personal oath of allegiance to Hitler, following the death of President Hindenburg in August 1934, only *after* the intentional and retrospectively 'legally sanctioned' use of murder as a political tool in the 'beheading' (not an inappropriate word, in this instance) of the SA in the days of late June and early July 1934. After 1936, with Himmler's growing control of his expanding SS and police empire, the exercise of state-sanctioned violence was ever less under the control of the traditional judicial authorities, ever more an affair of the party. Violent expressions of racism might not have been widely popular, as disapproving reactions to the boycott of Jewish shops on 1 April 1933 or the violent pogrom of 9 November 1938 demonstrated; but no one could really say they 'did not know' that the Nazi regime had unleashed, perpetrated, and sanctioned violence on a massive scale—even before Germany went to war in September 1939.

Under any 'normal' circumstances—say, a democratic state of the later twentieth or early twenty-first century—the violence of the 'peacetime' years would have been seen as murder and brutality on a massive scale. But in light of what was to come, this appeared to pale in comparison with the 6 million victims of Nazi policies of murderous racism and the more than 50 million casualties of Hitler's war. And where in September 1939 a 'mere' 21,400 people were imprisoned in the then six principal concentration camps, by the start of 1945—even despite the millions who had been murdered in the meantime—a staggering total of more than 700,000 people were held prisoner in the expanded concentration camp network.[1] To sustain and implement brutality on this scale involved millions of Germans; yet many later claimed they had never 'really known' anything about the brutal character of the Hitler regime and its murderous policies.

Once the country was at war, Germans were drawn into experiences of violence on an unprecedented scale.[2] To many people, the war might initially have appeared

---

[1] Figures taken from Mark Mazower, *Hitler's Empire: Nazi rule in occupied Europe* (London: Penguin Books, 2009), p. 11.

[2] The detailed course and character of the war will not be traced here. For a clear overview and summary, see Richard J. Evans, *The Third Reich at War* (London: Allen Lane, Penguin, 2008).

to be a 'normal' war, with the 'lightning strikes' and the easy occupations of large areas of Europe during 1939–40. It was even successfully and repeatedly presented as a pre-emptive or 'defensive' war, with Hitler portraying himself as the peace-loving *Führer* seeking to protect the German people against aggressors abroad at all costs, with some apparent success. As Luise S. put it on 10 September 1939 in a letter to her husband, Fritz, on the occasion of his birthday, when he had already been called away from home on clerical duties associated with the military campaign:

> Your 40th birthday—how differently we had thought we would spend it. Now we are in the middle of war and my Fritz is so far away from here. But I am, despite all, very close to you and so send you my most heartfelt good wishes for your birthday. May the dear God always protect you and let you remain healthy and come home to us again! ... It is beyond comprehension that governments like the French and English can so recklessly and without reason take their people into war, while our Führer right up to the last was concerned to maintain peace.[3]

But right from the outset, with the invasion and occupation of Poland, Hitler's war was fought with unprecedented brutality against civilians, fuelled by ferocious ideological ambitions, and informed by racial hatred. And as the war expanded into a pan-European and then a World War, ever more Germans were caught up in it, their lives radically affected whether through being mobilized to fight at the front or through the impact of 'total war' on the home front.

Moreover, knowledge of atrocities at the time was far more widespread than post-war protestations of ignorance and innocence would suggest. The 'euthanasia' campaign of 1939–41 was indeed at least publicly halted because of popular protestations. In the dedicated extermination camps which were developed from late 1941 and expanded massively in 1942, several thousand people could be murdered *daily* when the gas chambers and crematoria were in full operation. But it is worth remembering that more 'racial' victims of the regime were murdered outside the gas chambers than within, often not merely within sight of, but with the active participation of 'ordinary Germans'. Hundreds of thousands of letters home from the front reported on atrocities against civilians in the occupied territories as well as on the eastern front. But in the minds of self-defensive Germans later determined to prove their 'innocence' through 'ignorance', a sharp line was drawn, metaphorically, at the gates of Auschwitz. The SS and the concentration camp personnel later served as convenient, narrowly defined scapegoats; the myth of the 'decent' *Wehrmacht* was sustained in public for half a century after the end of the war. And, for a long time in both West and East Germany, a dominant focus on those who made policy at the top, and those who were at the front line of 'bestial' physical brutality, served to deflect attention from lower levels of the administration and from the wider context of racist policies of stigmatization, exclusion, and premature deaths, whether as a direct result of killing or as an indirect result of

---

[3] Archiv der Akademie der Künste, Kempowski-Biographienarchiv (henceforth Kempowski-BIO), 7076, Correspondence of Fritz S. (1899–1991), letter from Luise S. of 10 Sep. 1939.

Nazi maltreatment, including through the overcrowding, enforced starvation, and disease of the ghettoes.

No one, however far from direct military action, could emerge from this period untouched or unscathed in some way, emotionally, psychologically, or physically. But experiences of war and genocide were obviously significant in entirely different ways for different groups. There was all the world of difference—literally, the difference between life and death—between those who actively considered themselves members of a 'master race' and those destined for the gas chambers. There were gradations of difference among different victim groups, oppositionalists, old and young, males and females, committed or 'fanatical' Nazis, and 'fellow travellers', those who exploited forced labourers and those who were in fear of their own lives or simply sought to survive.

Here, perhaps even more than in any other period of twentieth-century German history, people faced massive common challenges. The ways in which they sought to make sense of their experiences, and to give meaning to what they were being required to do, or make it acceptable in terms with which they could live, varied not only with individual personalities, and particular political, moral, religious, and cultural commitments and heritages, but also betrayed the massive impact of Nazi propaganda, ideology, and peer-group pressure, as well as critical responses to these. It is remarkable how many common elements feature across quite different individual expressions and responses; and just how deeply individual perceptions and 'subjective experiences' were informed and framed by current discourses, despite registration of dissonance or discomfort. The character of the challenges and the impact of both ideology and experience varied not only with milieu and gender, but also according to generation: responses depended markedly on age and hence the character of an individual's exposure to different aspects of this genocidal war. And age-related experiences at this time gave way to different 'lessons' that were later drawn, different degrees of dissonance in post-war lives, and different possibilities for making new lives after the cataclysm.

I. MASS MOBILIZATION

The most homogeneous experiences were arguably those of adult males. But even here, age played a role in varying patterns of involvement and reaction to war, given the changing character of an increasingly violent war and the ways in which different age cohorts were called up at different stages of the war. Self-mobilization was accompanied by forcible mobilization.

The totals of those called up to fight for the Fatherland, or to serve in the Reich civil service in the occupied territories or at home, were staggering. In all, somewhere in the region of 17 to 18 million men were called up at one time or another to fight; around 11 million were at some point held as prisoners of war; a million or more were implicated in civilian administration of Nazi policies. Soldiers on the ground constituted around 90 per cent of all the armed forces of the Third Reich.

Involvement in military service was in large measure structured according to social origins, with men from upper-class backgrounds having different expectations and experiences from those of the ordinary '*Landser*'. Around 99 per cent of these soldiers were enlisted men, non-commissioned officers, or junior officers; only around 1 per cent were officers in the narrow sense of holding higher office in the army, at the level of major or above.[4] Only 3 per cent were ever intended to become officers at some point, although this level was never in fact reached; and only around 0.3 per cent were members of the real military elite, the generals, and admirals, whose memoirs and related publications have tended to shape later perceptions of 'what the war was like'.[5] What soldiers all had in common was experience of a war of ideologically driven brutality, however differently they drew on cultural frameworks to process and make sense of their experiences, and however differently they sieved these experiences internally. The marks left, on a personal level, were highly complex.

If there had been some degree of selection and choice involved at earlier stages with respect to involvement in state-sanctioned violence, this was no longer the case once war was declared and conscription was an unavoidable fact of life, even (perhaps especially) for those with no desire to be involved. Prior to 1939, both structural and cultural availability were important as selection mechanisms for those who were successfully mobilized for the Nazi project. After 1939, cultural responses continued to be significant as far as internal perceptions and strategies of reaction were concerned, but for millions of young men caught in the relevant age groups—which widened as the war proceeded and the need for manpower became more intense—'structural availability' became increasingly important, ultimately overriding all else; millions of Germans were sent, whether or not against their will, to participate in what was a highly ideologically driven fight. And the experience of participation in this most brutal war inevitably had an indelible impact on those who were lucky enough to survive.

Notions of who was held to be 'available for mobilization' in the military sense broadened as the war progressed. Even people in occupations where one could previously claim to be 'indispensable' (*unabkömmlich* or *uk*) on the home front found themselves subject to an embargo on leave with effect from 1 June 1941, given the need for manpower in 'Operation Barbarossa'.[6] More than 3 million men were involved in the June 1941 invasion of the USSR alone.[7] Not far short of

[4] Stephen Fritz, *Frontsoldaten: The German soldier in World War II* (Lexington, KY: University of Kentucky Press, 1995), p. 3. Despite the non-analytic style and approach, and the heavy dependence on a small selection of published sources, this book contains very useful and suggestive material on the experiences of 'ordinary soldiers'.

[5] Wolfram Wette, *Die Wehrmacht: Feindbilder, Vernichtungskrieg, Legenden* (Frankfurt-am-Main: S. Fischer Verlag, 2002), pp. 74, 176–7.

[6] Bernhard Kroener, 'The manpower resources of the Third Reich in the area of conflict between Wehrmacht, bureaucracy and war economy, 1939–1942' in Militärgeschichtliches Forschungsamt (ed.), *Germany and the Second World War* (Oxford: Clarendon Press, 2000; orig. German 1998), Vol. V, Pt 3, p. 913.

[7] Richard Bessel, *Nazism and War* (London: Weidenfeld and Nicolson, 2004), p. 94.

1 million (900,000) men served at some time as member of the ever expanding *Waffen-SS*.[8] In the autumn of 1944, given enormously heavy losses in the preceding months—more than one-third of a million German soldiers were killed in August 1944 alone—the so-called 'People's Fighting Force' (*Volkssturm*) was created, encompassing all males deemed fit to fight between the ages of sixteen and sixty. This last-ditch effort simultaneously brought into the war the cohorts born in both 1928 and 1929, with an entirely callous disregard for the lives of these youngsters.[9] Both their prior preparation and their experiences of war were distinctively different from those who had been involved from the start.

The experience of war thus differed quite markedly according to the different military campaigns at different stages of the war, and to time of call-up—which, of course, related directly to an individual's year of birth. Different birth cohorts thus could experience 'war' quite differently, in part because of the character of their prior socialization, as well as age-related degrees of responsibility and expectations, and because of the particular stages of the war and theatres of combat in which they were involved.

Many males who were already young adults in 1939 were moved widely across and around Europe, experiencing not only the easy victories of the early '*Blitzkrieg*' period, the invasion and occupation of areas of both eastern and western Europe, but also the atrocities of the racial war in the east and the long-drawn out suffering of the Russian campaign, as well as late, suicidal fighting for survival against all the odds on all fronts. Their responses to the experience of war shifted accordingly; but many of them appear also to have been strongly affected by the messages which Hitler, Goebbels, and others sought to put across, even in face of the most awful conditions. There were of course major differences according to political and moral viewpoints, family background, and levels of education. But the pervasiveness of Nazi ideology in the letters of soldiers from this generation when faced with perpetration of violence on those designated as 'the enemy' is quite extraordinary.

For many adults, this was a moment when careers could be made or destroyed; and active military service did not necessarily preclude other forms of involvement in the ever expanding machinery of the Third Reich. For many, stints at the front alternated with periods in the administration of racial policies across Europe.[10] Even those adults who were not called up into active military service were often involved in highly ideological practices in the employment of forced labourers in their farms and businesses, or in the 'Germanization' of the expanded Greater German Reich, putting racial policies into deadly practice through the oppression, exploitation, starvation, forced movement, and on occasion outright murder of subjugated peoples. Millions of Hitler's victims lost their lives as a result not of

---

[8] Evans, *Third Reich at War*, p. 505.

[9] Bessel, *Nazism and War*, p. 125.

[10] Cf. Michael Mann, 'Were the perpetrators of genocide "ordinary men" or "real Nazis"? Results from fifteen hundred biographies', *Holocaust and Genocide Studies*, 14(3) (2000), pp. 331–66; and M. Fulbrook, *Ordinary Nazis*.

military combat but rather as a consequence of policies of terrorization, 'reprisals', exploitation, and malnutrition under Nazi 'civilian' rule.[11]

For the men called up to fight and if necessary die for the Fatherland, the demands of the state could not be evaded and the effects were inescapable. This was the ultimate moment of mobilization. Yet for all the training and effort put into producing an ideologically homogeneous fighting force, responses varied. Many became convinced by their experiences and ideological training that the propaganda they had been subjected to before 1939 was 'true', and that the cause they were fighting for was just; others capitulated to peer-group pressure, and went along with the demands of the day, often alleviated by the periodic oblivion provided by alcohol; a few managed against the odds to retain some sense of inner distance, particularly if they already held strong inner convictions which provided a counter-vailing force to the demands of the Nazi regime.

Even so, there is a remarkable degree of patterning to the ways in which people wrote to each other about what they were witnessing and involved in. Mobilized as never before, Germans were constantly on the move, separated from families and friends; and they wrote to each other as never before. Although we can never know what went on inside people's heads, we certainly have vast quantities of evidence about the ways in which they were prepared to express their thoughts to others, and commit their views to paper.

Letters home (known as 'letters from the field', *Feldpostbriefe*) provide only veiled clues to soldiers' experiences; and they provide little by way of evidence of the longer-term impact or intergenerational transmission of wartime experiences.[12] Yet they are crucial to any understanding of the immediate impact of war on those mobilized to fight it, and the ways in which they sought to interpret and represent their experiences at the time.[13] They provide insights into how soldiers experienced different phases and arenas of war, insofar as men at the front were capable of articulating their experiences and tried to convey them to those at home, in face of both military censorship and the self-censorship entailed in not wanting to worry their loved ones. Letters from home to the front similarly provide valuable clues as to frameworks of interpretation, beliefs, values, and 'knowledge' of what was going on; and they provide glimpses of contemporary responses to what was later recognized as crime on such a scale that people subsequently professed that 'they knew nothing about it'.

---

[11] See Hans Umbreit, 'Towards continental domination' in Militärgeschichtliches Forschungsamt (ed.), *Germany and the Second World War*, Vol. V, Pt 1, p. 11.

[12] There is a frequent methodological problem encountered by researchers in this area, who rarely have access both to war-time material and later 'ego-documents' for the same individuals across long stretches of time.

[13] See e.g the use made of soldiers' letters in Omer Bartov, *Hitler's Army: Soldiers, Nazis and war in the Third Reich* (Oxford: Oxford University Press, 1991) and the analyses in Martin Humburg, *Das Gesicht des Krieges. Feldpostbriefe von Wehrmachtsoldaten aus der Sowjetunion 1941–1944* (Opladen/Wiesbaden: Westdeutscher Verlag, 1998); Klaus Latzel, *Deutsche Soldaten—nationalsozialistischer Krieg? Kriegserlebnis – Kriegserfahrung 1939–1945* (Paderborn: Ferdinand Schöningh, 1998); Hans Joachim Schröder, *Die gestohlenen Jahre. Erzählgeschichten und Geschichtserzählung im Interview: Der zweite Weltkrieg aus der Sicht ehemaliger Mannschaftssoldaten* (Tübingen: Max Niemeyer Verlag, 1992).

While millions of such letters have perished or still moulder in attics and cellars, large numbers of such letters have been collected, and some selections published; these, of course, have been pre-selected with certain aspects in mind.[14] Even the far vaster unpublished collections to be found in the archives are the result of almost arbitrary survival, selection, and deposit: no amount of trawling through the massive archival holdings will ever be able to provide any kind of comprehensive picture of mentalities and changing perceptions; there can, in short, be no 'inductive' method for writing about the changing subjectivities of this period. Nevertheless, key general issues and trends among certain groups of letter writers are very striking. It is difficult to ascertain precisely the extent to which they are representative. But the sheer prevalence of certain world views, reactions, and interpretative frameworks among ordinary soldiers is striking. It suggests, for all the differences in individual backgrounds and personalities, that there were certain common discourses which allowed soldiers and their friends and relatives at home to think about the war in certain ways, helping to construct notions of the self as part of a wider, often ethnically and culturally defined, community. Letters vary in terms of the degree of dissonance, distance, or internalization of dominant norms and values they express; the degrees of (generally rather unreflective) expression or surprised 'confirmation' of Nazi stereotypes; and the ways in which writers appeal to broader, quasi-philosophical considerations in seeking to overcome or deal with the challenges, discomforts, and fears of everyday life at war. On this evidence, the nazification of mentalities among a significant proportion of German adults in the preceding years had apparently run remarkably deep.

II. EARLY ATROCITIES

This was, right from the very start, a war like no previous war. It was not merely, as in all wars, a matter of soldiers fighting soldiers: it was, from the moment of the invasion of Poland in September 1939, a war against the whole Polish population, including civilians, who right from the start were construed as intrinsically dangerous, potential '*Freischarler*' (frequently translated into the quasi-French term, '*franctireurs*' or sharpshooters, also roughly translatable as 'insurgents', 'guerrillas', or 'terrorists', but in the German usage of the time going way beyond the Anglophone meaning of these terms). Ignoring all notions of taking defeated soldiers captive, German orders of September 1939 announced that '*Freischarler*' were liable to an instant death sentence: '*Franctireurs* are categorically subject to the death sentence.' (*Auf Freischärlerei steht grundsätzlich Todesstrafe.*)[15] Further orders

---

[14] See particularly Walther Bähr and Hans Bähr (eds.), *Kriegsbriefe gefallener Studenten 1939–1945* (Tübingen and Stuttgart: Rainer Wunderlich Verlag, 1952); Ortwin Buchbender and Reinhold Sterz (eds.), *Das andere Gesicht des Krieges. Deutsche Feldpostbriefe 1939–1945* (Munich: C. H. Beck, 1982); Walter Manoschek (ed.), *'Es gibt nur eines für das Judentum: Vernichtung'. Das Judenbild in deutschen Soldatenbriefen 1939–1944* (Hamburg: Hamburger Edition, 1995).

[15] Geheimes Staatsarchiv Preussischer Kulturbesitz (henceforth GStPK), HA XVII Rep. 201e. Ost 4 Reg. Kattowitz Nr. 3, Einrichtung einer deutschen Verwaltung nach Besetzung Ostoberschlesiens durch

authorized the taking of prominent civilians as hostages, who were—again in contravention of the previous conventions of warfare—to be shot dead on the slightest of pretexts, thus effectively seeking to terrorize the population into acquiescence with the German invasion:

> In order to combat any excesses on the part of the civilian population, prominent persons from among the civilian population can be arrested and held as hostages. The population is to be informed immediately that in the event of the slightest attack or act of sabotage against the troops the hostages will be shot dead.[16]

Civilians found or suspected of being in possession of weapons were to be shot dead instantly, without mercy:

> Anyone found with a weapon about him . . . is to be shot dead on the spot. Any attempts at escape are to be ruthlessly prevented by use of firearms, whether or not the perpetrator is armed while trying to escape.[17]

Interestingly, anyone trying to escape from German force was, in their construction of the situation, in principle designated a '*Täter*', here translated as 'perpetrator', a wholly inappropriate term in the circumstances—but one which is indicative of the prevalent German view that all victims of their violent aggression were legitimate prey if they failed to give in to German domination.

It was not only those who appeared to be actively engaged in a struggle to defend their invaded homeland who were to be arrested and if necessary murdered on the spot. In a remarkably vague phrasing, the order was given that all the males of any particular village or town should be rounded up and locked away in a suitable place, without any reason whatsoever and whether or not they were in possession of weapons; and that anyone should be shot if they tried to resist or escape:

> Under certain circumstances it can be necessary for the protection of the troops to hold the male population in a barn or other suitable place. Those held are to be guarded, and anyone trying to escape or to resist is to be shot.[18]

The photograph albums produced by ordinary soldiers, commemorating their time together during the invasion of Poland, contain horrifying scenes of barns burning, villages destroyed, and terrified civilians. In one such album, entitled 'For my comrade Franz D. in memory of the Polish campaign', photographs are adorned with captions such as 'On the march with hostages', 'Burning villages', 'A filthy Jew', and 'The Jews of Goworovo'. A series of photographs of scenes of utter devastation, with totally bombed-out houses and destruction are proudly labelled

---

deutsche Truppen—Anordnungen, Geschäftsverteilung und Stellenplan, Verwaltungsgliederung, Bd. 1 26. August – 20. September 1939. O.U. Kattowitz, 8.9.1939, Abschnittstagebefehl Nr. 2, Auszug aus dem Korpstagebuch Nr. 10, fol. 81.

[16] GStPK, HA XVII Rep. 201e. Ost 4 Reg. Kattowitz Nr. 3, Grenzabschnittskommando 3, Gleiwitz, den 3.9.1939, 'Richtlinien für die Tätigkeit der Ortskommandaturen', fol. 99.

[17] GStPK, HA XVII Rep. 201e. Ost 4 Reg. Kattowitz Nr. 3, 'Richtlinien für die Tätigkeit der Ortskommandaturen', fol. 100.

[18] GStPK, HA XVII Rep. 201e. Ost 4 Reg. Kattowitz Nr. 3, 'Befehl über die Bekämpfung von bewaffneten Zivilpersonen!', fol. 55.

'The complete works of our dive bombers on the way to Warsaw', culminating in a further series over the caption 'Warsaw's suburb of Praga burning'.[19] For ordinary soldiers, the use of violence against civilians had been unleashed with a vengeance. This approach to the rapidly defeated and ill-prepared Poland clearly prefigured the approach adopted in the campaign against Russia two years later.[20]

The devastation of Polish villages and towns, taking of hostages, and wanton murder of anyone resisting arrest or incarceration went way beyond previously accepted rules of warfare. But acts of violence were also targeted specifically against Jewish civilians. Immediately following the invasion of Poland, atrocities were committed against those perceived as 'racially' inferior, whether or not they could (also) be plausibly construed as dangerous in a political or military sense. Somewhat overlooked by accounts which focus on the actions of the *Einsatzgruppen*, or Special Task Forces, during the invasion of the Soviet Union in the summer of 1941, there were already *Einsatzgruppen* active in Poland in the first weeks of the war.[21] On some views the atrocities committed by these units, sometimes assisted by ethnic German 'self-defence' (*Selbst-Schutz*) units, already constituted the start of the 'war of extermination'.[22] Lists of people who were held to be members of the Polish political elites and intelligentsia were compiled already in June 1939; on Heydrich's orders four *Einsatzgruppen* were established by early July, and two additional ones set up in early September.

In September and early October 1939, in an orgy of violence several thousand Jewish civilians in Poland were killed: Jewish men, women and children were burnt alive in their houses or shot 'while trying to escape'; and synagogues were burnt down in towns and villages by the *Einsatzgruppen*, who on occasion sought to pin the blame on local Polish 'insurgents' who were later also murdered as 'culprits'. In the small Polish–Silesian border town of Będzin, for example, on the night of 8 September 1939 some 200 or more Jews were burnt alive in the synagogue, or in the surrounding houses, or shot while trying to save themselves by plunging into the nearby river—an incident still etched in the memories of Jewish survivors and elderly local Poles some seventy years later.[23] While the selective terrorization of the Jewish population was perhaps to persuade them to flee out of areas to be

---

[19] Feldpostsammlung Museum für Kommunikation (henceforth FMK), 3.2002.1325, Franz D., photographs numbered 83, 89, 101, 124, 131–8.

[20] Indeed, the description given by Omer Bartov of the treatment of 'partisans' and 'bandits' in Russia in 1941 could readily be transposed backwards to the Polish campaign of September 1939. See Bartov, *Hitler's Army: Soldiers, Nazis, and war in the Third Reich*, Ch. 4, particularly pp. 89–90.

[21] Klaus-Michael Mallmann, Jochen Böhler, and Jürgen Matthäus, *Einsatzgruppen in Polen: Darstellung und Dokumentation* (Darmstadt: Wissenschaftliche Buchgesellschaft, 2008); Helmut Krausnick and Hans-Heinrich Wilhelm (eds.), *Die Truppe des Weltanschauungskrieges. Die Einsatzgruppen der Sicherheitspolizei und des SD 1938–1942* (Stuttgart: Deutsche Verlags-Anstalt, 1981); Alexander Rossino, 'Nazi anti-Jewish policy during the Polish campaign: The case of the Einsatzgruppe von Woyrsch', *German Studies Review*, 24(1) (2001), 35–53.

[22] Mallmann, Böhler, and Matthäus, *Einsatzgruppen in Polen*, p. 15. Cf. also Alexander Rossino, *Hitler Strikes Poland: Blitzkrieg, ideology and atrocity* (Kansas: University Press of Kansas, 2003), pp. 135–6, who suggests lines of continuity with the atrocities of the Great War and even the genocidal practices in Africa a decade earlier; but see the discussion of this in previous chapters.

[23] On the case of Będzin, see Fulbrook, *A Small Town Near Auschwitz*.

incorporated by an expanded Reich—though in practice most Jews who initially fled eastwards found conditions no better elsewhere and soon returned—one of Hitler's principal aims at this time was the total destruction of the Polish elites, a goal he made quite clear to the leadership of the army in August, and which was discussed in detail by Himmler, Heydrich, and Best with the *Einsatzgruppen*. To this end, from the very start of the war Polish notables were rounded up, imprisoned, held as hostage, and in some instances murdered by members of these *Einsatzgruppen*, in cooperation with the army whose own orders were, as indicated, entirely in line with these aims.

Those primarily involved in leading positions at this early stage of proactive extreme violence were still what one might call 'self-mobilized' men. The biographical profiles of the *Einsatzgruppen* leaders reveal that the vast majority had been associated with the Free Corps movement after the Great War, and had already at that stage participated actively in violence on the German–Polish border, or in the Kapp putsch.[24] Around one-third had gained prior experience in warfare as members of the 'front generation'; around two-thirds were born in the first decade of the twentieth century, and were classic exemplars of the radical-right elements of the 'war-youth generation'. They had generally joined the NSDAP relatively early, either before or during 1933; many had academic qualifications, including doctorates; they had made their careers during the Third Reich with a degree of ideological commitment to the racial project, including working as police officers or civil servants at the forefront of driving racial polices.

In a context where there was clearly a general congruence of aims, army leaders were both well aware of and frequently provided the conditions for, but were also at times rather critical of, the radical violence of the *Einsatzgruppen*; the military also on occasion disapproved of the actions of the *Selbst-Schutz*. Yet they took no serious action against members of their own troops who participated in atrocities, and indeed often actively facilitated and participated in mass murders from the earliest days after the invasion of Poland; moreover, young soldiers, infused with ideological enthusiasm and no previous experience of warfare, seem to have been well-prepared for engaging in brutality sanctioned from above.[25] At the start, too, even with official encouragement and backing, the regular troops were somewhat uncertain of their role; but there seems to have been a relatively rapid development of ways of making disagreeable actions palatable, picking up on notions prevalent in the early weeks of the Great War. Fear of the activity of '*franctireurs*' or 'bandits'—people who looked like civilians and thus not legitimate military targets, but who might unexpectedly shoot at soldiers—was clearly high; and such fears were clearly encouraged, in order that German troops should respond mercilessly, casting aside

---

[24] See Mallmann, Böhler, and Matthäus, *Einsatzgruppen in Polen*, pp. 20 ff. for age profiles of *Einsatzgruppen*; pp. 42–5 for the more general biographical data.
[25] Hans Umbreit, 'Towards continental domination' in Militärgeschichtliches Forschungsamt (ed.), *Germany and the Second World War*, Vol. V, Pt 1, p. 57; Wette, *Wehrmacht*, pp. 104–7; Peter Longerich, *Politik der Vernichtung* (Munich: Piper Verlag, 1998), pp. 247–8; Klaus-Michael Mallmann and Bogdan Musial (eds.), *Genesis des Genozids: Polen 1939–1941* (Darmstadt: Wissenschaftliche Buchgesellschaft, 2004), p. 40.

any notion of protecting civilians, including women and children. As one soldier put it in a letter home, writing from East Prussia on 10 September:

> The war is hard and the Poles are fighting very viciously. We have ourselves been shot at by guerrillas [*franctireurs, Franktireurs*] and have finally come to the view that we have been too good-natured . . . The regular battle against the Polish army will probably soon be over, but the war against the gangs, which is no less bloody and is above all loathsome because it also often affects women and children here, will probably still go on for a while yet . . .[26]

Not yet two weeks into the war, this soldier was clearly echoing a collective framework of perception that supposedly 'legitimized' what might otherwise have been seen as excess violence, going beyond conceptions of 'regular' warfare.

The army and the *Einsatzgruppen* often worked together to try to impose order through policies of terror and mass reprisals. *Einsatzgruppen* reports—which cannot always be trusted as accurate—include, for example, comments such as the following:

> The shootings in Tschenstochau [Częstochowa, re-named by the Germans] on 4.9.1939 lasted into the late evening. On the part of the Wehrmacht [German army] we have to mourn for 9 dead and 40 injured. On top of this the Wehrmacht shot dead around 100 civilians. The Einsatzkommando 1 shot dead two franctireurs who were caught in the act. The military command in Tschenstochau is very nervous. Even if it is a fact that the German troops are being shot at by civilians, even so it was not in the end possible to determine who shot at whom . . . Apparently it is not a matter of a concerted attack but rather a nervousness and a desire on the part of the troops to shoot, noticeable here as everywhere else. I am of the view that through ruthless intervention the franctireur war will soon be brought to an end.[27]

Within a matter of days, according to these reports, the mutual cooperation of *Wehrmacht* and *Einsatzgruppe* had ensured a 'total pacification' of the area: 'Through the energetic, ruthless intervention of the Wehrmacht and the Einsatzkommando total peace has been brought to Tschenstochau.'[28] Yet there remained uncertainties and hesitations about the 'legality' of such an approach, at least as far as the paper trail of reporting was concerned. On 14 September 1939, one group found a way of making a mass shooting which was carried out as a reprisal measure for the death of a German appear almost like due legal process:

> The murder commission that was set up to investigate the murder of the Major General of the Order Police, General Rüttig, has come to the following conclusions:
> . . . By order of the AOK [*Armeeoberkommando*, Army High Command] shootings are strictly forbidden as a reprisal for the death of Major General Rüttig. The AOK in

[26] Buchbender and Sterz (eds.), *Das andere Gesicht des Krieges*, letter from Private W.K., 10 Sep. 1939, p. 40.

[27] Bundesarchiv Berlin (henceforth BAB) R / 58 / 7001, 'Meldung' of Einsatzgruppe II, 6 Sep. 1939, fol. 6. The inaccuracy of some reports can be demonstrated in cases where other sources reveal a dramatic underestimation of the damage caused by an *Einsatzgruppe* and its subsequent unwillingness to be associated, on paper at least, with the high numbers of casualties and actual destruction it had caused.

[28] BAB R / 58 / 7001, 'Meldung' of Einsatzgruppe II, bis 8.9.1939 8:00 Uhr, fol. 18.

this instance therefore arrested all male civilians from the age of 18 in Konskie and the surrounding area, in total about 5,000 individuals, and had them brought to a camp in Konskie. In agreement with the commandant for the locality and the camp, the prisoners were thoroughly searched. Then 20 individuals, Jews, Poles, and soldiers wearing civilian clothing, who although not injured wore clothes with blood on them and were in possession of German money and therefore could be seen as initiators of the slaughter of German soldiers, were shot dead.[29]

This was a transitional moment. Under peacetime circumstances, or under conditions of 'traditional' or 'regular' warfare, such indirect circumstantial evidence would hardly be considered sufficient to warrant an instant death penalty; and only a little later into the war, even this pretence at due legal process would be deemed unnecessary before carrying out mass 'reprisal' murders of people known to be entirely unconnected with an alleged offence. On 4 October 1939 Hitler effectively pronounced any 'excesses' as justified, amnestying anyone who might face disciplinary proceedings, and justifying the killings as appropriate responses to the behaviour of the Polish population who were resisting German conquest.

The notion of shooting 'partisans' or people 'while trying to escape' (*auf der Flucht erschossen*), and exercising 'collective retaliation', thus very soon became 'standard military practices', again well before the Russian campaign.[30] But interestingly, the responses of at least some 'ordinary soldiers' to the early activities of *Einsatzgruppen* were on occasion critical for a very different reason: they appear to have felt that those attacking defenceless civilians were not really proving anything at all by way of real courage, compared to those fighting against armed opponents.[31] Similarly, ordinary soldiers on occasion appear to have felt some sympathy for those they saw as innocent victims of German military action. As one soldier put it on 2 October 1939, on entering the devastated ruins of Warsaw:

> Yesterday we arrived in Warsaw, the saddest city in Europe...Misery in all its gruesome awfulness is nowhere as great as in this badly stricken heap of rubble. Our bombers and artillery have done their work too thoroughly...We often share our meagre rations because the misery of the children and women tears your heart-strings ...That is the horror, the awfulness of the city...[32]

Yet the initial shock of witnessing the effects of violence was, it seems, increasingly displaced by a blunting of reactions among some of those who were soldiers in the early stages of the war, even a brutalization.

Although much has been made of the fact that there were isolated protests on the part of the army at this stage, in contrast to the situation two years later in Russia, actually what is far more striking is the fact that such terror worried really very few people in the higher ranks of the military at the time. An exception was General Blaskowitz, an experienced veteran of the Great War and from October 1939

---

[29] BAB R / 58 / 7001, 'Meldung' of Einsatzgruppe II, EK II, 14.9.39, 8:00 Uhr, fol. 69.
[30] Cf. Rossino, *Hitler strikes Poland*, Ch. 5.
[31] *Ibid.*, pp. 42–3.
[32] Buchbender and Sterz (eds.), *Das andere Gesicht des Krieges*, Soldat J.S., 2 Oct 1939, pp. 40–1.

commander-in-chief in the east (*Oberbefehlshaber Ost*). He repeatedly raised his voice in criticism of the levels of excessive brutality characterizing the war in the east. Even so, and with all due allowances for the situation and what it was that he 'could say' in this context, it is also notable that Blaskowitz' criticisms were not so much of the horrendous consequences for the victims but rather the implications of such actions for the troops who were actively involved in perpetrating acts which went, in his view, way beyond the 'normal rules of warfare':

> The worst damage, however, that will be done to the German people by the current situation is the boundless brutalization and moral degeneration that will break out like the plague within a short space of time among this valuable resource, the German people. If people holding high office in the SS and the police demand acts of violence and brutality and openly praise such acts in public, then very soon only the violent will rule . . . There will be virtually no possibility of holding them in check; for they must consider themselves authorized by virtue of their office and feel they have a right to commit any atrocity.[33]

For voicing his concerns—and indeed articulating what proved to be a highly prescient criticism—Blaskowitz reaped the wrath of Hitler and was relieved of his command in May 1940; but he soon found himself engaged in other fronts of the war in the west. The brutalities in the east continued; and, as Blaskowitz predicted, those prepared and willing to carry out acts of brutality rose to dominance in the new structures of power. But physical brutality was not the only form that violence could take.

III. THE ROUTINIZATION OF SYSTEMIC VIOLENCE

The *Einsatzgruppen* were wound up within a matter of weeks, as the rapid conquest of Poland was followed by the installation of civilian occupation regimes. Military force, and the atrocities associated with the invasion, were soon augmented by routine daily violence, as new administrative systems were established to rule over the conquered territories. The character of German occupation differed between the rump Polish state of the so-called General Government under the German Governor Hans Frank, and those areas that were incorporated within the expanded German Reich—the new provinces of Wartheland and Danzig-West Prussia, and the enlarged provinces of East Prussia and Upper Silesia. But the fact that the *Einsatzgruppen* were no longer marauding across the countryside setting fire to houses, villages, or synagogues did not mean the end of violence, brutality, and murder in these areas: it was simply institutionalized and routinized. Similarly, much attention has rightly been devoted to the programme of 'euthanasia' or murdering those whose lives were considered by the Nazis to be 'lives unworthy of living' (*lebensunwertes Leben*), a programme which officially ran from 1939 to

---

[33] Generaloberst Johannes Blaskowitz, 'Vortragsnotiz für Vortrag Oberost beim Oberbefehlshaber des Heeres am 15.2. in Spala, 6.2.1940', repr. in *Topographie des Terrors: Eine Dokumentation*, 2nd edn (Berlin, 2009), p. 147.

1941. This should not however serve to deflect attention from the far wider system of brutality, exercised by far more people than the terror specialists of the *Einsatzgruppen* or the 'medical' specialists involved in murdering innocent people in institutions for the mentally ill and physically disabled.

The routine exercise of violence was a matter not only of continued acts of physical brutality committed by German troops, the SS, the Gestapo, or the regular police forces all the way through to local gendarmes; it was also, although in different and less obvious ways, a question of systemic violence carried by civilian administrators, employers, and 'ethnic Germans' out to make a profit from the exploitation and expropriation of Polish people—whether or not they were also Jewish, but especially if they were.[34] Individual acts of humiliation—jeering at Jews, pulling and cutting their beards—were frequent. 'Recrimination measures', or 'reprisals', were a standard means of imposing German domination and seeking to secure 'effective administration'. Thus for example in June 1940, thirty-two entirely innocent Poles were shot in the small hamlet of Celiny, in eastern Upper Silesia, in reprisal for the death of one German gendarme; on 'Bloody Wednesday', at the end of July 1940, all the adult males of the nearby small town of Olkusz were forced to lie flat face down on the ground in public places, as they were jeered at, trodden on, and in some cases murdered by German troops, with especially brutal treatment meted out to the Jewish residents of the town, many of whom were later taken away by truck and did not return.[35]

Such individual incidents of violence were complemented by forceful measures geared towards the attempted 'Germanization' of the incorporated territories. Already on 21 September 1939 Himmler had issued orders that the newly occupied territories should be made 'free of Jews'. Jews should be collected into what were at this time called 'concentration towns' (*Konzentrationsstädte*) close to railways stations or railway lines, pending deportation into the General Government.[36] 'Jewish Councils' (*Judenräte*) were set up with whom the German authorities could liaise and through whom the systematic robbery and restraint of Jewish communities could be organized at one remove; many victims later only remembered (often with

---

[34] See e.g. Isabel Heinemann, *'Rasse, Siedlung, deutsches Blut'. Die Rasse- und Siedlungspolitik der SS und die rassenpolitische Neuordnung Europas* (Göttingen: Wallstein Verlag, 2003); Diemut Majer, *'Non-Germans' under the Third Reich: The Nazi judicial and administrative system in Germany and occupied Eastern Europe with special regard to occupied Poland, 1939–1945* (Baltimore: Johns Hopkins University Press, 2003); Bogdan Musial, *Deutsche Zivilverwaltung und Judenverfolgung im General-gouvernement. Eine Fallstudie zum Distrikt Lublin 1939–1944* (Wiesbaden: Otto Harrassowitz, 1999); Hans Umbreit, *Deutsche Militärverwaltungen. Die militärische Besetzung der Tschechoslowakei und Polens* (Stuttgart: Deutsche Verlags-Anstalt, 1977). Martin Broszat, *Nationalsozialistische Polenpolitik 1939–1945* (Stuttgart: Deutsche Verlags-Anstalt, 1961), despite shortcomings in a variety of respects including evaluation of the role of the army, remains a classic and indeed path-breaking early study.

[35] For further details on these and related incidents, Fulbrook, *A Small Town Near Auschwitz*; on Olkusz, Ernst Klee, Willi Dreßen, and Volker Rieß (eds.), *'Schöne Zeiten'. Judenmord aus der Sicht der Täter und Gaffer* (Frankfurt: Fischer Verlag, 1988).

[36] See e.g. Ingo Haar, 'Biopolitische Differenzkonstruktionen als bevölkerungspolitisches Ordnungs-instrument in den Ostgauen: Raum- und Bevölkerungsplanung im Spannungsfeld zwischen regionaler Verankerung und zentralstaatlichem Planungsanspruch' in Jürgen John, Horst Möller, and Thomas Schaarschmidt (eds.), *Die NS-Gaue. Regionale Mittelinstanzen im zentralistischen 'Führerstaat'* (München: Oldenbourg, 2007).

hatred and contempt) their own 'leaders' who, they felt, had blocked attempts at resistance or escape, and failed to recognize the full parameters of a horrendous situation. In a desperate attempt to alleviate distress and ameliorate the conditions of their communities, Jewish leaders were effectively forced to collude in the systematic destruction of their own people; for some, this drove them beyond the limits of bearable despair, and they took their own lives even before the Germans disposed of them once they could no longer be of use.[37] Similarly, Jewish militia were deployed by the Germans to identify Jews for forced labour (and later for murder) and to maintain order, again at one remove from the German authorities overseeing and masterminding the apparatus of exploitation and brutality.

With variations according to area, civilian authorities made plans for the forced expulsion of Jews, and in many cases also Poles, from their homes, making way for the immigration of 'ethnic Germans'. The fulfilment of this policy in practice, which took place in fits and starts over the following months, was the official responsibility of the civilian authorities. Ordinary civil servants were thus involved at all levels in the implementation of racial policy: carrying out census exercises and drawing up registration lists of those in different 'racial' categories; forcing Jews out of their homes; confiscating their possessions and means of livelihood; rounding them up for forced labour; 'resettling' them in poorer housing, restricted living areas, or ghettoes; cutting rations; tightening regulations on where or when they could shop; forbidding the use of public transport; and subjecting them to highly restrictive regulations about curfew times, wearing armbands, even crossing the street at certain angles, and the appropriate manner of greeting Germans. Transgression of any of these regulations could incur severe penalties, including incarceration, deportation to a labour camp, or being shot dead on the spot. Horrendous living conditions and starvation rations, with Poles being given the basic minimum on which to live and work, and Jews even less, meant very high rates of mortality from malnutrition and disease, with variations depending on locality.

Conditions were worst in the enclosed ghettoes such as Warsaw (in the General Government) or Łódź (in Wartheland), and somewhat less atrocious in the highly industrial region of eastern Upper Silesia, where Jews were initially deployed in industries crucial to military purposes, including the production of armaments and uniforms.[38] Conditions for forced labourers varied: while some were able to remain living with their families—though rarely in their own homes, from which they had been ousted to make way for 'resettled' Germans—the majority were, over time, squeezed into ghettoes or snatched and deported to dedicated labour camps. Death by overwork, disease, and malnutrition was common. But whichever area is looked at, the policies of occupation caused immense suffering and in very many cases

---

[37] See e.g. Isaiah Trunk, *Judenrat: The Jewish Councils in Eastern Europe under Nazi occupation* (New York: Macmillan, 1972).

[38] A point emphasized in Sibylle Steinbacher, *'Musterstadt Auschwitz'*. The literature on ghettoes is large and growing; see e.g. the edited selection of sources for one ghetto, Sascha Feuchert, Erwin Leibfried, and Jörg Riecke, *Die Chronik des Gettos Lodz / Litzmannstadt* (Göttingen: Wallstein Verlag, 2007); and more generally Gustavo Corni, *Hitler's Ghettos: Voices from a beleaguered society 1939–1944* (London: Arnold, 2002).

premature death, whether by shooting, burning, hanging, maltreatment, or starvation. The later development of a well-organized system of mass extermination by bringing large groups of victims to places where execution was more rapid and 'efficient' should not blind us to the inherently murderous quality of Nazi rule in the years before the dedicated extermination centres were established.

Increasing impoverishment was often accompanied by a growing sense of hopelessness and apathy; or, in order simply to survive, a resort to what were designated by the occupying authorities as 'criminal activities', including fiddling with ration cards and black-market dealing. Processes of degradation and their inevitable outcome—a population living in squalor, filth, and misery—did not simply exist, to be 'witnessed' by 'bystanders'; they were actively created by the Germans who were administering these territories. And those targets of oppression who sought to resist or contest their fate were liable to be subjected to rapid, brutal measures: arrested, beaten up, imprisoned, shot, hanged. Civilian administrators later often appealed to the fact that it was the Gestapo or SS who had meted out such physical brutality, and sought thereby to protest their own 'innocence'.[39] But historians should not take such self-exculpatory sentiments as an accurate summary of the Nazi system, with its myriad of newly imposed repressive and exploitative regulations, which ultimately crushed its victims mercilessly for any minor infringement or transgression. Nor are post-war legal systems, with their emphasis on individual acts of extreme physical violence, a very good guide to the real system of power and enforcement of ultimately murderous rule. Involvement in the imposition of systemic violence went far beyond individual acts of brutality.

The new civilian administrations set up in the newly occupied territories, unlike in some area of the 'Old Reich' (*Altreich*), not only worked hand in hand with the local NSDAP organizations but were frequently synonymous.[40] In the occupied and incorporated territories in particular it was a complete myth that the 'civil service' remained a somehow untainted and honourable occupation (somewhat on the lines of the myth of the 'clean *Wehrmacht*'), separate from the party, the SS and the Gestapo, who could be blamed for doing all the dirty work. The overlap between party and state in these areas was almost complete. Thus the state role of president of the Province of Upper Silesia, for example, was at the same time coterminous with the party role of *Gauleiter*; and the incumbents of these posts, first Josef Wagner then from 1941 Fritz Bracht, were determined to build up a model Nazi province under the motto 'Upper Silesia—the new Ruhr area'.[41]

And here it was that those members of the war-youth generation who were willing to be mobilized in service of the Nazi cause found unprecedented

[39] Cf. the various defence statements and testimonies in Ludwigsburg, discussed further in Fulbrook, *A Small Town Near Auschwitz*.

[40] On the rather different situation in Württemberg, a rather distinctive area of the Old Reich (for many historical reasons) and where local functionaries could only hesitatingly be brought into line, retaining primary loyalties to relatives, friends and neighbours, see Stephenson, *Hitler's Home Front*.

[41] Ryszard Kaczmarek, 'Zwischen Altreich und Besatzungsgebiet. Der Gau Oberschlesien 1939/41–1945' in Jürgen John, Horst Möller, and Thomas Schaarschmidt (eds.), *Die NS-Gaue. Regionale Mittelinstanzen im zentralistischen 'Führerstaat'*, p. 352.

opportunities for very rapid promotion. The newly appointed district officials (*Landräte*) in the area of eastern Upper Silesia, a strip of land east of Katowice (Kattowitz) taken over beyond what had formerly been Prussian/German territory, were almost entirely young, keen, up-and-coming civil servants who were at the same time loyal party members. As many as ten of the eleven *Landräte* in this area, including by now Udo K., were born in the decade 1900–10, a pattern which was very typical for those holding leading positions in newly incorporated territories.[42] Very typically, again including Udo K., many of them alternated periods of military service at the front with periods administering the politics of occupation; only a few were successful in attempts at gaining, for longer or shorter periods of time, the status of 'indispensable' (*uk*) on the home front, and with varying degrees of ambivalence at that.[43] These civilian officials were responsible for implementing the new racial hierarchy and the associated 'resettlement' of populations within their territories—moving Jews and Poles out, moving 'ethnic Germans' in—and for issuing the decrees and regulations which governed who could go where, when, and how: passing down and ensuring the enforcement of decrees to do with curfews, wearing of armbands with the Star of David, policing restricted access areas and prohibitions on using public transport, and cutting allotted rations and access to shops and services. They implemented the racial system on the ground.

Involvement in the racial system thus went way beyond the physical violence exercised by the *Einsatzgruppen*, the SS, the Gestapo, and the various police forces down to the level of the local gendarmes. And it was not limited to people in the civilian administration. Racial oppression and systemic violence also involved large numbers of German entrepreneurs who took over 'Aryanized' Jewish businesses, or who ran factories and firms using slave labour 'bought' from the SS. Indirectly, but no less wittingly, it also involved those who knowingly benefited from the 'Aryanization' of Jewish property, living in formerly Jewish houses and buying furniture, clothes, and other goods at knock-down prices from the inappropriately named German 'trustees' (*Treuhändler*). Any German benefiting from these 'bargains' and windfalls was well aware of their background, but arguably chose to notice only the personal benefits and advantages of this system, and not think too hard about those from whom the property had been taken.

Even for those Germans who were not settling in these areas, the conditions under which Jews were forced to live, whether in the newly created ghettoes or in still 'open' areas of restricted residence, were no secret at this time. Soldiers passing through, civilians coming to do business, people visiting friends and family,

---

[42] Archivum Państwowe w Katowicach, Regierung Kattowitz, 119/703, fols. 17–18, for the ages of *Landräte* in Ostoberschlesien. See also more generally, Raul Hilberg, *Perpetrators, Victims, Bystanders* (New York: HarperCollins, 1993), pp. 36–50, and particularly pp. 38–9; and see also Lothar Kettenacker, 'Die Chefs der Zivilverwaltung im Zweiten Weltkrieg' in Dieter Rebentisch and Karl Teppe (eds.), *Verwaltung contra Menschenführung im Staat Hitlers. Studien zum politisch-administrativen System* (Göttingen: Vandenhoeck and Ruprecht, 1986), pp. 403–4, pointing out that the *Landräte* in the newly annexed province of Alsace were also all very young: most of them less than thirty-five years old, and only one aged sixty.

[43] See further Fulbrook, *A Small Town Near Auschwitz*.

frequently commented on the horrendous state of the impoverished population, with generally little conscious or at least explicit registration of the fact that it was German conquest and German policies that had caused this degree of poverty and degradation, bringing into physical effect the previous metaphorical claim that 'the Jews' were a 'danger' to the 'healthy German racial community'. Rather, they seemed to interpret what they saw as evidence that Nazi propaganda had been right all along. As one soldier put it in a letter home on 12 August 1940:

> This place [near Lublin] has around 16,000 inhabitants, of whom 14,000 are Jews. But real Jews, with beards and filthy, to be precise even worse than they are always described in *Der Stürmer*... The whole population is infested and filthy. You really can't imagine what one gets to see here. And this people of culture wanted to conquer Berlin![44]

The gulf between 'two worlds' which had been gradually created between Jewish and non-Jewish Germans through the peacetime years was thus apparently 'confirmed' with a vengeance by exposure to the horrendous state to which the Jews of Eastern Europe had been reduced even within the first few months of Nazi occupation. Moreover, those reacting in this way further betrayed the influence of Nazi propaganda in apparently thinking they were fighting a 'defensive war' against potentially dangerous enemies in the east. The reactions of Germans who witnessed these conditions appear to have been virtually untouched by the human tragedies. There was instead a widespread sense of distaste at having to live among 'creatures' whom they appear to have viewed in much the same way as animals about to go to the slaughterhouse, but with little evidence of any sense of common humanity. The fact that this was already a system which involved effective mass murder—deaths caused directly or indirectly by Nazi policies—seems to have escaped their attention.

Following Udo K.'s appointment as *Landrat* of Będzin in February 1940, Alexandra went in August with her husband to choose an appropriate house in which to live—in the event, the 'villa of the Jew Schein'—and, as she wrote to her mother, was not impressed by her new environment:

> The town is incredibly hideous, wretched, dilapidated, dirty, I've never seen anything like it. The streets are teeming with grimy, ragged, disgusting Jews. There is hardly anyone not wearing white armbands [bearing the Jewish star], but even they are filthy. Some of the Jews talk German, everyone else Polish.[45]

There seemed little evidence here of the 'humanist education' of the Augusta Schule days, and little conscious recognition that the all too visible impoverishment of a previously thriving and diverse Jewish community—including wealthy philanthropists such as the Scheins, in whose villa Alexandra and Udo were now to live—was directly due to the Nazi policies of seizing the housing, businesses, possessions, and livelihoods of the Jews. And as conditions worsened for those Jews subjected to

---

[44] Walter Manoschek (ed), *'Es gibt nur eines für das Judentum: Vernichtung'. Das Judenbild in deutschen Soldatenbriefen 1939–1944* (Hamburg: Hamburger Edition, 1995), 12.8.1940 Montag, Gefr. H.K., 3.Kp./Inf.Rgt.527, 298.Inf.Div., FPN 18 292D, p. 15.
[45] Letter from Alexandra to her mother, 28 August 1940, private family archive.

oppression, so the Germans became ever more willing to contemplate their 'removal' through 'resettlement' as a means of making these areas 'Jew free', and hence pleasanter for the remaining 'Aryan' population. This was a crucial precondition that made the 'Final Solution' eventually possible. The complicity of adults involved at this stage ranged from the passing 'witnesses', through the witting beneficiaries, to the willing functionaries of racist rule.

IV. IDEOLOGICAL WAR AND COLLECTIVE FRAMEWORKS OF INTERPRETATION

For all the ambivalence of Germans about going to war once again, the easy victories of the '*Blitzkrieg*' period, when the German army invaded and conquered vast swathes of Europe, from Poland in the east around through Denmark and Norway in the north to France in the west, allowed a sense of optimism to permeate even letters complaining about conditions at the front. For those serving under the relatively 'easy' conditions on the western front, the physical deprivations occasioned by living under military conditions were perhaps outweighed by the emotional deprivations of missing those at home. But even at this point, collective frameworks of interpretation and the notion of the self as part of a wider collectivity against an enemy (frequently caricatured and portrayed in the singular) helped to inform the sense of a social self as part of a national community.

Gerhard R. (born 1912), for example, was initially stationed in Western Europe, spending a considerable amount of time in Holland. Gerhard R. had a wife and young family at the time of his call up. His letters are full of love and concern for his wife and children, and memories of their times together; receiving a parcel of food reminds him of happy evenings at home; and, as he put it, 'There is always a beautiful memory, and a memory can keep you going for a long time.'[46] The dangers of warfare are treated relatively lightly, with a degree of distancing humour, a stereotyping of 'the enemy' in the singular ('Tommy'), and radically downplaying of the very real risks of warfare:

> Well, Tommy has recently been hiding himself away like a mouse, it's time that he got a rap on the head again soon. Here in our area he has recently also caused a few little eggs to fall, so among the civilian population there were quite a few dead, I haven't heard of any soldiers yet. Well, soon there'll be real pressure on him again, so that should take away any desire on his part to engage in this sort of fun and games.[47]

Even though the sentiments expressed here are likely to have been at least in part designed to reassure his wife, the confidence in German victory and the lack of any questioning of the broader project were relatively widespread at this time.

Moreover, once the victory over France was assured, many soldiers appear to have enjoyed their time as a form of tourism combined with licensed robbery. Even

---

[46] FMK, 3.2002.0990, Gerhard R., letter of 15 April 1942.
[47] *Ibid.*, letter of 30 April 1942.

young women seem to have gone along with the military in much this spirit, as evidenced by a rare sequence of letters. A school class of thirteen women from Chemnitz born in the last years of the Great War stayed in touch with each other after leaving school, and continued writing over a span of more than sixty years, in a series stretching from 1943 to 2004, including also many photos of their developments and exploits. One of these, Gretel, volunteered for the German Labour Front, and was sent to France with the *Wehrmacht*; her letters back to her school friends register a degree of apprehension at her new-found independence and need to make her way among predominantly male company, but also a great sense of excitement at and enjoyment of this unexpected foreign travel as a young woman.[48] The enjoyment by German soldiers of the riches of plunder following the invasion of France is evident too from other contemporary sources.[49] But matters changed once Hitler's attention turned eastwards; and letters to and from the eastern front betray an extraordinarily widespread internalization of official propaganda.

The announcement of the German invasion of the Soviet Union, after nearly two years in which the Hitler–Stalin pact had seemed to obviate any such possibility, was greeted in many quarters with a degree of surprise; and yet the official theory of an honourable and indeed 'defensive' or 'pre-emptive war' was widely prevalent. As one young soldier, Walter E., put it in a letter home:

> You will probably have been astonished when the news came, war with Russia. It was to be foreseen, and it was something that had to be. What we have seen up to now was always one and the same thing, Russia and England want to annihilate Germany. But the Führer got in before them.[50]

Within a matter of weeks, the parents of this particular 24-year old had to post his death notice, according to which: 'In faithful fulfilment of his duty [Walter] gave his young life for Führer, nation [*Volk*] and Fatherland in the fight against Bolshevism.'[51] Solace was to be sought by relativizing the worth of the individual life in relation to the national ethnic collective and its ideologically driven struggles—an attempt which arguably increasingly wore thin as the war progressed.

Initially at least, a spirit of what might be called joyous apprehension at finally tackling the 'real enemy' is evident. Sergeant (*Feldwebel*) Hans M., for example, rhetorically asked his wife 'Well, what do you say about our new enemy?' and reminded her that he had already said, on his last leave at home, 'that in the long term there's no way of maintaining friendly relations with the Bolsheviks. On top of that, there are still far too many Jews there.'[52] On the same day, Kurt U. wrote home that:

---

[48] Bibliothek für Zeitgeschichte Stuttgart, 'Klassenbriefe', Vol. I, 30.5.43–6.10.53, fols. 40–6.

[49] See e.g. Götz Aly, *Hitlers Volksstaat* (Frankfurt: Fischer, 2005); but see also Adam Tooze, *The Wages of Destruction: The making and breaking of the Nazi economy* (London: Penguin, 2007).

[50] Bibliothek für Zeitgeschichte Stuttgart, Sammlung Sterz (henceforth BfZ, SSt), O'Gefr. Walter E., 28816 E, 8.Kp./Inf.Rgt.499, 268.Inf.Div., 9 Jul. 1941.

[51] BfZ, SSt, O'Gefr. Walter E., 28816 E, 8.Kp./Inf.Rgt.499, 268.Inf.Div., death notice, Heidelberg, 29 Aug. 1941.

[52] BfZ, SSt, Fw. Hans M., 28193 B, 9.Kp./Inf.Reg.226, 79.Inf.Div., Sunday 22 Jul. 1941.

Early today thank God we finally got going against our deadly enemy, Bolshevism. I felt like a weight had been lifted from my heart. Finally this uncertainty has come to an end and we know what we are about.[53]

Soldiers seem to have felt it relevant to rehearse in some detail in their letters home what they had obviously taken from propagandistic representations of the 'preventive war', although writers portrayed such interpretations as being entirely their own:

> But who would have thought that we would now be fighting against the Bolsheviks? The whole thing was kept fabulously secret! But when I think about it properly, then the Führer has yet again done the best thing he could have done . . . And now it's all stations go in the east, and it's definitely a good thing that this is so. Because in the shorter or longer term it would have come to this clash . . . Now Jewry has declared war on us all along the line, from one extreme to the other, from the plutocrats in London and New York to the Bolsheviks. All that is Jewish stands together in one front against us. The Marxists are fighting shoulder to shoulder with High Finance—just like in Germany before 1933 . . . But we managed to get a nose-length ahead of the Reds by our preventive attack . . .
>
> If you might perhaps be thinking that we've all broken out into cheering enthusiasm, then that would be mistaken. We ourselves know exactly what's at stake, and that this is one of the most decisive armed combats, yes if it turns out victorious [for us], the most decisive.[54]

In the event, for all the ideological posturing and in retrospect extraordinary statements in these letters, betraying deep internalization of Nazi world views in some quarters, no one really knew exactly what they were about to face. What from this point on developed in the east proved virtually beyond imagining, and for many of these soldiers it was almost beyond description too.

At this stage, even the smaller everyday difficulties of war, whether at home or at the front, were widely put into a broader, heavily ideological perspective. Appeals to a notion of a community above the self, and constructions of a 'real soldier' as one who would defend the Fatherland in order to return to peacetime work could help people in facing the new challenges. As Annaliese N., in a letter of letter of 22 June 1941, wrote to her husband:

> When I turned on the radio this morning and then, totally without any idea [this would happen], heard the Führer's proclamation, I was at first quite speechless . . . Today I have just realized in wonderment the greatness of his diplomacy . . . And if you stop to think about it, you feel quite small. What is our little bit of suffering, our cares and the tiny privations that arise from the war economy. But that's the way we are, actually we don't really think about things enough, and then we get so caught up by personal matters and so we just live without really thinking. In any event, the struggle will likely be hard, and yet many will breathe more easily after the long weeks of waiting, for a real soldier yearns, after all, for battle and for victory, in order then to be able to turn again to his [peacetime] work . . .[55]

---

[53] BfZ, SSt, Sold. Kurt U., 31040, 1.San.Kp.91, 6.Geb.Div., Sunday 22 Jun. 1941.
[54] BfZ, SSt, Uffz. Alfred N., L 33281, Fliegerhorst Lyon, 23 Jun. 1941.
[55] BfZ, SSt, Annaliese N., Haisberge / Porta, 22 Jun. 1941.

Anneliese N. clearly felt she had to rise beyond her personal experiences, the worries and cares of her own daily life, and appropriate a broader current framework of interpretation to deal with the new developments. These interpretive frameworks included both notions of a 'hard struggle' and a decent soldier: a particular construction of a social self, not purely as an individual following personal concerns but one committed to and part of a wider national community; and one, moreover, which was at heart a peace-loving self, fighting only temporarily in order to create the conditions for a peaceful life.

Similar sentiments placing the community above the individual are to be found in the framework appropriated by Private Wilhelm H.:

> today a great struggle began, of great world historical significance, against a traitor to Germany, a bitter enemy of people bent on building for the future . . . And only the Führer and his closest followers, who always have trust in him and will give their last for him, have taken this danger from us, and just in time. This is why I find it ever harder to understand why there are still German people who do not have blind trust in this Führer, who either can't or won't believe in him, if not absolutely everything is going just as they imagined or as they would like from their own egocentric perspective [*ichsüchtigen Standpunkt*].[56]

While it is clear that letters to and from the field were censored, such that soldiers were hardly likely to write critical comments, it was certainly not necessary from the censorship point of view to write in these overwhelmingly enthusiastic, indeed quasi-religious, terms.[57]

Letters such as these can be seen not (or not only) as supposed evidence of political attitudes or degrees of faith in the *Führer*; they betray rather (or also) a real and very personal urgency in trying to 'make sense' of what people were being mobilized to do, and to make sense of this mobilization in ways with which individuals could live, even by which they could feel enthusiastic. This might otherwise have seemed an appalling way to spend what, in purely personal terms as young adults, would potentially have been seen under 'normal' peacetime circumstances as the 'best years of one's life'. Commitment to a wider sense of community and purpose was arguably the only way to deal with the deprivations of the self; or rather, constructions of the self at this point had repeatedly to emphasize the self as part of this wider community, and not as an individual entitled to the happiness of the privacy of family and work, now denounced or demoted as 'self-serving'. The private idyll had to be postponed until after the 'final victory' (*End-sieg*). External mobilization, in short, was for at least some of these soldiers and their families accompanied by an astonishing reflection of official frameworks of interpretation in personal strategies of self-mobilization along the prescribed lines.

---

[56] BfZ, SSt, Gefr. Wilhelm H., 13063, Stab/Bau-Btl.46, Monday 23 Jun. 1941.

[57] To point to elements arguably appropriated from and certainly having something in common with the imagery and practices of religious faith communities does not also necessarily entail buying into broader interpretations of Nazism as a 'political religion', a topic that has intermittently been the subject of much debate among historians; see e.g. Michael Burleigh, *The Third Reich: A new history* (New York: Hill and Wang, 2001).

Thus what is striking in a large number of letters following the invasion of the Soviet Union in the early summer of 1941 is the way in which soldiers were imbued with an ideological outlook betraying both the influence of recent Nazi propaganda and ideological training, and of longer-term notions of being a 'decent soldier' doing one's 'duty', drawing on pre-Nazi traditions—on which of course Hitler had also drawn in gaining a following for the Nazi cause. Another soldier justified his return to his division precisely in terms of a triple, and to him apparently mutually confirming, set of allotted collective self-identifications:

> I have reported back to my Division . . . Now, I will do everything I can to make it [in time] for the attack. Ultimately, as a soldier, Nazi and East Prussian I am trebly bound to fight against the Reds.[58]

A young soldier, Erwin Z., wrote home to his mother: 'You write that you are very proud of me, I'm very glad about that but I am doing no more than my duty as a German youth, helping to protect the homeland [*Heimat*].'[59] Here, any justification for his mother's pride in her son as an individual was explicitly rejected in terms of his internalized sense of doing nothing more than his 'duty' as a 'German youth' helping to 'defend' his 'homeland'.

An appeal to selected historical traditions could also help in making the connections between the *Führer* and the self. As Lance Corporal Gerhard S. put it in a letter of 22 June 1941:

> Recently in a 46° degree heat we had a 20 km march . . . But I am nevertheless still the old marcher. It should never be possible to say that the 'boys' are the first to hit the wall [*schlapp machen*, reach the point of total exhaustion]. I'm doing my duty as a decent soldier. May the little part that I play do its bit for Germany's victory in the war. Look, right now it is ever more a matter of being hard with oneself. Personal wishes have to be suppressed. We have gradually to become ever more like the front soldiers of 1918. I will gladly give everything for our people, for in these fateful times this is our highest and purest experience . . .
>
> I believe in our German people, because in these hours of difficulty it shows itself to be so powerful and radiant. The spirit of freedom of 1813 is blowing through the German lands. 'And if you do not venture your own life, you will never have gained it for yourself' [quotation from Friedrich Schiller, 1797].[60]

Nazi emphases on 'hardness' are here tacked lightly on to appeals to long-standing German military experiences and traditions, with successful wars of 'liberation' and unacceptable defeats coming together with traditions of German high culture in the new campaign against the east.

At the most basic physical level, the campaign in the east was from the outset far harder than that in the west. Soldiers needed every shred of ideological commitment they could muster simply to keep going. Letters contain innumerable

---

[58] BfZ, SSt, Lt. Curt J., Höh.Kdo.XXXII, 23 Jun. 1941.
[59] BfZ, SSt, O'Gefr. Erwin Z., 07 226 C, 10.Kp./Inf.Rgt.447, 137 Inf.Div., 19 Jul. 1941.
[60] BfZ, SSt, Gefr. Gerhard S., 38002, 1.Kp./Inf.Div.Nachr.Abt.198, 98.Inf.Div., Sunday 22 Jun. 1941.

complaints about heat and dust and thirst and mosquitoes. As one soldier put it in a
letter home of 8 July 1941:

> You can hardly imagine how much we are sweating. As wet as if we had just been
> pulled out of the water. Crazy! And on top of that, this dust! We look as black as
> niggers, or better, as stripy as zebras, since the sweat runs down our faces in broad
> streams and slowly makes wave marks on our hands.[61]

And as another soldier put it in his diary: 'Marching on through Ostrog. Indescribable pictures. Houses destroyed, barren and deserted, everywhere the smell of
burning and corpses...The numbers of dead can't even be imagined.'[62] But
even in face of basic discomforts, belief in the *Führer* seemed not merely to survive,
but to provide some form of comfort or support, as another letter suggested:

> Amongst much dust and much heat and much thirst and many mosquitoes Stalin's
> pupils are retreating...Again and again it is something unfathomable and powerful—
> this faith in the Führer in the midst of all this deprivation and exertion...[63]

Everything could be thrown in together—the physical discomforts and the significance of the ideological fight—as illustrated by a letter from Paul B:

> It is a battle against all the elements that the Asiatic peoples, Jewry, Bolshevism etc. can
> throw up. And we can thank the Führer and the German soldiers for the fact that the
> Heimat and Europe have been spared these. And then the battle against the mosqui-
> toes. Swarms beyond counting and huge specimens descend on us, the beasts can get
> through anything, even gloves on your fingers and a turban on your head, and all of
> this in this extreme heat. But we keep on going: forwards, into battle, to victory.[64]

In this state of physical distress and exhaustion, constantly struggling with heat and
dust, and plagued by mosquitoes, young German males marched into terrain where
they would be mobilized for mass murder in ways for which they were, to a startling
degree, already ideologically softened up.

As they travelled further east, for many soldiers a sense of self as part of a
supposedly superior national-ethnic community was constantly reaffirmed by
'confirmation' of the 'primitivity' of the 'inferior' peoples about whom they had
previously heard but were now encountering personally for the first time. Quasi-
anthropological travelogues begin to pervade soldiers' accounts:

> The mosquitoes that have already made these woods famous and notorious since the
> World War were the most annoying thing...The image of war is always the same,
> piteous yet all the same always overpowering; burning villages, churned up streets,
> people chased away, cattle without masters, dust, smoke, gunfire...Small low wooden
> houses along long village-like streets. The people meeting us in the villages ragged,
> filthy, bare-footed, the women dressed colourfully, headscarves and blouses...[65]

---

[61] BfZ, SSt, Sold. Manfred V., 02544, 3.Kp./Pz.Jäg.Abt.32, 32. Inf.Div., 8 Jul. 1941.

[62] BfZ, SSt, Tagebuch, Gefr. G., 13517 A, Stab III/Art.Reg.119, 11.Pz.Div., 2 Jul. 1941.

[63] BfZ, SSt, Mj. Hans Sch., 33691, Stab/Pi.Btl.652, 24 Jun. 1941.

[64] BfZ, SSt, Gefr. Paul B., L 46 281, Flak-Sondergeräte-Werkst.Zug 13., 16 Jul. 1941.

[65] BfZ, SSt, Gefr. Heinrich V., 07405, Stab/Beob.Abt.9, 23 Jun. 1941.

Such observations of ill-clad, dirty, bare-foot and hence clearly 'inferior' peoples inevitably shored up notions of the supposed cultural superiority of the Germans. As Private Paul H. expressed it: 'We could never in our lives manage to get as dirty as the Russians are, we would have to live all over again in order to catch up on that front.'[66]

In the early weeks following the invasion of the Soviet Union, there was apparent confirmation of Goebbels' propaganda about the 'Soviet paradise', and a sense of German superiority as a 'people of culture' (*Kulturvolk*) in contrast to 'Asiatic primitivity'. As one soldier put it: 'Finally we are in the Soviet paradise... It looks dismal here, the people are impoverished and covered in dirt. The roads here are indescribable, it's impossible to write about, you can't even talk about it.'[67] Or in the words of another: 'Ruins of churches, ... ragged, listless people, filth and decay everywhere, a nice paradise. We can thank our dear God that we live in Germany.'[68] Such views remained closely linked to continuing notions of a 'defensive' or 'preventive' war: an essentially pre-emptive war against what the Russians and 'Jews' would, it was assumed, have done to Germany if Hitler had not chosen the right time to take action in order to 'prevent' it.

This interpretation was furthermore echoed back through letters from those at home. Similar views were expressed by people who were clearly influenced by the *Wochenschau* newsreels and Nazi-dominated newspaper reports, and had no personal experience of any such encounters, as expressed for example in a letter from Frau W., resident in Hamburg, on 6 July 1941:

> Isn't it all ghastly, what they are experiencing in the east? The newspaper reports made me feel quite sick, these aren't people any more, but beasts. And they want to bring culture and civilization to Europe? What would it have been like if they had invaded us? I believe we would really have had an experience then. Well, thank God the Führer went on the attack first...[69]

But soldiers often felt they were experiencing 'more' than mere propaganda, and that those at home could not really imagine what it was, in their interpretation of their perceptions, 'really' like. Their attempts to deal with new experiences were sometimes faltering.

It is hard to gauge whether, on occasion, soldiers really held to any coherent framework of interpretation; sometimes it appears that the almost overwhelming impressions they gained on their travel to the east were too much for them to describe. As Emil E. put it: 'But nevertheless there are still a great many incidents [*Zwischenfälle*], it's simply beyond description. Later, if we get together again sometime in a fit state, [I'll tell you] the details.'[70] But soldiers clearly clutched at any attempt to make sense of what they were witnessing—and to make sense in a way that would also seem to justify their own actions. Letters often included a not

---

[66] BfZ, SSt, Gefr. Paul H., 21663, 12.Kp./Geb.Jäg.Rgt.98, 1.Geb.Div., 23 Jun. 1941.
[67] BfZ, SSt, Sold. Siegfried Sch., 02 466 E, 4.Kp./Inf.Rgt.34, 35.Inf.Div., Monday14 Jul. 1941.
[68] BfZ, SSt, Gefr. Paul Sch., 21 046, Bäck.Kp.54, 1.Geb.Div., 13 Jul. 1941, 19 Jul. 1941.
[69] BfZ, SSt, Frau W., Hamburg, 6 Jul. 1941.
[70] BfZ, SSt, Gefr. Emil E., 37 664 C, 2.Kp./Ldsschtz.Btl.874, 14 Jul. 1941.

entirely logical leap to reiteration of faith in the *Führer* and the 'preventive' war, as in the following letter, first describing the Warsaw ghetto:

> We drive through the disease-ridden Jewish quarter, fenced off with barbed wire, the state of this area and its inhabitants is beyond description . . . As we were driving by we saw a man collapse without any obvious cause, it was probably hunger that caused the collapse, since every day a number of this rabble [*Gesindel*] die of starvation. A few are still well dressed in pre-war clothing, most are shrouded in sacks and rags, a frightful picture of hunger and misery. Children and women run after us crying 'bread, bread'.[71]

Despite traces of racist terminology here ('*Gesindel*' is a pejorative term that can also be translated as trash, riff-raff, or vermin), the letter writer is clearly shocked by these scenes. He even implicitly registers that the rags in which the Jews are dressed are a product of wartime conditions, since some people still provide evidence of a pre-war life in which they were well-dressed. Yet he fails to reach the obvious conclusion that the current situation is the result of Nazi maltreatment of the Jewish population in the ghetto; and he arrives at safer ideological territory later on in the letter, when he finally manages to draw more securely on prevalent Nazi discourse in the description of his subsequent experiences:

> Our first destination was <u>Siedlce</u>, a medium-sized town . . . 80% of the population are Jews, the appearance of the whole town correspondingly [awful] . . . the houses ooze with dirt and decay . . . Then we reached somewhere close to the Russian border . . . 52 Russian and 31 Polish snipers were shot dead here yesterday . . . So yet again the Führer has struck at precisely the right moment.[72]

Here, the filthy appearance of the town can readily be put down to the high percentage of the Jewish population, with no apparent shift from pre-war to current conditions; and the onset of 'real' warfare, with the shooting dead of some eighty-three snipers, can be slotted without further problems into the concept of the *Führer*'s pre-emptive strike.

For all the influence of propaganda and prior ideological training, soldiers were on occasion aware of discrepancies between what they were now witnessing, and what they had expected—certainly what they assumed those still at home would be imagining, based on war reports. As one soldier put it:

> All around us is war and horror, struggle and sacrifice. The newspaper will describe the victory more easily than the experience of it is really like. Later we will be in the same position as many from the other Great War. Only we know what happened!—But loyalty remains!—[73]

Soldiers often registered both a 'recognition' of Nazi stereotypes, and at the same time a degree of shock about what they were seeing, as well as a sense that all was not being accurately reported home. The dissonance between perceptions cast in

---

[71] BfZ, SSt, Uffz. Heinrich Z., 07794, Stab/Heeres-San.Abt.601, 30 Jun. 1941.
[72] *Ibid.*
[73] BfZ, SSt, Gefr. Heinz Sch., 20 158, Pi.Rgts.Stab 514 z.b.V., Sunday, 13 Jul. 1941.

the terms of ideological stereotypes, and more immediate personal reactions of revulsion at scenes of horror, was often difficult to convey, particularly when aware of the very different images being screened at home. In the words of Manfred V.:

> In the little town here live almost exclusively Jews. Revolting people; typical caftan Jews; they simply talk too much with their hands as well as their mouths . . . One sees frightful and terrible scenes. But this can never be written about in letters; it can hardly be captured in words. It's just a good thing that you don't get to see such scenes in the newsreel. Many a young man would lose all desire to go to war.[74]

However difficult this was to describe, the reality or prospect of atrocities against Jews could nevertheless still be twisted and incorporated into the wider version of the 'defensive war', as another soldier, Christoph B., intimated:

> Now I've already been here on Russian soil for two days . . . In the towns the population generally consists of 50–80% Jews. This gives you an idea of what the members of the chosen people are like. The Jews are also the ones who led the way in committing atrocities against Ukrainians. And not a few German soldiers have fallen prey to the deviousness of these filthy rats. We Germans therefore have no reason to go about treating these creatures with any kind of consideration. For this reason they are lower than dogs as far as we are concerned. For us soldiers this is taken for granted.[75]

Again, the appeal to the self as part of a wider collective—'we Germans' and 'us soldiers'—as well as explicit repetition of the allegedly reasonable grounds for severe maltreatment of those no longer considered even to be human beings, are used to assist this individual in coping with what it is he is being mobilized to do, and in trying to explain it to those back home.

One letter more or less summed up the entire gamut of topoi evident across a wide range of letters to and from the front. It is worth quoting in full, for the way in which it configures these various elements into one relatively coherent whole, and stands for a dominant world view which, on this evidence, was not only a matter of propagandistic pronouncements. To write a private letter home in this way, going well beyond the 'individual' messages of greetings and cares for family members, suggests that the official interpretive framework was apparently internalized to a high degree in some quarters, or at least learnt and rehearsed sufficiently to explain actions which the soldier was being constrained to engage in. These sorts of dissonant rationalizations are found repeatedly in letters home, and appear to have been widely prevalent among collectively informed subjectivities and constructions of the social self at the time. On Thursday 10 July 1941, a little over two weeks into the Russian campaign, Heinz B. wrote home:

> One thing we know for certain, particularly we soldiers, and that is the absolute fact and certainty that we are heading towards a great and glorious victory, one that will outshine all that has gone before in its greatness, achievements and sacrifice. And being able to be a small cog in the great machine helps us to forget a lot and relieve the pain.

---

[74] BfZ, SSt, Sold. Manfred V., 02544, 3.Kp./Pz.Jäg. Abt.32, 32. Inf.Div., 2 Jul. 1941.
[75] BfZ, SS, St'Fw. Christoph B., L34215, Trsp. Kol.d.Lw.9/VII, 7 Jul. 1941.

For each day that breaks afresh always has something new to show us, partly human, partly cultural, and one thing always stands out large and clear, how endlessly proud and joyful we can be that we are Germans and that our Heimat is called Germany. Only we can so precisely confirm anew, every day, that there are many countries and peoples with culture and education, but that there is only one German people and that this is many classes higher than anything else in the world. Every German, even the poorest, has it a hundred times better, yes, he lives magnificently in comparison to the lower cultures and lives of other peoples. When we come eventually to take off our uniform, then we'll have a life before us that we know how to treasure, however stormy the times ahead may be. But the German people has an enormous indebtedness towards our Führer, since if these beasts who are our enemies here had come to Germany, there would have been murder on a scale the world has not yet seen. If countless thousands of their own inhabitants are already being murdered by the Soviets, and Ukrainians, a people without any defence, are being brutally mutilated and killed, how would they have even begun to deal with the Germans? What we have seen can't be described by any newspaper. It borders on the unbelievable, even the Middle Ages can't compete with what has happened here. And even if in Germany you read the *Stürmer* and see the pictures, that is only a tiny glimpse of what we are seeing here and of what Jews are committing here by way of crimes. Believe me, even the most sensationalist reports in the newspapers convey only a fraction of what is going on here.[76]

In this one long passage, in which Heinz B. does not even use the first person voice in the singular but rather speaks in the plural throughout, the entire set of collective representations are present. For all the heaping of guilt for atrocities on the Soviets, and hence reiterating the significance of the allegedly defensive war, this is not least an extraordinary testimony to the power which could, even if only among a minority, be exercised by the dominant mentalities of the time.[77] However much others may have managed to retain some sense of individuality and even internal distance from the regime, clearly among many soldiers the only way to deal with the horrendous scenes they were not merely witnessing, but in which they were also actively participating, was to engage in explicit reiteration of the received views and the collective identities as soldiers and Germans that appeared to legitimize this venture.

There were exceptions: how atypical these were we cannot know. One such voice is that of Siegbert Stehmann, a theologian and poet whose letters to his wife are full of tenderness, thoughtfulness, and a sense of utter isolation.[78] It is clear that endless exposure to violence had a numbing effect on Stehmann:

We ourselves are staggering with tiredness, hunger and exhaustion, a little heap of soldiers against a mighty enemy. The air is filled with the repulsive sweet smell of the rotting corpses which lie on the roads. It is gruesome. The only strange thing is how

---

[76] BfZ, SSt, Uffz. Heinz B., 29 524 C, 11. Btr./Art.Rgt.125, 125.Inf.Div., 10 Jul. 1941.

[77] As ever, it is not possible to make statements on percentages or the degrees to which any testimony is 'representative'.

[78] Siegbert Stehmann, *Die Bitternis verschweigen wir. Feldpostbriefe 1940–1945* (Hannover: Lutherisches Verlagshaus, 1992). See also Konrad Jarausch and Klaus Jochen Arnold (eds.), *Das stille Sterben . . . Feldpostbriefe von Konrad Jarausch aus Polen und Russland 1939–1942* (Paderborn: Ferdinand Schöningh, 2008).

one can look at this all without being touched by it. Yesterday at midnight I sat for a couple of minutes on the side of the road in order to rest, next to a dead Russian, and ate up my last piece of bread. The image of war here is how it is depicted in Goya's 'Horrors of War'.[79]

But there is no evidence in Stehmann's letters of either the 'brutalization' that often accompanied involvement in violence on the eastern front, nor of a sense of 'comradeship' (*Kameradschaft*) that was alleged to exist among soldiers sharing a common fate. As he ruminated in late August 1941:

> In these days of late summer I feel more alone than ever before. Heavy personal disappointments and bitterness, repeatedly poisoned by the troop of those united in quiet, silently fulfilled duty; personal misunderstandings, from which I suffer more than from the fact of war, lead me to yearn dreadfully for a return to the realm of orderliness, thoughts, love and friendship. Despite sobering experiences, hearts are fundamentally on idle. Egoism and thoughtlessness are growing in strange contrast to the natural recognition of the truly essential, a recognition that everyone should have in a state of emergency.[80]

A week later, Stehmann continued:

> Clouds of grief are hanging over tens of thousands. The pace of war has grown from month to month and it has become lonely around those who see such a fate from the inside, yes, who are destined to participate in it with their lives. I sense this in myself to a frightening degree. One lives totally isolated, even as a comrade who is in a relationship of comradeship. Existence would no longer be existence without this cloak of isolation, which provides protection against the floods dragging you down. Within this however is the connection with values, thoughts, love, friendship. Within this I have unison with you, who would otherwise become an almost foreign image of memory. Within this the spirit thinks, dreams and creates, as though that still had any sense. Yes, it does probably have sense, hidden, muted, and one day a new world will arise from it. But perhaps that belongs more in the realm of fantasy and poetic imagination than in the realm of reality. Let God decide.[81]

Like so many of his compatriots, Stehmann—who bore no responsibility at all for this war or the way it was carried out—did not survive to reflect on his experiences later, or to help bring up the son whom he never knew. He died in January 1945. Even if Stehmann was far from typical, and indeed his sense of isolation was rooted precisely in the capacity of the majority of his comrades to go along with the prevailing tide, it is important that voices such as his should also be heard.

---

[79] Stehmann, *Die Bitternis verschweigen wir*, entry of 23 Jul. 1941, p. 116. The original Goya title is generally translated as 'The Disasters of War', but this does not accurately convey the flavour of the German term '*Schrecknisse*' used by Stehmann in this context.

[80] *Ibid.*, entry of 24 Aug. 1941, p. 123. On the notion of '*Kameradschaft*' more generally, see Thomas Kühne, *Kameradschaft: Die Soldaten des nationalsozialistischen Krieges und das 20. Jahrhundert* (Göttingen: Vandenhoek und Ruprecht, 2006); and on the question of 'brutalization' see also Ben Shepherd, *War in the Wild East: The German army and Soviet partisans* (Cambridge, MA: Harvard University Press, 2004).

[81] Stehmann, *Die Bitternis verschweigen wir*, entry of 1 Sep. 1941, p. 126.

Many letters provide only snapshots or moments in time; we know little or nothing about the longer-term developments of an individual's views and attitudes. But some sequences do allow insights into the ways in which people of different ages developed and changed with their experiences through the war. And they suggest that patterns were not entirely dissimilar across the older age groups, although there were differences in perceptions between those older soldiers who were already family men, and younger ones, members of the 'first Hitler Youth generation', who were often both highly influenced by the conditions of their upbringing and had not as yet made long-term commitments with respect to marriage partners or children.

Once Gerhard R., who had begun to come to terms with military life on the western front, was moved to the east, the tone of the letters shifts distinctly, and concern about family is but one theme among many.[82] For one thing, the physical discomforts were now much greater:

> for the first time in 35 hours we have a period of rest and now would like to sleep, but the heat and the flies do not allow it . . . The dust and ever more dust is the same, day and night . . . When you get out of the carriage you look like a chimney sweep and then on top of that no water to wash with, barely any for cooking or drinking.[83]

Nor was the landscape of much solace, although the Germans themselves were doing little to improve matters:

> Otherwise the area here is everywhere equally barren, no trees, no shrubs far and wide. For kilometres not a single human habitation . . . Well, when we finally get to Stalingrad, we'll get to see something of culture again, since that is a big city with more than a million inhabitants. That is, if it hasn't all been burnt down. Since it has been burning now for several days. We can observe it well from here, by day the gigantic clouds of smoke and by night the fiery glow that can be seen from far away.[84]

Altogether, Gerhard R. was only now beginning to realize quite how good conditions had been on the western front, by comparison:

> those were also different and I think better times. Yes, if I think back on the time in Holland or even in Belgium, then I realize for the first time really how good we still had it then despite all, and we already thought things were bad. Today I can understand already why those comrades who came from the east looked a little askance at the soldiers who were stationed in the west, you get tempted into this view yourself now and then. At the same time it is of course clear to me that even there one has to be on one's guard, but only someone who has been here too can get any real idea of life at the front and any real idea of this Russian campaign. And already we have experienced and also had to withstand an awful, awful lot here.[85]

Gerhard R. remained relatively quiet on what it was that the Germans themselves were doing, and what was implied by the last sentence of this letter. But he

---

[82] See above, p. 186.
[83] FMK, 3.2002.0990, Gerhard R., letter of 10 Aug. 1942.
[84] *Ibid.*, letter of 13 Sep 1942.   [85] *Ibid.*

remained clear that the Germans were culturally 'superior', and, without much further reflection, entirely entitled to do what they were doing. Even the burial customs (or lack of them) of the Russians during a period of heavy fighting gave cause for criticism:

> Here in our section the Russian has, alongside his last eastern-asiatic butt of an army, already mobilized quite young, 15-year-old youths, who have hardly been given any military training yet . . . How often already we have been amazed by the fact that dead Russians lie around in the villages after battle, none of the civilians even think of burying them, absolutely no one is bothered by this, they can stay lying there like dead animals . . . Well, there is scarcely anything here that one could describe as culture, the people are completely apathetic.[86]

It is a sad irony that an appeal to the superiority of German 'culture' is here, even as late as September 1942, evidenced with respect to the perceived Russian practice of leaving dead bodies to lie around 'like dead animals'. Gerhard R. made no reference to the other heaps of corpses caused by murderous German policies: openly hung on trees as a warning, burned alive in barns, houses, and synagogues, rounded up, shot and buried in mass graves in the woods, or gassed and burned in open fires or specially designed crematoria and scattered as ashes.

Appeals to related and more specific notions within the broader categories of the cultural superiority of the Germans were also of some use. When writing to his parents Gerhard R. sought to make it clear how a sense of 'comradeship' was a very real experience, and indeed essential given the conditions under which the soldiers were living. For Gerhard R., a young member of the war-youth generation, it also provided some sort of bond with his father and echoed with what he assumed was his father's experience and understanding of the Great War:

> But a person can endure a lot and adapt to changed living conditions, however different . . . Here everyone is in practice dependent on everyone else and so a quite different sort of comradeship develops. If it were not for this, then a number of things could not have been accomplished which have already been accomplished. Well, Father will know too how things look when you only have Mother Earth as your quarters.[87]

Perhaps the reference to his father's experience in the Great War was momentarily of some comfort to this particular member of the war-youth generation. But it was not to be of very enduring solace.

Like so many of his comrades, Gerhard R. did not survive Stalingrad to return to his wife and children. The last letter he wrote was on New Year's Day 1943. The version retained in the archival collection is, unlike the handwritten originals of all the other letters, a typed up copy sent to the family posthumously, stamped as authentic (*beglaubigt*) by the NSDAP, and including what might have been the somewhat embellished sentiments that:

> Even if things don't look too rosy for us here at the moment, nevertheless our belief in the final victory remains unshakable. And with faith in God, who will certainly not

---

[86] FMK, 3.2002.0990, Gerhard R., letter of 4 Sep. 1942.   [87] *Ibid.*, letter of 6 Sep. 1942.

desert us, and faith in our Führer, who will not leave us in the lurch, we will simply persevere here until we can breathe somewhat more freely again.[88]

Gerhard R. had, up to this point, been what one might call 'apolitically nationalist' in his letters. He had not queried the purpose of war, implicitly assuming natural superiority over the various enemies, and was in that sense an uncritical representative of German nationalist and Nazi discourses; for all the individuality of his experiences, reactions, and selection of points for commentary, he had also echoed tropes that were widely current at the time. But he had also not explicitly paraded any enthusiastic pro-Nazi sentiments. He had simply been effectively mobilized, going wherever he was sent, doing the best he could for himself and his 'comrades', seeking to make the best sense of it all that he could, in the context of the frameworks available to him, while continually yearning for his family at home. In some respects, this is a relatively typical profile, often found among the vast numbers of letter-writers whose relatively mundane letters did not make it out of the archives and into the edited and published selections.[89] The phrase alluding to faith in the *Führer*, highly uncharacteristic in light of Gerhard's earlier letters, may well have been written in by the Nazi stenographer. It was in any event a spin which the NSDAP sought desperately to get across to the millions of German soldiers and their families who shared similar fates—falling in the senseless slaughter of Stalingrad, or waiting anxiously at home for news of sons, husbands, brothers, friends, lovers, relatives, and neighbours away at the front—and yet who were expected, in face of it all, to retain an absolute and unconditional faith in the *Führer*. Whether or not Gerhard R. penned these sentiments himself in the last letter before he died, these were the ways in which such deaths were to be interpreted by those of his compatriots who were part of the exclusive national ethnic community.

Karl S., born in late November 1922 and some ten years younger than Gerhard R. (born 1912), was desperate to be allowed to join in the war. An enthusiastic member of the Hitler Youth organization, he joined the NSDAP straight from the HJ. In early August 1941, when still only eighteen, he was involved in pre-military training and had already applied to join the SS. His early experiences of the war were registered as little more than a free railcard around Europe; even his arrival in Russia was almost like a holiday to him, with the occasional roughing it built in for an extra sense of adventure:

> It was a wonderful journey from Wednesday to Sunday. It seemed to me like a holiday trip. The journey led in a curve like on a fever chart via the Reich capital city to the granary of Prussia, from here up again to the capital of Lithuania and then south-east to the capital of White Russia, a town that has now been annexed to the German Reich. A wonderful region, in midst of woods . . . But [the roads], they are simply indescribable. Our field paths at home are golden in comparison . . . And then the Russian economy.

---

[88] *Ibid.*, letter of 1 Jan. 1943.
[89] For a variety of fairly obvious methodological reasons, it would be impossible to guess at percentages or degrees of 'typicality'. But Gerhard R.'s letters have been chosen as representing a highly prevalent profile.

I've already seen some of the houses close by to us. I can only say that I would feel more comfortable in our chicken coop.[90]

As far as the social and racial hierarchy in the camp was concerned, Karl S. repeated the ideological sentiments about both Jews and Russians—his reference is unclear, though the two seem more or less coterminous for him—in which he had been socialized: 'Jews and prisoners of war are now working in this camp. I can tell you, a people even worse than the gypsies.'[91] And he remained delighted with his own career and rapid progress in comparison to others from his school class and age group: 'That I'm the first to go to the front, or at least near the front is for me a quite special honour. I am proud of it.'[92] Even a year later, when he had experienced a great deal more by way of military service across Europe, this highly committed member of the 'first Hitler Youth generation' was apparently very happy with his lot, still seeing it more in terms of adventure and tourism than as the tragedy of war. Most of his letters are to his parents, and he did not have the kinds of family ties of those men a few years older. The spirit of adventurous travel seems to have taken precedence for Karl S. over family ties or other relationships. In a letter to a girl by the name of Liesel of 9 September 1942 he commented:

> I greatly liked Paris, which was excellent. You feel like a real bon viveur. Today in Russia, tomorrow in France and the day after tomorrow God knows where. Days spent lying around in fast trains, seeing all the beautiful towns of every country, learning about the languages, customs and traditions of foreign peoples. I am only 28 km away from one of the most beautiful and well-known palaces of France.[93]

Along with around half of his age group, Karl S.'s adventures were to be short-lived, his youthful enthusiasm for the Nazi cause ultimately bearing little fruit. He was killed in action on the eastern front on 15 February 1943.

Karl S. clearly came from a family of highly committed Nazis. His younger brother Walter S., born 1924, seems equally keen to have been called up. Walter's letters home are purely formulaic: he generally restricts his remarks to comments about the weather, and repeatedly asserts that all is well with him. In March 1944, for example, and despite the loss of his brother the previous autumn, he writes home that:

> Otherwise everything is tip-top here with me. It is a quite glorious day again today. It all looks wonderful in this area. The fruit trees are nearly all in bloom. The meadows are also full of flowers already. And at home where you are there is still snow on the ground.[94]

Even allowing for the evidently limited capacity for expression of this young man, his repeated expressions of delight in landscapes and weather and seasons suggest that enjoyment of life took precedence over any thoughts about the project in which he was engaged. In the summer of 1944, when Walter S. was uncharacteristically

---

[90] FMK, 3.2002.1276, Karl S., letter of 9 Sep. 1941.   [91] *Ibid.*, letter of 21 Sep. 1941.
[92] *Ibid.*   [93] *Ibid.*, letter of 9 Sep. 1942.
[94] FMK, 3.2002.1277, Walter S., letter of 13 Mar. 1944.

registering real news of the numbers of wounded troops and lost planes, he retained a staggering kind of dumb optimism:

> Everything is still tip-top here with me . . . Well I guess in England too it's not looking so rosy now . . . I'll get leave once the war is over and that won't last long now.[95]

On 15 September 1944 Walter S. too died, at the age of twenty, following an unsuccessful attempt at amputation of one of his limbs in a field hospital.

It is instructive to place the evidence of these letters in a comparative context, looking at a selection coming from more highly educated Germans. Given the way in which the German system of higher education still operated, even in the 1930s, an academic university degree (let alone a doctorate) was also a proxy for higher social standing, allowing something of a glimpse of class differences in perceptions.

A collection of selected letters was published a few years after the end of the war when there was a strong concern to be able to grieve for 'honourable' or 'decent' soldiers, providing evidence from a small number of generally well-educated and literate young men mainly from the 'first Hitler Youth generation' born towards or just after the end of the Great War.[96] This collection is of some considerable interest for what it reveals about the mentalities of those educated and 'decent' young men whose letters were included. It has of course to be remembered that there were also later, post-war processes of selection of which letters to forward for publication, and which to include in the final volume, which may have served somewhat to present a more 'acceptable' rather than fully representative sample of the young soldiers' writings. Nevertheless, certain features stand out. It is clear from the letters that for many of these young soldiers knowledge of the Great War— including often specific reference to what their fathers had or might have experienced—played a considerable role in both their anticipation of and in some cases eventual disillusionment with Hitler's War. This generation appears at first to have been less fearful of, more excited about, the prospect of war than were those of an older generation who had experienced the Great War at first hand and had viewed the prospect of another war with foreboding. Yet very soon many of these letters register a sense, not exactly of disappointment, but rather of disillusion: that war was not all a matter of heroism (*Heldentum*), or as spiritual and glorious as they felt they had been led to expect, but both more mundane and more awful. These 'fallen students' were of the same generation as those who participated in the youth gangs perpetrating 'spontaneous' acts of violence in the 1930s. The violent youth gangs were of course only a minority of the age group, and—although the sources do not allow complete certainty on this point—probably less likely to have come from the kind of educated, professional, and bourgeois backgrounds from which the 'fallen students' had emerged. The 'fallen students' were very probably not themselves participants in the street violence of the 1930s; and, before being called up, all had

---

[95] *Ibid.*, letter of 28 Jun. 1944.
[96] Walther Bähr and Hans Bähr (eds.), *Kriegsbriefe gefallener Studenten 1939–1945* (Tübingen and Stuttgart: Rainer Wunderlich Verlag, 1952).

been in some way involved in the education system, whether as students, researchers, or junior teaching assistants. But nevertheless, they would have been exposed to
the Hitler Youth organization and Nazi propaganda throughout the 1930s. It is,
then, quite striking just how patchily this seems to have affected the ways in which
they described their perceptions of and responses to the physical experience of
brutality in war once at the front.

Shattered by the atrocious physical conditions in which they sought to survive,
and horrified by the evidence of brutality and slaughter all around, many of these
student letter-writers sought solace in 'Nature', God, and the German classics.
Letters are filled with quotations from well-known German poets from Goethe
onwards. A few seek reassurance—in also reassuring their loved ones at home—that
they will have fallen for the Fatherland; some suggest that their death will not have
been in vain; but relatively little of this is couched in Nazi propaganda terms.[97]
A source of comfort, or at least momentary escapism, for some was to indulge in
day-dreaming, mentally escaping into happy memories of home, childhood, and
everyday things. In the atrocious physical conditions in which they had to struggle,
young soldiers empathized with fallen comrades and even dead horses, pitying
themselves for having to live among the hideous evidence of so much death and
destruction, rather than explicitly reflecting on why they were there and what they
were doing to their own victims and enemies. Yet when mentioned, the latter are
not universally shunned or presented in the Nazi stereotypes, even in the ideologically highly charged Russian campaign against the Slavic, Bolshevist *Untermenschen*
(inferior beings). There are occasionally remarkably kind words about individual
Russians; and also positive comments about Russian culture, the works of great
Russian writers, and the Russian landscape—although the latter was perhaps more
frequently contrasted unfavourably with the familiar German *Heimat*, and once
winter set in with a vengeance the climate was experienced as unbearably harsh.

These 'letters from the field' were of course effectively trebly censored: first by
the writers of the letters exerting a degree of self-restraint in what they wrote
(although this would have been unlikely to excise any authentic pro-Nazi sentiments); secondly by the military censorship of the time (again, this would not have
filtered out pro-Nazi expressions); and finally by the editors' selection of letters for
publication which would seem acceptable in the climate of the early 1950s, when
there was a desire to be able to mourn fallen youngsters without the complications
entailed by any taint of Nazism (which would have exercised a filter in the opposite
direction from the first two). Nevertheless, and even taking this treble sieving into
account, it is striking how little space is given in any of these letters to querying the
purpose of war or critiquing those who inaugurated and steered it. Even among
those who appear most disaffected at the experiences of war, any anger at 'those
who are responsible' is utterly non-specific. If anything, the dominant mood in the
letters runs in the other direction: a sense of pride in the *Vaterland* is often palpable.
Again, with all due recognition not merely for the constraints of censorship but also

---

[97] See also Michael Kater, *Hitler Youth* (Cambridge, MA: Harvard University Press, 2004).

for the enhancing effects of 'cognitive dissonance' among letter writers at the time—if one has to die, then the cause has to be worth it—the rhetoric seems to have been sufficiently entrenched inside soldiers' heads for relatively plausible attempts to be made at persuasion of both oneself and those at home that the battles and sacrifices were not (and could not be) in vain. Even so, overall in these private letters there is perhaps more about survival and 'getting through' by sheer strength of character and attitude (*durchhalten*), and about the unimaginably awful conditions the soldier himself was enduring, than about any high ideals which might make it all worthwhile.

Letters from a more general selection published in 1982 illustrate to a greater extent the impact of Nazi propaganda and ways of seeing things. Russians, for example, are described as 'these uncultivated, multi-racial people'; the fight is an ideological one, since 'We are not fighting against the Russian people, but against the world enemy, Bolshevism.'[98] Ordinary soldiers seem to have had greater difficulties in finding words for communicating the horrors all around. Key concerns revolve around how to remain 'decent' (*anständig*) under conditions of warfare. 'Decency' was closely related to 'comradeship' (*Kameradschaft*): it related basically to one's fellow soldiers, to the small group of peers with whom one lived and might die; it related to 'doing one's duty' (*Pflicht*), being prepared to sacrifice oneself, and having the 'hardness' required in order to keep fighting despite numerous deprivations and atrocious physical conditions.[99]

But perhaps what is most striking about the vast majority of field-post letters is what is most absent. There is virtually no apparent sense of shame at what they were doing; and they appear to have raised no real questions about the ultimate morality of the enterprise, mostly—if they addressed this at all—merely parroting contemporary propaganda about why they were doing what they were doing. The repetition of these reasons, however, does give some cause for wondering whether there was indeed on occasion an inner sense of dissonance, or at least fear that those at home would have little understanding, psychologically perhaps requiring the explicit reproduction of reasons which did not necessarily quite match the horror of the situation. As far as the 'racial war' was explicitly mentioned, soldiers appear either to have largely internalized the Nazi world view (*Weltanschauung*) before arriving in the field, or to have interpreted what they now saw as confirmation or 'proof' of what they had previously viewed more sceptically as merely propaganda, or perhaps to have sought, through writing, to adopt the prevalent language and line of interpretation and hence by repetition to convince themselves about the rightness of the actions in this new and awful world. In other letters, there are hints that what has been witnessed cannot be described in writing, or needs talking about at length; such hints provide intimations of a substantial group who witnessed but

---

[98] Buchbender and Sterz (eds.), *Das andere Gesicht des Krieges*, pp. 78, 81.
[99] See the summary in Wette, *Die Wehrmacht*, p. 179. For detailed analyses of the processes of brutalization on the eastern front and the extent of army involvement in atrocities, see e.g. Omer Bartov, *The Eastern Front, 1941–45: German troops and the barbarisation of warfare*, 2nd edn (Houndmills: Palgrave, 2001; orig. 1985); and Shepherd, *War in the Wild East*.

were, for whatever reasons (including of course censorship and self-censorship), not prepared or able to commit their reactions to writing. It is again impossible to quantify the relative proportions. Yet had it not been for the significant numbers who willingly went along with the regime propaganda or the peer-group pressures of the moment to interpret their encounters with 'eastern Jews' in the sense provided by Hitler, the architects of genocide would have had a far harder job in finding willing agents of destruction in the field.

V. FROM MASS MURDER TO THE 'FINAL SOLUTION'

The invasion of the Soviet Union in the summer of 1941 is generally held to represent something of a turning point in the character of the ideological and racial war.[100] It was made clear from the spring of 1941 that this was to be a campaign of a different character from the conventional notions of warfare. As *Generaloberst* (Colonel-General) Franz Halder noted in his diary, on 30 March 1941, following a speech of Hitler's which lasted some two and a half hours:

> *The struggle of two worldviews against each other.* A verdict of annihilation against Bolshevism, it's equivalent to asocial criminality. Communism a great danger for the future. We have to distance ourselves from the standpoint of soldierly comradeship. The Communist is not a comrade—neither beforehand nor afterwards. It's about a war of extermination [*Vernichtungskampf*]. If we don't conceive of it in this way, then we may well beat the enemy, but in 30 years time the communist enemy will stand against us yet again. We are not waging war in such as way as to preserve the enemy . . .

Halder noted further at the side of this entry:

> The battle will be very different from the war in the west. In the east ruthlessness now means lenience for the future.
> The leaders must ask of themselves the sacrifice of suppressing their qualms.[101]

---

[100] There has been a recent tendency to query these sharp distinctions, however. See e.g. Klaus-Michael Mallmann and Bogdan Musial (eds.), *Genesis des Genozids: Polen 1939–1941* (Darmstadt: Wissenschaftliche Buchgesellschaft, 2004), 'Einleitung'. Historians over the decades have debated intensively over when, if at all, Hitler may have reached a definitive decision that the 'final solution' of the 'Jewish question' should be not simply the exclusion but rather the active extermination of all Jews in Europe. Current historiography on the whole prefers to approach this in terms of an evolving process rather than seeking to identify a key turning point, although it is clear that there were significant moments of escalation. See e.g. the magisterial narrative by Saul Friedländer, *The Years of Extermination: Nazi Germany and the Jews, 1933–45*, 2 vols. (New York: HarperCollins, 2007), Vol. II; and for significant earlier contributions, Christopher Browning, *The Path to Genocide: Essays on launching the Final Solution* (Cambridge: Cambridge University Press, 1998); and Browning, *The Origins of the Final Solution: The evolution of Nazi Jewish Policy, September 1939–March 1942* (Lincoln: University of Nebraska Press, 2004); Philippe Burrin, *Hitler and the Jews: The genesis of the Holocaust* (London: Edward Arnold, 1994); and Longerich, *Politik der Vernichtung*.

[101] Reprinted in Gerhard Ueberschar and Wolfram Wette (eds.), *'Unternehmen Barbarossa'. Der deutsche Überfall auf die Sowjetunion 1941* (Paderborn: Ferdinand Schöningh, 1984), p. 303, from *Generaloberst Halder: Kriegstagebuch Bd II* (Stuttgart: Kohlhammer, 1962–4), pp. 335 ff.; emphasis in the original.

As at the start of the Polish campaign, special orders were issued concerning the necessity for special task forces: 'The deployment of special commandos of the Security Police in the area of operations is necessary in order to carry out exceptional security police tasks . . .' These special units were to work together closely with the military forces in the area:

> An appointee of the Chief of the Security Police and the SD will be deployed to provide central guidance to these Commandos in the region covered by each Army . . . The appointees are constantly to work closely with the Ic . . . The Ic is to ensure that the tasks of the Special Commandos are coordinated with military intelligence and the activities of the secret field police and in line with the demands of the operations.[102]

Thus from the outset the actions of the special task force units were fully coordinated with the actions of the army with the role of the 'Ic' officer acting as official go-between.

Furthermore, right from the outset the rules of regular warfare and distinctions between criminal acts and 'acceptable' violence were lifted. On 13 May 1941, a special order explicitly removed any legal penalties for committing acts of violence against civilians, including shooting civilians 'while trying to escape' (*auf der Flucht erschossen*), and 'extermination' (*Vernichtung*) of anyone representing a threat to the Germans:

> Also all *other attacks by enemy civilians on the Army*, their associated members and entourage, are to be combated on the spot by the most extreme means possible including the annihilation of the assailant . . .
>
> For *treatment meted out by members of the Army* and its retinue *against enemy civilians*, there is *no need for prosecution*, even when the action is at the same time equivalent to a military crime or misdemeanour.[103]

On 19 May, a further set of 'Guidelines for the Behaviour of Troops in Russia' was issued, once more underlining the ideological character of warfare in this arena:

> 1. *Bolshevism is the deadly enemy of the National Socialist people. Germany's struggle is directed against this destructive worldview and its carriers.*
>
> 2. This struggle demands ruthless, energetic and drastic measures against *Bolshevik rabble-rousers, franctireurs, saboteurs, Jews* and total elimination of every form of active or passive resistance.[104]

In effect, Germans had been given the official go ahead to engage in indiscriminate murder, unbound by any previous constraints of law, or considerations of possible

---

[102] 'Regelung des Einsatzes der Sicherheitspolizei und des SD im Verbande des Heeres' signed by von Brauchitsch, and 'Zusammenarbeit zwischen den Sonderkommandos und den militärischen Kommandobehörden im rückwärtigen Armeegebiet', repr. in Ueberschar and Wette (eds.), '*Unternehmen Barbarossa*', pp. 303–4.

[103] Der Führer und Oberste-Befehlshaber der Wehrmacht, 13. Mai 1941, 'Erlaß über die Ausübung der Kriegsgerichtsbarkeit im Gebiet 'Barbarossa' und über besondere Maßnahmen der Truppe', repr. in Ueberschar and Wette (eds.), '*Unternehmen Barbarossa*', p. 306, emphases in original.

[104] 'Anlage 3 zur Weisung Nr. 21 (Fall Barbarossa) von 19.5.1941: Richtlinien für das Verhalten der Truppe in Rußland', repr. in Ueberschar and Wette (eds.), '*Unternehmen Barbarossa*', p. 312, emphases in original.

penalties for their actions, or conventional guidelines for appropriate conduct and distinctions between 'legitimate' and 'illegitimate' targets in times of war.

Such boundaries had in practice already been crossed, by the thousandfold, since the invasion of Poland in September 1939; but now they were the subject of further, highly explicit emphasis and widespread distribution. The 'anti-partisan' warfare following the invasion of the Soviet Union was fought with extraordinary ferocity and brutality, with inevitable consequences for all involved, however diverse their initial reactions. And there is some evidence to suggest that here, as in so many aspects of the tale of Nazi brutality, officers who themselves came from the eastern provinces of Germany and were brought up among the anti-Slav sentiments of the post-Versailles era, were among the most ideologically committed to brutal notions of racial war in the east.[105] Yet as the war proceeded, more and more troops, of an ever widening age distribution, were called up to replace those who were maimed, captured, or killed in combat. Individual variations in degrees of willingness or otherwise to be involved were increasingly swept away by the wider logic of the escalating situation.

Moreover, military conquest was followed by brutal civilian administration of occupied territories, again accompanied by violence and the administrative facilitation of policies of exploitation and genocide.[106] Massacres of Jews from whole villages often took place in open-air sites, where they were forced to dig their own graves before being shot into them. Sometimes preparations for such killings took several days, and involved the cooperation of significant numbers of the local non-Jewish populations, as well as being widely witnessed by civilians who were not directly involved.[107]

What accompanied and followed the invasion of Russia is not only by now well known, but was also extremely widely known at the time.[108] The convenient postwar myth that, in the convenient and widely used phrase, 'we never knew anything about it' ('*davon haben wir nichts gewusst!*') was predicated on a widespread failure to register and respond appropriately to what was known, on a failure of imagination or empathy, and on a lack of willingness to put different details of the mosaic

---

[105] Shepherd, *War in the Wild East*, p. 231.

[106] There are growing numbers of regional and local studies; see e.g. Karel Berkhoff, *Harvest of Despair: Life and death in the Ukraine under Nazi rule* (Cambridge, MA: Harvard University Press, 2004); Wendy Lower, *Nazi Empire Building and the Holocaust in the Ukraine* (Chapel Hill: University of North Carolina, 2005).

[107] Much of this has escaped official memorialization, while remaining highly alive in the memories of local residents; see for recent attempts to raise such sites of mass killing to a higher public consciousness, Father Patrick Desbois, *The Holocaust by Bullets: A priest's journey to uncover the truth behind the murder of 1.5 million Jews* (Houndmills, Basingstoke: Palgrave Macmillan, 2008); see also Ray Brandon and Wendy Lower (eds.), *The Shoah in the Ukraine: History, testimony, memorialisation* (Bloomington and Indianapolis: Indiana University Press, 2008).

[108] See also Frank Bajohr and Dieter Pohl, *Der Holocaust als offenes Geheimnis. Die Deutschen, die NS-Führung und die Alliierten* (Munich: C. H. Beck, 2006); Bernward Dörner, *Die Deutschen und der Holocaust. Was niemand wissen wollte, aber jeder wissen konnte* (Berlin: Ullstein, 2007); Peter Longerich, *'Davon haben wir michts gewusst!' Die Deutschen und die Judenverfolgung 1933–1945* (Munch: Siedler Verlag, 2006); and the more general collection, Otto Dov Kulka and Eberhard Jäckel (eds.), *Die Juden in den geheimen NS-Stimmungsberichten 1933–1945* (Düsseldorf: Droste Verlag, 2004).

together to form a wider picture; in short, on an unwillingness to construct what precisely was implied by the 'about it' ('*davon*') of which one had allegedly 'known nothing', until confronted with the full horrors and forced to acknowledge the wider picture after the war. 'Ignorance' was not a lack of knowledge with respect to individual atrocities, nor a lack of knowledge that civilians were being murdered in extraordinarily large numbers, but rather an incapacity or unwillingness on the part of many, but by no means all, Germans to recognize what these atrocities cumulatively amounted to. It was also, in part, rooted in an extreme narrowing down in post-war conceptions of 'responsibility' to the legal sense of acts of individually motivated, excessive brutality, and to a related if rarely explicit view that responsibility somehow only 'really' began at the gas chambers of Auschwitz, and not in any prior acts of extreme inhumanity (maltreatment, forced labour, expropriation, ghettoization, and rationing amounting to enforced starvation) or killing 'while trying to escape' (without asking from what). It also has to be remembered that only a fraction—perhaps around one-fifth—of the total number of victims of what has come to be known collectively as the 'Holocaust' were actually killed in Auschwitz itself, however iconic that particular site has become. Violence against Jews more generally was certainly well-known, even if the details were (a not always well-kept) secret.

In effect, then, what people did not 'know' was what all the small acts of inhumanity and brutality would cumulatively amount to; and what they did not consciously register, then or later, was the part that their own actions and roles, however small, played in the larger scheme of things. Most of those involved were merely tiny cogs in the system, with no responsibility for the direction or character of policy-making. Neither the overall shape and functioning of this system, nor the ultimate and cumulative results of disparate 'actions' across Europe, were within the scope of most people's knowledge or imaginings at the time (or indeed later). Having been caught up and complicit in the preconditions and practices of this system, people could subsequently only appeal to the lack of 'knowledge' of the whole in order to exonerate themselves from blame for their own small, often tiny, part in it.

What changed in the summer and autumn of 1941? The notion of Jewish life as being in principle 'unworthy of living' had been prevalent in the Third Reich for many years, with individual deaths being caused, directly and indirectly, by acts of brutality and maltreatment as well as suicides arising out of despair, and had escalated dramatically already with the annexation of Austria; the pogrom of November 1938; the occupation of the Sudetenland, Bohemia, and Moravia; and, more dramatically and on a larger scale, with the invasion of Poland in the September 1939. The major shifts of 1941–2 were not so much a matter of transgressing a moral boundary in principle, but rather of the scale, methods, and ultimate explicit goal of killing civilians on 'racial' grounds, as well as the concomitant prevention of emigration and the progressive concentration of intended victims in specific locations. There were also a series of escalations in the programme, in part related to the changing fortunes of the Russian campaign in the summer and autumn of 1941, in part related to the transition from a European to a World War in December 1941, and in part related to the death in early June 1942 of Himmler's close collaborator in the persecution and extermination of Jews, Reinhard Heydrich, following the assassination attack a week earlier.[109]

With the invasion of Russia far larger numbers of Jewish civilians were encountered, and almost immediately murdered. Not only members of the SS special squads or *Einsatzgruppen*, but also 'ordinary soldiers' and Order Police units were involved in mass killings, whether by shooting into graves which the victims themselves had been forced to dig, or through a variety of other means, including locking victims up in barns and buildings and burning them alive. Troops were readily mobilized to carry out Hitler's orders through a combination of the brutalizing effects of existence at the front and a heightened susceptibility for cultural mobilization, especially as a result of the ideological work of relatively young, highly convinced, junior officers in enhancing and consolidating a Nazi world view 'legitimating' actions of utmost brutality against civilians through appeals to notions of 'inferior races', 'reprisals' for 'partisan activity', and the like.[110] But none of the methods of killing current on the eastern front in the summer of 1941 was, from the point of view of the murderers, very 'efficient', for a range of physical, material, political, and psychological reasons.

In the autumn of 1941, major new developments in the methods of murderous violence occurred. In addition to killing large numbers of Jews in the places where they were found (being shot, hanged, burned, or beaten to death in or near the villages and towns of Eastern Europe in which they lived), or proactively encouraging their deaths by policy-created 'natural causes' such as starvation, disease, and exploitation in places where they had been brought together (concentration camps, slave labour camps, and ghettoes), the scope and potential goals of mass murder were massively expanded by the construction of specifically designed extermination centres, and the deportation of Jews from their places of residence (or refuge) to these designated centres of death. In this way, the killers themselves did not have to go to find their prey; the victims were brought to the specialists in killing. And both the physical methods and psychological procedures of the killing centres were constantly subject to review and enhancement, such that the scale of killing could be hugely increased, lending a degree of wild credibility to the most extreme Nazi aspiration that, by murdering every last member of what was defined as a discrete 'racial' community, the very 'final solution' to the self-defined 'Jewish question' could be achieved. This ultimate aspiration was summarized in the Wannsee conference of January 1942, a meeting which implicated virtually all the key state authorities in the coordination of practical arrangements for mass murder as the mutually agreed 'final solution' of the 'Jewish question', explicitly replacing the previous programme of enforced emigration which had been finally

---

[109] On Heydrich, see e.g. Mario Dederichs, *Heydrich: The face of evil* (London: Greenhill Books, 2006; orig. German Piper Verlag, 2005).

[110] See Bartov, *The eastern front*, Chs. 2–3, for the relatively young age range of the junior officers, committed to the Nazi cause and responsible for ideological indoctrination, and the character and impact of the material they presented.

forbidden the previous autumn. The discussion also revisited some of the ambiguities persisting around the definition of who actually was to be included in the 'biological community' designated for murder, including startlingly bureaucratic distinctions between '*Mischlinge*' of various 'degrees', within and outside of marriage with others in a similar variety of categories, with and without children, and with and without extenuating circumstances and distinctions, and turning over the possible 'choices' for '*Mischlinge*' between 'voluntary' or 'forced' sterilization or deportation and murder.

If the senior civil servants were involved in detailed planning at the top, so too were civil servants, political leaders, and technical experts as well as a multiplicity of other interested parties at regional and lower levels of the apparatus. For to implement the movement, exploitation and murder of people on this scale had massive logistical implications, even beyond the coordination of train timetables which implicated every station master along rail routes across Europe.[111] By the time the 'Final Solution' was officially implemented, the prior work of population counting—deciding who was in which of many possible categories for varying degrees of disadvantage, reduction of rations, loss of the means of livelihood, restrictions on movement, ghettoization—had already been largely carried out in the areas which were already firmly under German occupation and administration. Now, those Jews who had not yet fallen prey to disease and starvation, or died as a result of random shootings, hangings, and other forms of 'retribution', and who were deemed not still 'useful' as slave labour for the Germans, had to be rounded up under pretexts ranging from 'resettlement' to the 'stamping' or 'reissue' of identity cards; held in guarded temporary waiting areas if the trains and trucks available could not cope with the numbers involved; policed and shot at if trying to escape. The remaining property and valuables had to be collected and 'disposed of', and housing reallocated. Nor were the forces of brutality the only ones to be involved; logistics demanded a great deal by way of detailed planning and coordination among technical experts, political officials, and civil servants, as well as the SS, particularly as, during the course of 1942, dedicated extermination centres were set up to develop ever more 'efficient' ways of killing. The existing extermination facilities of the concentration camps of Auschwitz and Majdanek, and the gas vans of Chełmno (put into operation in December 1941), were in 1942 rapidly augmented by the killing centres of Bełżec (construction of which had already begun the previous autumn), Sobibór and Treblinka, as part of 'Operation Reinhard', so named after the assassination of Reinhard Heydrich. And all these brought with them—as at every previous stage in this monstrous project—new 'problems' which had to be 'solved', involving the efforts of far wider circles of people than the front-line killers themselves.

The extension of involvement, and the corresponding extension of 'knowledge', may be illustrated by what might at first glance seem a very banal and, in the

---

[111] A point made particularly by Raul Hilberg: see his classic work on *The Destruction of the European Jews* (Yale: Yale University Press, updated edn, 2003; orig 1961). On the Auschwitz area in particular, see Sybille Steinbacher, *'Musterstadt' Auschwitz. Germanierungspolitik und Judenmord in Ostoberschlesien* (München: K. G. Saur, 2000).

context, almost trivial example. Yet it is precisely in the detailed logistics of these operations at the grass roots that so many beyond the front-line killers were involved. The presence of large numbers of people forced to live in highly unsanitary conditions in the Auschwitz concentration camp at Oświęcim (the Polish name of the town), and the construction in 1942 of the huge extermination and slave labour camp at Auschwitz-Birkenau in a little village on the outskirts of the town, had major implications for the supply of fresh water and the removal of waste water from an area where the health not only of the local Polish population but also increasing numbers of Germans was being endangered by the spread of disease. Not only members of the SS, but also civilian workers in the large chemical works of IG Farben in the neighbouring hamlet of Monowitz, and many other Germans were now living and working in the area. The discussion of town planning and engineering questions relating to drains—which might seem the most grotesquely mundane of subjects in this connection—is highly illuminating with respect to the sheer extent of the wider circles involved.[112] The difficulties of deciding where to put a waste-water disposal plant near the concentration camp complex that would not carry with it disease and water pollution issues absorbed the energies of a wide range of groups and individuals. Members of the SS, the civilian administration of the town, the *Landrat* of the district of Bielitz, regional government representatives including *Gauleiter* Bracht and regional government president Springorum (Udo K.'s immediate superior in Kattowitz), consulted extensively with technical experts about the possible siting of a large waste-water disposal area in relation to the railway station, the concentration camp areas, the Sola and Weichsel rivers, the huge IG Farben plant at Monowitz (on the other side of town from Birkenau), while also taking into consideration the extension of the SS and railway personnel residential areas, and the building of a new railway shunting station (*Verschiebungsbahnhof*) in the area. Discussions were slowed not merely by technical considerations which were difficult to resolve, but also by questions of the respective responsibility of the concentration camp administration, the industrial managers of IG Farben and the civilian town administration with respect to decisions over where to site the new drainage facilities, who was responsible for their upkeep, and how they should be maintained. The files of correspondence between different offices, including back and forth to Berlin as well as extensively through these local networks, make it quite clear that large numbers of people were involved in all these discussions, which included periodic site visits to see the scale and details of the problem at first hand. Discussions rumbled on from 1940 through 1941 and 1942, with continuing postponements in finding any kind of solution or reaching practical decisions as the scale of the problem itself grew ever larger.

The minutes of a meeting followed by a site visit to Auschwitz on 23 September 1942 listed among those present not only Camp Commandant Rudolf Höss and several senior SS officials, and the regional political hierarchy from *Gauleiter* Bracht

---

[112] Archivum Państwowe w Katowicach, Rejencja Katowcije / Regierung Kattowitz, 119 / 2909, 'Wasserversorgung und Abwasserbeseitigung'.

and Regional District President Springorum down to the local district administrator (*Landrat*) Ziegler and even more local functionary (*Amtskommissar*) Butz, but also a number of technical experts including building advisors, engineers, and architects, as well as representatives from the Reich Ministry of the Interior, the town planning department of the Reich Ministry for Employment, and several experts from the Reich Water and Light Office in Berlin-Dahlem.[113] By now, it seemed that it was almost a matter of pride (or indication of political status) to show that one was included among the group of those possessed of knowledge that was still held in some way to be 'secret' or at least a matter of being privy to top level *Führer* orders. *SS-Brigadeführer* Dr Ing. Kammler explained that the problem of water supplies and drainage had now been under discussion for over a year, but that in view of the dramatically increased numbers now passing through the camp the question was becoming increasingly urgent:

> In view of the extraordinary growth by leaps and bounds of the number of inhabitants of the K.L. [Concentration Camp] Auschwitz, an independent water supply for the K.L. Auschwitz would be and is necessary . . . Disposal of the sewage from this high number of inhabitants via a special facility of the K.L. Auschwitz is urgently required.[114]

SS-Obergruppenführer Pohl underlined the fact that the coming year would bring even larger numbers into the area, making it even more essential to ensure 'an adequate water supply even with the highest average occupancy numbers of the year 1943'.[115] Further supporting the urgency of this issue and not awaiting a major health catastrophe, it was noted in the minutes of this meeting that 'Gauleiter Bracht here confided that he is aware of the Führer's order with respect to the special task that is currently in hand.'[116]

Gauleiter Bracht was not merely 'aware': he had indeed been personally present when Himmler toured Auschwitz on 17 July 1942, and had hosted a dinner for him that evening at his residence near Katowice. On 18 July Himmler returned to Auschwitz, this time making an inspection with senior officials from IG Farben. Clearly the topic of mass killing was the subject of explicit discussion among wider circles at Bracht's dinner party that evening. The Bracht villa was owned by a firm called Giesche, under the management of one Eduard Schulte, who appears on this occasion to have acquired remarkably detailed knowledge about the precise methods of killing, down to the use of what he called 'Prussic acid'. This was apparently the occasion for an attempt by Schulte to get the news out to the wider world, and particularly the USA, by way of senior Jewish connections in Switzerland.[117] Whether or not Himmler actually witnessed the gassing of some 449 Jews in

---

[113] Archivum Państwowe w Katowicach, Rejencja Katowcije / Regierung Kattowitz, 119 / 2909, Niederschrift über die Besprechung in Auschwitz am 23.9.1942 betr. K.L. Auschwitz, Berlin 26.9.1942, fols. 93–100.
[114] *Ibid.*, fol. 99.
[115] *Ibid.*, fol. 100.
[116] *Ibid.*
[117] Walter Laqueur and Richard Breitman, *Breaking the Silence: The secret mission of Eduard Schulte, who brought the world news of the Final Solution* (London: The Bodley Head, 1986).

what was known as Bunker 2, a converted farm building, he now authorized the building of specifically designed crematoria. For, as Auschwitz Commandant Rudolf Höss explained in his early post-war biography:

> It became apparent during the first cremations in the open air that in the long run it would not be possible to continue in that manner. During bad weather or when a strong wind was blowing, the stench of burning flesh was carried for many miles and caused the whole neighbourhood to talk about the burning of Jews, despite official counter-propaganda. It is true that all members of the SS detailed for the extermination were bound to the strictest secrecy over the whole operation, but... [e]ven the most severe punishment was not able to stop their love of gossip.[118]

Moreover, the killings were by this time due to escalate massively in scale: the very day after this visit, on 19 July 1942, Himmler issued an order that the entire Jewish population of Poland should have been removed and dealt with by the end of the year: 'I hereby order that the resettlement of the entire Jewish population of the General Government is to be carried out and completed by 31 December 1942.'[119]

Just as the engineers employed by the Erfurt-based firm of Topf and Sons were figuring out the technically most efficient means for constructing crematoria which could 'process' several hundreds of bodies *daily*, so too the various officials and experts involving planning for a 'Jew-free' living area for Germans in Europe were considering it from all the relevant practical angles, as were the municipal authorities who administered the disposal of housing, valuables, and other possessions that had been stolen from those who were deported, without ever being willing to acknowledge explicitly quite what sort of a murderous enterprise they were engaged in supporting. The surrounding exploitation of slave labour—in which the average life expectancy of those 'selected' for work rather than instant death was around three months—was no secret either. As one person employed at IG Farben wrote home, after giving a remarkably precise description of conditions in the plant: 'Here is a murderous enterprise, everything is topsy-turvy... In Poland it doesn't take much to get yourself into a striped suit'.[120]

It hardly needs saying that from the perspective of those who were victims of Nazi persecution, what was meant by 'Auschwitz' was not even an 'open secret'; it was an ever present threat, known about intimately among Polish people, both Jewish and non-Jewish, living for miles around. Numerous survivor accounts report how they themselves managed to escape, or were forced to witness the transport of loved ones to their certain deaths during this period. Nor were 'selections' carried out only on the infamous 'ramp' at Auschwitz, which has gained notoriety through associations with the 'medical' selections by Josef Mengele: for many Jews, 'selections' already took place in their ghetto or home town, at 'collection points' where

[118] *Autobiography of Rudolf Höss*, repr. in *Kl Auschwitz Seen by the SS*, trans. Constantine Fitzgibbon (Oświęcim: Publications of Państwowe Muzeum w Oświęcimiu, 1972), p. 122.

[119] Helmut Heiber (ed.), *Reichsführer!... Briefe an und von Himmler* (Stuttgart: Deutsche Verlags-Anstalt, 1968), p. 131, Himmler's letter of 19 Jul. 1942.

[120] Feldpostsammlung Museum für Kommunikation, 3.2002.1277, Walter S., letter of 16 Feb. 1942.

members of the SS, Gestapo and often also local employers distinguished between those who were still 'useful' for labour and those who should immediately be sent to their deaths. The significance of the distinctions being made between the very young, very old, ill, and weak on the one hand, and the able-bodied young on the other, were not lost on anyone involved in these processes. It hardly bears saying that the Holocaust, too, was a phenomenon patterned by generations: survivors tend predominantly to be those who were strong young adults at the time. Nor was the fact that, unlike in the case of those who had earlier been sent away to camps for forced labour, there were rarely postcards or any further signs of life from those who had been shipped to Auschwitz or the other death camps.[121] Meanwhile, of course, surrounding populations were often actively involved in the process, whether through forms of collusion with the Germans, including betrayal of Jews living under 'Aryan' identities, or attempts at resistance, sometimes in collaboration and sometimes in conflict with Jewish resistance activities. It is notable that, alongside well-known incidents such as the massacre of Jews by non-Jewish Polish neighbours in Jedwabne, tending to confirm the stereotype of Poles as antisemitic, it is also the case that Polish people have received the single largest number of nominations by Yad Vashem for the status of 'Righteous among Nations' for attempts to help persecuted Jews.[122]

As far as German soldiers at the front were concerned, it was not only the special task forces, or *Einsatzgruppen*, who were involved in mass murder; many ordinary soldiers were also actively involved or witnessed—and wrote home about—incidents of mass murder on an extraordinary scale.[123] While it is difficult to obtain exact figures or percentages, there is sufficient evidence to suggest that a significant number of ordinary soldiers in the army were caught up in racial atrocities and became more or less willing participants in actions of mass murder, and many interpreted what they saw as confirmation of previous Nazi teachings about the alleged 'inferior people' (*Untermenschen*).[124] Some echoed regime propaganda in representing the murder of Jews as appropriate 'punishment' for their presumed collective misdeeds, such as the soldier who wrote home from Tarnopol on 6 July 1941: 'Up to now we have dispatched around 1,000 Jews [with clubs and spades] into eternity but that is far too little for what they have done.'[125] There were staggering details given at the time of the mass murder of Jews in the Ukraine with the full cooperation of the *Wehrmacht* in the summer of 1941.[126] In Kamenec

---

[121] Oral history interviews in the area, 2008 and 2009; see also e.g. testimonies in the Visual History Archive, USC Shoah Foundation Institute; and for further references to survivor testimonies, Fulbrook, *A Small Town Near Auschwitz*.

[122] Jan T. Gross, *Neighbours: The destruction of the Jewish community in Jedwabne, Poland, 1941* (London: Random House, Arrow, 2003; orig. Princeton University Press, 2003); for Yad Vashem, see <http://www1.yadvashem.org/yv/en/righteous/index.asp>.

[123] See e.g. the printed selections in Klee, Dreßen, Rieß (eds.), '*Schöne Zeiten*'; Walter Manoschek (ed.), '*Es gibt nur eines für das Judentum: Vernichtung' Das Judenbild in deutschen Soldatenbriefen 1939–1944* (Hamburg: Hamburger Edition, 1995).

[124] Wette, *Die Wehrmacht*, p. 180.

[125] Manoschek (ed.), '*Es gibt nur eines für das Judentum*', Tarnopol, 6 Jul. 1941, p. 33.

[126] Dieter Pohl, 'Schauplatz Ukraine: Der Massenmord an den Juden im Militärverwaltungsgebiet und im Reichskommissariat 1941–1943' in Norbert Frei, Sybille Steinbacher, and Bernd C. Wagner

Podol'skij, 4,200 Jews were murdered on 27 August 1941; on the next day, a further 11,000 were killed; and the final total reported to Berlin was in the region of 23,600. There were also mass shootings further south, on the north shore of Black Sea area; the local military administration was fully involved in and aware of these incidents, which were far from being the allegedly hidden, well disguised operations of the later extermination camps of eastern Poland.[127]

There are horrifying passages in large numbers of soldiers' letters, providing more than ample evidence of the prevalence of antisemitic views and actions among ordinary soldiers.[128] As one described an incident of mass murder in extraordinarily trivializing terms:

> In Bereza-Kartuska, where I stopped for lunch, they had just shot dead around 1,300 Jews the previous day. They were brought to a pit outside the place. Men, women and children had to get totally undressed there and were dispatched with a shot in the back of the neck. The clothes were disinfected and put to new use. I am convinced: if the war lasts for much longer, the Jews will also have to be turned into sausages and set before the Russian prisoners of war or the Jewish skilled workers.[129]

We cannot be sure how typical these excerpts are of *Landser* views more generally. They do however suggest that the soldiers' experience of 'eastern Jews' (*Ostjuden*) in the state to which they had been reduced by Nazi occupation policies had successfully strengthened the attitudes that pre-war propaganda had sought less successfully to induce. There is repeated evidence to suggest that the Nazi newspaper *Der Stürmer* was now believed more readily. Previously, many soldiers had had no real conception of what 'the Jew' was 'really like'; now they were for the first time exposed to large numbers of Jews in Eastern Europe, some of whom had genuinely been extremely poor, but many of whom had been herded by the Nazis into ghettoes, expropriated from their own homes and means of livelihood, and starved on rations insufficient to sustain life. It was hardly surprising that their appearance now seemed to conform to Nazi stereotypes, confirming for the unthinking *Landser* the caricatures of propaganda; pre-existing 'taught' antisemitism thus became 'experienced' antisemitism. As one put it, in a letter home on 6 August 1941:

> You won't find conditions like these in any German town. I can't describe to you how the Jewish quarter looks, since you wouldn't believe it anyway. Images of Jews like those we already had in the STÜRMER, you can find masses of here in reality. Shrouded in rags, which are mostly torn as well, they run around here by the dozen. We in the Main region couldn't really get a proper idea of the Jew. But here in the east you only need to look at the wretches and you know what sorts of wretches you have

(eds.) *Ausbeutung, Vernichtung, Öffentlichkeit. Neue Studien zur nationalsozialistischen Lagerpolitik* (München: K. G. Saur, 2000), pp. 140–3.
[127] Pohl, 'Schauplatz Ukraine', pp. 135–73.
[128] Manoschek (ed.), *'Es gibt nur eines für das Judentum'*.
[129] Manoschek (ed.), *'Es gibt nur eines für das Judentum'*, 18.7.1942, Zahlm.d.R. H.K., H.K.P. 610 (Brest/Bug), FPN 37 634, p. 58. On this incident see also the Groscurth diaries, and the discussions in: Friedländer, *Years of Extermination*; and Klee, Dreßen, and Rieß, *'Schöne Zeiten'*.

before you, without even having had to speak to them. Anyone who is German doesn't talk at all to this vermin.[130]

Some appear now to have seen what they called, in the stereotypical singular, 'the Jew', as the feared enemy to be fought at all costs: they seem to have approved of and thought within the discourse of 'revenge' killings of communists, Jews, partisans, all of which were constructed as acceptable targets for killing even on the slightest pretext. The notion propagated by Hitler of a 'defensive war' persisted. In the words of one clearly highly committed party man as well as soldier:

> As an SA man I have long recognized the Jewish poison in our people; we are seeing how far this could have gone only now, in this campaign . . . [E]ven the last doubter must be cured here, in the light of the facts. We must and will succeed in freeing the world from this pest, the German soldier at the eastern front stands as guarantee of this, and we won't return before we have ripped out the roots of all evil here and the central headquarters of the Jewish-Bolshevik 'world benefactor' has been exterminated.[131]

Or, as another put it:

> The great task which has been set us in the fight against Bolshevism lies in the extermination of eternal Jewry. If one sees what the Russian has set up here in Russia then one can for the first time really understand why the Führer began the fight against Jewry. What manner of suffering would have befallen our Fatherland if this beast of a human had kept the upper hand?[132]

Caution only started to enter much later in the war, with fear for what the position would be after a lost war. In many such letters, there is barely a whispering of conscience; few seemed to see—or dared to write in terms of—the Jews as human beings. And the Home Front was certainly well aware of mass killings of Jews, shootings of large groups, and shootings of individuals, as well as maltreatment through slave labour—an issue which was very present even at the heart of the old Reich too.

What effects did participation in such a war have on people? The answer has to be manifold. But that it had effects (beyond the sheer physical question of survival without serious injury) was unquestionable. As one soldier put it, writing home in January 1943:

> The beautiful time of our youth is passed and will not come again. You will all be surprised at what sorts of 'old men' in the truest sense of the word your sons have become . . . One has no interest in anything any more, no desire for anything . . .[133]

It is also possible to trace, through the letter of Gertrud S. to one of her female friends, the long-term effects on her husband Hans of involvement in mass killings.

---

[130] Manoschek (ed), *'Es gibt nur eines für das Judentum'*, 6.8.1941, Sold. J.Z. 3. Kp./Ldsschtz. Btl.619, FPN 20 355 D, p. 40.

[131] *Ibid.*, 14.8.1942, Uffz. F.K., 4. Kp./Bau-Btl. 55, p. 61.

[132] *Ibid.*, San.Uffz. K.G., Stab/Lw.Bau-Btl.6/VII, FPN L 08 440, p. 59.

[133] BfZ, SSt 1943-1, Sold. Hans-Joachim H., 28 942 C, 10.Kp. / Gren. (Feldausb.) Div., 10 Jan 1943.

Referring back to the 'November days', it seems that Hans had been asked to play some administrative role in the November pogrom of 1938; he also had a role, though not one of direct shooting, in the mass killings on the eastern front. It is clear that he was plagued by his part in these murderous operations, and continually plagued by the images he had witnessed and which he could not get out of his mind; he seems also to have suffered from—presumably—pangs of conscience over what was going on; and while he appealed to religion, this seemed only to serve to strengthen and uphold his sense of obedience to worldly authority with respect to the tasks which he was being asked to carry out. The reaction of Hans's wife Gertrud is interesting for the way in which she pities her husband for having to be directly involved in scenes of gruesome murders, and wishes 'younger men' could have been co-opted instead; but she does not seem to have queried, at least on paper, the ghastly developments themselves as being, in the long run, the right policies. There is of course the question of what could actually be said in such a context, given that even though such letters between female civilians were not subject to the military censorship of letters home from the front, they might nevertheless be opened and read, with predictable adverse consequences if crucial lines had been overstepped. It is all the more interesting, then, that Gertrud ruminates even as explicitly as she does to her friend on the cumulative effects on her husband of his involvement in violence—although without going into details on what precisely he was asked to do—from the November pogrom of 1938 through to the current atrocities on the eastern front:

> Now Hans has admitted it to me: even if this meant he would have been shot, he does not believe that he would have carried out orders expected of him in pursuit of this handiwork which has nothing to do with war. That was the key moment which, after he knew about the anti-partisan campaign, no longer let him sleep a wink! . . . We lay awake nights, as he moaned into the pillow: 'Why always me, always me for such tasks? In November [1938] (at the time when the soul of the people was seething) I was given the order to blow up the mortuary of the Synagogue community! Will I never again lose the images of Charkow [Kharkov, Ukraine, a site of atrocities] from my mind? Oh, how can you know what scenes one is exposed to during the interrogation and rounding up of hostages? No—no—I won't go along with it; no—they'll have to send someone else!' . . . In those November days Hans had suffered dreadfully, he lay awake at night just like now and stared into the darkness and asked himself and asked his God and then did what his conscience and his heart suggested to him: before carrying out these orders he went to the Head of the Synagogue Community, Prof F., a—well, let's not go into that now! Anyway I had been friends with his daughters since my childhood and every single person in Königsberg respected and valued this meritorious doctor.—Hans wrote to me from Charkow: 'You cannot possibly imagine what it means to have to walk through streets in which the bodies of people who have been hanged are bundled together likes bunches of grapes hanging from windows and balconies. When these images plague me at night, then I flee ever more into the world of the abstract, that's the image of my father, the image of you; these are my altars, before which I have always been able to find myself again, in order to be able to stand up straight the next morning and not have to disobey orders . . . ' And so during that time I was, just like Hans, simply choked up. I was equally horrified, and everything in

me cried out: Why don't they send out to these commandos 'young, insensitive officers, to whom it means nothing if women are tied up to trees and thrashed and shot dead' (as Frau M. once wrote to me...), why do they use for this task men who are soldiers but not hangmen?[134]

It is interesting that both Gertrud S. and a mutual friend, Frau M., whose letter she quotes here, appear to have registered generational differences in reactions to having to be involved in such acts of brutality and murder: younger men, building on their experiences and socialization in the 1930s, were more likely to see it as part of their ideologically defined roles as soldiers in a 'racial war' in a way that older, more traditional military men apparently did not. It is also somewhat curious, to say the least, that Gertrud S. appears to have been opposed to her husband having to do the dirty work, given the consequences for his psychological state, and yet—at least on the evidence of this letter—did not appear to have been against what was being done in principle, which she seems to have considered an appropriate task not for 'soldiers' but for 'hangmen'. Yet she is unable fully to complete her thoughts on what happened in November 1938, acts of brutality that clearly affected those whom she knew and valued personally.

This is a reaction found in the letters of other women too, who protest at having to witness frightful scenes themselves but do not seem to register any sense of outrage at what is being done; they would simply rather not have to see it for themselves, or not register explicitly quite what they knew it really entailed in a broader picture. Similar responses can be seen, for example, in Alexandra von S.'s letters to her mother about the violent mass 'resettlement' of the Jews of Będzin in August 1942 and again in June 1943. In early August 1942, Udo K.'s wife Alexandra wrote to her mother about the 'resettlement' of 1,500 Jews from Będzin, eastern Upper Silesia, adding the comment that 'Russia is as nothing to this'—a betrayal of her knowledge (and that of her mother) of what had been going on in Russia since the invasion of the previous summer.[135] In her case, the response both now and during the bloody mass clearance of the ghetto the following summer was essentially one of distaste at having to witness the scenes in person, having to hear screams and shots and see dead bodies lying everywhere, but in her letters there is no evidence of any disagreement with the policy of forcible removal of Jews from their home town; the programme in principle of rendering Będzin 'Jew-free', however distasteful such scenes appeared to be in practice, did not appear to occasion any adverse comments on the part of the *Landrat*'s wife at the time.[136]

There seems, then, to have been for some time an arguably widespread acceptance of the ultimate ends, even if the means were seen as particularly distasteful—or at least, there appears to have been an explicit attempt to persuade oneself and others of this standpoint, however hard this might be. It is possible that the anguish—not too extreme a word in some cases—apparently experienced when registering or witnessing or having to participate in the brutality of this racial war,

---

[134] BfZ, SSt 1943-1, Gertrud S., Königsberg/Ostpr., 2 Jan. 1943.
[135] Alexandra K., letter to her mother, 12 August 1942, private family archive.
[136] See for further discussion Fulbrook, *A Small Town Near Auschwitz.*

often having to act in ways which were in conflict with other personal values, led to a need to register one's feelings about the means while not daring to query the ultimate goals. At the time, arguably, the theory of the 'defensive war' may have helped many to accept the apparent need for such violence. Later, after the war, the individual incidents would not be packaged as part of the bundle that was collectively castigated—more easily accomplished if brutality was condensed into the iconic gas chambers, away from the shooting on the streets or the corpses dangling from trees and balconies.

These dissonances and difficulties in terms of personal responses to violence were even explicitly addressed by Himmler in his 'Posen speeches', first to SS leaders on 4 October and then again two days later to a group of central and regional political leaders (*Reichs-* and *Gauleiter*) on 6 October 1943. Arguing for the separation of immediate emotional reactions from recognition of the allegedly long-term 'service' being performed for the 'national community' by these murders, Himmler acknowledged the difficulties of dealing with this topic:

> Allow me, in this connection and in this very close circle, to touch on a question that you, my Party comrades, have all taken for granted, but which has become the most difficult question of my life, the Jewish question.[137]

At this stage, and despite his reference to the small circle of comrades, Himmler appears to have been quite consciously seeking to draw wider circles into the community of the explicitly implicated.[138] He simultaneously acknowledged both that the mass murder of civilians was widely known about, and yet that it should not be discussed or only under conditions of strictest secrecy, thus effectively binding in the circle of those complicit both in the project of mass murder and in its attempted cover-up and denial. Moreover, for once, he 'translated' the typical Nazi euphemisms shrouding murder into words explicitly saying what was meant:

> I beg you really only to listen to what I am saying to you in this circle, and never to talk about it. The question has been put to us: But what about the women and children?—I decided to find a quite clear solution here too. For I did not think it justifiable to exterminate the men—in other words, then, to kill them or to have them killed—and yet allow the children to grow up to take revenge against our sons and grandchildren. The hard decision had to be taken that this people should be wiped from the face of the earth.[139]

At the end of these remarkable comments, Himmler again emphasized both the significance and the inherent difficulty of the task, and the long-term significance of what was being done:

> With this I would like to end the discussion of the Jewish question. You now know for certain, and you will keep it to yourselves. Much later, perhaps, we may be able to

---

[137] Bradley Smith and Agnes Peterson (eds.), *Heinrich Himmler. Geheimreden 1933 bis 1945* (Propyläen Verlag, 1974), p. 169.
[138] See also Peter Longerich, *Heinrich Himmler: Biographie* (Siedler Verlag, 2008), pp. 709–10.
[139] Smith and Peterson (eds.), *Himmler. Geheimreden*, p. 169.

consider whether the German people should be told somewhat more about it. I believe it is better that we—we collectively—have done this for our people, have taken the responsibility upon ourselves (the responsibility for an action, not for an idea) and that we take the secret with us into our graves.[140]

Yet even at this stage, as wider political circles were formally implicated in 'knowledge' of that which they later sought to claim was the sole responsibility of the SS and about which they had 'known nothing', what was going on was far from being the 'secret' that Himmler claimed and intended.

VI. BEYOND TWO WORLDS

Reports of the Nazi murder of Europe's Jews reached the outside world already at a relatively early stage. The routes by which news travelled ranged from accounts by individuals to the more official reports of organizations, whether Jewish, Red Cross, or governmental.[141] Readers of any international newspaper of note could be well-informed of what was going on in Nazi-occupied Europe; *The Daily Telegraph* reported on extermination as early as June 1942, as did the BBC; by early July, *The New York Times* was carrying similar reports.

Merely going through the files of one internationally reputable newspaper indicates just how widespread and relatively accurate—in gist if not in detail—knowledge was of the unfolding horror of mass murder under Nazi auspices. Readers of the London-based British newspaper, *The Times*, were as well informed as could be under the conditions of war that murder of civilians was taking place on a simply massive scale, and by a wide variety of means. Nor, without the historian's 'benefit of hindsight', did they represent 1941 as a significant turning point: murder by a wide variety of means had, after all, been going on for a long time before this, and it was rather the rapid escalation in killings as well as enhancement of methods of killing that was worthy of note in 1942. As early as 16 December 1939, there was an article under the prescient title 'Lublin for the Jews. The Nazi plan. A stony road to extermination'. Describing Nazi plans for the 'barren district around Lublin' designated as a 'Jewish reserve', the *Times*' correspondent noted that 'it is clear that the scheme envisages a place for gradual extermination, and not what the Germans would describe as *Lebensraum*'. Reviewing the sheer numbers of Jews to be deported from the Reich (180,000), Austria (65,000), the Czech Protectorate (75,000), the annexed parts of Poland (450,000), and the rump Polish state (1,500,000) *The Times* commented that already 'the number of the dead rises into tens of thousands, and of refugees into hundreds of thousands. But again the size of the programme is very nearly irrelevant: it amounts to a mass massacre such as Nazi imagination can conceive but even Nazi practice can hardly carry through

---

[140] *Ibid.*, pp. 170–1.
[141] See e.g. Walter Laqueur, *The Terrible Secret: Suppression of the truth about Hitler's 'Final Solution'* (Boston, Toronto: Little, Brown, 1980).

in full.'[142] While commenting with remarkable foresight on the 'Nazi imagination', on the point concerning impossibility in practice the correspondent proved to be wildly wrong. Subsequent issues documented the unfolding programme in striking detail. An article of 20 May 1941 on 'German Atrocities in Poland' reported on 'photographs unfit for publication in a newspaper', including pictures of people 'hanged by the Germans in front of their own houses or hanged in public squares with children grouped around ... women being taken off by the execution squad; men rounded up for forced labour', and spoke of the way in which even German newspapers, such as the *Krakauer Zeitung*, reported on the internment and deaths of Poles in Oświęcim—Auschwitz, although *The Times* did not as yet call it by this name, and stayed with the Polish name of the town where the infamous concentration camp was based, and where, the following year, the extermination facilities of Birkenau would be developed.[143] And indeed, by the end of 1942, the reports were even more grim. On 11 December 1942 *The Times* reported in some detail the Polish government's 'Note on the German Persecution of the Jews'. The article included:

> The new methods of mass slaughter applied during the last few months confirm the fact that the German authorities aim with systematic deliberation at the total extermination of the Jewish population of Poland and of the many thousands of Jews deported ... The Note gives details already published in the Press about Himmler's decree of March, 1942, for the extermination of 50 per cent. of Polish Jews by the end of 1942, liquidation of the ghettoes, the suicide of Mr. Czerniakow, chairman of the Jewish Council, on receiving an order to deliver up 7,000 persons daily, and the transports to the 'Extermination Camps'.[144]

The Note included the estimate that 'of the 3,130,000 Jews in Poland before the war over one third have perished during the last three years'.[145] Ten days later, on 21 December 1942, summarizing a statement released by the Inter-Allied Information Committee, *The Times* carried an article entitled 'Persecution of the Jews' and again subtitled 'Plan of Extermination'. This summarized the way in which, from 'the middle of 1942 there was a general intensification of measures against Jews ... [A] plan of extermination which transcends anything in history.' The article quoted the figure given by Dr Stephen F. Wise, president of the American Jewish Congress, to President Roosevelt on 8 December, to the effect that some 2,000,000 Jews had been deported and perished, and that 'another 5,000,000 were in danger of extermination'.[146] Four years to the day after the invasion of Poland, on 1 September 1943, *The Times* carried an article headed: 'Poland's Martyrdom. Four Years of Nazi Occupation and Terror. A Policy of Extermination.' Referring to Polish men who had sought to escape from Nazi forced labour or conscription in the army, the correspondent noted that:

> To discourage them from this the Nazis retaliated on their families. Wives, mothers or daughters of men reported to have deserted were taken to a camp at Oświęcim and

---

[142] *The Times*, Issue 48490, Saturday 16 Dec. 1939, p. 9.
[143] *Ibid.*, Issue 48930, 20 May 1941, p. 4.   [144] *Ibid.*, Issue 49416, 11 Dec. 1942, p. 3.
[145] *Ibid.*   [146] *Ibid.*, Issue 49424, 21 Dec. 1942, p. 3.

there murdered in gas chambers. Six thousand are said to have died in this way up to date.[147]

Although this report—expressed with a sense of restrained outrage—concentrated on the fate of the non-Jewish Polish population, it is clear that knowledge of the gas chambers as a method of killing was explicit. On 8 July 1944, under the heading 'Hungarian Jews' Fate. Murder in Gas Chambers', more details were given to *Times* readers of figures, methods and locations of killing. *The Times* reported on the 'fate of more than 400,000 Hungarian Jews' who were deported to Poland, including '62 railway carriages filled with Jewish children, aged between two and eight years'. Reports suggested that the majority 'were sent to Oświęcim, and most of them have been put to death in the gas chambers of that dreaded concentration camp'. Again, the details available to *The Times* were hazy and slightly inaccurate, but the gist of the message was entirely clear:

> In 1942 the Germans erected in Oświęcim gas chambers with installations enabling them to kill daily 6,000 and even more of their victims. Many prominent Poles and thousands of Jews were sent to Oświęcim and put to death there.
> When the Germans, in the second half of 1942, started their extermination of Polish Jewry the gas chambers of Oświęcim could not cope with all the victims, so two more death camps were erected—Tremblinka [*sic*] and Rawa Ruska, near Lwow. In these three camps more than 2,000,000 Polish Jews have been murdered since 1939.[148]

No educated reader in Britain of just this one newspaper alone—leaving aside comparable (and indeed earlier) reports in the *Daily Telegraph* and elsewhere—could have failed to 'know' that murder on a major scale was underway in German-occupied Europe. *The Guardian* too had reported in similar terms, carrying for example an article in December 1942 which summarized the situation as conveyed by the Polish government in exile:

> The Note on Jewish persecution in Poland which the Polish Government in London has addressed to the respective Governments of the United Nations contains a comprehensive account of the horrors being perpetrated by the Germans on Polish soil. The Note mentions 'new methods of mass slaughter' and tells the ghastly story of the Warsaw Ghetto. It declares that the total number of Jews killed in Poland since the German occupation runs into many hundreds of thousands and that of the 3,130,000 Jews in Poland before the war over one-third have perished in the last three years whilst many millions of the Polish population have been either deported to Germany as slave labour or evicted from their homes and lands, and many of their leaders murdered.[149]

Yet Germans claimed in their millions after the war that 'we never knew anything about it'.

One thing Germans certainly did know was the Jews were being 'resettled' and areas of the Reich rendered 'Jew-free'. This was evident for many Germans through

---

[147] *Ibid.*, Issue 49639, 1 Sep. 1943, p. 5.
[148] *Ibid.*, Issue 49903, 8 Jul. 1944, p. 3.
[149] *The Guardian*, 'The German massacres of Jews in Poland', 11 Dec. 1942.

witnessing deportations from neighbouring houses and streets, particularly in cities
such as Berlin where many Jewish Germans were still resident—evidenced now in
the ubiquitous '*Stolpersteine*' or golden 'stumbling stones' set among the cobbles in
the pavements outside the former residences of Jews who were forcibly ousted from
their homes and transported to their deaths. As the journalist Ursula von Kardorff
commented in a letter to a friend, Hanna Boye, on the deportation of the Jews from
Berlin:

> Here the most depressing things are happening at the moment. All Jews up to the age
> of 80 are being deported to Poland. You see only tear-stained figures on the streets. It is
> beyond measure and quite heartbreaking. Above all that one has to stand by and watch
> so helplessly and can do so frightfully little to help. They are only allowed to take with
> them a very small bundle the size of a briefcase. And this in face of all the world-
> shattering things, beyond measure, which are going on out there.[150]

Not merely were deportations open for all to see; the results were even trumpeted in
German newspapers when particular locations were rendered 'Jew free'.[151]

The claim was later made that people believed Jews were indeed simply being
'resettled' in their 'own' areas in the east; but this claim too was being undermined
by reports at the time. Even given the difficulties of obtaining news from outside
sources in Nazi Germany, including severe penalties for listening to foreign radio
broadcasts, there was plenty enough by way of first-hand knowledge—indeed
knowledge gained from active involvement—to ensure that Germans, too, knew
full well what was going on, even if not in all the details, and even if they could not
or did not want to believe what they were hearing. There can be no doubt at all,
despite the widespread claims to the contrary made after the war, that very many
adults in Germany knew very well that Jews were being murdered in large numbers.
On 13 January 1942, for example, Viktor Klemperer, now living in the 'Jews'
house' in Dresden, confided in his diary the rumours that were coming back about
the fate of Jews who were being 'resettled' in the east: 'Paul Kreidl reports—a
rumour, but very credibly conveyed from various quarters—, that evacuated Jews
were *shot dead* in rows as they left the train in Riga.'[152] While victims of racial
persecution might be more aware than most of rumours, these circulated too
among 'Aryan' Germans with little to fear as far as they themselves were concerned.
Interestingly, even they seem to have known about planned transports in advance.
Daniel L., an elderly German who had retained a capacity to empathize with the
fates of others, and who lived in Bavaria far away from the eastern front, wrote in
his diary as early as 21 March 1942:

> Tomorrow morning the rest of the Jewish people still abiding in Furth will be taken away
> on a transport. The fate which awaits them is terrifying. Many have preferred to take their

---

[150] Ursula von Kardorff, *Berliner Aufzeichnungen 1942 bis 1945*, ed. Peter Hartl (München:
Deutsche Taschenbuch Verlag, 1994), p. 44, fn 1.
[151] See e.g. the *Ostdeutscher Beobachter*, Nr. 135, 17 May 1942, article on 'Krakau wird wieder rein
deutsch'.
[152] Victor Klemperer, *Ich will Zeugnis ablegen bis zum letzten. Tagebücher 1942–1945*, ed. Walter
Nowojski with Hadwig Klemperer (Berlin: Aufbau Verlag, 1995), entry of 13 Jan. 1942, p. 9,
emphasis in the original.

own lives. Certain rumours are emerging, the truth of which can hardly be doubted any more, that report that thousands of Jewish men, women and children have been and are being murdered in Poland. The executors of this inhumanity are allegedly the SS. Woe to those who lower German soldiers to the accomplices of hangmen!

Interestingly Daniel L. was concerned not only about the fate of those 'Jewish people' who were being deported (or who had committed suicide for fear of what lay ahead), but also distinguishes between 'soldiers' and 'hangmen' and worries about the 'Germans' whose loyalty to the regime was being misappropriated: 'My heart bleeds if I have to believe that German people are capable of such misdeeds.'[153] Here, Daniel L. appeared to some extent to have internalized regime distinctions between 'Jewish people' and 'Germans', and yet utterly rejected the murderous consequences of this distinction, in a sense mourning for both sides in the unfolding tragedy.

By January 1943, rumours with quite considerable detail on particular incidents were clearly spreading widely, again as far as Bavaria. As Daniel L. now commented in his diary:

A pastor who was recently staying here on holiday asked me if I had also already heard that whole trainloads of poor Jews, who had been squashed in together, had been simply gassed. I had to reply that I had already heard repeatedly from trustworthy sources of similar and other appalling acts of murder against these poor people, but that I was baulking at believing news of such atrocities. Yesterday a lawyer told me that Jews who had been held in a train that was sealed up had been pleading without success for water. When the train carriage was opened the corpses of martyred and suffocated Jews fell out in front of the railway workers. Such reports are being passed around by word of mouth—and believed.[154]

Even so, it should also be borne in mind that not all Germans were exposed to such rumours about killings. Nor by any means were all Germans as complicit in the functioning of the system, let alone the practices of systemic violence, brutality, and murder, as were those involved in the civilian administration and military campaigns of Hitler's state. Unwilling and often only partial belief in rumours is not at all the same thing as positive action sustaining the system or culpable acts of violence, and to ask of people who were often uncomfortably aware that something awful was going on why they did not do more to resist or oppose it is in part to ask the wrong question, or at least to ask the right question of largely the wrong groups of people.

At the very same time as many Germans were more or less aware of the murder in large numbers of Jewish civilians, the vast majority of those old enough to notice were also perfectly conscious of and indeed often actively involved in the employment of forced labourers.[155] Some 20 million Europeans were employed as forced

---

[153] DTA Emmendingen, 1315, *Das Tagebuch des Daniel L. 1934–1946*, p. 150, entry of 21 Mar. 1942.
[154] *Ibid.*, p. 173, entry of 20 Jan. 1943.
[155] See for an overview of the use of forced labour in the Third Reich, Ulrich Herbert, *Hitler's Foreign Workers: Enforced foreign labour in Germany under the Third Reich*, trans. William Templer (Cambridge: Cambridge University Press, 1997; orig. German 1985); and in broader historical

or slave labourers, either in the occupied and annexed territories or brought into the Reich to replace the German manpower now away at (or already maimed or killed in) war. From 1943 onwards, perhaps half of the agricultural labourers in Germany were forced workers from abroad. This enormous system of employment of foreign labour often served to reinforce a sense of German 'racial superiority', largely unexamined and taken for granted. Forced labourers were engaged in the most menial and demeaning of work, while 'better' jobs were reserved for the 'racially superior' Germans: thus the hierarchies of work and of course local power over 'inferior' workers echoed the hierarchy of 'race', even if this did not quite serve to massage away class differences among members of the supposed 'master race'.

Strict regulations governed the (non-)relationships between Germans and the 'inferior' forced labourers, with severe penalties for infringements—particularly when romantic or at least sexual relations were involved. There is much evidence to suggest that at a fairly low level many Germans further abused their state-sanctioned position of dominance over foreign workers, and in some cases sub-jected them to extreme brutality. People working in agriculture often lived with their German employers at close quarters in family farms and in relatively small communities, and were thus particularly vulnerable and exposed—whether to maltreatment with no hope of redress, or by contrast to a degree of common decency and humanity. After the war, acts of physical brutality and maltreatment were, particularly in the GDR, often prosecuted as having been culpable in terms of criminal law—unlike, for decades, the system itself: the right to compensation was only conceded some half a century later, when for most former forced labourers it was far too late to receive anything by way of 'compensation' for the brutality and injustices suffered. On the other hand, some Germans recall that they—or mem-bers of their families, if they were still young at the time—treated 'their' foreign workers particularly nicely, inviting them to eat together at the family table or giving them more by way of food and other comforts than they were 'supposed to'. Thus the exploitation of forced labourers could simultaneously give Germans first-hand experience of deeply racist practices, reinforcing their own sense of superiority on 'racial' grounds, and yet also provide the basis for a post-war clean conscience and sense of having been rather virtuous in face of state-ordained callousness.

Vast numbers of 'racially pure' and conformist Germans also were able to witness the state of the slave labourers from concentration camps and their numerous external sub-camps within the territory of the Reich, and some interacted in one capacity or another with these and with inmates of prisoner-of-war camps. It was not as if the racist and deeply repressive character of the Nazi state was in any sense a secret for anyone living there at the time: indeed, callous and often also murder-ous racism was trumpeted from all sides. That its practical outcome in terms of mass murder should have come to Germans as such as a 'surprise' after the war is perhaps itself the greater surprise, although this allegation was clearly part of

context, Herbert, *Geschichte der Ausländerpolitik in Deutschland: Saisonarbeiter, Zwangsarbeiter, Gastarbeiter, Flüchtlinge* (Munich: C.H. Beck. 2001), Pt III.

widespread attempts to find ways of living with an uncomfortable past and an individual biography that no longer fitted what was required.

For those decreasing numbers of Jews still remaining in Germany, life was increasingly desperate. Separation, gradual debasement, stigmatization, and loss of social contacts and stimulation, increasing restrictions on where and when they could move, where and when they could buy what, how indeed they would be able to survive, were from October 1941 replaced by the threat or actuality of deportation. Some few sought on occasion to try to retain a sense of being a cultured human being, engaging in a fearful refusal to be completely separated off from the rest of their fellow Germans, sneaking out without wearing the yellow star and going out at night to the cinema, theatre, or other form of entertainment forbidden to Jews. One of the few who survived in Berlin by virtue of assistance from individuals who were prepared to hide her was Inge Deutschkron, who recalled vividly the sense of living in two worlds; she constantly had to be aware that she was acting a role, and having to act even to the tiniest details, such that she would not draw attention to herself as someone who did not belong to the *Volksgemeinschaft* of the living but was, if she gave herself away, effectively doomed to death.[156] Similar experiences were registered by Ruth Klüger, who was ripped from her Viennese childhood first to Theresienstadt then to Auschwitz, and survived the last stages of the war by escaping and hiding under cover of an 'Aryan' identity; she too was acutely sensitive to the differences between the worlds.[157] Both these and many others survivors who survived in hiding or adopted 'Aryan' identities highlight the ways in which they had to force themselves to play a role so as not to attract attention to themselves. They also recall, along with many others, the ways in which Germans simply appeared 'not to see', or 'looked away from', the victims of Nazi persecution—perhaps one of the most significant gestures fostered by the Nazi state.[158]

Across Europe, anyone who did not conform to Nazi beliefs and demands, norms of behaviour or of 'racial purity' was at risk: not only Jews but also Sinti, Roma, Jehovah's Witnesses, and countless others had, if they were to have any hope of physical survival, to 'behave as if' through identities which were not ones of their choosing.[159] 'Acting the part' was in different ways, for example, crucial to the

---

[156] Inge Deutschkron, *Ich trug den gelben Stern* (München: Deutscher Taschenbuch Verlag, 1985).
[157] Ruth Klüger, *weiter leben* (München: Deutscher Taschenbuch Verlag, 1994).
[158] See also M. Fulbrook, 'Embodying the self: Gestures and dictatorship in twentieth-century Germany' in M. Braddick (ed.), *The Politics of Gesture: Historical perspectives, Past and Present* Supplement 4 (Oxford: Oxford University Press, 2009), pp. 257–79.
[159] For a couple of decades, the appellation 'Sinti and Roma' has been preferred to the previously used and more generic 'gypsies', although technically the broader term 'Roma' can also be used to encompass the 'Sinti' subgroup. Like the choices between 'Holocaust' versus 'Shoah', or 'Kristallnacht' versus 'November pogrom', a heightened sensitivity (particularly among Germans) about potentially causing posthumous linguistic offence seems to be a form of over-compensation for, or at least explicit self-distancing from, far worse offences that can no longer be repaired. The German word 'Zigeuner' derived from a Greek root referring to 'untouchables'. Richard J. Evans has opted for the all-encompassing (and in English more neutral) term 'Gypsies', with a capital letter, in *The Third Reich at War*. The key issue here as elsewhere is to ensure avoidance of offensive terminology, even if the various linguistic arguments about particular terms tend to go in and out of fashion.

survival of homosexuals. While lesbians were not subjected to the same criminal penalties, for gay males 'masquerading' was often the only way to avoid arrest, imprisonment, torture, and in many cases death. Some 50,000 men were convicted under Paragraph 175 of the Criminal Code for having committed what were seen as homosexual 'offences', and between 10,000 to 15,000 interned in concentration camps, of whom around two-thirds did not survive.[160] Among those who did survive, 'masquerading' had to continue through the early post-war decades, since homosexuality remained a criminal offence even if the penalties it attracted were no longer so severe. What different strategies for survival among all these groups might mean for a fractured sense of identity in either the short or the long term was highly complex.[161]

Even for those who were, on all counts, upright and committed members of the *Volksgemeinschaft*, there could be inner conflicts. One extraordinary example of what was later so often repressed is given by a series of letters involving a so-called 'euthanasia' case. Hildegard and Wolfgang S. were the parents of a child, Gudrun, who was killed in the later phase of the 'euthanasia' programme, when death was caused by enforced malnutrition culminating in rapid starvation or falling prey to a fatal disease. Gudrun, referred to in letters by her nicknames of 'Dulala' or the affectionate diminutive 'Dulachen', had been born as a perfectly healthy baby in July 1938, but had later apparently received brain damage following a blow to her head. Although the family tried to hush this up even among themselves, their whispered view was that Gudrun's elder sister had delivered this blow in a fit of sibling jealousy; how the sister later felt, given the ultimately fatal consequences of her childish action, is beyond imagining. In any event, Gudrun's condition was soon held to be 'hopeless in the view of the doctors', and, as her father somewhat heartlessly put it in a letter to his brother-in-law, 'Father Christmas will hopefully bring a replacement [*Ersatz*] for Gudrun.'[162] (Or perhaps he had adopted an enforced lightness of expression to cover up the pain and pretend there could be such a thing as an '*Ersatz*' for a unique child.) Shortly before her fourth birthday, her father voluntarily handed Gudrun ('Dulala') into the 'care' of one of the institutes specializing in 'euthanasia', and the child was killed by enforced starvation within a matter of weeks, as her mother recounted:

> Two weeks ago today, on the 18th of July, at 12.30 in the morning our Dulala died in the regional institution of Görden near Brandenburg an der Havel. Wolfgang had

---

[160] Claudia Schoppmann, *Days of Masquerade: Life stories of lesbians during the Third Reich* (New York: Columbia University Press, 1996), p. 10. For personal accounts see e.g. Heinz Heger, *The Men with the Pink Triangle*, trans. David Fernbach (London: Gay Men's Press, 1980; orig. German, 1972); Richard Plant, *The Pink Triangle: The Nazi war against homosexuals* (Edinburgh: Mainstream Publishing, 1987); Frank Rector, *The Nazi Extermination of Homosexuals* (New York: Stein and Day, 1981).

[161] This is a topic that cannot be pursued here in the depth that would be required to begin to do it any kind of justice. But see e.g. Charlotte Delbo, *Auschwitz and After* (New Haven and London: Yale University Press, 1995); Lawrence Langer, *Holocaust Testimonies: The ruins of memory* (New Haven and London: Yale University Press, 1993); Aaron Hass, *The Aftermath* (Cambridge: Cambridge University Press, 1996).

[162] FMK, 3-2002-1248, letter of 27 Nov. 1941, p. 9.

brought her here without my knowledge on 26.6, when I was away for about three weeks in Upper Bavaria near Königssee and Chiemsee for rest and recuperation, in order, as he tells me, to have D. undergo another thorough investigation. As I have now heard from our Elspeth, he took her there in order never to bring her back again and there he gave them full authority over Dulachen. They then treated Dulachen accordingly. When we visited on 15.7 Dulachen had already got so thin that she was virtually unrecognizable, it hurt me to the depths of my soul, and I reproached myself dreadfully that I hadn't chosen, instead of going to Upper Bavaria, to stay home, and that I bore the guilt of her poor condition . . .[163]

How this bereaved mother managed to retain her relationship with a husband who had knowingly delivered their daughter into the murderous 'care' of this institution, without involving her in the decision and clearly against every instinct in her emotional repertoire, is beyond imagining. But together they had several more children, boys, although the emotional legacies were not easily dealt with. A letter of 8 March 1943 from Wolfgang S. to his brother-in-law Helmut informed him that:

Hilde yesterday gave birth to a little boy—Gunter. Well, our joy is great, as you can well imagine. Hilde did in fact wish for a little girl for Gudrun, but perhaps it is better like this, that she is not reminded so much of our former misfortune; and three boys so close together is also quite nice.[164]

Wolfgang and Hildegard seem, on the evidence of their letters, to have remained supporters of the Nazi regime and its war effort to the last, and to have found ways of coping with this personal tragedy, or suppressing any sense of loss or guilt. Wolfgang's work was sufficiently important to allow him to remain largely based in Berlin. But eventually he too was called up in the *Volkssturm* and was killed in the very last few days of the war, just two doors away from his own home.[165]

Several decades later, when the by now adult son of the brother-in-law, Helmut, came to read through and seek to understand the import of these wartime letters to his father from his uncle and aunt, he tried to talk it through with one of his cousins, Hildegard and Wolfgang's fourth son. But the latter refused even to touch on the matter of the murdered sister whom he had never known, as Helmut's son recounted:

My attempt to provide the fourth son, Volker, of Hildegard and Wolfgang S. with the findings of these letters and the facts they contained met with the greatest resistance on his part (telephone call on 7.7.1994). He [said that] he did not know all these facts, and also didn't want to know anything about it. Ultimately there were only a few meaningful bits of information contained in the letters, the background must inevitably remain in the dark. His tone was disconcertingly deterrent and aggressive. I had the

---

[163] *Ibid.*, letter of 1 August 1942, p. 12. Helmut was the husband of Hildegard's sister, and father of the person who donated the collection of wartime letters to the archive.
[164] *Ibid.*, letter of 8 March 1943, p. 18.
[165] FMK, 3-2002-1248, Wolfgang-D. Schröer, 'Tötung behinderter Kinder unter dem Deckmantel der Eugenik im "Dritten Reich". Vorbemerkungen', p. 5.

impression that he certainly knew more and precisely because of this did not want to be pestered with it any further. That has to be respected.[166]

The matter was repressed as best the family could at the time, and it remained repressed into the next generation; the murder of the child Gudrun effectively disappeared from the family's collective memory, while the father was probably mourned as a late 'victim' of Nazism. It is hard to tell how many families in post-war Germany were affected in this way by enforced silence on such matters, such rewriting of family histories, but the numbers were immense.

Many Germans lived with a combination of constant fear and grief and yet at the same time a degree of freedom and the superficiality of seeking to maintain at least the outward appearance of a 'normal life'. Only relatively late in war, and only in the worst-targeted areas for bombing raids, did that change radically with mass civilian casualties. While many children were sent out to what was supposed to be the safety of life 'on the land', 'Mischling' children such as Ilse J. remained within the cities and sought to survive with adults as best they could. In Ilse J.'s case, the fear was made worse following the deportation of her Jewish grandmother and aunt, neither of whom she ever saw again. Her 'Aryan' father was sent to a forced labour camp, where he was put under immense pressure to divorce her mother, who would then have been deported too; a pressure to which he refused to succumb.[167] This family was highly fortunate that the war did not continue longer and that, unlike many of her mother's relatives, Ilse's parents both survived.

The worst worries for virtually all Germans who remained at home were losses of loved ones at the front—made even worse for those who could not share any world view which made those losses seem at all meaningful, let alone worthwhile in light of a wider cause. For women who were 'internally' opposed to the regime, but not excluded from the 'people's community' by virtue of 'race', finding ways of dealing with the war was difficult. The diaries of a journalist, Ursula von Kardorff, give insights into the mind of a young woman from a background of high social standing and associated socialization into 'Prussian' virtues. In a diary entry of 17 October 1942, Ursula von Kardorff deeply regretted the inactivity, indeed almost fatalism, of her conforming contemporaries:

> Those who are cautious are usually right. But this lack of action on all sides is shocking. I don't know a single convinced Nazi, and yet everything is accepted as though it is unalterable.[168]

Within Kardorff's social circle, there was a constant shifting of topics of conversation from how awful everything was and constant fear and crying to superficial or very false jollity, a Titanic-style life playing cards as though nothing were wrong in the world. Von Kardorff speaks of the way in which Prussian humour was intended to cover up emotions which were unbearable on saying farewell as yet another

---

[166] FMK, 3-2002-1248, Wolfgang-D. Schröer, 'Tötung behinderter Kinder unter dem Deckmantel der Eugenik im "Dritten Reich". Vorbemerkungen', p. 6.
[167] Interview with Ilse J., 2007.
[168] Von Kardorff, *Berliner Aufzeichnungen*, entry of 17 Oct. 1942, p. 43.

friend or relative left for the front: 'We went through the motions of a cosy family breakfast with the sort of tense jollity that always sets in at a time of farewells. Spoke of the most trivial things. Just no emotions.'[169] With respect to the battle of Stalingrad (to which 250,000 men had been despatched, of whom only 90,000 survived the winter and the campaign itself; and only 6,000 eventually returned after periods of imprisonment), von Kardorff commented: 'Unbelievable. It makes you go crazy, simply crazy . . . And yesterday, despite all, again this ludicrous gaiety, disconnected from the world.' Two days later, she noted: 'A grotesque life: in the depths of grief, and then again for hours on end as though living in peaceful times in which our comfort matters.'[170]

Moving in circles where she felt many were like-minded, yet also that she could never fully trust anyone, von Kardorff constantly sought to maintain her Prussian 'bearing' (*Haltung*), yet with ever less success, particularly after one of her brothers, Jürgen, was killed and her other brother, Klaus, was called up and left to fight. When von Kardoff got Jürgen's belongings back, she found he had written a draft of a letter of condolence to one Frau Beheim, whose son died in January, professing religious grounds for maintaining a sense that the war was not without purpose. Von Kardorff quoted it in her diary, seeking desperately to find some comfort in it, but with little success:

'Despite all unhappiness I have not lost faith that this war too has a meaning, only that we don't yet recognize the meaning, for there is nothing which happens in the world without meaning, nothing which is not God's will.'[171]

Among others who were trying, almost literally, to drown their sorrows was Franziska, one of the former classmates of Helga Paasche and Alexandra von S. from the Augusta Schule. Unlike Alexandra von S., Franziska had not gone along with the politics of the Third Reich; and her father, Alexander Schwab, a former colleague of Hans Paasche's in the German youth movement, was actively involved in the anti-Nazi resistance group called the 'Red Fighters' (*Rote Kämpfer*). In November 1936 Schwab was caught and in 1937 sentenced to eight years' imprisonment; moved around through four different prisons and subjected to brutal maltreatment, he died while still in captivity on 12 November 1943.[172] Franziska was forced, along with her brother Felix, to go to the prison and identify the body of their father. Even decades later, Franziska confessed a continuing sense of guilt that she had tried so hard to live on a superficial plane of existence that would somehow give a sense or at least an appearance of a 'normal life' during the Third Reich. Yet she had a continuing sense that she was really only 'half present', seeing neither the need to emigrate nor wanting to leave her father while there still remained some hope that he might survive and even be released from prison, but at the same time having a strong sense of being cut off from any kind of identification

---

[169] *Ibid.*, entries of 27 Dec. 1942, 9 Nov. 1942, pp. 50, 41.

[170] *Ibid.*, entries of 23 Jan. 1943, 25 Jan. 1943, p. 61.

[171] *Ibid.*, entry of 15 Apr. 1943, p. 76.

[172] See also the brief biographical details in Hans-Joachim Fieber, *Widerstand in Berlin gegen das NS-Regime, 1933- bis 1945. Ein biographisches Lexikon* (Berlin: trafo verlag, 2004), Vol. 7, p. 191 (which inaccurately lists him as only having a son).

with her own country and its people—a sense that continued right up into old age, decades after the end of the Nazi regime.[173]

But in the meantime there was little hope for political change either. Von Kardorff was a journalistic colleague of Franziska's brother Felix Schwab, who had attended the same school as her brother Jürgen. Schwab's comments on the mood among the students he was acquainted with was depressing, as was the likelihood of any kind of revolutionary or mutinous developments among soldiers:

> He said that the atmosphere of mistrust among students was so great that no one spoke openly. Friends barely trusted each other; impossible to raise such a topic, even only tangentially, in a larger circle . . . No opposition will arise from the Russian trenches. Anyone fighting for his own life has no leisure to brood over the question of whether he likes his government or not.[174]

Von Kardorff briefly toyed with the idea of distributing leaflets from the White Rose resistance group, associated with Hans and Sophie Scholl, but her then boyfriend ripped the only copy of a flyer from her hands and burnt it. By the summer of 1943, von Kardorff was highly critical of all the acquired and learned mechanisms for coping with the situation, complaining to her diary of 'my mood in two minds' and the 'shit-word bearing' (*Scheißwort Haltung*):

> As though I had not demonstrated that, if it is needed, I more than have this stupid 'bearing'. But these inner debates are about something more important than external composure, which I hope I will always have, they are about conscience. And that you can't always shrug off. One has to become more consistent, that's all that I wanted to achieve . . . That these people don't always latch on that it's not enough for me to have done enough for some people just by my sheer 'existence'. That is after all cowardly and self-sufficient. Self-satisfied. How hateful.[175]

But von Kardorff found no resolution for her sense of dissonance and desire for effective action. Her Berlin social circle was by the later years of the war engaged in a mad round of socializing and partying, as people claimed they wanted to use their flats to the full before they were bombed out. The joke, reported also in many other sources, was going the rounds: '"Children, enjoy the war, for the peace will be terrible".'[176]

Others too felt they were living within, effectively, two worlds within one person. The partially aristocratic, partially Jewish Mascha Razumowsky, now living in Vienna, was highly aware of the two worlds in which she was herself living: on the one hand, a world of indulgence in her chosen field of music, attending concerts and enjoying happiness with friends; but aware, on the other, of what she was trying to repress, in trying to ignore both war and the future:

> That is the world in which I have been living since Aunt Olga's death, into which I have artificially spun myself, and which is too nice to be true. Everything else, the real, terrible world, is shut out . . . In this way one experiences everything far more

[173] Letter to a school friend, 6 Nov. 1980, private family archive.
[174] Kardorff, *Berliner Aufzeichnungen*, entry of 15 May 1943, pp. 84–5.
[175] *Ibid.*, extract from *Tagebuch* of 22 Jun. 1943, p. 90, fn. 3.
[176] *Ibid.*, p. 95, p. 94.

intensively, and the memory of these days will hopefully give me strength and courage when the bad times come, since otherwise my whole current life would be nothing but wasted time. I have by now become quite a pessimist, looking at the dark side of everything. If you look at what is going on around us, how brutalized [*verroht*] people are, if you hear what will happen if Germany wins the war; if on the other hand . . . you get told about Russia, then there is only one conclusion: for us there <u>can</u> be no future; people like us don't fit into today's times.[177]

And further, Razumowsky recognized that she and her family, as the 'hybrid' offspring of a family including both Jews and aristocrats, had every reason to fear what the future might hold in this 'age of ideologies':

> Least of all do I understand why we always and everywhere are supposed to be worse than all other people. Once our sort was held to be better, but those were probably not very good times . . . The old world is dead—how the outcome of the new will look one cannot say as yet. But it will depend on the victors whether in the 'new Europe' there will be a place for us or not.[178]

Ousted by all ideologies, whether Nazi racism or Soviet class warfare, and fearful of whoever might eventually win this devastating war, all Razumowsky could do was try to shut out thoughts both of present 'reality' and of future possibilities and artificially try to throw herself, as best she could, into enjoyment of her social life and indulgence in music in what was likely to be a very short-lived present.

VII. THE MOBILIZATION OF THE YOUNG

If 80 per cent of all German troops fought on the eastern front in Russia, a very large majority of these did not return to tell the tale. The males of the war-youth generation and the 'first Hitler Youth generation' were decimated by war. Those who survived were not merely aware of the ways their ranks had been thinned, but were also in a large proportion of cases both physically and mentally deeply scarred by their experiences of war and also often imprisonment. The most highly ideologically charged generations were also the most widely maimed, and the most deeply tainted by their support for Nazism as adults. Their entry into the post-war world would be very different from that of those only a few years younger.

The generation of '1929ers' had a markedly different experience of war from that of older or younger cohorts (the latter, of course, not being called up at all).[179] Those younger males who as soldiers entered the war late were by 1944–5 drawn into what was a very different kind of war in the last year of defensive fighting

---

[177] Mascha, Dolly, and Olga Razumovsky, *Unsere versteckten Tagebücher 1938–1944. Drei Mädchen erleben die Nazizeit* (Wien, Köln, Weimar: Böhlau Verlag, 1999), 28 Mar. 1944 (Mascha), pp. 185–6, underlining in original.

[178] *Ibid.*, pp. 186–7.

[179] On children's experiences, see Nicholas Stargardt, *Witnesses of War: Children's lives under the Nazis* (London: Jonathan Cape, 2005).

against the approaching enemy forces on German soil.[180] All, including those who never came to serve at the front, such as females and younger males, had distinctive prior experiences of collective socialization and ideological preparation for war.

These cohorts were uniquely subjected to what has been called 'total education for total war', exposed to the most far-reaching attempts at ideological influence, paramilitary training, and eventually mobilization for a whole variety of aspects of the war effort—including playing a crucial role in the war economy—going way beyond what might be conceived of as the 'typical' activities of a mass youth organization.[181] In particular, these cohorts were the most removed from the influence of parents, the most absorbed into the ever growing landscape of 'camps' for a variety of purposes, the most subjected to Nazi indoctrination—and arguably the most affected by the experience of violence at a relatively young, impressionable age, a violence for which they themselves held extremely little or no responsibility. Yet the consequences were somewhat more ambiguous than one might expect.

Most had still been at school when war broke out. This meant, in many cases, also being among those school groups who were evacuated from cities where the dangers of air raids were high, and being sent away to pursue their studies in country areas supposedly well away from any risk of bombing. Letters home from such camps combine comments about everyday life—particularly the quality and quantity of food—and concerns about the well-being of members of their families at home. The combination of the extraordinary and ordinary for these youngsters was taken for granted in ways which can, for later readers, seem quite disconcerting. Wolfgang M. (born June 1929), for example, wrote home on 14 September 1943 from his camp in the Wartheland:

> I haven't had any post from you yet. How are you? Is our house still standing? I'm well, yesterday I ate up the last sandwiches; and I've only got one pear left now too.[182]

The first few letters report on the details of life in the camp, sleeping on a 'straw sack, on the floor due to lack of space'. There was no electricity, so 'we can't listen to the Führer's speech here'. The daily round of organized activities started at 7:00, with school lessons for most of the morning, a 'march' or 'darning' or 'mending' in the afternoon, and going to sleep at the 'onset of darkness'. Many letters are concerned with food, as this growing teenager, like his fellow students, appears to have been perpetually hungry. Within a matter of weeks homesickness was taking over; by 22 September, Wolfgang M. was counting down the days until he could go home, having been given a probable date of 'February', a rather general indication

---

[180] For the age ranges called up in different years of the war, see Bernhard Kroener, 'The manpower resources of the Third Reich in the area of conflict between Wehrmacht, bureaucracy, and war economy, 1939–1942' in Militärgeschichtliches Forschungsamt (ed.), *Germany and the Second World War*, Vol. V, pt 3, p. 831.

[181] Michael Buddrus, *Totale Erziehung für den totalen Krieg: Hitlerjugend und nationalsozialistische Jugendpolitik*, Institut für Zeitgeschichte, Texte und Materialien zur Zeitgeschichte (München: K.G. Saur, 2003), Vols. 13/1 and 13/2.

[182] FMK, 3.2002.7614, Wolfgang M. letter of 14 Sep. 1943.

from which he developed a detailed calculation: 'so in approximately 145 days. Christmas is in 93 days.'[183]

Students in another evacuated school camp in southern Bavaria were making similar comments about conditions and food supplies. One of the adults in charge of five camps in the Garmisch-Partenkirchen and Mittenwald area sent a circular letter to all parents seeking to reassure them that, despite difficulties caused by shortages of books and materials, everything was being done to look after their children and they should not believe everything in their children's letters. As he put it: 'Monitoring their letters has demonstrated that the younger pupils easily give a false impression of provisions.'[184] The censorship of children's letters would continue, and there should be no attempt to circumvent this rule:

> We kindly ask parents never to cause your children to keep their letters secret from the camp leadership, which has unfortunately occurred on occasion. In this way mistrust and lack of honesty are sown and the consistent education of character by both school and home is endangered.[185]

This generation was, then, being brought up to conform to the norms and practices of the state as transmitted through the school and camp leadership.

For many, the transition from such schooling into military service was seamless. In the file of Fritz W. (born 1927) was a little card entitled 'The waiting one' [*Der Wartende*] with the following rhyme on it, beautifully written out in careful handwriting:

> For Fritz the time is dragging out long
> Until to the army he can go
> Because the year group to which he belongs
> Still has to weather a year or so.[186]

In the event, they did not have to wait so very long. By 24 May 1943, some four months after the schoolchildren had settled into their evacuation quarters, Fritz W. and his schoolmates had been called up as air force auxiliaries (*Luftwaffenhelfer*). In the words of the 8th Flak-Division commander in charge of Fritz:

> With numerous comrades he is fulfilling his service with enthusiasm, cheerfully subordinating himself to military discipline and by his efforts replacing a soldier who is thus freed up to serve at the front.[187]

And from the air force auxiliary service, like those just old enough to enter the final and most murderous phase of the war, Fritz soon joined the regular troops. He was last heard of on 18 March 1945, when his left leg was in plaster; there was then no further news. His parents sought desperately to trace him; as they put it in a letter to the Red Cross in January 1946, 'Fritz is our only child and this hoping against hope is very difficult.'[188] Despite a correspondence going through until the 1960s, Fritz

---

[183] *Ibid.*, letter of 22 Sep. 1943.
[184] FMK, 3.2002.7256, Gerfried Ahrens, circular letter from *Lagerleiter* of February 1943.
[185] *Ibid.*   [186] FMK, 3.2002.7256, Fritz W. (1927), no date.
[187] *Ibid.*, letter of 24 May 1943.   [188] *Ibid.*, letter of 24 Jan. 1946.

was never heard of again. Wolfgang M., two years younger than Fritz, was luckier: he was only called up on 1 May 1945, and survived the last week of the war intact.

Unlike members of the war-youth generation, who had reached adulthood well before the Third Reich entered its most violent phase, and who had, like Udo K., been in a position to make informed choices about compromises and career goals, however uncomfortable they may or may not have found subsequent developments, for many of these youngsters 'life projects' had been almost entirely informed by Nazi socialization. Individuals such as Fritz W. and his near contemporary Siegfried H., born in 1926, had available to them little by way of alternatives to officially given 'scripts' with respect to valued character traits and 'racial types', constructions of personal identity in terms of 'national' commitments, and future aspirations in which their own lives and that of the national community were intricately bound together.[189] This was particularly the case when there were no strong alternative moral communities (of the sort represented by Maria K.'s family, who had stood by and supported her in aiding Jews in November 1938), or when there appeared to be little by way of practical alternatives in terms of achieving a sense of self-worth and fulfilment, let alone broader social recognition.

Siegfried H., for example, left school before he turned fourteen and worked as a gardening assistant, a job which he had to give up for health reasons; he then managed to obtain work as an office assistant, but was desperate to be called up into the Reich Labour Service (RAD) with a view to going on into the *Waffen-SS* at the earliest possible age; in the surviving letters, the family at some stage after the war blacked out every mention of the particular SS unit he sought to join, before the letters were finally deposited in an archive. As Siegfried H. put it in his letter to the registration office of the RAD:

> I hereby beg you politely to call me up finally for the RAD after all, so that by the end of my 17th year I can be called up in the [SS unit blacked-out]. I know that with my modest strength I cannot make a big contribution to the victory, but in the difficult times of today where every man is needed, I don't want to stand back and I would like to place myself at the service of the Fatherland . . .
> Heil Hitler![190]

Having successfully obtained a place in the Reich Labour Service, Siegfried H. wrote to his mother on 1 August 1943 that he had heard that his 'comrades from the year group 1926 now must also join the RAD' whereas he would soon be out and able to join the *Waffen-SS*. His youthful enthusiasm for this sudden advancement, as he saw it, is almost painful to read:

> Then at least I can say with pride that at the age of 16¾ I was already serving in enemy territory for my Führer, for my people [*Volk*], and for my wonderful Sudeten German Heimat.[191]

---

[189] FMK, 3.2002.1377, Siegfried H. (28 Aug. 1926–24 Aug. 1944).
[190] *Ibid.*, letter from Siegfried H. to RAD-Meldeamt Trautenau Sudetenland, 4 May 1943.
[191] *Ibid.*, letter from Siegfried H. to his mother, 1 Aug. 1943.

Here, a young person's entire identity seems bound up with the national cause; and in the case of a person who was highly unlikely to have had many other options available to him, either structurally or culturally. He was, in short, fully mobilized, in mind as well as body.

Even after experiencing the privations of inadequate food and excessive exercise, as well as some apparently stomach-turning experiences while in training school for the SS near Berlin ('sometimes you see things that can ruin your appetite for weeks on end'), Siegfried H. remained enthusiastic:

> Well I too certainly didn't dream of it being all fun and games with the [SS unit blacked-out], but nevertheless my eyes have also really been opened here. But the harder the exertion, the better for us in the upcoming mobilization at the front . . . Despite all the tribulations and exertion I'm unspeakably proud to be able to belong to precisely this, the best troop of our German people and quite particularly the core unit [SS unit blacked-out], of our [blacked-out]. When I look at the black lapels with the white runes [SS unit blacked-out] on my uniform, then the sacredness of the words 'My honour is to be faithful' comes to my mind and I want to and will always and under all circumstances put into practice this oath of fidelity that I carry on my belt buckle. Even if there are sometimes moments in which one thinks about things differently or because of the unfamiliar circumstances would like to mutiny, they nevertheless pass quickly and that happens even to the best of soldiers and is here in order to be overcome.[192]

When Siegfried H. finally went to serve on the eastern front, the inevitable soon happened. He was wounded at Tarnopol on 10 March 1944, but on recovery rapidly volunteered himself back to the front, where he died. In the words of one of his superiors in *SS-Sturm* 10/95: 'After his recovery he volunteered himself back to the front and on 24.8.44 during the battles in Tuckum, Latvia, his hero's death for Greater Germany befell him.'[193] Siegfried himself had, earlier, tried to give a meaning to his death with almost Christian overtones, claiming to his mother that, in the event of his death, his girlfriend Ella should feel that (echoing Christ's words) 'he died that we may live': 'Should fate determine for me that I do not survive to experience the victorious peace, then Ella should and must say, he has died for me. He had to give his life in order that I can live!'[194]

The death notices and related material make for miserable reading. As Siegfried's family put it:

> The deepest sorrow was brought to us by the news that our beloved, good son, brother, nephew and cousin, the volunteer SS Infantryman of the Adolf Hitler Bodyguard Regiment,
>
> SIEGFRIED H.,
>
> bearer of the insignia of the wounded, found a hero's death during an attack in the East on 24.8.1944, 4 days before his 18th birthday, joyfully giving his life in willing service for the Führer and the Heimat. He was denied the chance to see his beloved Heimat

---

[192] *Ibid.*, letters from Siegfried H. to his mother, 6 Dec. 1943, 10 Dec. 1943.
[193] *Ibid.*, 'Lebenslauf', SS-Sturm 10/95.
[194] *Ibid.*, letter from Siegfried to his mother of 10 Dec. 1943.

again. With cheerful courage he made the ultimate sacrifice of his own life, and we of our most beloved.

The family also produced a verse which from an aesthetic point of view can only be described as doggerel, but which is significant for the way in which it remains full of pain despite all the attempts at making Siegfried's death at such a young age seem to mean something more than the utterly useless loss of a much loved son:

> When the great reunion eventually takes place
> With much rejoicing on the streets
> We will stand silently and with a sad face
> Alone and bereft.

> He will not return in glory to these parts
> Home to the quiet hearth,
> He whom we pressed to our hearts
> Rests in foreign soil.

> Sleeps the long, deep sleep
> Without hope of morning
> The bullet that hit him deep
> Has hit us too.

While still talking about a 'hero's death . . . for Führer and Fatherland', the family nevertheless registered their own private pain: 'All our hopes sank with him into a distant soldier's grave. Only those who have shared the same fate can appreciate our pain.'[195] The tragedy for so many Germans after the war was that, while the personal pain of bereavement remained acute, the supposedly comforting cultural wrappings of the allegedly higher 'meaning' of the premature death had either faded away and disintegrated entirely, or had become unspeakable, effectively censored in post-war, post-Nazi society: there could later be no solace, no 'good' reasons to have died so young, to have lost one's loved ones. Those on the side of the fight against Nazism could still have reason to believe that their loved ones had died in a 'good cause', however much they wished it had not had to be; but those who mourned for loved ones who had lost their lives on behalf of 'Führer and Fatherland', and whose leaders had, furthermore, been responsible for instigating the war, had no such framework for rendering suffering and bereavement less unbearable.

Siegfried H. may or may not have been unusual (like Wilhelm B. before him) in the way he identified so fully with the Nazi cause. But he was far from alone in his outlook. And his family were among the millions of bereaved, whose reactions can at best have clutched at the notion of death in service of something higher. Whether towards the end a concern for defence of family and homeland against what were seen as the invading hordes of rapacious Russians displaced faith in the *Führer* as the prime motive for fighting on with commitment, rather than allowing a widespread collapse of morale as in 1918, remains a somewhat moot point; there is only suggestive and partial evidence to this effect. Arguably for the vast majority of

---

[195] *Ibid.*, materials relating to the memorial service.

adults a tremendous fear of 'Bolshevism' and what would come after this most horrendous 'racial war' was a major incentive in balancing the fear of peace against the hatred of a continuing and by now suicidal war.

Other youngsters appear to have been far more shocked and traumatized by what they went through. In 1943 the sixteen- and seventeen-year-olds were called up, and in 1944 also whole classes of fifteen-year-olds were removed from their school classrooms and mobilized as '*Luftwaffenhelfer*', '*Flakhelfer*' or anti-aircraft auxiliary forces.[196] Not only the youngest but also the oldest German males still capable of bearing arms were now being called up in the 'People's militia' (*Volkssturm*), to replace the vast numbers of men who had already been maimed or fatally wounded and killed in their prime; in February 1945, this decree was extended also to women. The young in particular were at a stage of life when their primary personal concerns had been narrowly focused on home, school, and relationships, with Nazi socialization resulting in a sense of the significance of fulfilling duties; unlike those who were somewhat older, they had no experience at all of life outside or before Nazi Germany, and nothing with which they could personally compare it. Many came from homes where parents had accommodated themselves to the regime in one way or another.[197] They were mentally entirely unprepared for what now faced them.

Diary entries of the time by Sepp Nuscheler suggest a certain bravado and sense of adventure at first, as his whole school class served together and had some near misses and lucky escapes while 'defending' the town of Saarbrücken. Having been brought up to believe in the cause, Nuscheler's tone at first is almost stridently triumphant, or at least has periodic echoes of the bombastic tone of officialese at the time; and *Flakhelfer* activities appeared initially more worthwhile than time spent in the classroom. But it was not long before the tone of the diary entries turned distinctly more sombre, as Nuscheler's friends, classmates and superior were killed before his eyes:

---

[196] See Rolf Schörken, *Luftwaffenhelfer und Drittes Reich. Die Enstehung eines politischen Bewußtseins* (Stuttgart: Klett Cotta, 1985), p. 17. On the anti-aircraft auxiliary forces, see also e.g. Horst-Adalbert Koch (with Heinz Schindler and Georg Tessin), *Flak. Die Geschichte der Deutschen Flakartillerie und der Einsatz der Luftwaffenhelfer*, 2nd edn (Bad Nauheim: Podzun Verlag, 1965; orig. 1954); Hans-Dietrich Nicolaisen, *Die Flakhelfer. Luftwaffenhelfer und Marinehelfer im Zweiten Weltkrieg* (Berlin: Ullstein, 1981); Hans-Dietrich Nicolaisen, *Der Einsatz der Luftwaffen- und Marinehelfer im II. Weltkrieg. Darstellung und Dokumentation* (Büsum: Selbstverlag Dr. Hans-Dietrich Nicolaisen, 1981); Ludwig Schätz, *Schüler-Soldaten. Die Geschichte der Luftwaffenhelfer im zweiten Weltkrieg* (Darmstadt: Thesen Verlag, 1974); Rolf Schörken, 'Sozialisation inmitten des Zusammenbruchs. Der Kriegseinsatz von 15- und 16-jährigen Schülern bei der deutschen Luftabwehr (1943–1945) in Dittmar Dahlmann (ed.), *Kinder und Jugendliche in Krieg und Revolution* (Paderborn etc.: Ferdinand Schöningh, 2000), pp. 123–43.

[197] See e.g. the personal accounts in Hans Scherer, *Ich war Oberschüler und Luftwaffenhelfer. Teil I, II und II, 1927–1948* (Selbstverlag, Staffelstein 1996); Hans-Martin Stimpel, *Schülersoldaten 1943– 1945. Gymnasiasten als Luftwaffenhelfer in Berlin, bei Auschwitz, und als Fallschirmjäger in der 'Festung Harz'* (Göttingen: Cuvillier Verlag, 2004); and Wulf Schröder, *Luftwaffenhelfer 1943–44. Erlebnisse einer Gruppe Flensburger Schüler im Zweiten Weltkrieg*, Kleine Reihe der Gesellschaft für Flensburger Stadtgeschichte, Heft 16 (Gesellschaft für Flensburger Stadtgeschichte, 1988).

19 July 1944
Already at 8.00 the sirens went off. Wave after wave came over . . . Then there was a
humming noise quite close by, the ghastly humming noise. It gets quite dark from the
bomb's impact, it must be really close by . . . I threw myself down immediately . . .
What sort of a picture then lay before me . . . I will never so easily forget. Pelzel covered
in stones up to his chest, back to back with Scheibe. His face streaming with blood.
A picture of horror. The death rattles and the groaning of the wounded are still
resounding in my ears. Friedemann . . . had severe injuries. Walter died instantly. Pelzel
we dug out with our hands, he died a few minutes later. The same with our Chief. One
I took away, I don't any more know who it was. The faces were disfigured. Doctors
arrived, up until then our paramedics had already done makeshift bandaging.[198]

From then on, until the end of his diary in December, the entries record the shock
of deaths, and the meaninglessness of the military awards for bravery which were
made even in posthumous 'compensation':

20th July 1944
. . . Cadet Barthen, Labour Service men Koch and Schmal died of their wounds today.
General Buffa came to us, praised our attitude by awarding us the Iron Cross II and the
War Merit Cross Class II. Cadet Barthen did not survive to receive his Iron Cross II.[199]

The following day, this teenager noted in his diary:

21st July 1944
Everyone is rather nervous here, the latest attacks made themselves rather notice-
able.[200]

There was, at this time, no comment about the attempt on Hitler's life the previous
day. But the position of the *Flakhelfer* was rapidly becoming more precarious, and
the accompanying shift in mood was registered in the diary:

11th August 1944
. . . An impact extremely nearby. Everyone lay on the ground. Again everything was
dark and only gradually lightened to a grey haze . . . A direct hit on an artillery piece of
the 5th Battery. Ten dead and five injured, mostly 16- and 17-year-old air force
auxiliaries.[201]

By the autumn, Sepp was clearly shifting in his perceptions of what he understood
as 'good':

14th October 1944
. . . Now Saarbrücken has been completely destroyed . . . The war is getting ever more
threatening. When will the world come to peace? When will goodness make a break-
through?[202]

---

[198] Sepp Nuscheler, 'Kriegstagebuch (12. Juni bis 21. Dezember 1944)', repr. in Ernst Itschert,
Marel Reucher, Gerd Schuster, and Hans Stiff, *'Feuer frei—Kinder!' Eine mißbrauchte Generation—
Flakhelfer im Einsatz* (Saarbrücken: Buchverlag Saarbrücker Zeitung, 1984), pp. 181–94, quotation here
from pp. 186–7.
    [199] *Ibid.*, p. 187.   [200] *Ibid.*   [201] *Ibid.*, p. 189.   [202] *Ibid.*, p. 192.

Some six weeks later, he commented:

28th November 1944
We are now leaving Saarbrücken. We experienced good but also hard times this year. The town has in the meantime been completely destroyed, it's like a city of the dead.[203]

Finally, war became a deadly reality in Sepp's own family, which he records with a startling factuality and possible numbness in his diary:

7th December 1944.
I received today a telegram informing me of the death of my father. The Chief immediately gave me special leave.[204]

The same collection includes photographs of the occasion when, on 11 May 1944, families stood around a mass grave with mothers and younger brothers and sisters looking down on a row of coffins covered in flags (including swastikas), and the inscription 'Here on 11.5.1944 died air force auxiliaries at the young age of 15–17' followed by the names of sixteen young people who, in times of peace, would have still had a couple of years of schooling before them; victims of total mobilization, at an age when few had a choice either over what to do, or even what to believe.[205]

The utter pointlessness of their service to the cause, alongside shock at the loss of their classmates and comrades, made a long-lasting impact on these young people. Hans-Martin Stimpel, a former *Luftwaffenhelfer*, later recalled his time 'defending' the capital city, Berlin in quite graphic terms:

The skies were covered in exploding shrapnel, tracer bullets and bright illuminated parachutes falling to the ground. In between, every so often burning planes plummeted down, spiralling as they fell . . . On top of that the fiery glow of detonating mines and fire-spewing phosphorous canisters lit up the night. Searchlights searched the skies for planes . . . The smell of burning and black smoke damage still gave evidence the following day that tens of thousands of fire bombs had turned whole areas of the town into a blazing sea of flames. We knew: yet again hundreds if not thousands of people had died appalling deaths in the affected areas, under their collapsing houses or while attempting to escape through blazing streets in the firestorm. We could not prevent it. So this was our experience, in danger of our own lives, of how we had been mobilized to defend our population, as in each of these bombing nights we made futile attempts to fight against this and great sections of the capital city fell into ruins . . . Sixteen- and seventeen-year-olds were torn to shreds, and anyone who survived would never be rid of these traumatic impressions.[206]

Many youngsters went into the fight apparently willingly, only to be shattered by the realization of what violence actually meant once they witnessed it at first hand. A massive sense of shock at the realities of violence, at having been sent out on a hopeless and dangerous mission in vain, and at seeing one's friends and classmates being blown into pieces, was soon followed, after the war, by a sense of 'having been

---

[203] *Ibid.*, p. 193.   [204] *Ibid.*, p. 194.
[205] Itschert, *'Feuer frei—Kinder!'*, pp. 92–3.
[206] Stimpel, *Schülersoldaten*, pp. 6–7.

betrayed'—a feeling which appears to have been very widespread among both males and females of the 1929er generation.[207]

Hans-Martin Stimpel only published his recollections of his time as a *Luftwaffenhelfer* some sixty years after he was called up into service of the Third Reich as a teenager. His traumatic memories of air raids, nightly bombing, and firestorms echo those of many others of his generation, whose experiences as victims of air raids have recently been the subject of increased attention.[208] There can be little doubt that, unlike those a few years older, this generation could bear no responsibility for the violence which was now returning to Germany with a vengeance, towards the end of a war of unprecedented brutality. Like many of his age group in later life, Stimpel appears to have been most affected by the consequences for himself and his classmates of the horrendous circumstances into which they were quite innocently thrown. In these memoirs, however, written with the benefit of later knowledge, he remained what can best be described as somewhat coy about his own and his classmates' knowledge of Nazi atrocities and violence against others. Stimpel recounts that many from his school and his *Flakhelfer* group were stationed at Grojec, six kilometres south of Auschwitz, for some six months until the Russian advance in January 1945; thus they were there during the latter half of 1944, a period which included the gassing of the massive transports of Hungarian Jews in the summer of 1944, and the attempt by a resistance group among the prisoners to blow up the crematoria at Birkenau in October 1944. The young *Flakhelfer* working in nearby Grojec saw the slave labourers—who must, if they were at all typical, have been in a shocking state of starvation and near collapse—but, according to Stimpel's account, despite their close proximity (where both sights and smells should have alerted them, even if they were 'not told' what was happening in the camp) neither knew nor believed what was going on in Auschwitz-Birkenau. As Stimpel puts it:

> Most people had only vague knowledge, limited to concepts such as 'prison camp', 're-education camp' or 'work camp for the enemies of National Socialism'. They had heard nothing as yet of 'gassing'. Any form of contact with or talking to the prisoners was strictly forbidden, and apart from that the women, who were being misused for construction work, mostly spoke only Hungarian. When rumours nevertheless occasionally arose that made one suspect worse in the camp, the head of the Flak unit maintained that such 'idle talk' was based solely on 'enemy lies'. The prisoners were 'enemies of the people, who have been locked up here and have to carry out penal labour'.[209]

---

[207] See further below, Ch. 7. Cf. also Gabriele Rosenthal, 'Einleitung' in Gabriele Rosenthal (ed.), *Die Hitlerjugend-Generation. Biographische Thematisierung als Vergangenheitsbewältigung* (Essen: Verlag Die blaue Eule, 1986), p. 17.

[208] Cf. Jörg Friedrich, *Der Brand. Deutschland im Bombenkrieg 1940–1945* (Munich: Propyläen Verlag, 2002).

[209] Stimpel, *Schülersoldaten*, p. 9. See also his more comprehensive account in Hans-Martin Stimpel, *Getäuscht und mißbraucht. Schülersoldaten in Zentren des Vernichtungskrieges* (Göttingen: Cuvillier Verlag, 2001), pp. 41–83, particularly pp. 74–6.

It is quite possible that the teenagers believed what those in charge of them claimed, and accepted the picture portrayed. Yet at the same time this account echoes what became, in the post-war decades, a familiar trope: that true evil only really began at the gates of Auschwitz-Birkenau, indeed only really at the doors of the gas chambers. On this version, one could effectively remain innocent if one had 'only' participated in upholding a system characterized by practices of utmost brutality, generally causing death within months by enforced starvation or killing on the spot for collapsing on the job, and had not actually 'realized' that the 'rumours' of 'gassings' were actually true. By so massively restricting what was held to be the key issue, people could claim with conviction that they really had 'never known anything about it', even at these extremely close quarters. It is interesting that even in this late account, too, there is an odd and inappropriate gesture towards what can perhaps be best described as chivalry: to say that women were 'misused' for construction work implies that lighter work might have been acceptable or that for men such work would not have constituted an abuse; an extraordinary implication in the circumstances.

Stimpel was perhaps somewhat unusual in the proximity of his unit to Auschwitz. But evidence of abuse of slave labourers, not to mention the condition of those on the death marches, was far more widespread in the last few months of the war, as survivors of concentration camps were brought ever closer to the heart of the Reich in face of the Soviet advance. There were very few Germans, then, who did not witness horrific scenes of one sort or another in late 1944 and the early months of 1945. And some youngsters, on the evidence of contemporary material, do seem to have retained a sense of moral qualms or conscience in a way that those somewhat older, already 'made raw' by their earlier experiences, apparently no longer registered. The comments of one young person who was still only an air force auxiliary helper (*Luftwaffenhelfer*), and who was utterly shocked by what he saw as the 'burdens on his soul' of being involved in guarding concentration camp prisoners, are interesting in this regard:

> There are however other burdens on the soul, of a weighty character. For example the Jewish problem, held before our eyes here in all its naked reality. Here . . . in large KZ.-camps there are thousands of Jews living in conditions of mud and slime . . . During the day, they receive as their provisions two pieces of army bread and also a watery soup . . . On this basis they have to . . . carry out the heaviest of physical labour: excavating deep shafts in the ground, laying sewerage, cutting down trees and much else. In order to drive them on to higher productivity, naturally guards of the Jews have to run along behind them with rifles, punishing them with blows if they work too slowly and shooting them dead if they are separated by more than 3 metres from the group. And this is the task that we have to fulfil. To find the right path here between sympathy, charity, and duty, is very very hard. At first I avoided this job. But now I sign up for it all the more often, in order thereby to achieve some amelioration for the 'insulted and humiliated' [a reference to the title of a book by the Russian writer Fyodor Dostoyevsky, based on a biblical phrase]. That is of course forbidden, and I have already often got into trouble for this, but I nevertheless still think this is more the right thing to do than how the SS is going about it . . . Every day 30 die naturally

and 20 commit suicide . . . you have to be really down in the dirt to find God, it doesn't work in a confirmation suit.[210]

This youngster, presumably not so long out of his own confirmation lessons, was clearly having something of a difficult time squaring the morality he had learnt in church with that propagated by his country's leadership.

VIII. BOOMERANG VIOLENCE

In the ten months between July 1944 and capitulation on 8 May 1945, nearly as many Germans died as a result of Hitler's war as in the whole previous five years since the outbreak of war in 1939. Of the total of 5,300,000 who died in the war, around 2,600,000 million—virtually one half—died in the last ten months alone.[211] Yet Germans appear generally to have been far more willing to 'fight to the bitter end' in 1944–5 than they were in 1918, when it was mutiny on the part of soldiers and sailors that precipitated the collapse of the imperial government and the ending of the war.

There are a number of reasons for continuing to fight against all the odds in 1944–5, including not only the military mobilization of ever broader sections of the population whatever their views, but also a widespread, shared, and increasingly desperate sense of the need to defend 'Fatherland' and family, massively spurred by rising fear about revenge if Germany were to lose the war. There was particular anxiety as far as likely 'Bolshevik' treatment of the Germans was concerned, based not only on the years of propaganda about the 'defensive war' against the 'inferior peoples' of the east, but also the response which Hitler's aggressive war of utmost brutality had indeed unleashed on the part of those who had been invaded and attacked. As one soldier put it, reporting on a Russian propaganda leaflet:

> Yesterday I got a copy of a Russian flyer that was targeted at Russian soldiers. Probably no proclamation or newspaper article could be more arousing than the order of the Jew Ehrenburg: 'Soldiers of the Red Army, now collect your booty, German women and girls! Enjoy the scent of their flesh and your sexual lust. Then revel in murdering the fascists. Take for yourselves the blond Germanic women, and break the German arrogance!' I must say, on reading this, an ice-cold shiver ran down my spine. One shouldn't think about these words further: they are terrifying. Hatred without limits and offering ourselves to the last is the only answer that we can give to them. We *must* nail the colours of victory to our flag![212]

Even though faith in the invincibility or infallibility of the *Führer*'s judgement might have been wavering after Stalingrad, a determination to save the 'beloved

---

[210] Manoschek (ed.), *'Es gibt nur eines für das Judentum'*, 20.11.1944, L.w.Helfer, Dormettingen, p. 80.

[211] Wette, *Wehrmacht*, p. 182.

[212] Manoschek (ed.), *'Es gibt nur eines für das Judentum'*, 17.9.1944, Hptm.H.G.E., Stab/Pz.Aufkl. Abt.12, 12. Pz.Div., p. 78.

Fatherland' and avoid the potential horrors of revenge following defeat seem to have provided a powerful motivating force, particularly among the more committed soldiers who had been most influenced by Nazi ideology. As one put it, in August 1944:

> We can no longer think of resting, now it's all or nothing, make or break, we have to gain victory, Germany must live. It must never go under, our beautiful Germany, however much by way of sacrifices this may claim... [F]or it cannot and shall not be the case that we lose the war, for then we Germans are lost without hope. The Jews will then overwhelm us and annihilate everything that is German, there would be a frightful and ghastly massacre...[213]

There is in comments such as this no sense whatsoever of the irony of the German perspective. As soldiers began to worry about what might follow, they played down, even trivialized, what it was that they had already done, and began to create a differentiation of identity between 'Germans' and 'Nazis'. As another soldier put it on 4 September 1944:

> What if we lose the war after all? That would be frightful, and one would have to have doubts about destiny, we Germans have after all not been such criminals, even if the Nazis occasionally went a bit too far with the Jews [*es mal ein bisschen toll mit den Juden getrieben*]. So I would rather die in action before I get sent to Russia for forced labour, then at least this shit would have an end...[214]

Soldiers' views clearly varied according to prior convictions, but the sheer numbers who still—despite or perhaps even because of the mass crimes they had witnessed and participated in—were strongly imbued with Nazi ideology while yet distancing themselves from any responsibility is quite remarkable. To reduce the murder of millions of people to a phrase more frequently found in the context of a playground scuffle is extraordinary.

Even those no longer in the thick of fighting were locked into mentalities and ways of viewing the world which allowed them to dismiss or evade any real confrontation with the enormity of what the Nazi regime had been doing. An intriguing insight into views among German prisoners of war in North Africa is given in the manuscript notes of Fritz Beyling, commenting on reactions among fellow POWs to reports on discoveries of concentration camps and mass murders committed by the Germans in France and Poland:

> The reaction amongst circles of Nazi prisoners of war to the reports about <u>fascist atrocities</u> in France and Poland... is quite various. A small number reject these things as 'bogus enemy propaganda'. That's particularly the case concerning reports of gas chambers and corpse factories [*Kadaverfabriken*]. A far larger proportion support the view that the Führer and Himmler are 'still being far too humane' (Sergeant E.,... among those who in their circles support the principle of 'root and branch'

---

[213] Manoschek (ed.), '*Es gibt nur eines für das Judentum*', 16.8.1944, Uffz. O. D., 4. Kp./Trsp. Sich.Rgt.882, p. 74.

[214] Manoschek (ed.), '*Es gibt nur eines für das Judentum*', 4.9.1944, Wm. L. D., 7. Bttr./Pz.Art.Rgt. 103, 4.Pz.Div., FPN 03 711 B, p. 77.

extermination.) Corporal W. averred with respect to the SS crimes in Oradour that it
was the view of the whole 4th Company . . . that this had happened 'with good reason'.
The only mistake had been that such measures had been used too sparingly in France
. . . Anyone who had themselves been involved in terror actions like those at the
moment in the East has been forced under threat into remaining silent about them
even in the prisoner of war camp (evidence of Party member L . . . .)

For many it is the case that a certain anxiety about possible post-war penalties has
precipitated a particularly 'courageous' Nazi stance.[215]

At this stage, clearly, most of those who had been implicated in fighting for Nazism
were unsure of what response to adopt—but the last thing on their minds, it would
appear, was any real concern with the central issues of morality and mass murder.
Moreover, they were increasingly concerned with the safety and well-being of their
own, as the violence unleashed by Nazism across the world boomeranged back into
the heartlands of Germany itself.

If some Germans had managed to live relatively comfortably in many areas for
much of the war, from 1943 at the latest most families began to realize and fear for
the worst. With the growing threat of air raids, children were removed from the big
cities and sent to what were held to be safe areas in the countryside; people who had
been bombed-out sought new lodgings; and gradually those in the east began to
fear for the likely advance of a revengeful Red Army. There was no longer any
possibility of evading the effects of war. As Fritz Sch.'s sister wrote to his wife Luise
in late August 1943:

> Recent weeks have been full of commotion, the long stream of refugees would never
> come to an end, we had all the misery at first hand . . . I helped a lot [in the assembly
> camp for refugees], I saw misery without end . . . Berlin is also being cleared of school-
> children . . . How many families are now separated. Hopefully this will all soon come to
> a good end.[216]

At times, it may have seemed to soldiers in some parts of the front as if the exposure
to the violence of air raids at home was even worse than what they were experiencing. Fritz Sch. wrote home from Italy in the final stages of the war barely ruffled by
his own circumstances:

> Healthwise I'm fine now . . . Now and then I've swapped some of my tobacco for a
> piece of sausage, I could well use it. I can't complain about our provisions, if I compare
> it to the war years of 1917–1918.[217]

But he was at the same time well aware of what was going on at home, and was
shattered by the implications:

> I came into possession of the newspaper 'The Reich' of 4th March, from a comrade.
> The article about the attack on Dresden gave me an insight into the horrendous

---

[215] SAPMO BArch, NY 4500/1, Fritz Beyling, undated manuscript notes, late 1944/early 1945.
[216] Kempowski-BIO, 7076, Correspondence of Fritz Sch. (1899–1991), letters from Emilie Kraft
(Fritz's sister) to Luise (his wife), 28 Aug. 1943, Bad Segeberg, pp. 1–2.
[217] *Ibid.*, letter from Fritz to Luise and his mother, 3 May 1945.

catastrophe that has hit Dresden. It's just impossible to grasp. A city with all its cultural treasures was destroyed in one night.[218]

The front had, in short, reached home.

Violence was now experienced by German civilian populations too on an unprecedented scale. In the winter of 1944–5, the vast majority of those Germans who lived in territories at risk of being overrun by advancing Soviet troops fled for fear of what would happen if they stayed. Even those who were not affected by the 'treks' themselves often knew very well about the experiences of the refugees, whether through news about acquaintances, friends or relatives, or whether being at the receiving end when refugees arrived in search of housing, food, and clothing. On 23 January 1945 Ursula von Kardorff received a letter from a friend in Prague, 'Gretl', from which she quoted in her diary:

> The downfall of the Bohemian aristocracy . . . Anyone still there is either living hopelessly in the past or has found some arrangement with the future entailing the devaluation of the label 'aristocrat'. So everything on which we had pinned our hopes, in which we still believe, is slowly perishing. To have to watch this consciously is hard.[219]

Two days later, on 25 January, von Kardorff reported on stories she heard from a couple who had escaped from Breslau:

> They told of refugees who virtually trampled each other to death, of corpses that had been thrown out from unheated goods trains along the way, of treks that had got stuck on the road, of mothers who had gone crazy and would not believe that the babies they carried in their arms were already dead. But one is already so stupefied that one can barely imagine such ghastly scenes any more.[220]

On 30 January 1945 von Kardorff records the fate of those who did not leave in time:

> Willy Beer's wife did not come back from Silesia. Daily his desk is covered with ghastly news about misdeeds carried out against people who remained there: children bludgeoned to death, women raped, farms set on fire, farmers shot dead.[221]

Such tales were widely repeated: few did not know personally someone who had been thus affected; and this significantly coloured the views of Germans who had not themselves been part of the westwards flight in the closing months of the war.

While hundreds of thousands were fleeing ahead of the Red Army's advance on the ground, the heartland of the Reich was far from safe, as Allied air raids over German cities took on a new intensity. On 3 February 1945 Ursula von Kardorff was in Berlin with Franziska's brother, Felix Schwab, when the heaviest air raid of the war to hit Berlin thus far took place. Around 23,000 people were killed within

---

[218] *Ibid.*, letter from Fritz to Luise and his mother, 10 Feb 1945.
[219] Von Kardorff, *Berliner Aufzeichnungen*, p. 283.
[220] *Ibid.*, p. 284.   [221] *Ibid.*, p. 285.

barely one hour. When von Kardorff and Schwab came out of the air raid shelter, they found the editorial building in flames. As von Kardorff recorded in her diary:

> While we were talking together—a nice little secretary, blackened with soot, was trying to cheer us up with jokes—I thought now and then that I would suffocate, there were such clouds of smoke. Not a single bit of the sky to be seen, only yellow, poisonous wads of smoke.
>
> ...On Potsdamer Platz the Columbus House was burning like a torch. We wandered in midst of a stream of grey, bent over figures, carrying their possessions with them. Bombed-out, cumbersomely laden creatures, who seemed to be coming out of nowhere and going nowhere. The evening sinking over the glowing town was barely noticeable, it had been so dark already throughout the day...

But von Kardorff—unlike the majority of her contemporaries—then posed the question that, for all the appeals to 'defence of Fatherland and family', or Germans' fear of 'Bolshevism', still remains essentially unanswerable:

> Why does no one go out onto the street and shout 'enough, enough', why does no one go mad? Why is there no revolution?
>
> Just keep on going [*durchhalten*], the stupidest of all phrases. So they will keep on going until they are all dead, there is no other redemption.[222]

And for some, when Germany was finally defeated, the only way out did indeed appear to be that of taking their own lives. But for all affected by Hitler's war, the end, even for those for whom it really should signify liberation, was to inaugurate a very hard transition.

---

[222] Von Kardorff, *Berliner Aufzeichnungen.*, p. 287.

Epilogue

For many Germans, with the military defeat of the Third Reich and Hitler's suicide, their world seemed to be coming to an end. People who were severely compromised by their roles under Nazism had to fear potential penalties; those who had been infused by faith in the Führer could barely imagine a life beyond the Thousand Year Reich; all who had been on the 'perpetrator side', however grudgingly and unwillingly, faced an uncertain future under new political conditions. The situation was very different for those who had managed to survive severe persecution and had now been liberated; but for them, too, the transition to new lives with the cessation of hostilities in May 1945 was far from easy. Physically and emotionally exhausted, injured and ill, many who had survived the camps or in hiding were too weak to make it through the early weeks after liberation. Others who recovered often only now began to register the extent of their losses, the devastation of their former worlds. For all, living uncertainly amid ruined landscapes, the world was in a moment of extreme transition.

Over the course of the next four years, defeated Germany was occupied by the victorious Allies, had its borders redrawn, and saw new regimes established. By 1949, in the western zones of occupation, the democratic capitalist Federal Republic of Germany was founded; in the Soviet zone of eastern Germany (formerly 'middle Germany', having lost territory to Poland), the communist German Democratic Republic was founded. In the Cold War between the new American and Soviet superpowers, now both involved on German soil and glaring at each other across the 'Iron Curtain' that divided Europe, the two new German states played very different roles. The experiences of different generations differed accordingly.

The cohorts whose lives had been stamped by responses to the challenges of two world wars and continuing violence through the earlier half of the century now faced entirely new situations. In West Germany, there were significant continuities in both personnel and social and economic structures, despite the transition to a new democratic political regime. Following a period of denazification, many former Nazis were reinstated in their former jobs or gained other comparable employment. Those Germans who were young enough to be relatively untainted by their roles and actions under Nazism were often culturally ready to seize new opportunities; but the reinstatement of former elites, the return of soldiers from prisoner of war camps, and the influx of refugees and expellees from eastern Europe and from the GDR prior to the building of the Berlin Wall in 1961, meant that structurally the opportunities for rapid upward mobility for young people were less extensive than they were in the East. Even so, marked by their life-changing experiences, some members of the 1929er generation went on to play particularly prominent roles in intellectual and cultural life in West Germany.

Generational experiences in West Germany are relatively well-researched, particularly with respect to the phenomenon of '1968'. Arguably, this phenomenon began much earlier; and further sea changes in both attitudes and institutional make-up took place only from the 1970s, as the older generations who had dominated West German life began to retire from the stage. But that is a quite different story, and is not one of responses to dictatorial rule.

In East Germany, by contrast, under communist auspices there was a more radical and far-reaching social, political and economic revolution. For young people from the right backgrounds—generally disadvantaged, preferably left-wing—and who were politically willing to put their energies at the disposal of communist conceptions of a 'better' Germany, there were unprecedented opportunities for upward mobility. Under the tutelage of the 'antifascist' founding fathers of an older generation, now returning from exile or released from imprisonment, the 1929ers came to play a distinctive, prominent role in the GDR, affecting its character, sustaining its system, and disproportionately upholding it until the bitter end in 1989—which came just as this generation, too, entered into retirement age. The experiences and mentalities of the 1929ers cannot be ignored if we want to understand the East German dictatorship from within. Nor can the very different orientations of new generations who were 'born into' the GDR, as they engaged with the challenges of a communist dictatorship in the Cold War world.

Volume Two turns, then to explore the roles and outlooks of different generational groups, through the period from the end of the Third Reich to the collapse of the GDR and the unification of Germany in 1990.

Select Bibliography

This bibliography lists only the principal secondary works and some published primary sources that were cited in the footnotes, for ease of reference. Archival sources cited in the footnotes are not listed again separately here. Given the scope of this book, it would be impracticable to list all relevant secondary works; suggestions for further reading will be found in many of the works listed below.

Ahonen, Pertti et al., *People on the Move*: *Forced Population Movements in Europe in the Second World War and its Aftermath* (Oxford and New York: Berg, 2008)

Ahrberg, Edda, Hans-Hermann Hertle, Tobias Hollitzer and the Stiftung Aufarbeitung der SED-Diktatur (eds.), *Die Toten des Volksaufstandes vom 17. Juni 1953* (Münster: Lit Verlag, 2004)

Allinson, Mark, *Politics and Popular Opinion in East Germany, 1945–1968* (Manchester: Manchester University Press, 2000)

Aly, Götz, *Hitlers Volksstaat* (Frankfurt: Fischer, 2005)

Aretz, Jürgen and Wolfgang Stock (eds.), *Die vergessenen Opfer der DDR. 13 erschütternde Berichte mit Original-Stasi-Akten* (Bergisch-Gladbach: Bastei Verlag, 1997)

Bähr, Walther and Hans Bähr (eds), *Kriegsbriefe gefallener Studenten 1939–1945* (Tübingen and Stuttgart: Rainer Wunderlich Verlag, 1952)

Bajohr, Frank and Dieter Pohl, *Der Holocaust als offenes Geheimnis. Die Deutschen, die NS-Führung und die Alliierten* (Munich: C. H. Beck, 2006)

—— and Michael Wildt (eds.), *Volksgemeinschaft. Neue Forschungen zur Gesellschaft des Nationalsozialismus* (Frankfurt am Main: S. Fischer Verlag, 2009)

Baldwin, Peter (ed.), *Reworking the Past: Hitler, The Holocaust, and the Historians' Debate* (Boston: Beacon Press, 1990)

Bankier, David, *The Germans and the Final Solution*: *Public Opinion under Nazism* (Oxford: Blackwell, 1992)

Bartov, Omer, *Hitler's Army. Soldiers, Nazis and War in the Third Reich* (Oxford: Oxford University Press, 1991)

—— *The Eastern Front, 1941–45: German Troops and the Barbarisation of Warfare* (Houndmills: Palgrave, 2nd edn., 2001, orig 1985)

Bauerkämper, Arnd, *Ländliche Gesellschaft in der kommunistischem Diktatur. Zwangsmodernisierung und Tradition in Brandenburg 1945–1963* (Cologne, Weimar, Vienna: Böhlau Verlag, 2002)

Becker, Felicitas and Jigal Beez (eds.), *Der Maji-Maji-Krieg in Deutsch-Ostafrika 1905–1907* (Berlin: Ch. Links Verlag 2005), pp. 154–67.

Benedict, Nina, *Böse Briefe über Deutschland* (Schkeuditz: GNN-Verlag 1993)

Bergerson, Andrew Stuart, *Ordinary Germans in Extraordinary Times*: *The Nazi Revolution in Hildesheim* (Bloomington and Indianapolis: Indiana University Press, 2004)

Berkhoff, Karel, *Harvest of Despair: Life and Death in the Ukraine under Nazi Rule* (Cambridge, Mass.: Harvard University Press, 2004)

Bertram, Barbara, *Adam und Eva heute* (Leipzig: Verlag für die Frau, 1988)

Bessel, Richard (ed.), *Life in the Third Reich* (Oxford: Oxford University Press, 1987)

Bessel, Richard and Ralph Jessen (eds), *Die Grenzen der Diktatur. Staat und Gesellschaft in der DDR* (Göttingen: Vandenoeck and Ruprecht, 1996)

Bessel, Richard, *Germany 1945. From War to Peace* (London; HarperCollins, 2009)

—— *Germany after the First World War* (Oxford: Oxford University Press, 1993)

—— *Nazism and War* (London: Weidenfeld and Nicolson, 2004)

—— *Political Violence and the Rise of Nazism: The Storm Troopers in Eastern Germany 1925–1934* (New Haven and London: Yale University Press, 1984)

Bielenberg, Christabel, *The Past is Myself* (London: Chatto and Windus, 1968)

Biess, Frank, *Homecomings: Returning POWs and the Legacies of Defeat in Postwar Germany* (Princeton and Oxford: Princeton University Press, 2006)

Bjork, James and Robert Gerwarth, 'The Annaberg as a German-Polish Lieu de Mémoire' *German History* 2007, Vol. 25 no. 3, pp. 372–400

Blackbourn, David and Geoff Eley, *The Peculiarities of German History* (Oxford: Oxford University Press, 1984)

Brandon, Ray and Wendy Lower (eds.), *The Shoah in the Ukraine. History, Testimony, Memorialisation* (Bloomington and Indianapolis: Indiana University Press, 2008)

Brecht, Bertolt, 'An die Nachgeborenen', in Karl Carstens (ed.), *Deutsche Gedichte* (C. Bertelsmann Verlag 1983)

Broszat, Martin, *Nationalsozialistische Polenpolitik 1939–1945* (Stuttgart: Deutsche Verlags-Anstalt, 1961)

Browning, Christopher, *The Origins of the Final Solution: The Evolution of Nazi Jewish Policy, September 1939 – March 1942* (Lincoln: University of Nebraska Press, 2004)

—— *The Path to Genocide: Essays on launching the Final Solution* (Cambridge: Cambridge University Press, 1998)

Bruce, Gary, *Resistance with the People: Repression and Resistance in Eastern Germany, 1945–1955* (Lanham, Md.: Rowman and Littlefield, 2003)

—— *The Firm: The Inside Story of the Stasi* (Oxford: Oxford University Press, 2010)

Buchbender, Ortwin and Reinhold Sterz (eds), *Das andere Gesicht des Krieges. Deutsche Feldpostbriefe 1939–1945* (Munich: C. H. Beck, 1982)

Buddrus, Michael, *Totale Erziehung für den totalen Krieg: Hitlerjugend und nationalsozialistische Jugendpolitik,* Institut für Zeitgeschichte, Texte und Materialien zur Zeitgeschichte, vols. 13/1 and 13/2 (München: K. G. Saur, 2003)

Burleigh, Michael, *The Third Reich: A New History* (New York: Hill and Wang, 2001)

Burrin, Philippe, *Hitler and the Jews: The Genesis of the Holocaust* (London: Edward Arnold, 1994)

Caplan, Jane (ed.), *Nazi Germany* (Oxford: Oxford University Press, 2008)

Chickering, Roger, *Imperial Germany and the Great War, 1914–1918* (Cambridge: Cambridge University Press, 1998)

—— *The Great War and Urban Life in Germany: Freiberg, 1914–1918* (Cambridge: Cambridge University Press, 2007)

Clarke, David and Ute Wölfel (eds.), *20 Years After: Remembering the German Democratic Republic* (Basingstoke: Palgrave Macmillan, 2011)

Conze, Eckart and Monika Wienfort (eds.), *Adel und Moderne. Deutschland im europäischen Vergleich im 19. und 20. Jahrhundert* (Köln: Böhlau Verlag, 2004)

Corner, Paul (ed.), *Popular Opinion in Totalitarian Regimes* (Oxford: Oxford University Press, 2009)

Corni, Gustavo, *Hitler's Ghettos: Voices from a beleaguered society 1939–1944* (London: Arnold, 2002)

Crew, David (ed), *Nazism and German Society, 1933–45* (London: Routledge, 1994)

Dahlmann, Dittmar (ed.), *Kinder und Jugendliche in Krieg und Revolution* (Paderborn etc: Ferdinand Schöningh, 2000)

de Bruyn, Günter, *Vierzig Jahre. Ein Lebensbericht* (Frankfurt: Fischer, 1998)

Dederichs, Mario, *Heydrich. The Face of Evil* (London: Greenhill Books, 2006; orig. German Piper Verlag, 2005)

Delbo, Charlotte, *Auschwitz and After* (New Haven and London: Yale University Press, 1995)

Dennis, Mike, *The Rise and Fall of the German Democratic Republic 1945–1990* (Harlow: Pearson, 2000)

—— *The Stasi: Myth and Reality* (London: Pearson, 2003)

Desbois, Father Patrick, *The Holocaust by Bullets*: *A Priest's Journey to uncover the truth behind the murder of 1.5 Million Jews* (Houndmills, Basingstoke: Palgrave Macmillan, 2008)

Deutschkron, Inge, *Ich trug den gelben Stern* (München: Deutscher Taschenbuch Verlag, 1985)

Diedrich, Torsten, Hans Gotthard Ehlert, Rüdiger Wenzke (eds.), *Im Dienste der Partei: Handbuch der bewaffneten Organe der DDR* (Berlin: Ch. Links Verlag, 1998)

Diewerge, Wolfgang, *Als Sonderberichterstatter zum Kairoer Judenprozeß. Gerichtlich erhärtetes Material zur Judenfrage* (München: Zentralverlag der NSDAP. Franz Eher Nachf., 1935)

Dohmen, Karin, *Märkisches Tagebuch* (Frankfurt am Main: edition fischer im Rita G. Fischer Verlag, 1981)

Donat, Helmut (ed.) in collaboration with Wilfried Knauer, with an Introduction by Helga Paasche, *"Auf der Flucht" erschossen . . . Schriften und Beiträge von und über Hans Paasche. Zum hundertsten Geburtstag von Hans Paasche* (Bremen/Zeven: Schriftenreihe das andere Deutschland, 1981)

—— and Helga Paasche (eds.), *Hans Paasche, Ändert eueren Sinn! Schriften eines Revolutionärs* (Bremen: Donat Verlag, 1992)

Dönhoff, Marin Gräfin, Rudolf Walter Leonhardt and Theo Sommer, *Reise in ein fernes Land. Bericht über Kultur, Wirtschaft und Politik in der DDR* (Hamburg: Nannen Verlag, Die Zeit Bücher, 1964)

Dörner, Bernward, *Die Deutschen und der Holocaust. Was niemand wissen wollte, aber jeder wissen konnte* (Berlin: Ullstein, 2007)

Dowe, Dieter (ed), *Jugendprotest und Generationenkonflikt in Europa im 20. Jahrhundert. Deutschland, England, Frankreich und Italien im Vergleich* (Bonn: Verlag Neue Gesellschaft, 1986)

Drobisch, Klaus and Günther Wieland, *System der NS-Konzentrationslager 1933–1939* (Berlin: Akademie Verlag, 1993)

DuMont, Alfred Neven (ed.), *Jahrgang 1926/27. Erinnerungen an die Jahre unter dem Hakenkreuz* (Cologne: DuMont Buchverlag, 2007)

Eisenfeld, Bernd, Ilko-Sascha Kowalczuk and Ehrhart Neubert (eds.), *Die verdrängte Revolution. Der Platz des 17. Juni in der deutschen Geschichte* (Bremen: Edition Temmen, 2004)

Eley, Geoff (ed.) *The Goldhagen Effect: History, Memory, Nazism—Facing the German Past* (Ann Arbor: University of Michigan Press, 2000)

Engelmann, Roger and Ilko-Sascha Kowalczuk (eds.), *Volkserhebung gegen den SED-Staat. Eine Bestandaufnahme zum 17. Juni 1953* (Göttingen: Vandenhoeck and Ruprecht, 2005)

Eppelmann, Rainer, Bernd Faulenbach and Ulrich Mählert (eds.), *Bilanz und Perspektiven der DDR-Forschung* (Paderborn: Ferdinand Schöningh, 2003)

Evans, Richard J., *The Coming of the Third Reich: How the Nazis Destroyed Democracy and Seized Power in Germany* (London: Penguin 2004)

—— *The Third Reich in Power* (London: Penguin, 2006)

—— *The Third Reich at War* (London: Allen Lane, Penguin, 2008)

Fadermann, Lillian and Brigitte Eriksson (eds), *Lesbians in Germany: 1890s–1920s* (NP: The Naiad Press, 1990)

Feinstein, Joshua, *The Triumph of the Ordinary: Depictions of Daily Life in the East German Cinema, 1949–1989* (Chapel Hill: University of North Carolina Press, 2002)

Fenemore, Mark, *Sex, Thugs and Rock 'n' Roll, Teenage Rebels in Cold-War East Germany* (Berghahn, 2007)

Festinger, Leon, *A Theory of Cognitive Dissonance* (Stanford: Stanford University Press, 1957).

Feuchert, Sascha, Erwin Leibfried und Jörg Riecke, *Die Chronik des Gettos Łódź / Litzmann-stadt* (Göttingen: Wallstein Verlag, 2007)

Fieber, Hans-Joachim, *Widerstand in Berlin gegen das NS-Regime, 1933- bis 1945. Ein biographisches Lexikon* (Berlin: trafo verlag, 2004)

Finkelstein, Norman and Ruth Bettina Birn, *A Nation On Trial: The Goldhagen Thesis and Historical Truth* (New York: Henry Holt, 1998)

Fischer, Thomas, *Polizeisoldaten. Kasernendienst – Straßenkämpfer – Atombunker* (Aachen: Helios, 2006)

Frei, Norbert, Sybille Steinbacher and Bernd C. Wagner (eds.) *Ausbeutung, Vernichtung, Öffentlichkeit. Neue Studien zur nationalsozialistischen Lagerpolitik* (München: K. G. Saur, 2000)

Friedländer, Saul, *Nazi Germany and the Jews, vol. 1, The Years of Persecution, 1933–1939* (London: HarperCollins, 1998)

—— *Nazi Germany and the Jews, Vol. 2, The Years of Extermination. 1933–45,* (New York: HarperCollins, 2007)

Friedrich, Jörg, *Der Brand. Deutschland im Bombenkrieg 1940–1945* (Munich: Propyläen Verlag, 2002)

—— , Walter and Hartmut Griese (eds.), *Jugend und Jugendforschung in der DDR: Ge-sellschaftliche Situationen, Sozialisation und Mentalitätsentwicklung in den achtziger Jahren* (Opladen: Leske and Budrich, 1991)

Fritz, Stephen, *Frontsoldaten: The German Soldier in World War II* (Lexington, Kentucky: University of Kentucky Press, 1995)

Fritzsche, Peter, *Life and Death in the Third Reich* (Cambridge, Mass: Harvard University Press, 2008)

Fulbrook, Mary (ed.), *Power and Society in the GDR, 1961–1979: The 'Normalisation of Rule'?* (New York and Oxford: Berghahn, 2009)

—— (ed.), *Un-Civilizing Processes? Excess and Transgression in German Culture and Society: Perspectives Debating with Norbert Elias* (Amsterdam: Rodopi, 2007)

—— 'Embodying the Self: Gestures and Dictatorship in Twentieth-Century Germany', in M. Braddick (ed.), *The Politics of Gesture: Historical Perspectives* (Oxford: Oxford University Press; *Past and Present* Supplement 4, 2009), pp. 257–79

—— 'Generationen und Kohorten in der DDR. Protagonisten und Widersacher des DDR-Systems aus der Perspektive biographischer Daten' in Annegret Schüle, Thomas Ahbe and Rainer Gries (eds.), *Die DDR aus generationengeschichtlicher Perspektive. Eine Inventur* (Universitätsverlag Leipzig, 2005), pp. 113–30

—— *Anatomy of a Dictatorship: Inside the GDR, 1949–1989* (Oxford: Oxford University Press, 1995)

—— *History of Germany 1918–2008: The Divided Nation* (Oxford: Blackwell, 3rd edn., 2008)

—— *The People's State: East German Society from Hitler to Honecker* (New Haven and London: Yale University Press, 2005)

—— *A Small Town Near Auschwitz: Ordinary Nazis and the Holocaust* (Oxford: Oxford University Press, 2012)

Funder, Anna, *Stasiland* (London: Granta, 2003)

Gellately, Robert, *Backing Hitler: Consent and Coercion in Nazi Germany* (Oxford: Oxford University Press, 2001)

—— *The Gestapo and German Society* (Oxford: Oxford University Press, 1990)

Gieseke, Jens (ed.), *Staatssicherheit und Gesellschaft. Studien zum Herrschaftsalltag in der DDR* (Göttingen: Vandenhoeck & Ruprecht, 2007)

—— *Hauptamtlichen Mitarbeiter der Staatssicherheit: Personalstruktur und Lebenswelt 1950–1989/90* (Berlin: Ch. Links, 2000)

—— *Mielke-Konzern. Die Geschichte der Stasi 1945–1990* (Stuttgart and Munich: Deutsche Verlagsanstalt, 2001)

Glombowski, Friedrich, *Organisation Heinz (O.H.). Das Schicksal der Kameraden Schlageters* (Berlin: Verlag von Reimar Hobbing, 1934)

Goeschel, Christian, *Suicide in Nazi Germany* (Oxford: Oxford University Press, 2009).

Goffman, Erving, *The Presentation of Self in Everyday Life* (Harmondsworth: Penguin, 1959)

Goldhagen, Daniel Jonah, *Hitler's Willing Executioners* (New York: Knopf, 1996)

Götzen, G. A. Graf von, *Deutsch-Ostafrika Afrika im Aufstand 1905/06* (Berlin: Dietrich Reimer (Ernst Vohsen) 1909)

Greiffenhagen, Martin, *Jahrgang 1928: Aus einem unruhigen Leben* (Munich: Piper, 1988)

Grieder, Peter, *The East German Leadership 1946–1973* (Manchester: Manchester University Press, 1999)

Groß, Gerhard P. (ed.), *Der vergessene Front. Der Osten 1914/15. Ereigniß, Wirkung, Nachwirkung* (Paderborn: Ferdinand Schöningh, 2006)

Gross, Jan T., *Neighbours. The Destruction of the Jewish Community in Jedwabne, Poland, 1941* (London: Random House, Arrow, 2003; orig, Princeton University Press, 2003)

Gründel, E. Günther, *Die Sendung der jungen Generation. Versuch einer umfassenden revolutionären Sinndeutung der Krise* (München: C. H. Beck'sche Verlagsbuchhandlung, 1933; orig, 1932)

Grundmann, Siegfried, *Felix Bobek. Chemiker im Geheimapparat der KPD. (1932 bis 1935)* (Berlin: Dietz Verlag, 2004)

Gruner, Wolf, *Judenverfolgung in Berlin 1933–1945. Eine Chronologie der Behördenmassnahmen in der Reichshauptstadt* (Berlin: Stiftung Topographie des Terrors, 1996)

Gwassa, G. C. K. and John Iliffe (eds.), *Records of the Maji Maji Rising* (Nairobi, Kenya: East African Publishing House, 1968: Historical Association of Tanzania, Paper no. 4)

Haffner, Sebastian, *Geschichte eines Deutschen. Die Erinnerungen 1914–1933* (Munich: Deutscher Taschenbuch Verlag, 2002)

Harrison, Hope, *Driving the Soviets up the Wall: Soviet-East German Relations, 1953–1961* (Princeton and Oxford: Princeton University Press, 2003)

Hass, Aaron, *The Aftermath* (Cambridge: Cambridge University Press, 1996)

—— , Kurt (ed), *Jugend unterm Schicksal. Lebensberichte junger Deutscher, 1946–1949* (Hamburg: Christian Wegner Verlag, 1950)

Heer, Hannes, *Vom Verschwinden der Täter. Der Vernichtungskrieg fand statt, aber keiner war dabei* (Berlin: Aufbau Taschenbuch Verlag, 2004)

—— and Klaus Naumann (eds.), *Vernichtungskrieg. Verbrechen der Wehrmacht 1941–1944* (Hamburg: Hamburger Edition, 1995)

Heger, Heinz, *The Men with the Pink Triangle* (London: Gay Men's Press, 1980; transl. David Fernbach, orig. German 1972)

Heiber, Helmut (ed.), *Reichsführer!... Briefe an und von Himmler* (Stuttgart: Deutsche Verlags-Anstalt,1968)

Heinemann, Isabel, *'Rasse, Siedlung, deutsches Blut'. Die Rasse- und Siedlungspolitik der SS und die rassenpolitische Neuordnung Europas* (Göttingen: Wallstein Verlag, 2003)

Heinemann, Ulrich, *Ein konservativer Rebell. Fritz-Dietlof Graf von der Schulenburg und der 20. Juli* (Berlin: Siedler Verlag, 1990)

Henke, Klaus-Dietmar and Roger Engelmann (eds.), *Aktenlage. Die Bedeutung der Unterlagen des Staatssicherheitsdienstes für die Zeitgeschichtsforschung* (Berlin: Ch. Links Verlag, 1995)

Herbert, Ulrich, *Geschichte der Ausländerpolitik in Deutschland: Saisonarbeiter, Zwangsarbeiter, Gastarbeiter, Flüchtlinge* (Munich: C. H. Beck. 2001)

—— *Hitler's Foreign Workers: Enforced Foreign Labour in Germany under the Third Reich* (Cambridge: CUP, transl. William Templer, 1997; orig. German 1985)

Hilberg, Raul, *Perpetrators, Victims, Bystanders* (New York: HarperCollins, 1993)

—— *The Destruction of the European Jews* (Yale: Yale University Press, updated edition, 2003; orig. 1961)

Hobsbawm, Eric, *Age of Extremes: The Short Twentieth Century 1914–1991* (London: Penguin, 1994)

Hodenberg, Christina von, *Konsens und Krise. Eine Geschichte der westdeutschen Medienöffentlichkeit 1945–1973* (Göttingen: Wallstein Verlag, 2006)

Horne, John and Alan Kramer, *German Atrocities: A History of Denial* (New Haven and London: Yale University Press, 2001)

Höss, Rudolf, *Autobiography of Rudolf Höss*, reprinted in *Kl Auschwitz seen by the SS* (Oświęcim: Publications of Państwowe Muzeum w Oświęcimiu, 1972, transl. Constantine Fitzgibbon)

Hull, Isabel, *Absolute Destruction. Military Culture and the Practices of War in Imperial Germany* (Ithaca and London: Cornell University Press, 2005)

Humburg, Martin, *Das Gesicht des Krieges. Feldpostbriefe von Wehrmachtsoldaten aus der Sowjetunion 1941–1944* (Opladen/Wiesbaden: Westdeutscher Verlag, 1998)

Ide, Robert, *Geteilte Träume. Meine Eltern, die Wende und ich* (Munich: Luchterhand Literaturverlag, 2007)

Iliffe, John, *A Modern History of Tanganyika* (Cambridge: Cambridge University Press, 1979)

—— *Africans: The History of a Continent* (Cambridge: Cambridge University Press, 1995)

Irmela Nagel, *Fememorde und Fememordprozesse in der Weimarer Republik* (Köln u. Wien: Böhlau Verlag, 1991)

Itschert, Ernst, Marel Reucher, Gerd Schuster and Hans Stiff, *"Feuer frei – Kinder!" Eine mißbrauchte Generation – Flakhelfer im Einsatz* (Saarbrücken: Buchverlag Saarbrücker Zeitung, 1984)

Jaide, Walter, *Generationen eines Jahrhunderts. Wechsel der Jugendgenerationen im Jahrhunderttrend. Zur Geschichte der Jugend in Deutschland 1871 bis 1985* (Opladen: Leske und Budrich, 1988)

—— and Barbara Hille (eds.), *Jugend im doppelten Deutschland* (Köln: Westdeutscher Verlag, 1977)

Janka, Walter, *Schwierigkeiten mit der Wahrheit* (Berlin und Weimar: Aufbau-Verlag, 1990)

Jarausch, Konrad (ed.), *Dictatorship as Experience: Towards a socio-cultural history of the GDR* (New York: Berghahn, 1999)

—— and Klaus Jochen Arnold (eds.), *'Das stille Sterben…' Feldpostbriefe von Konrad Jarausch aus Polen und Russland 1939–1942* (Paderborn: Ferdinand Schöningh, 2008)

Jobel, Johannes, *Zwischen Krieg und Frieden. Schüler als Freiwillige in Genzschutz und Freikorps* (Berlin: R. Kittlers Verlag, 3rd edn, 1934)

John, Jürgen, Horst Möller and Thomas Schaarschmidt (eds.), *Die NS-Gaue. Regionale Mittelinstanzen im zentralistischen "Führerstaat"* (München: Oldenbourg, 2007)

Johnson, Eric, *The Nazi Terror: Gestapo, Jews and Ordinary Germans* (London: John Murray, 2000)

—— and Karl-Heinz Reuband, *What we knew: Terror, mass murder and everyday life in Nazi Germany* (London: Hodder, 2005)

Judt, Matthias (ed.), *DDR-Geschichte in Dokumenten. Beschlüsse, Berichte, interne Materialien und Alltagszeugnisse* (Berlin: Chr. Links, 1997)

Jureit, Ulrike, *Generationenforschung* (Vandenhoeck and Ruprecht, 2006)

—— and Michael Wildt (eds.), *Generationen* (Hamburg: Hamburger Edition, 2005)

Kaelble, Hartmut, Jürgen Kocka and Hartmut Zwar (eds.), *Sozialgeschichte der DDR* (Stuttgart: Klett Cotta, 1993)

Kahane, Anetta, *Ich sehe was, was du nicht siehst. Meine deutschen Geschichten* (Berlin: Rowohlt, 2004)

Kaiser, Monika, *Machtwechsel von Ulbricht zu Honecker* (Berlin: Akademie Verlag, 1997)

Kaplan, Marion, *Between Dignity and Despair: Jewish Life in Nazi Germany* (Oxford: Oxford University Press, 1998)

Kardorff, Ursula von, *Berliner Aufzeichnungen 1942 bis 1945* (München: Deutsche Taschenbuch Verlag, 1994; ed. and commentated by Peter Hartl)

Karstädt, Christina und Anette von Zitzewitz, *… viel zuviel verschwiegen. Eine Dokumentation von Lebensgeschichten lesbischer Frauen aus der Deutschen Demokratischen Republik* (Berlin: Hoho Verlag Christine Hoffmann, 1996)

Kater, Michael, *Hitler Youth* (Cambridge, Mass: Harvard University Press, 2004)

Kershaw, Ian, *Hitler: Hubris* (Harmondsworth: Penguin, 1998)

—— *Hitler: Nemesis* (Harmondsworth: Penguin, 2000)

—— *Popular Opinion and Political Dissent in the Third Reich: Bavaria, 1933–45* (Oxford: Oxford University Press, 1983)

—— *The 'Hitler Myth': Image and Reality in the Third Reich* (Oxford: Oxford University Press, 1987)

—— and Moshe Lewin (eds.), *Stalinism and Nazism* (Cambridge: Cambridge University Press, 1997)

Killinger, Manfred von, *Kampf um Oberschlesien 1921* (Leipzig: v. Hase und Koehler Verlag, 1934)

Klee, Ernst, Willi Dreßen and Volker Rieß (eds.), *"Schöne Zeiten". Judenmord aus der Sicht der Täter und Gaffer* (Frankfurt: Fischer Verlag, 1988)

Klemperer, Victor, *Curriculum Vitae. Erinnerungen eines Philologen, 1881–1918. Zweites Buch: 1912–1918* (Berlin: Rütten and Leoning, 1989)

—— *Ich will Zeugnis ablegen bis zum letzten. Tagebücher 1933–1945* (Berlin: Aufbau Verlag, 1995)

Klemperer, Victor, *So sitze ich denn zwischen allen Stühlen. Vol. 2: Tagebücher 1950–1959* (Berlin: Aufbau Verlag, 1999)

Klessmann, Christoph and Georg Wagner (eds.), *Das gespaltene Land: Leben in Deutschland 1945 bis 1990. Texte und Dokumente* (Munich: C.H. Beck, 1993)

Klüger, Ruth, *weiter leben* (München: Deutscher Taschenbuch Verlag, 1994)

Koch, Horst-Adalbert (with Heinz Schindler and Georg Tessin), *Flak. Die Geschichte der Deutschen Flakartillerie und der Einsatz der Luftwaffenhelfer* (Bad Nauheim: Podzun Verlag, 2nd edn, 1965; orig. 1954)

Kocka, Jürgen (ed.), *Historische DDR-Forschung. Aufsätze und Studien* (Berlin: Akademie Verlag, 1993)

—— and Martin Sabrow, *Die DDR als Geschichte. Fragen, Hypothesen, Perspektiven* (Berlin: Akademie Verlag, 1994)

Koonz, Claudia, *Mothers in the Fatherland* (London: Jonathan Cape, 1987)

Kopstein, Jeffrey, *The Politics of Economic Decline* (Chapel Hill: University of North Carolina Press, 1997)

Kott, Sandrine, *Le communisme au quotidien. Les enterprises d'État dans la société est-allemande* (Paris: Belin, 2001)

Kramer, Alan, *Dynamic of Destruction: Culture and Mass Killing in the First World War* (Oxford: Oxford University Press, 2007)

Krausnick, Helmut and Hans-Heinrich Wilhelm (eds.), *Die Truppe des Weltanschuaung-skrieges. Die Einsatzgruppen der Sicherheitspolizei und des SD 1938–1942* (Stuttgart: Deutsche Verlags-Anstalt, 1981)

Kühne, Thomas, *Kameradschaft: Die Soldaten des nationalsozialistischen Krieges und das 20. Jahrhundert* (Göttingen: Vandenhoek und Ruprecht, 2006)

Kulka, Otto Dov and Eberhard Jäckel (eds.), *Die Juden in den geheimen NS-Stimmungsber-ichten 1933–1945* (Düsseldorf: Droste Verlag, 2004)

Landsman, Mark, *Dictatorship and Demand: The Politics of Consumerism in East Germany* (Cambridge, Mass: Harvard University Press, 2005)

Lange, P. Werner, 'Die Toten im Maisfeld. Hans Paasches Erkenntnisse aus dem Maji-Maji-Krieg' in Felicitas Becker and Jigal Beez (eds.), *Der Maji-Maji-Krieg in Deutsch-Ostafrika 1905–1907* (Berlin: Ch. Links Verlag, 2005)

—— *Hans Paasche: Militant Pacifist in Imperial Germany* (Trafford Publishing, 2005)

Langer, Lawrence, *Holocaust Testimonies: The Ruins of Memory* (New Haven and London: Yale University Press, 1993)

Laqueur, Walter, *The Terrible Secret: Suppression of the Truth about Hitler's "Final Solution"* (Boston, Toronto: Little, Brown, 1980)

—— and Richard Breitman, *Breaking the Silence: The secret mission of Eduard Schulte, who brought the world news of the Final Solution* (London: The Bodley Head, 1986)

Last, George, *After the 'Socialist Spring'. Collectivisation and Economic Transformation in the GDR* (New York and Oxford: Berghahn. 2009)

Latzel, Klaus, *Deutsche Soldaten – nationalsozialistischer Krieg? Kriegserlebnis – Kriegserfah-rung 1939–1945* (Paderborn: Ferdinand Schöningh, 1998)

Leide, Henry, *NS-Verbecher und Staatssicherheit. Die geheime Vergangenheitspolitik der DDR* (Göttingen: Vandenhoeck and Ruprecht, 2005)

Lemke, Jürgen (ed.), *Gay Voices from East Germany*, English-language version edited and with an introduction by John Bornemann (Bloomington: Indiana University Press, 1991)

Lengsfeld, Vera, *Von nun an ging's bergauf . . . Mein Weg zur Freiheit* (Munich: LangenMüller, 2nd edn., 2007)

Lindenberger, Thomas (ed.), *Herrschaft und Eigen-Sinn* (Cologne: Böhlau, 1999)

Longerich, Peter, *"Davon haben wir nichts gewusst!" Die Deutschen und die Judenverfolgung 1933–1945* (Munch: Siedler Verlag, 2006)

—— *Heinrich Himmler: Biographie* (Siedler Verlag, 2008)

—— *Politik der Vernichtung* (Munich: Piper Verlag, 1998)

Lovell, Stephen (ed.), *Generations in Twentieth-Century Europe* (Basingstoke: Palgrave Macmillan, November 2007)

Lower, Wendy, *Nazi Empire Building and the Holocaust in the Ukraine* (Chapel Hill: University of North Carolina, 2005)

Madarász, Jeannette, *Conflict and Compromise in East Germany, 1971 to 1989: A Precarious Stability* (Basingstoke: Palgrave, 2003)

—— *Working in East Germany: Normality in a Socialist Dictatorship, 1961 to 1979* (Basingstoke: Palgrave, 2006)

Mählert, Ulrich (ed.), *Der 17. Juni 1953: ein Aufstand für Einheit, Recht und Freiheit* (Bonn: Dietz, 2003)

—— —— and Gerd-Rüdiger Stephan, *Blaue Hemden, rote Fahnen. Die Geschichte der Freien deutschen Jugend* (Opladen: Leske and Budrich, 1996)

Majer, Diemut, *'Non-Germans' under the Third Reich. The Nazi Judicial and Administrative System in Germany and Occupied Eastern Europe with special regard to Occupied Poland, 1939–1945* (Baltimore: Johns Hopkins University Press, 2003)

Major, Patrick, *Behind the Berlin Wall: East Germany and the Frontiers of Power* (Oxford: Oxford University Press, 2010)

—— and Jonathan Osmond (eds.), *The Workers' and Peasants' State* (Manchester: Manchester University Press, 2002)

Mallmann, Klaus-Michael and Bogdan Musial (eds.), *Genesis des Genozids: Polen 1939–1941* (Darmstadt: Wissenschaftliche Buchgesellschaft, 2004)

—— Jochen Böhler, and Jürgen Matthäus, *Einsatzgruppen in Polen: Darstellung und Dokumentation* (Darmstadt: Wissenschaftliche Buchgesellschaft, 2008)

Mann, Michael, 'Were the perpetrators of genocide "ordinary men" or "real Nazis"? Results from fifteen hundred biographies', *Holocaust and Genocide Studies* 2000, pp. 329–66

Mannheim, Karl, 'Das Problem der Generationen', in Mannheim, *Wissenssoziologie* (Berlin: Luchterhand, 1964; orig. 1928), pp. 509–565

Manoschek, Walter (ed), *"Es gibt nur eines für das Judentum: Vernichtung". Das Judenbild in deutschen Soldatenbriefen 1939–1944* (Hamburg: Hamburger Edition, 1995)

Martel, Gordon (ed.), *Modern Germany Reconsidered* (London: Routledge, 1992)

Mazower, Mark, *Hitler's Empire: Nazi Rule in Occupied Europe* (London: Penguin Books, 2009)

McDougall, Alan, 'A Duty to Forget? The "Hitler Youth Generation" and the Transition from Nazism to Communism in Postwar East Germany, c.1945–49', *German History* Vol. 26, No. 1, pp. 24–46

—— *Youth Politics in East Germany. The Free German Youth Movement 1946–1968* (Oxford: Oxford University Press, 2004)

Merkel, Ina, *Utopie und Bedürfnis. Die Geschichte der Konsumkultur in der DDR* (Cologne, Weimar, Vienna: Böhlau Verlag, 1999)

Meyer, Beate, *Jüdische Mischlinge: Rassenpolitik und Verfolgungserfahrung 1933–1945* (Hamburg: Dölling & Galitz, 1999)

Militärgeschichtliches Forschungsamt (ed.), *Germany and the Second World War,* (Oxford: Clarendon Press, 2000; orig, German 1998)

Miller, Barbara, *Narratives of Guilt and Compliance in Unified Germany. Stasi informers and their impact on society* (London: Routledge, 1999)

Mitter, Armin and Stefan Wolle, *Untergang auf Raten. Unbekannte Kapitel der DDR-Geschichte* (Munich: C. Bertelsmann Verlag, 1993)

Mogge, Winfried and Jürgen Reulecke (eds), *Hohe Meißner 1913. Der Erste Freideutsche Jugendtag in Dokumenten, Deutungen und Bildern* (Köln: Verlag Wissenschaft und Politik, 1988)

Moses, Dirk, *German Intellectuals and the Nazi Past* (Cambridge: Cambridge University Press, 2007)

Müller, Hans-Harald, *Intellektueller Linksradikalismus in der Weimarer Republik. Seine Entstehung, Geschichte und Literatur – dargestellt am Beispiel der Berliner Gründergruppe der Kommunistischen Arbeiter-Partei Deutschlands* (Kronberg/Ts: Scriptor Verlag, 1977)

Müller-Enbergs, Helmut, *Inoffizielle Mitarbeiter des Ministeriums für Staatssicherheit* (Berlin: Chr. Links Verlag, 2008)

—— Jan Wielgohs and Dieter Hoffman (eds), *Wer war wer in der DDR? Ein biographisches Lexikon* (Berlin: Christoph Links Verlag and Bundeszentrale für politische Bildung, 2001 edn.)

Musial, Bogdan, *Deutsche Zivilverwaltung und Judenverfolgung im Generalgouvernement. Eine Fallstudie zum Distrikt Lublin 1939–1944* (Wiesbaden: Otto Harrassowitz, 1999)

Naimark, Norman, *The Russians in Germany* (Cambridge, Mass.: Harvard University Press, 1995)

Nastola, Edgar, *Individuelle Freiheit und staatliche Reglementierungen. Lesben und Schwule in der DDR* (Marburg: Tectum Verlag, 1999)

Netzker, Wolfgang, *Bereit und fähig zur Verteidigung des Sozialismus. GST-Mitglieder* (Leipzig, Juli 1986)

Nicolaisen, Hans-Dietrich, *Der Einsatz der Luftwaffen- und Marinehelfer im II. Weltkrieg. Darstellung und Dokumentation* (Büsum: Selbstverlag Dr. Hans-Dietrich Nicolaisen, 1981)

—— *Die Flakhelfer. Luftwaffenhelfer und Marinehelfer im Zweiten Weltkrieg* (Berlin: Ullstein, 1981)

Niethammer, Lutz, Alexander von Plato and Dorothee Wierling, *Die volkseigene Erfahrung* (Berlin: Rowohlt, 1991)

—— —— *Die Mitläuferfabrik. Die Entnazifizierung am Beispiel Bayerns* (Berlin: Dietz, 1982; orig, 1972)

Noakes, Jeremy, 'The Development of Nazi Policy towards the German-Jewish "Mischlinge" 1933–1945', *Leo Baeck Institute Yearbook,* 1989, 34(1), pp. 291–354.

Nolte, Ernst, 'Die Vergangenheit, die nicht vergehen will. Eine Rede, die geschrieben, aber nicht gehalten werden konnte', *Frankfurter Allgemeine Zeitung,* 6 June 1986, reprinted in *"Historikerstreit": Die Dokumentation der Kontroverse um die Einzigartigkeit der national-sozialistschen Judenvernichtung* (Munich: Piper, 1987)

Nothnagle, Alan, *Building the East German Myth* (Ann Arbor: University of Michigan Press, 1999)

Oertzen, F. W. von, *Kamerad reich mir die Hände. Freikorps und Grenzschutz Baltikum und Heimat* (Berlin: Im Verlag Ullstein, 1933)

Ohse, Marc-Dietrich, *Jugend nach dem Mauerbau. Anpassung, Protest und Eigensinn (DDR 1961–1974)* (Berlin: Ch. Links, 2003)

Orth, Karin, *Die Konzentrationslager-SS. Sozialstrukturelle Analysen und biographische Studien* (Göttingen: Wallstein Verlag, 2000)

Osterloh, Jörg, *Nationalsozialistische Judenverfolgung im Reichsgau Sudetenland 1938–1945* (München: R. Oldenbourg Verlag, 2006)

Ostermann, Christian (ed.), *Uprising in East Germany 1953: the Cold War, the German question, and the first major upheaval behind the Iron Curtain* (Budapest and New York: Central European University Press, 2001)

Paasche, Hans, *"Im Morgenlicht". Kriegs-, Jagd- und Reise-Erlebnisse in Ostafrika* (Berlin: Verlag von C. A. Schwedtke und Sohn, 1907)

—— *Das verlorene Afrika* (Berlin: Verlag Neues Vaterland, E. Berger and Co., 1919; Flugschriften des Bundes Neues Vaterland Nr. 16)

—— *Lukanga Mukara. Die Forschungsreise des Afrikaners Lukanga Mukara ins innerste Deutschland* (Berlin: Verlag Eduard Jacobson, 1980)

Pakenham, Thomas, *The Scramble for Africa 1876–1912* (London: Weidenfeld and Nicolson, 1991)

Pearce, Caroline and Nick Hodgin (eds), *The GDR Remembered: Representations of the East German state since 1989* (New York: Camden House, 2010)

Pence, Katherine and Paul Betts (eds.), *Socialist Modern. East German Everyday Culture and Politics* (Michigan: University of Michigan Press, 2008)

Peukert, Detlev, *Inside Nazi Germany* (London: Batsford, 1987)

—— *The Weimar Republic: The Crisis of Classical Modernity* (New York: Hill and Wang, 1993)

Plant, Richard, *The Pink Triangle: The Nazi War against Homosexuals* (Edinburgh: Mainstream Publishing, 1987)

Poiger, Uta, *Jazz, Rock and Rebels: Cold War Politics and American Culture in Divided Germany* (Berkeley: University of California Press, 2000)

Port, Andrew, *Conflict and Stability in the German Democratic Republic* (Cambridge: Cambridge University Press, 2006)

Poste, Burkhard, *Schulreform in Sachsen 1918–1923. Eine vergessene Tradition deutscher Schulgeschichte* (Frankfurt-am-Main, Berlin, Bern, NY, Paris, Wien: Peter Lang, 1993)

Rahden, Till van, *Jews and Other Germans: Civil Society, Religious Diversity and Urban Politics in Breslau, 1860–1925* Transl. by Marcus Brainard (Madison: University of Wisconsin Press, 2008)

Rauhut, Michael, *Beat in der Grauzone. DDR-Rock 1964 bis 1972 – Politik und Alltag* (Berlin: BasisDruck, 1993)

—— *Schalmei und Lederjacke. Udo Lindenberg, BAP, Underground: Rock und Politik in den 80er Jahren* (Berlin: Schwarzkopf und Schwarzkopf, 1996)

Razumovsky, Mascha, Dolly and Olga, *Unsere versteckten Tagebücher 1938–1944. Drei Mädchen erleben die Nazizeit* (Wien, Köln, Weimar: Böhlau Verlag, 1999)

Rebentisch, Dieter and Karl Teppe (eds.), *Verwaltung contra Menschenführung im Staat Hitlers. Studien zum politisch-administrativen System* (Göttingen: Vandenhoeck and Ruprecht, 1986)

Rector, Frank, *The Nazi Extermination of Homosexuals* (NY: Stein and Day, 1981)

Reese, Dagmar, *Growing up Female in Nazi Germany* (University of Michigan Press, transl. William Templer, 2006; orig 1989)

Reimann, Brigitte, *Aber wir schaffen es, verlaß dich drauf! Briefe an eine Freundin im Westen* (Berlin: Elefanten Press, 1995)

Renger, Annemarie, *Ein politisches Leben* (Stuttgart: Deutsche Verlags-Anstalt, 1993)

Renn, Ludwig, *Adel im Untergang* (Berlin: Das neue Berlin, 2001)

Reulecke, Jürgen (ed.), with Elisabeth Müller-Lückner, *Generationalität und Lebens-geschichte im 20. Jahrhundert* (München: R. Oldenbourg Verlag, 2003)

Richthofen, Esther von, *Bringing Culture to the Masses: Control, Compromise and Participation in the GDR* (New York and Oxford: Berghahn, 2009)

Roden, Hans (ed), *Deutsche Soldaten, Vom Frontheer und Freikorps über die Reichswehr zur neuen Wehrmacht* (Berlin: Paul Franke Verlag, 1935)

Roseman, Mark (ed.), *Generations in Conflict* (Cambridge: Cambridge University Press, 1995)

Rosenthal, Gabriele (ed.), *Die Hitlerjugend-Generation. Biographische Thematisierung als Vergangenheitsbewältigung* (Essen: Verlag Die blaue Eule, 1986)

Ross, Corey, *Constructing Socialism at the Grass-Roots: The Transformation of East Germany* (Basingstoke: Macmillan, 2000)

Rossino, Alexander, 'Nazi Anti-Jewish Policy during the Polish Campaign. The Case of the Einsatzgruppe von Woyrsch', *German Studies Review*, Vol. 24, no.1, Feb 2001, pp. 35–53

—— *Hitler strikes Poland. Blitzkrieg, Ideology and Atrocity* (Kansas: University Press of Kansas, 2003)

Roth, Bert (ed), *Kampf: Lebensdokumente deutscher Jugend von 1914–1934* (Leipzig: Philipp Reklam jun., 1934)

—— Joseph, *The Spider's Web* (London: Granta Books, transl. John Hoare, 2004)

Rubin, Eli, *Synthetic Socialism: Plastics and Dictatorship in the German Democratic Republic* (University of North Carolina Press, 2008)

Rüdenauer, Erika (ed.), *Dünne Haut. Tagebücher von Frauen* (Halle, Leipzig: Mittel-deutscher Verlag, 1987)

Rusch, Claudia, *Meine freie deutsche Jugend* (Frankfurt: Fischer, 2003)

Salomon, Ernst von, *Das Buch vom deutschen Freikorpskämpfer* (Berlin: Wilhelm-Limpert Verlag, 1938)

—— *Fünf Jahre Unterschied*, reprinted in Bert Roth (ed.), *Kampf. Lebensdokumente deutscher Jugend von 1914–1934* (Leipzig: Philipp Reklam jun., 1934)

Sarotte, M. E., *Dealing with the Devil: East Germany, Détente and Ostpolitik, 1969–1973* (Chapel Hill and London: University of North Carolina Press, 2001)

Sauer, Bernhard, *Schwarze Reichswehr und Fememorde* (Berlin: Metropol Verlag, 2004)

Schätz, Ludwig, *Schüler-Soldaten. Die Geschichte der Luftwaffenhelfer im zweiten Weltkrieg* (Darmstadt: Thesen Verlag, 1974)

Schelsky, Helmut, *Die skeptische Generation* (Düsseldorf and Cologne: Diederichs Verlag, 1957)

Scherer, Hans, *Ich war Oberschüler und Luftwaffenhelfer. Teil I, II und II, 1927–1948* (Selbstverlag, Staffelstein 1996)

Schmidt-Pauli, Edgar von, *Geschichte der Freikorps 1918–1924* (Stuttgart: Robert Lutz Nachfolger Otto Schramm, 1936)

Schmitt, Hans, *Quakers and Nazis. Inner Light in Outer Darkness* (Columbia: University of Missouri Press, 1997)

Schoeps, J. H. (ed.), *Ein Volk von Mördern? Die Dokumentation zur Goldhagen-Kontroverse um die Rolle der Deutschen im Holocaust* (Hamburg: Hoffmann & Campe, 1996)

Schollwer, Wolfgang, *Potsdamer Tagebuch 1948–1950. Liberale Politik unter sowjetischer Besatzung*, ed. Monika Faßbender (Munich: Oldenbourg, 1988)

Schoppmann, Claudia, *Days of Masquerade. Life Stories of Lesbians during the Third Reich* (New York: Columbia University Press, 1996)

Schörken, Rolf, *Luftwaffenhelfer und Drittes Reich. Die Enstehung eines politischen Bewußtseins* (Stuttgart: Klett Cotta, 1985)

Schröder, Hans Joachim, *Die gestohlenen Jahre. Erzählgeschichten und Geschichtserzählung im Interview: Der zweite Weltkrieg aus der Sicht ehemaliger Mannschaftssoldaten* (Tübingen: Max Niemayer Verlag, 1992)

——— , Wulf, *Luftwaffenhelfer 1943–44. Erlebnisse einer Gruppe Flensburger Schüler im Zweiten Weltkrieg* (Gesellschaft für Flensburger Stadtgeschichte, 1988; Kleine Reihe der Gesellschaft für Flensburger Stadtgeschichte, Heft 16)

Schroeder, Klaus, *Der SED-Staat* (Munich; Carl Hanser Verlag, 1998)

Schubert, Helga, *Das verbotene Zimmer* (Darmstadt: Luchterhand, Neuwied, 1982)

Schüle, Annegret, Thomas Ahbe and Rainer Gries (eds.), *Die DDR aus generationgeschichtlicher Perspektive: Ein Inventur* (Leipzig: Leipziger Universitätsverlag, 2006)

Schulenburg, Tisa von der, *Ich hab's gewagt. Bildhauerin und Ordensfrau – ein unkonventionelles Leben* (Freiburg im Breisgau: Verlag Herder, 1995)

Schulz, Hermann, Hartmut Radebold, and Jürgen Reulecke, *Söhne ohne Väter. Erfahrungen der Kriegsgeneration* (Berlin: Christoph Links Verlag, 2004)

Schulze, Hagen, *Freikorps und Republik, 1918–1920* (Boppard am Rhein: Harald Boldt Verlag, 1969)

Schwantje, Magnus, 'Hans Paasche: Sein Leben und Wirken' *Flugschriften des Bundes Neues Vaterland* Nr. 26/27 (Berlin: Verlag Neues Vaterland, E. Berger and Co., 1921), pp. 1–28

Schwartz, Michael, *Vertriebene und "Umsiedlerpolitik". Integrationskonflikte in den deutschen Nachkriegs-Gesellschaften und die Assimilationsstrategien in der SBZ/DDR 1945–1961* (München: R. Oldenbourg Verlag, 2004)

Seeberg, Karl-Martin, *Der Maji-Maji-Krieg gegen die deutsche Kolonialherrschaft. Historische Ursprünge nationaler Identität in Tanzania* (Berlin: Dietrich Reimer Verlag, 1989)

Seegers, Lu, Jürgen Reulecke (eds.), *Die "Generation der Kriegskinder". Historische Hintergründe und Deutungen* (Gießen: Psychosozial Verlag, 2009)

Shandley, Robert R. (ed.), *Unwilling Germans? The Goldhagen Debate*, essays translated by Jeremiah Riemer (Minneapolis and London: University of Minnesota Press, 1998)

Shepherd, Ben, *War in the Wild East: The German Army and Soviet Partisans* (Cambridge, Mass: Harvard University Press, 2004)

Siegfried, Detlev, *Das radikale Milieu. Kieler Novemberrevolution, Sozialwissenschaft und Linksradikalismus, 1917–1922* (Wiesbaden: Deutscher Universitäts-Verlag, 2004)

Sillge, Ursula, *Un-Sichtbare Frauen. Lesben und ihre Emanzipation in der DDR* (Berlin: Christoph Links, LinksDruck Verlag, 1991)

Smith, Bradley and Agnes Peterson (eds.), *Heinrich Himmler. Geheimreden 1933 bis 1945* (Propyläen Verlag, 1974)

Sopade, *Deutschland-Berichte der Sozialdemokratischen Partei Deutschlands (Sopade) 1934–1940* (Frankfurt am Main: Verlag Petra Nettelbeck und Zweitausendeins, 1980)

Stachura, Peter, *The German Youth Movement 1900–1945* (London: Macmillan, 1981)

Stargardt, Nicholas, *Witnesses of War: Children's Lives under the Nazis* (London: Jonathan Cape, 2005)

Starke, Kurt, *Schwuler Osten. Homosexuelle Männer in der DDR* (Berlin: Ch. Links Verlag, 1994)

Stehmann, Siegbert, *Die Bitternis verschweigen wir. Feldpostbriefe 1940–1945* (Hannover: Lutherisches Verlagshaus, 1992)

Steinbacher, Sybille, *"Musterstadt" Auschwitz. Germanierungspolitik und Judenmord in Ostoberschlesien* (München: K. G. Saur, 2000)

Stephenson, Jill, *Hitler's Home Front: Württemberg under the Nazis* (London: Hambledon Press, 2006)

—— *The Nazi Organisation of Women* (London: Croom Helm, 1981)

—— *Women in Nazi Germany* (London: Pearson, 2001)

—— *Women in Nazi Society* (London: Croom Helm, 1975)

Stern, Frank, *The Whitewashing of the Yellow Badge: Antisemitism and philosemitism in postwar Germany* (London: Heinemann, 1991)

Stimpel, Hans-Martin, *Getäuscht und mißbraucht. Schülersoldaten in Zentren des Vernichtungskrieges* (Göttingen: Cuvillier Verlag, 2001)

—— *Schülersoldaten 1943–1945. Gymnasiasten als Luftwaffenhelfer in Berlin, bei Auschwitz, und als Fallschirmjäger in der "Festung Harz"* (Göttingen: Cuvillier Verlag, 2004)

Stokes, Raymond, *Constructing Socialism: Technology and Change in East Germany 1945– 1990* (Baltimore: Johns Hopkins University Press, 2000)

Stöver, Bernd, *Berichte über die Lage in Deutschland. Die Meldungen der Gruppe Neu Beginnen aus dem Dritten Reich 1933–1936* (Bonn: Verlag J. H. W. Dietz Nachfolger, 1996)

Suckut, Siegfried (ed.), *Das Wörterbuch der Staatssicherheit. Definitionen zur "politisch-operativen Arbeit"* (Berlin: Ch. Links Verlag, 1996)

—— (ed.), *Die DDR im Blick der Stasi 1976* (Göttingen: Vandenhoeck and Ruprecht, 2009)

Süß, Dietmar and Winfried Süß (eds.), *Das "Dritte Reich": Eine Einführung* (Munich: Pantheon, 2008)

Tent, James F., *In the Shadow of the Holocaust: Nazi Persecution of Jewish-Christian Germans* (Lawrence, Kansas: University Press of Kansas, 2003)

Ther, Philip, *Deutsche und polnische Vertriebene. Gesellschaft und Vertriebenenpolitik in der SBZ/DDR und in Polen 1945–1956* (Gottingen: Vandenhoeck and Ruprecht, 1998)

Thiedemann, Elviera, *Es kam ein langer lichter Herbst. Tagebuch der Wendezeit* 1989/90 (Berlin: trafo verlag, 2000)

Thomas Lindenberger, *Volkspolizei. Herrschaftspraxis und öffentliche Ordnung im SED-Staat 1952–1968* (Cologne: Böhlau, 2003)

Thoms, Robert and Stefan Pochanke, *Handbuch zur Geschichte der deutschen Freikorps* (MTM Verlag, 2001)

Thoß, Bruno (ed.), *Volksarmee schaffen – ohne Geschrei! Studien zu den Anfängen einer 'verdeckten Aufrüsting' in der SBZ/DDR 1947–1952* (Munich: R. Oldenbourg Verlag, 1994)

Tooley, T. Hunt, *National Identity and Weimar Germany: Upper Silesia and the Eastern Border, 1918–1922* (Lincoln and London: University of Nebraska Press, 1997)

Tooze, Adam, *The Wages of Destruction: The Making and Breaking of the Nazi Econoomy* (London: Penguin, 2007)

Topographie des Terrors: Eine Dokumentation (Berlin, 2nd edn, 2009)

Trunk, Isaiah, *Judenrat: The Jewish Councils in Eastern Europe under Nazi Occupation* (NY: Macmillan, 1972)

Ueberschar, Gerhard and Wolfram Wette (eds), *"Unternehmen Barbarossa". Der deutsche Überfall auf die Sowjetunion 1941* (Paderborn: Ferdinand Schöningh, 1984)

Ulrich, Bernd and Benjamin Ziemann (eds.), *Frontalltag im ersten Weltkrieg* (Essen: Klartext, 2008)

Umbreit, Hans, *Deutsche Militärverwaltungen. Die militärische Besetzung der Tschechoslowakei und Polens* (Stuttgart: Deutsche Verlags-Anstalt, 1977)

Verhey, Jeffrey, *The Spirit of 1914* (Cambridge: Cambridge University Press, 2000)

Waite, R. G. L., *Vanguard of Nazism* (Cambridge, Mass: Harvard Historical Studies, Vol. LX, 1952)

Watson, Alexander, *Enduring the Great War. Combat, Morale and Collapse in the German and British Armies, 1914–1918* (Cambridge: Cambridge University Press, 2008)

Wehrmeister, Pater Cyrillus, *Vor dem Sturm: Eine Reise durch Deutsch Ostafrika vor und bei dem Aufstande 1905* (St. Ottilien: Missionsverlag, 1906)

Weinke, Annette, *Die Verfolgung von NS-Tätern im geteilten Deutschland* (Paderborn: Ferdinand Schöningh, 2002)

Weitz, Eric, *Weimar Germany: Promise and Tragedy* (Princeton: Princeton University Press, 2007)

Wensierski, H.-J. von, *Mit uns zieht die alte Zeit. Biographie und Lebenswelt junger DDR-Bürger im Umbruch* (Opladen: Leske and Budrich, 1994)

Wette, Wolfram, *Die Wehrmacht: Feindbilder, Vernichtungskrieg, Legenden* (Frankfurt-am-Main: S. Fischer Verlag, 2002)

Wienfort, Monika, *Adel in der Moderne* (Göttingen: Vandenhoeck and Ruprecht, 2006)

Wierling, Dorothee, *Geboren im Jahr Eins* (Berlin: Ch. Links Verlag, 2002)

Wildt, Michael, *Generation des Unbedingten* (Hamburg: Hamburger Edition, 2002)

—— *Generation of the Unbound. The Leadership Corps of the Reich Security Main Office* (Jerusalem: Yad Vashem, 2002)

—— *Volksgemeinschaft als Selbstermächtigung. Gewalt gegen Juden in der deutschen Provinz, 1919 bis 1939* (Hamburg: Hamburger Edition, 2007)

Wilke, Manfred (ed.), *Die Anatomie der Parteizentrale. Die KPD/SED aud dem Weg zur Macht* (Berlin: Akademie Verlag, 1997)

Wohl, Robert, *The Generation of 1914* (Cambridge, Mass: Harvard University Press, 1979)

Wolf, Christa, 'Unerledigte Widersprüche. Gespräch mit Therese Hörnigk (June 1987–October 1988), in C. Wolf, *Im Dialog. Aktuelle Texte* (München, 1994)

—— *Kindheitsmuster* (Darmstadt: Luchterhand, 1979; orig. 1976)

Wolfrum, Edgar, *Geschichtspolitik in der Bundesrepublik Deutschland. Der Weg zur bundesrepublikanische Erinnerung, 1948–1990* (Darmstadt: Wissenschaftliche Buchgesellschaft, 1999)

Wollenberger, Vera *Virus der Heuchler* (Berlin: Elefanten Verlag, 1992)

Ziemann, Benzamin, *Front und Heimat. Ländliche Kriegserfahrungen im südlichen Bayern, 1914–1923* (Essen: Klartext, 1997)

Zwahr, Hartmut, *Die erfrorenen Flügel der Schwalbe. DDR und "Prager Frühling". Tagebuch einer Krise 1968–1970* (Bonn: Dietz, 2007; Archiv für Sozialgeschichte vol. 25)

Index